AF825759

Financial Modelling

Contributions to Management Science

Ulrich A. W. Tetzlaff
Optimal Design of Flexible Manufacturing Systems
1990. 190 pages. Softcover DM 69,-
ISBN 3-7908-0516-5

Fred von Gunten
Competition in the Swiss Plastics Manufacturing Industry
1991. 408 pages. Softcover DM 120,-
ISBN 3-7908-0541-6

Harald Dyckhoff/Ute Finke
Cutting and Packing in Production and Distribution
1992. 248 pages. Hardcover DM 120,-
ISBN 3-7908-0630-7

Hagen K. C. Pfeiffer
The Diffusion of Electronic Data Interchange
1992. 257 pages. Softcover DM 85,-
ISBN 3-7908-0631-5

Evert Jan Stokking / Giovanni Zambruno (Eds.)
Recent Research in Financial Modelling
1993. 174 pages. Softcover DM 90,-
ISBN 3-7908-0683-8

Richard Flavell (Ed.)
Modelling Reality and Personal Modelling
1993. 407 pages. Softcover DM 120,-
ISBN 3-7908-0682-X

Lorenzo Peccati · Matti Virén (Eds.)

Financial Modelling

Recent Research

With 40 Figures

Physica-Verlag
A Springer-Verlag Company

Series Editor
Werner A. Müller
Peter Schuster

Editors
Professor Lorenzo Peccati
Università Commerciale Luigi Bocconi
Istituto di Metodi Quantitativi
via U. Gobbi, 5
I-20136 Milano, Italy

Professor Matti Virén
University of Turku
Department of Economics
SF-20500 Turku, Finland

CIP-Kurztitelaufnahme der Deutschen Bibliothek
Financial modelling : recent research / Lorenzo Peccati ; Matti Virén (eds.). - Heidelberg : Physica-Verlag., 1994
(Contributions to management science)
ISBN-13: 978-3-7908-0765-3 e-ISBN-13: 978-3-642-86706-4
DOI: 10.1007/978-3-642-86706-4

NE: Peccati, Lorenzo [Hrsg.]

This work is subject to copyright. All rights are reserved, whether the whole or part of the material is concerned, specifically the rights of translation, reprinting, reuse of illustrations, recitation, broadcasting, reproduction on microfilms or in other ways, and storage in data banks. Duplication of this publication or parts thereof is only permitted under the provisions of the German Copyright Law of September 9, 1965, in its version of June 24, 1985, and a copyright fee must always be paid. Violations fall under the prosecution act of the German Copyright Law.

© Physica-Verlag Heidelberg 1994

The use of registered names, trademarks, etc. in this publication does not imply, even in the absence of a specific statement, that such names are exempt from the relevant protective laws and regulations and therefore free for general use.

2201/2202-543210 - Printed on acid-free paper

PREFACE

The volume collects a selection of papers presented and discussed during the two Meetings held in 1992 of the EURO Working Group on Financial Modelling. In April the works were held in Cogne (Aosta Valley - Italy) and in November in Turku (Finland).

The Group was founded eight years ago and at present is formed by some hundreds of people from over ten European countries and from the United States.

The unusually high rythm of two Meetings per years has been always kept, with the exception of one of the first years. This reveals the strong vitality of this community. The wide variety of papers presented and discussed, together with the originality of their approach and of the results, also witnesses the quality of the work the Group is doing in Finance.

There are more than one way to work in this fastly growing field. A largely diffused approach is mainly oriented in building theories to be cast within some general economic paradigm. If some simplifications are needed to get perfect theoretical coherence with the preferred paradigm, they are easily accepted. The most diffuse approach within the Group, although attenctive to general theories, tries sometimes to build workable models where many relevant details of the reality are captured even if the price is not to adhere to some general theory. This does not mean, of course, that the Group is against general paradigms. This simply means that general paradigms are welcome as long as they are useful, but need not to be fully respected when the reality appears clearly in contrast with their assumptions.

In our mind this is a sort of *incipit* for a *Manifesto* of a European way to think of Finance. European banks, insurance companies and other financial intermediaries are expected in the next decades to bet more and more efficiently over two partially distinct gaming-tables: on the wide and efficient world financial markets but also on the non-necessarily wide, inefficient and thin local markets. For the first gaming-table the standard theory of Finance provides a robust guide to the decision maker. Too often the problems common on the second gaming table are (im)pudically hidden under the familiar categories of "imperfections", "irrationalities" and "noises" and the task to cope with them is blindly committed to the otherwise powerful use of some standard brownian motion. A European way to Finance should take seriously account of these simple points. A gap between standard Finance theory and common financial reality must be covered with a bridge. The bricks of the bridge are (at least partially) provided twice per year by the components of our Group.

The papers in this volume cover a wide range of topics. Thus, the papers deal with insurance and risk management, stock market behavior, taxation and market imperfections, pricing and bargaining in financial markets, empirical tests of financial market models and currency market applications. Although some of the papers are purely theoretical, most of papers represent some sort of application, theoretical or empirical. Quite often, the applications are related to European institutions and/or to European features of financial markets. Take, for instance, the various rules affecting the behaviour of pension funds, or take into account market imperfections which are so often encountered in European financial markets.

The high quality of the papers is determined by the original quality of the researches, by the discussion of the results during the Meetings, by a refereeing and selection process ensuing yearly after the November Meeting. We are very grateful to the referees who have helped a lot to select the papers. They have also given numerous good suggestions of how to improve their contents and style.

The good success of the Meetings depends both on the scientific quality of our work, and on many facilities that are found by the organizers. As concerns the Meeting in Cogne, L. Peccati must be grateful to the Faculty of Economics and the Business Administration School of Torino University, to the Finance Department of the Aosta Valley Regional Government, to the National Research Council, to the Compagnia di San Paolo, to the Banque de la Vallée, to the Banca CRT, to Fidis SpA, to Fondiaria SpA and to ADB SIMpA. For the Meeting in Turku, M. Virén thanks the Foundation for Economic Education, the Yrjö Jahnsson Foundation, the Sampo Group, the Savings Bank of Finland SBF (Turku) and the Turku School of Economics and Business Administration for help and facilities generously put at disposal of the participants.

The Editors and the EURO Working Group on Financial Modelling wish to express their appreciation to the following persons who acted as referees in preparing the proceedings volume:

Phelim P. Boyle
Elio Canestrelli
Erio Castagnoli
A. Corhay
Massimo De Felice
Steinar Ekern
Robert W. Grubbström
Robin Hewins
Robert Kast
Johan Knif
Marco Li Calzi
Elisa Luciano
Eva Liljebom
Otto Loistl
Umberto Magnani
Sergio Margarita
Benedetto Matarazzo
Brian Mathews

Piera Mazzoleni
Nigel Meade
Fausto Mignanego
Carlo Mottura
Michael B. Ormiston
Fulvio Ortu
Andrew Pollock
Vesa Puttonen
Luciano Sigalotti
Silvana Stefani
Jan Stokking
Frans M. Tempelaar
Pietro Terna
Anders Thorstenson
Marcello Torrigiani
Giovanni M. Zambruno.

Lorenzo Peccati
Matti Virén

Torino-Turku - February 1994

Table of Contents

SINGLE AND PERIODIC PREMIUMS FOR GUARANTEED EQUITY-LINKED LIFE INSURANCE UNDER INTEREST-RATE RISK: THE "LOGNORMAL + VASICEK" CASE (')

Anna Rita Bacinello
Fulvio Ortu (*)

Dipartimento di Matematica Applicata alle Scienze Economiche Statistiche e Attuariali "Bruno de Finetti"
University of Trieste, ITALY

ABSTRACT

Interest-rate risk, while significantly affecting the pricing of almost all life-insurance products, has been up to now disregarded in the analysis of equity-linked policies for which a minimum-amount-guaranteed provision operates. The purpose of the present paper is to build on the work of Brennan and Schwartz(1976,1979a,b) and Delbaen(1990) to show how uncertainty in interest rates influences both single and periodic premiums for equity-linked life insurance. To this end, we consider a model in which the unit price of the fund to which benefits are referred follows a lognormal process, while the spot rate of interest is described as in Vasicek(1977), and we employ the martingale approach to contingent-claims pricing introduced by Harrison and Kreps(1979) to obtain pricing formulae for guaranteed equity-linked policies that account for interest-rate risk. The paper includes a detailed comparative static analysis of our extended formulae, as well as some numerical examples.

(') We thank Leonardo Felli for helpful comments and suggestions. Financial support from MURST Fondo 40% on The Theory of the Term Structure of Interest Rates is gratefully aknowledged.

(*) also at Department of Economics, University of Chicago, Chicago Il, USA.

1. Introduction

In the last two decades, the life insurance market has witnessed an increasing popularity of products in which the financial aspects play a role as crucial as the (more traditional) demographic ones [(1)]. Among these products, guaranteed equity-linked policies have attracted not only the interest of investors but also, as a consequence, the curiosity of researchers in financial and actuarial studies. Brennan and Schwartz (1976, 1979b) have been the first to pursue a theoretical analysis of this type of policies. They have supplied a closed form valuation formula, based on the celebrated stock option model of Black and Scholes (1973), for single premium contracts, and have proposed a numerical scheme, based on a finite-difference approximation method, for the valuation problem in the periodic premium case. Subsequently, Delbaen (1990) has presented an alternative approach to the valuation of equity-linked policies, based on the martingale theory of contingent claims successfully pioneered by Harrison and Kreps (1979). More recently, Bacinello and Ortu (1993a) have extended both approaches in order to account for endogenously determined minimum amounts guaranteed.

All the above-mentioned results rest on the maintained hypothesis of a non-stochastic (and flat) term structure of interest rates so that, mortality risk aside, the only uncertainty is in the behaviour of the reference fund to which the benefits are linked. The assumption of a constant, non-stochastic term structure can be however criticized on behalf of the empirical evidence that displays, at least in the last decade, long periods of highly volatile interest rates. This assumption may then lead to relevant mispricings of contracts that include long-lived options, as equity-linked policies implicitly do.

A first, partial step towards removing the non-stochastic-interest-rate assumption has been taken by Bacinello and Ortu (1993b) in a more general model where fixed-income securities may enter the composition of the reference fund, and the analysis is however concentrated only on single premium policies. They show, in particular, that a closed form solution for the single premium can be obtained when interest rates are described by the Vasicek model and the reference fund follows a lognormal process. They observe, however, that the analysis of this particular case needs still to be completed, and they recommend a sharper investigation of the comparative static properties of their single premium formula, in order to build a sound basis for comparisons with the standard model of Brennan and Schwartz. They point out, moreover, that the periodic-premiums scheme, most common for equity-linked policies, remains still to be studied.

The objective of our contribution is to fill the above-mentioned gaps, and to this end

(1) See Delvaux and Magnée (1991) for a detailed description of products of this type offered on European markets.

we structure the paper as follows. In Section 2 we briefly outline the framework of Frigerio, Ortu and Pressacco (1992) for pricing "equity-dependent" contingent claims when the spot rate follows the model of Vasicek, and the unit price of the "equity" (reference fund, in our case) follows a lognormal process. Such a framework is employed in Section 3 to develop a pricing formula for periodic-premiums equity-linked policies. While a closed form solution is not available, the pricing formula that we obtain can be numerically evaluated via simulation, with little additional effort than that needed in evaluating the corresponding formula in the standard model. For the sake of completeness, and for further reference, the single-premium pricing formula of Bacinello and Ortu (1993b) is obtained in this Section as well . Comparative statics are dealt with in Section 4, where an in-depth analysis of the single-premium model is carried out, along with some other relevant issues. In particular, we argue that in both the single and the periodic premium cases a constant, non-stochastic interest rate that equates the premiums in the standard framework to those obtained in our extended one, is uniquely determined. We observe that such a rate can be usefully employed in evaluating the rate of "interest-profit" (or "loss") of insurance companies that disregard interest-rate risk in pricing equity-linked products, using instead a constant *technical* rate. Since no closed form comparative statics are available in the periodic-premiums scheme, Section 5 exhibits simulations of our periodic premium formula for different sets of parameters, so that the sensitivity of the periodic premium to different scenarios is established. Other relevant numerical experiments are collected in that Section, while Section 6 summarizes and hints at possible further extensions.

2. The valuation framework for contingent claims

We collect in this Section some results on contingent claims pricing when the default-free rate of interest is stochastic, results that are fundamental in our development of single and periodic premium formulae for equity-linked policies. The basic references, along with Frigerio, Ortu and Pressacco (1992), are Cheng (1991) and Harrison and Kreps (1979).

We envison an arbitrage-free economy in which both equities and fixed-income securities are traded. We consider in particular a reference fund, composed all by equities, whose unit price S is a stochastic process that obeys, on some time interval [0,T], the following lognormal process [(2)]

(2) The lognormality assumption is justified when, for instance, the unit price of the fund is a geometric mean of the prices of the equities composing it, and all following lognormal processes. An example of an index with this characteristic is the Value Line Index traded on the American markets (see Ingersoll (1987)).

$$S(t) = S(0)\exp\{(\mu_S - \sigma_S^2/2)t + \sigma_S W_1(t)\} \tag{2.1}$$

where $S(0)$, μ_S, σ_S, are (strictly) positive constants, and W_1 is a standard brownian motion.

We model the market for fixed-income securities as a single-factor one, with the spot market rate of interest as the state variable. We follow Vasicek (1977) in assuming an Ornstein-Uhlenbeck process for the spot rate r, i.e.

$$dr(t) = a\,[\theta - r(t)\,]\,dt - \eta\,dW_2(t) \tag{2.2}$$

with $r(0)$ given, and a, θ, η positive constants (3). We assume W_2 to be a standard brownian motion as well, and $(W_1(t), W_2(s))$ to be jointly normally distributed $\forall$ t, s, with

$$\text{cov}(W_1(t), W_2(s)) = \begin{cases} \rho t & \text{if } t=s \\ 0 & \text{otherwise} \end{cases} \tag{2.3}$$

and $|\rho| \leq 1$. The market for fixed-income securities is fully described once the price of zero-coupon bonds is determined. To this end, one lets $b_T(t)$ represent the time t price of such an asset, $t \leq T$, and recalls that the cash-flow associated to it is identically 0 for $t < T$, and equal to 1 if $t = T$. The single-factor hypothesis underlying fixed-income securities is formalized by assuming a functional relationship between $b_T(t)$ and the couple $(t,r(t))$, with $r(t)$ the spot rate value prevailing at time t. Letting then $b_T(t) = f_T(t,r(t))$, standard arguments (see, among others, Vasicek (1977), Cox, Ingersoll and Ross (1981, 1985) and Artzner and Delbaen (1989)) show that viability (4) of the fixed-income market requires the existence of a function $\lambda(t,r(t))$, known as the market price for interest-rate risk, such that f_T is the solution of the following partial differential equation:

$$x f_T(t,x) = \frac{\partial f_T(t,x)}{\partial t} + [a(\theta - x) + \eta\lambda(t,x)]\frac{\partial f_T(t,x)}{\partial x} + \frac{1}{2}\eta^2\frac{\partial^2 f_T(t,x)}{\partial x^2} \tag{2.4}$$

with boundary conditions $f_T(t,x) \geq 0\ \forall x,t$, and $f_T(T,x) = 1\ \forall x$.

When the function λ is assumed constant, say $\lambda(t, r(t)) = \bar{\lambda} \in R$, then (5)

(3) The minus sign that preceeds η in (2.2) allows us to obtain a positive volatility for pure-discount bond prices.

(4) We recall that the concept of viability, as introduced by Harrison and Kreps (1979), captures the idea of banning arbitrage opportunities in economies with an infinite number of states, where the absence of simple free-lunches (i.e. simple arbitrage opportunities) is in general only a necessary condition for the model to be sensible from an economical point of view.

(5) See Vasicek, (1977).

$$f_T(t,r(t)) = \exp\{-\frac{1}{a}(1-e^{-a(T-t)})r(t) + H(T-t)\} \tag{2.5}$$

where

$$H(\tau) = -\tau(\theta + \frac{\eta\bar{\lambda}}{a}) + \frac{1}{a}(\theta + \frac{\eta\bar{\lambda}}{a})(1-e^{-a\tau}) + \frac{1}{4}\frac{\eta^2}{a^3}(4e^{-a\tau} - e^{-2a\tau} + 2a\tau - 3) \tag{2.6}$$

Note that, in this case, b_T follows itself a diffusion process, i.e.

$$db_T(t) = \mu_T(b_T(t),t)\, b_T(t)\, dt + \sigma_T(b_T(t),t)\, b_T(t)\, dW_2(t) \tag{2.7}$$

with $\sigma_T(b_T(t),t) = \frac{\eta}{a}(1 - e^{-a(T-t)})$, as it can be easily shown upon observing that f_T is continuous and invertible in x $\forall t$, and using Ito's Lemma.

Fix now some time $T \in R$, and consider the economy in which the reference fund and the zero-coupon bond with maturity T are traded. Let x be the time T payoff of any contingent claim traded in such an economy, and assume that x has finite second moment. We are interested in giving conditions under which a unique time 0 price can be assigned to such a claim, and to present a valuation formula for it. Assume to this end that

$$\varphi^2(t) = \sigma_S^2 - 2\rho\sigma_S\frac{\eta}{a}(1-e^{-a(T-t)}) + \frac{\eta^2}{a^2}(1-e^{-a(T-t)})^2 > 0 \quad \forall t \in [0,T]\ ^{(6)} \tag{2.8}$$

and let the process S^* be defined in [0,T] by

$$S^*(t) = \frac{S(0)}{b_T(0)} \exp\{-\frac{1}{2}\int_0^t \varphi^2(s)\,ds + \int_0^t \varphi(s)\,dW(s)\} \tag{2.9}$$

where the standard brownian motion W(t) satisfies

$$\varphi(t)\,dW(t) = \sigma_S\,dW_1(t) - \sigma_T(b_T(t),t)\,dW_2(t) \tag{2.10}$$

Letting $\pi(x)$ denote the time 0 price of x, Frigerio, Ortu and Pressacco (1992) show that (2.8) is a necessary and sufficient condition for $\pi(x)$ to be well defined, and moreover that there exists a measurable functional $h: \mathcal{C}[0,T] \to R$ (7) such that

$$\pi(x) = b_T(0)E[h(S^*)] \tag{2.11}$$

(6) Observe that condition (2.8) is always satisfied if $\rho<1$. If $\rho=1$ (2.8) is satisfied if and only if $\frac{a\sigma_S}{\eta} \neq 1 - e^{-a(T-t)}$ $\forall t \in [0,T]$, which is equivalent to $\frac{a\sigma_S}{\eta} > 1 - e^{-aT}$.

(7) $\mathcal{C}[0,T]$ denotes here the vector space of continuous real functions on [0,T].

The idea underlying the valuation formula (2.11), as well as the necessary and sufficient condition (2.8), is as follows. Given the economy in which the reference fund and the pure-discount bond are traded, consider a "normalized" economy in which a reference fund with unit price $S'(t) = \frac{S(t)}{b_T(t)}$ and a zero-coupon bond with constant unit price are present. One shows that the viability of this "normalized" economy is equivalent to the viability of the first one, and that a claim x can be priced by arbitrage in the original economy if and only if a corresponding claim x' can be priced by arbitrage in the second one. Moreover, if $\pi'(x')$ is the arbitrage price of x' in the "normalized" economy, one shows that $\pi(x) = b_T(t)\pi'(x')$. Eventually, one notices that the "normalized" economy satisfies the assumptions of Theorem 3 (page 396) of Harrison and Kreps (1979), so that this theorem (along with its corollary) can be invoked to obtain $\pi'(x') = E[h(S^*)]$, from which (2.11) follows [8].

3. Pricing single and periodic premium policies

We are now ready to tackle the problem of pricing, in arbitrage-free financial and insurance markets, equity-linked life insurance of the endowment type for which a minimum amount guaranteed provision operates.

We assume that the fund to which benefits are referred has unit price following the lognormal process introduced in Section 2, and that fixed-income securities are priced according to the Vasicek model, with (constant) market price for interest-rate risk $\bar{\lambda}$, introduced in Section 2 as well. The remaining notation relevant in our pricing problems is as follows:

x entry age of the insured,

N term of the policy,

α_n probability that the benefit becomes due to be paid at the (end of the) n-th year. Since the policy is of the endowment type, we have

$$\alpha_n = \begin{cases} {}_{n-1/1}q_x & n=1,\ldots,N-1 \\ {}_{N-1/1}q_x + {}_Np_x = {}_{N-1}p_x & n=N \end{cases}$$

We assume that events concerning the insured's life are independent from those regarding financial markets.

(8) See also Appendix 2 of this paper for a few more details.

g_n exogenously given minimum amount guaranteed at time n, n=1,...,N.

We consider equity-linked policies of both the single and the level periodic premium type. For the first case we let:

U single premium, due to be paid immediately,

D part of the single premium deemed to be immediately invested in the reference fund.

For the second type we let:

P (level) periodic premium, due to be paid at the beginning of each year if the insured is alive,

d part of the periodic premium deemed to be invested in the reference fund at each payment date, when the insured is alive.

In both cases it is useful to define the following variable, whose value will depend crucially from the policy being of the single or periodic premium type:

m(t) units of the reference fund deemed to be held up to (and including) time t.

The principal peculiarity of an equity-linked endowment policy with an asset value guaranteed (ELEPAVG henceforth) is that at each n=1,...,N the benefit v_n constitutes the maturity value of a portfolio of m(n) units of the reference fund insured at level g_n, i.e. $v_n = \max\{m(n)S(n), g_n\}$. Observe that, as long as benefits are concerned, the difference between single and periodic premium contracts is completely reflected in different values taken up by m(n). In the analysis that follows we discuss separately single and periodic equilibrium premiums, exploiting in both cases the following two alternative decompositions of the benefit:

$$\begin{aligned} v_n &= g_n + \max\{m(n)S(n) - g_n, 0\} \\ &= m(n)S(n) + \max\{g_n - m(n)S(n), 0\}, \quad n=1,...,N \end{aligned} \tag{3.1}$$

3.1 The single premium case

The single premium of an ELEPAVG contract is said to be an equilibrium premium when it is computed as the linear combination, with weights $\{\alpha_n\}_{n=1}^{N}$, of the time 0 market values of the single benefits v_n, i.e.

$$U = \sum_{n=1}^{N} \alpha_n \pi(v_n) \tag{3.1.1}$$

with π as introduced in Section 2.

The rationale behind this definition is in our assumption of independence of life contingencies and events concerning financial markets, along with the hypothesis that each insurance company underwrites enough contracts so that mortality risk is made (almost) irrelevant. On this basis, the effect of competition among insurance companies forces, in equilibrium, the single premium to be equal to the value of the benefits payable [9].

The valuation of the equilibrium single premium goes then through the pricing of the contingent claims v_n, n=1,...,N. In this case we have

$$\begin{aligned} v_n &= g_n + \frac{D}{S(0)} \max\left\{ S(n) - \frac{S(0)g_n}{D}, 0 \right\} \\ &= \frac{D}{S(0)} S(n) + \frac{D}{S(0)} \max\left\{ \frac{S(0)g_n}{D} - S(n), 0 \right\}, \quad n=1,\dots,N \end{aligned} \tag{3.1.2}$$

with (3.1.2) obtained by observing that here $m(t) = \frac{D}{S(0)}$ $\forall t \geq 0$, substituting it in the expression for the benefit and rearranging.

We assume now that condition (2.8) is satisfied with T=N, so that financial markets are viable and every finite-variance contingent claim can be priced by arbitrage. Exploiting the value-additivity principle (i.e. the linearity of π) implied by the viability of the model, we obtain

$$\begin{aligned} U &= \sum_{n=1}^{N} \alpha_n g_n b_n(0) + \frac{D}{S(0)} \sum_{n=1}^{N} \alpha_n \pi\left(\max\left\{ S(n) - \frac{S(0)g_n}{D}, 0 \right\}\right) \\ &= D + \frac{D}{S(0)} \sum_{n=1}^{N} \alpha_n \pi\left(\max\left\{ \frac{S(0)g_n}{D} - S(n), 0 \right\}\right) \end{aligned} \tag{3.1.3}$$

where $b_n(0) = f_n(0, r(0))$, and $f_T(t, r(t))$ as in (2.5).

---

(9) For a more detailed discussion of these principles see Brennan and Schwartz (1979b), p. 32-33.

The contingent claims $x_1^n = \max\{S(n) - \frac{S(0)g_n}{D}, 0\}$ and $x_2^n = \max\{\frac{S(0)g_n}{D} - S(n), 0\}$ are easily seen to be the maturity values of a european call, respectively put, option on the reference fund with maturity n and striking price $\frac{S(0)g_n}{D}$.

Exploiting the framework introduced in Section 2, observing that $h(S^*) = \max\{S^*(n) - \frac{S(0)g_n}{D}, 0\}$, and applying (2.11), we obtain [10]

$$\pi(x_1^n) = S(0)F(A_n) - \frac{S(0)g_n}{D} b_n(0)F(B_n) \tag{3.1.4}$$

where

$$A_n = \frac{\ln(D/(g_n b_n(0)))}{\sqrt{C_n}} + \frac{1}{2}\sqrt{C_n}$$

$$B_n = A_n - \sqrt{C_n}$$

$$C_n = \int_0^n \varphi^2(s)\, ds$$

with F the cumulative distribution function of a normal standard variate, and $\varphi^2(s)$ as defined in (2.8) [11].

Simple algebraic manipulations lead now to the following expression for the equilibrium single premium of an ELEPAVG:

$$U = D\sum_{n=1}^{N} \alpha_n F(A_n) + \sum_{n=1}^{N} \alpha_n g_n b_n(0)\,[1-F(B_n)] \tag{3.1.5}$$

which is the formula originally presented in Bacinello and Ortu (1993b).

An in-depth analysis of the comparative static properties of (3.1.5) is carried out in Section 4, where we also compare our extended formula to the standard one of Brennan and Schwartz for the case with no interest-rate risk. We note, to this end, that when $\eta=0$ and $\theta=r(0)$ the two formulae coincide, since $b_n(0)=e^{-r(0)n}$ and $C_n=n\sigma_S^2$. This is hardly surprising since, when $\eta=0$ and $\theta=r(0)$, the unique solution to (2.2) yields a deterministic and flat yield curve. Before turning to these issues, we direct our attention to the most relevant problem of pricing periodic premium policies.

(10) See Appendix 1 for details.
(11) European put values are easily obtained by put-call parity.

3.2 The periodic premium case

The definition of an equilibrium periodic premium for an ELEPAVG parallels the one given for the single premium case, once track is kept of the two basic differences. The first one is related to the fact that premium payments are made, subject to the contingencies on the insured's life, at more instants in time. If exactly n (n=1,...,N) premiums are paid, one has to compute the market value of a stream of (constant) payments, each one in the amount of P, made at the instants 0,1,...,N-1 [(12)]. It is easily seen that, under our assumption of viable financial markets, the time 0 market value of such an amount is given by $P\sum_{j=0}^{n-1} b_j(0)$, once again with $b_j(0)=f_j(0,r(0))$ defined in (2.5). The second difference is in the way the quantity m(t) that enters the benefits is defined. Recalling that d is the part of the premium P invested in the reference fund at each time premium payments are made, we have in this case

$$m(t) = \begin{cases} \dfrac{d}{S(0)} & t=0 \\ \displaystyle\sum_{j=0}^{n-1} \dfrac{d}{S(j)} & n-1<t\leq n;\ n=1,\dots,N \end{cases} \tag{3.2.1}$$

so that the benefits v_n can be expressed in the following two equivalent ways

$$v_n = g_n + \max\left\{d\sum_{j=0}^{n-1}\frac{S(n)}{S(j)} - g_n,\ 0\right\}$$

$$= d\sum_{j=0}^{n-1}\frac{S(n)}{S(j)} + \max\left\{g_n - d\sum_{j=0}^{n-1}\frac{S(n)}{S(j)},\ 0\right\},\quad n=1,\dots,N \tag{3.2.2}$$

The equilibrium periodic premium P is then obtained by equating the linear combination, with weights $\{\alpha_n\}_{n=1}^{N}$, of the market values of the annuities introduced above, to the linear combination, with the same weights, of the market values of the benefits, i.e.

$$P\sum_{n=1}^{N}\alpha_n\sum_{j=0}^{n-1}b_j(0) = \sum_{n=1}^{N}\alpha_n\pi(v_n) \tag{3.2.3}$$

Exploiting the decompositions (3.2.2) one obtains

(12) Recall that the periodic premium is due to be paid at the beginning of the year, if the insured is alive.

$$P = \frac{\sum_{n=1}^{N} \alpha_n g_n b_n(0)}{\sum_{n=1}^{N} \alpha_n \sum_{j=0}^{n-1} b_j(0)} + \frac{\sum_{n=1}^{N} \alpha_n \pi(\max\{d\sum_{j=0}^{n-1} \frac{S(n)}{S(j)} - g_n, 0\})}{\sum_{n=1}^{N} \alpha_n \sum_{j=0}^{n-1} b_j(0)}$$

$$= d + \frac{\sum_{n=1}^{N} \alpha_n \pi(\max\{g_n - d\sum_{j=0}^{n-1} \frac{S(n)}{S(j)}, 0\})}{\sum_{n=1}^{N} \alpha_n \sum_{j=0}^{n-1} b_j(0)} \tag{3.2.4}$$

The second of the two equivalent expressions for the equilibrium periodic premium follows upon observing that, as a simple arbitrage argument shows, $\pi(d\sum_{j=0}^{n-1} \frac{S(n)}{S(j)}) = d\sum_{j=0}^{n-1} b_j(0)$ [13], so that $\sum_{n=1}^{N} \alpha_n \pi(d\sum_{j=0}^{n-1} \frac{S(n)}{S(j)}) = d\sum_{n=1}^{N} \alpha_n \sum_{j=0}^{n-1} b_j(0)$. In order to value the contingent claims $x_1^n = \max\{d\sum_{j=0}^{n-1} \frac{S(n)}{S(j)} - g_n, 0\}$ and $x_2^n = \max\{g_n - d\sum_{j=0}^{n-1} \frac{S(n)}{S(j)}, 0\}$, n=1,...,N, we exploit once again the framework introduced in Section 2. We show in Appendix 2 that, as long as condition (2.8) is satisfied with T=N, the arbitrage prices of the contingent claims x_1^n, x_2^n, n=1,...,N, can be written as follows

$$\pi(x_1^n) = b_n(0)E\Big[\max\Big(d\sum_{j=0}^{n-1} a(j,n)\exp\{\alpha(Y_1(n)-Y_1(j))+\beta(Y_2(n)-Y_2(j))\} - g_n, 0\Big)\Big] \tag{3.2.5}$$

and respectively

$$\pi(x_2^n) = b_n(0)E\Big[\max\Big(g_n - d\sum_{j=0}^{n-1} a(j,n)\exp\{\alpha(Y_1(n)-Y_1(j))+\beta(Y_2(n)-Y_2(j))\}, 0\Big)\Big] \tag{3.2.6}$$

where $\alpha = \sqrt{\frac{1+\rho}{2}}$, $\beta = \sqrt{\frac{1-\rho}{2}}$ and

$$a(j,n) = \exp\Big\{-\frac{1}{2}\int_j^n \varphi^2(s)\, ds + \frac{1}{a}\,(1 - e^{-a(n-j)})\,[r(0)e^{-aj} + \theta(1-e^{-aj})] - H(n-j)\Big\}$$

---

(13) Recall to this end that the contingent claim $d\sum_{j=0}^{n-1} \frac{S(n)}{S(j)}$ can be obtained by investing in the reference fund the amount d at each j=0,1,...,n-1.

with H(n-j) defined in (2.6). The expectation is taken with respect to the joint distribution of the random vectors $Y_1^n = (Y_1(1),\dots,Y_1(n))$ and $Y_2^n = (Y_2(1),\dots,Y_2(n))$. In Appendix 2 it is shown that Y_1^n, Y_2^n are jointly normally distributed with zero mean-vector and block-diagonal variance-covariance matrix, with blocks V_1^n, V_2^n depending only on σ_S, a, η. This means that $\text{cov}\{Y_1(s),Y_2(t)\} = 0 \ \forall s,t=1,\dots,N$, hence the random vectors Y_1^n, Y_2^n are independent.

Unfortunately, (3.2.5) and (3.2.6) do not yield to closed form solutions as it is the case for single premium contracts. It is however possible to frame our pricing problem in such a way that for any given set of parameters the equilibrium periodic premium can be computed via simulation in a very simple way. Indeed, it is easily seen that exploiting (3.2.6) P can be expressed as follows:

$$P = d + \frac{\sum_{n=1}^{N} \alpha_n b_n(0) E\left[\max\left(g_n - d\sum_{j=0}^{n-1} \alpha(j,n) \exp\left\{\alpha \sum_{h=1}^{N} (\gamma^1_{n,h} - \gamma^1_{j,h}) Z_1(h) + \beta \sum_{h=1}^{N} (\gamma^2_{n,h} - \gamma^2_{j,h}) Z_2(h)\right\}, 0\right)\right]}{\sum_{n=1}^{N} \alpha_n \sum_{j=0}^{n-1} b_j(0)} \tag{3.2.7}$$

The random vectors $Z_1 = (Z_1(1),\dots,Z_1(N))$ and $Z_2 = (Z_2(1),\dots,Z_2(N))$, whose components enter (3.2.7), are both normally distributed with zero mean-vector and variance-covariance matrix the identity one, and they are independent. The coefficients $\{\gamma^i_{k,h}\}$ are the elements of matrices Γ_i such that $V_i^N = \Gamma_i^T \Gamma_i$, i=1,2 (14).

The fact that our formula for the equilibrium periodic premium of an ELEPAVG yields to numerical valuations in a simple way should now be appearent. Indeed, one needs only to simulate 2N independent normal standard variates, since the other ingredients of (3.2.7) are given, non-random parameters. The comparative static properties of P will be investigated mainly in Section 5, by evaluating the premium for different sets of parameters. In Section 4 we discuss some comparative statics that can be ascertained without the help of numerical valuations, and we compare our pricing formula to the one obtained by Delbaen (1990) for the equilibrium periodic premium when interest-rate risk is assumed away.

We conclude this Section observing that, once again, (3.2.7) coincides with Delbaen's valuation formula if $\eta=0$ and $\theta=r(0)$, since in this case the term structure is non-stochastic and flat. To verify this claim directly, note that $\alpha(j,n)$ simplifies to $\exp\{(r(0) - \frac{\sigma_S^2}{2})(n-j)\}$, while $\alpha(Y_1(n)-Y_1(j))+\beta(Y_2(n)-Y_2(j))$ becomes $\sigma_S(W_1(n)-W_1(j))$.

---

(14) Such a Γ_i exists since V_i^N is a symmetric, positive (semi) definite matrix. Standard linear algebra arguments (see, for instance, Hadley (1961)) show that $\Gamma_i = T_i D_i^{1/2}$, where the columns of T_i are an orthonormal system of eigenvectors of V_i^N, and $D_i^{1/2}$ is a diagonal matrix with the square-root of the eigenvalues of V_i^N on its diagonal.

4. Comparative statics and comparisons with the standard model

The presence in our framework of an additional source of uncertainty, the stochastic market rate of interest, makes the comparative static analysis more interesting, though somewhat more complicated. The first-glance effect of interest-rate stochasticity is in the increased number of parameters on which both the single and the periodic premium depend. Indeed, along with the effect of changes in the amount(s) deemed to be invested, in the minimum amounts guaranteed, in the spot rate and in the volatility of the unanticipated return on the fund, parameters that are common to both the standard and our extended models, it is now important to account for the reactions of U and P to changes in the correlation coefficient ρ, the parameters a, θ, η identifying the spot rate process, and the market price of interest-rate risk, $\bar{\lambda}$.

We start our analysis fixing the attention on the single premium formula (3.1.5), and observing that changes in D, the g_n's and r(0) affect it in the same directions (although in general with different strenghts) as in the standard case, i.e $\frac{\partial U}{\partial D} > 0$, $\frac{\partial U}{\partial g_n} > 0 \; \forall n$ and $\frac{\partial U}{\partial r(0)} < 0$. As for the remaining parameter common to both frameworks, namely σ_S, we have

$$\frac{\partial U}{\partial \sigma_S} = \sum_{n=1}^{N} \alpha_n g_n b_n(0) \frac{F'(\sqrt{C_n} - A_n)}{\sqrt{C_n}} \left[\sigma_S n + \frac{\eta\rho}{a^2}(1\text{-}an\text{-}e^{-an})\right] \tag{4.1}$$

A first difference between the two models arises here. While in the standard case it is shown that the single premium is in any case an increasing function of σ_S, the same can be ascertained here analytically only for $\rho \leq 0$, since $1\text{-}an < e^{-an}$ whenever $n > 0$. Indeed, some numerical experiments show that $\frac{\partial U}{\partial \sigma_S}$ becomes negative for high values of ρ and when the spot rate is highly volatile. The intuition of why $\frac{\partial U}{\partial \sigma_S}$ changes in sign is conveyed by the analysis of the comparative statics with respect to the remaining parameters. In particular, the partial derivative of U with respect to ρ, the instantaneous correlation coefficient between W_1 and W_2, is as follows

$$\frac{\partial U}{\partial \rho} = \sum_{n=1}^{N} \alpha_n g_n b_n(0) \frac{F'(\sqrt{C_n} - A_n)}{\sqrt{C_n}} (1\text{-}an\text{-}e^{-an}) \frac{\sigma_S \eta}{a^2} < 0 \tag{4.2}$$

An explanation for the inverse relationship between the equilibrium single premium U and ρ follows from the way the correlation coefficient influences the covariance between the continuously compounded return on the reference fund, $\ln(S(t)/S(0))$, and the spot rate $r(t)$. We have in fact, for all s,t [(15)]

$$\mathrm{cov}\left\{ \ln\left(\frac{S(s)}{S(0)}\right), r(t) \right\} = -\rho\sigma_S\eta\, e^{-a\min\{t-s,0\}}\,(1-e^{-as}) \tag{4.3}$$

so that, *for given values of the other parameters*, a positive (negative) shift in ρ corresponds to a negative (positive) shift in the covariance between the continuously compounded return on the fund and the spot rate, thus making the equilibrium single premium an increasing function of such a covariance [(16)]. The above discussion sheds also some light on why there may be a reversal in the sign of $\frac{\partial U}{\partial \sigma_S}$: along with the usual, positively-signed effect of σ_S on the options intervening in U, in our extended framework, and when $\rho > 0$, an increment in σ_S decrements the covariance between $\ln(S(s)/S(0))$ and $r(t)$ and has then also an effect of the opposite sign on U. As we mentioned before our numerical analysis suggests that, in certain cases, the negative effect prevails on the positive one.

As for the comparative statics with respect to θ and $\bar{\lambda}$, let $\Theta = \theta + \frac{\eta\bar{\lambda}}{a}$ and interpret it as a risk-neutralized long-term spot rate of interest. We have

$$\frac{\partial U}{\partial \Theta} = \sum_{n=1}^{N} \alpha_n g_n b_n(0)\, \frac{F(\sqrt{C_n} - A_n)}{a}\,(1-an-e^{-an}) < 0 \tag{4.4}$$

so that $\frac{\partial U}{\partial \theta} = \frac{\partial U}{\partial \Theta} < 0$ and $\frac{\partial U}{\partial \bar{\lambda}} = \frac{\eta}{a}\frac{\partial U}{\partial \Theta} < 0$. Since Θ is the long-term rate relevant for the investors, and given the mean-reverting property of the process assumed for the spot rate, increments in either θ or $\bar{\lambda}$ imply increments in Θ that are reflected in a lower equilibrium single premium, as it is to be expected.

The two remaining comparative statics, those with respect to a and η, yield as a result quite complicated partial derivatives whose sign is in general undetermined, so that numerical valuations are called for. We briefly comment on such a numerical analysis in the next Section, and we try here to understand the reasons of such an indeterminacy, starting with the instantaneous volatility of the spot force of interest, η. Part of the story for this

---

(15) Formula (4.3) is obtained by applying standard results on linear systems of stochastic differential equations (see, for instance, Karatzas and Shreve (1988), pages 354, 355).

(16) A similar explanation for the effect of ρ on U rests on observing that, since $\sigma_T(b_T(t),t) = \frac{\eta}{a}(1-e^{-a(T-t)})$, then $\mathrm{cov}\left\{\frac{dS(t)}{S(t)}, \frac{db_T(t)}{b_T(t)}\right\} = \frac{\rho\sigma_S\eta}{a}(1-e^{-a(T-t)})$, so that, *through ρ and for given values of the remaining parameters*, U is a decreasing function of the covariance between the unanticipated instantaneous return on the fund and on the bonds.

parameter parallels the one already seen for σ_S: an increase in η on the one side increases the instantaneous volatility of the unanticipated return on bonds (see (2.7)), while on the other side it influences the covariance between the continuously compounded return on the fund and the spot rate, increasing it when $\rho<0$ and decreasing it when $\rho>0$. Contrary to what happens with σ_S, however, an increase in the volatility of $\frac{db_T}{b_T}$ does not imply an increase in the options composing U, since not even the effect of $\sigma_T(b_T(t),t)$ on the bond price is a priori determined. In particular if $\bar{\lambda}\leq 0$ then b_T increases with $\sigma_T(b_T(t),t)$, while the contrary may happen when the market price for interest-rate risk is positive. The indeterminacy in the sign of $\frac{\partial U}{\partial \eta}$ is then the natural result of an indeterminate response of the total variance C_n and of the bond price $b_n(0)$ to changes in η. As for the influence on U of the mean-revertion coefficient a, eventually, a similar story can be told.

The comparisons between U^{BS}, the equilibrium premium of Brennan-Schwartz for the case of no interest-rate risk and our extended formula (3.1.5) can be based on two different hypotheses concerning the behaviour of an insurance company selling ELEPAVGs and disregarding interest-rate risk. The company can choose the spot rate r(0) as the constant rate prevailing up to the term N, and use it in the formula U^{BS}. In this case the mispricing can be easily evaluated numerically, as we do in Section 5. It is however standard practice in the life-insurance business not only to disregard interest-rate risk, but to employ, instead of the prevailing spot rate r(0), a constant force of interest δ, usually lower than r(0) and referred to as a "technical rate". A second comparison can then be obtained by finding the unique constant force of interest δ^*, that equates U to U^{BS} (17). Any insurance company selling ELEPAVGs and pricing them according to the standard model in which a *technical* rate δ is employed, will overprice them when setting δ below the critical level δ^*, and viceversa. Since the equilibrium single premium gives the time 0 value of the investment strategy allowing a company to perfectly hedge the ELEPAVGs sold, the critical level δ^* allows us to obtain some preliminary, although significant, answers to the solvency problems of the companies that are active in this line of business. Quite a bit of caution, however, is required in interpreting the above findings. Indeed, while it is true that any insurance company selling ELEPAVGs with a technical rate higher than δ^* will incur with positive probability in solvency problems, it is also true that a company setting $\delta<\delta^*$ will avoid with certainty any problem related to the solvency of its business as long as the company will take into account, in its investment strategy, the interest-rate uncertainty present in the economy in which it operates. We return on this issue briefly in our conclusive Section 6.

(17) Unicity of δ^* follows upon recalling that U^{BS} is a strictly decreasing, continuous function of δ that converges to D when δ goes to $+\infty$ and diverges positively when δ goes to $-\infty$.

Before turning our attention to the periodic premium case, two further remarks on the comparison between U and U^{BS} are in order. We first notice that, along with the one mentioned above, another possible interpretation for δ^* is as the internal rate of return (as of time 0) a company earns on its equity-linked business. Such a parameter can then be employed in comparing the profitability of the equity-linked line to other more traditional ones. We observe, moreover, that the comparative statics of δ^* with respect to the parameters relevant in pricing single premium ELEPAVGs under interest-rate risk show that δ^* increases (at least locally) with the spot rate r(0), the correlation coefficient ρ and the risk-neutralized long-term rate Θ (hence with both θ and $\bar{\lambda}$), while it is undetermined the effect on δ^* not only of shifts in σ_S, a and η (for which it is to be expected) but also of shifts in D and g_n, n=1,...,N. This last fact does not come as a surprise, however, after realizing that the sign of $\frac{\partial\delta^*}{\partial D}$ and $\frac{\partial\delta^*}{\partial g_n}$ is the sign of the differences $\frac{\partial U^{BS}}{\partial D} - \frac{\partial U}{\partial D}$, $\frac{\partial U^{BS}}{\partial g_n} - \frac{\partial U}{\partial g_n}$ respectively. Indeed, it is not clear which one of U, U^{BS} reacts more strongly to increases in D and in the g_n's [18].

We turn now our attention to the analysis of the equilibrium periodic premium. The lack in this case of a closed form solution for which the existence of partial derivatives can be established makes the numerical procedure almost compelled. Indeed, the only parameters for which the comparative statics can be ascertained analytically are the amount deemed to be invested at the beginning of each year the insured is alive, d, and the minimum amounts guaranteed, $\{g_n\}_{n=1}^{N}$. As it is to be expected, P increases with both d and any of the g_n's, and this fact can be established by applying standard distribution-free-arbitrage arguments to the two alternative expressions for the equilibrium periodic premium presented in (3.2.4). As for the remaining parameters, we show numerically in the next Section that they display on P the same type of influence they have on U, and in particular P decreases with r(0), ρ and Θ, while the effect of σ_S, a and η is undetermined.

The comparisons between P and P^D, the periodic premium obtained by Delbaen (1990) for the no-interest-rate-risk case, is based on the same observations on which the comparisons between U and U^{BS} were based. In particular, the possibility of computing the critical *technical* rate δ^* is based here on the numerical valuation of P^D, suggesting that P^D decreases with the (constant) force of interest employed in computing the premium. For further comments concerning the comparisons between P and P^D based on these remarks, we refer to the observations made about the comparisons between U and U^{BS}, and that apply to the periodic premium case as well.

---

(18) The derivatives of δ^* with respect to the parameters can be obtained applying the implicit function theorem to the equation $U-U^{BS}=0$, that defines implicitly δ^* as a function of D, $\{g_n\}_{n=1}^{N}$, σ_S, r(0), a, θ, η, $\bar{\lambda}$, ρ.

5. Numerical Experiments

In this Section we present the results of some numerical experiments concerning an endowment policy with entry age x=45 and term N=10. The life table used in order to value the probabilities α_n, n=1,...,N is the Italian Statistics about Males Mortality published after the general census of 1981. In all our experiments the guarantees g_n, n=1,...,N are set equal to $g_n = De^{\gamma n}$, for the single premium case, and $g_n = d\sum_{j=0}^{n-1} e^{\gamma(n-j)}$, for the periodic premium one. The minimum guarantee is then the value, in n, of the amounts deemed to be invested in the reference fund up to that time, value computed at a contractually specified force of interest γ. Such an exemplification for the minimum guarantees is suggested by standard actuarial practice concerning equity-linked policies. The fact that the guarantees are linear homogeneous functions in D (d respectively) makes both the single and the periodic premiums to be themselves linear homogeneous in these parameters (see (3.1.5) and (3.2.7)). This fact allows us to set, in all our experiments, D=d=1 so that the cost for providing the guarantee can be captured at first sight. In order to obtain some numerical information on the comparative static properties of both the single and the periodic equilibrium premiums, along with some comparisons with the standard Brennan-Schwartz and Delbaen models, we choose to start from the following "basic" set of parameters:

$$r(0)=0.1, \quad \gamma=0.05, \quad \sigma_S=0.3, \quad \rho=0, \quad a=0.5, \quad \theta=0.08, \quad \eta=0.05, \quad \bar{\lambda}=0.2$$

and to move them one at the time. Although our "basic" set does not collect estimates for the parameters obtained from data on a specific market, we believe that most of our figures may constitute a sensible basis for the description of actual markets.

In Tables 1 and 2 we report some numerical results pertaining to our single and periodic equilibrium premiums respectively. In the first column of each table, in particular, we present the value of the parameter changed from its "basic" value, in the second column the value of the premium, U, respectively P, in the third column ΔU, respectively ΔP, the difference in the premium due to the change in the parameter. The fourth column reports U^{BS} and P^{D} respectively, the premiums obtained with no interest rate risk, i.e. setting η=0 and θ equal to the current spot rate. The fifth column collects the differences $U-U^{BS}$ and $P-P^{D}$, and the sixth column, eventually, displays the values of δ^*, the force of interest that equates U to U^{BS} and P to P^{D} respectively. The data in Table 2 are computed by means of Montecarlo simulation of the expectation in (3.2.7) [19].

Parameter moved	U	ΔU	U^{BS}	$U-U^{BS}$	δ^*
Basic	1.1514	-	1.1322	+0.0192	0.0937
$r(0)=0$	1.2275	+0.0761	1.8481	-0.6206	0.0738
$r(0)=0.05$	1.1862	+0.0348	1.3597	-0.1735	0.0838
$r(0)=0.15$	1.2223	-0.0291	1.0413	+0.0810	0.1036
$r(0)=0.2$	1.0982	-0.0532	1.0110	+0.0872	0.1135
$\gamma=0$	1.0498	-0.1016	1.0413	+0.0085	0.0924
$\gamma=0.1$	1.3964	+0.2450	1.3597	+0.0367	0.0947
$\gamma=0.15$	1.9105	+0.7591	1.8481	+0.0624	0.0955
$\gamma=0.2$	2.8796	+1.7282	2.7798	+0.0998	0.0960
$\sigma_S=0.1$	1.0211	-0.1303	1.0063	+0.0148	0.0827
$\sigma_S=0.2$	1.0780	-0.0734	1.0588	+0.0192	0.0911
$\sigma_S=0.5$	1.2981	+0.1467	1.2789	+0.0192	0.0954
$\sigma_S=0.7$	1.4192	+0.2678	1.3995	+0.0197	0.0960
$\sigma_S=1$	1.5391	+0.3877	1.5186	+0.0205	0.0963
$\rho=-1$	1.2052	+0.0538	1.1322	+0.0730	0.0790
$\rho=-0.75$	1.1928	+0.0414	1.1322	+0.0606	0.0820
$\rho=-0.5$	1.1798	+0.0284	1.1322	+0.0476	0.0854
$\rho=-0.25$	1.1660	+0.0146	1.1322	+0.0338	0.0893
$\rho=0.25$	1.1358	-0.0156	1.1322	+0.0036	0.0987
$\rho=0.5$	1.1192	-0.0322	1.1322	-0.0130	0.1047
$\rho=0.75$	1.1013	-0.0501	1.1322	-0.0309	0.1121
$\rho=1$	1.0820	-0.0694	1.1322	-0.0502	0.1214
$a=0.25$	1.1441	-0.0073	1.1322	+0.0119	0.0960
$a=0.75$	1.1600	+0.0086	1.1322	+0.0278	0.0911
$a=1$	1.1665	+0.0151	1.1322	+0.0343	0.0891
$\theta=0.05$	1.2443	+0.0929	1.1322	+0.1121	0.0703
$\theta=0.11$	1.0908	-0.0606	1.1322	-0.0414	0.1170
$\theta=0.15$	1.0436	-0.1078	1.1322	-0.0886	0.1479
$\eta=0.025$	1.1620	+0.0106	1.1322	+0.0298	0.0904
$\eta=0.075$	1.1507	-0.0007	1.1322	+0.0185	0.0939
$\eta=0.1$	1.1586	+0.0072	1.1322	+0.0264	0.0915
$\bar{\lambda}=-0.4$	1.3819	+0.2305	1.1322	+0.2497	0.0468
$\bar{\lambda}=-0.2$	1.2845	+0.1331	1.1322	+0.1523	0.0624
$\bar{\lambda}=0$	1.2090	+0.0576	1.1322	+0.0768	0.0781
$\bar{\lambda}=0.4$	1.1080	-0.0434	1.1322	-0.0242	0.1092

Table 1

(19) The complete eigensystems for the matrices V_i^N needed to build the matrices Γ_i i=1,2 are computed via the Jacobi Transformation Routine.

Parameter moved	P	ΔP	P^D	$P-P^D$	δ^*
Basic	1.0918	-	1.0774	+0.0144	0.0916
$r(0)=0$	1.1109	+0.0191	1.4103	-0.2994	0.0820
$r(0)=0.05$	1.1011	+0.0093	1.1961	-0.0950	0.0868
$r(0)=0.15$	1.0832	-0.0086	1.0243	+0.0589	0.0965
$r(0)=0.2$	1.0752	-0.0166	1.0060	+0.0692	0.1013
$\gamma=0$	1.0341	-0.0577	1.0254	+0.0087	0.0879
$\gamma=0.1$	1.2219	+0.1301	1.2027	+0.0192	0.0947
$\gamma=0.15$	1.4815	+0.3897	1.4634	+0.0181	0.0973
$\gamma=0.2$	1.9419	+0.8501	1.9379	+0.0040	0.0996
$\sigma_S=0.1$	1.0199	-0.0719	1.0029	+0.0170	0.0755
$\sigma_S=0.2$	1.0603	-0.0315	1.0358	+0.0245	0.0831
$\sigma_S=0.5$	1.1546	+0.0628	1.1453	+0.0093	0.0952
$\sigma_S=0.7$	1.2037	+0.1119	1.2011	+0.0026	0.0987
$\sigma_S=1$	1.2758	+0.1840	1.2734	+0.0024	0.0989
$\rho=-1$	1.1650	+0.0732	1.0774	+0.0876	0.0709
$\rho=-0.75$	1.1431	+0.0513	1.0774	+0.0657	0.0740
$\rho=-0.5$	1.1233	+0.0315	1.0774	+0.0459	0.0791
$\rho=-0.25$	1.1068	+0.0150	1.0774	+0.0294	0.0849
$\rho=0.25$	1.0781	-0.0137	1.0774	+0.0007	0.0993
$\rho=0.5$	1.0652	-0.0266	1.0774	-0.0122	0.1076
$\rho=0.75$	1.0526	-0.0392	1.0774	-0.0248	0.1174
$\rho=1$	1.0411	-0.0507	1.0774	-0.0363	0.1275
$a=0.25$	1.0791	-0.0127	1.0774	+0.0017	0.0989
$a=0.75$	1.0981	+0.0063	1.0774	+0.0207	0.0883
$a=1$	1.0939	+0.0021	1.0774	+0.0165	0.0905
$\theta=0.05$	1.1479	+0.0561	1.0774	+0.0705	0.0664
$\theta=0.11$	1.0545	-0.0373	1.0774	-0.0229	0.1162
$\theta=0.15$	1.0252	-0.0666	1.0774	-0.0522	0.1486
$\eta=0.025$	1.0928	+0.0010	1.0774	+0.0154	0.0911
$\eta=0.075$	1.0974	+0.0056	1.0774	+0.0200	0.0887
$\eta=0.1$	1.0906	-0.0012	1.0774	+0.0132	0.0923
$\bar{\lambda}=-0.4$	1.2032	+0.1114	1.0774	+0.1258	0.0478
$\bar{\lambda}=-0.2$	1.1579	+0.0661	1.0774	+0.0805	0.0627
$\bar{\lambda}=0$	1.1213	+0.0295	1.0774	+0.0439	0.0773
$\bar{\lambda}=0.4$	1.0687	-0.0231	1.0774	-0.0087	0.1055

Table 2

We believe that Tables 1 and 2, once coupled with the discussion of Section 4, give a fairly good idea of the main properties of our extended formulae. We add here few further remarks, noting first of all that the influence of changes in the parameters is reflected in substantially the same way by the single and the periodic premiums. In particular , the mispricing due to disregarding interest-rate risk has the same sign in both cases. Indeed, our findings show that the standard formulae in which interest-rate risk is not accounted for and the constant force of interest is set equal to the *current* spot rate underprices the contracts under scrutiny for most sets of parameters. Any "naive" insurance company pricing its ELEPAVGs in such a way would face, under our maintained assumptions, solvency problems with positive probability (and most likely with probability one if more overlapping generations of such contracts are considered).

In Section 4, however, we have observed that the standard approach of most companies is different, and consists in using a constant, non-stochastic *technical* force of interest in pricing their products. Such a technical rate is usually fairly low, never exceeding 4% on a per-annum basis (at least on European life insurance markets). Noting now that δ^* never goes below 4%, and actually exceeds 7% for almost all the sets of parameters we have considered, we are induced to claim that insurance companies using low technical rates should have enough funds to operate an investment strategy that allows them to perfectly hedge their claims. We stress however once again the fact that an insurance company may incur in solvency problems even in this case, if it adopts an investment strategy that does not replicate the payoffs of the options (implicitly) sold.

We conclude this Section recalling that the derivatives of the single premium with respect to the volatility parameter in the interest rate process, η, has undetermined sign whenever at least one of $\bar{\lambda}$ and ρ are strictly positive, while the derivative of U with respect to the mean reversion coefficient a is undetermined in general. Our numerical experiments confirm the difficulty in identifying a wide range of parameters on wich such derivatives maintain a constant sign.

6. Concluding remarks

The model presented in Section 3 for the valuation of single and periodic equilibrium premiums of ELEPAVGs, along with the discussion of its main comparative static properties and the numerical experiments, suggest that interest rate risk undoubtedly influences the terms at which such contracts should sell for on arbitrage-free financial and insurance markets. The behaviour of the term structure should then enter as a relevant parameter in both the pricing and the investment decisions of the issuers of such products.

We believe, however, that our analysis may still be improved by accounting for three further important issues. The first two pertain still to the pricing problem and are somewhat correlated. In using the Vasicek model for the spot rate, one trades off the capability of obtaining pricing formulae that are either in closed form or otherwise easy to simulate, with the (rather unrealistic) phenomenon of interest rates that go negative with strictly positive probability. While this problem is likely to be a minor one when the contingent claims at hand have a short life [20], it may have a major effect when analysing the long-lived option components of an ELEPAVG.

This problem can be avoided by modelling the spot rate as a mean-reverting process of the type introduced by Cox, Ingersoll and Ross (1985), which prevents it from going negative. This issue stands clearly as an objective for future research.

A second, related issue is identified in the possibility of coupling the hypothesis of interest rates stochasticity with the presence of endogenously determined minimum amounts guaranteed, as defined in Bacinello and Ortu (1993a). The relation between these two issues is in the fact that the results in Bacinello and Ortu for the flat term structure case can be extended to the present framework only *as long as* the interest rate, although stochastic, does not go negative. To model the spot rate as in Cox, Ingersoll and Ross would then allow us to consider a stochastic and non-negative spot rate together with minimum amounts guaranteed that depend functionally on the premium paid, hence that are endogenous.

The third, major issue on which future research is to be directed is the identification of feasible hedging strategies for the issuers of ELEPAVGs. To this end, one may follow the lead of Brennan and Schwartz (1979a), and see how their results are to be amended when the flat term structure hypothesis is removed.

Appendix 1

In order to value the contingent claim $x_1^n = \max\{S(n) - \frac{S(0)g_n}{D}, 0\}$, we need to evaluate $E(\max\{S^*(n) - \frac{S(0)g_n}{D}, 0\})$, i.e. (see (2.9)):

$$E(\max\{\frac{S(0)}{b_n(0)} \exp\{-\frac{1}{2}\int_0^n \varphi^2(s)\,ds + \int_0^n \varphi(s)dW(s)\} - \frac{S(0)g_n}{D}, 0\}) \tag{A1.1}$$

Recalling that W as defined in (2.10) is a standard brownian motion, we observe that the random variable $Z=\exp\{-\frac{1}{2}\int_0^n \varphi^2(s)\,ds + \int_0^n \varphi(s)dW(s)\}$ has a lognormal distribution, with $E(Z)=1$ and $Var(Z)=\exp(C_n)-1$ (see for instance Karatzas and Shreve(1988), pages 355 and 361). Denoting by f(z) its density in z, and letting

(20) See on this point the discussion in Rabinovitch (1989).

$\kappa_n = \frac{g_n b_n(0)}{D}$, the formula for the expected value of a truncated lognormal distribution (see for instance Johnson and Kotz(1970), page 129, or Ingersoll(1987), page 14) can be employed to obtain

$$\int_{\kappa_n}^{+\infty} z f(z)\, dz = F(A_n) \tag{A1.2}$$

Observing that $\int_{\kappa_n}^{+\infty} f(z)\, dz = F(B_n)$, our formula (3.1.3) is derived as follows

$$\begin{aligned}\pi(x_1^n) &= b_n(0)E(\max\{\frac{S(0)}{b_n(0)}Z - \frac{g_n S(0)}{D}, 0\}) \\ &= S(0)E(\max\{Z - \kappa_n, 0\}) \\ &= S(0)\{ \int_{\kappa_n}^{+\infty} z f(z)\, dz - \kappa_n \int_{\kappa_n}^{+\infty} f(z)\, dz \} \\ &= S(0)F(A_n) - \kappa_n S(0)F(B_n)\end{aligned} \tag{A1.3}$$

While Rabinovitch(1989) has been the first to present a formula for european options in the "Lognormal +Vasicek" case, his approach requires from the outset the differentiability assumption on the option price. The framework outlined here yields Rabinovitch's formula without the a-priori differentiability assumption, and highlighting the necessary and sufficient condition (2.8).

Appendix 2

We show here how to obtain (3.2.5), the pricing formula for the contingent claim $x_1^n = \max\{d\sum_{j=0}^{n-1}\frac{S(n)}{S(j)} - g_n, 0\}$. We start by letting $S'(t) = \frac{S(t)}{b_n(t)}$ for all t in [0,n], and noting that

$$x_1^n = \max\{d\sum_{j=0}^{n-1}\frac{S'(n)}{S'(j)}\frac{1}{b_n(j)} - g_n, 0\} \tag{A2.1}$$

In (A2.1) the contingent claim x_1^n is expressed as a measurable functional of the trajectories of the process S', say $x_1^n = h(S')$ with $h : \mathcal{C}([0,n]) \rightarrow R$. This fact allows us to invoke Proposition 1 of Harrison and Kreps(1979, page 395) to claim that x_1^n is a well defined contingent claim in the "normalized" economy where a reference fund with unit price S' and a pure-discount bond with constant unit price are traded. As shown by Frigerio, Ortu and Pressacco(1992), (2.8) is a necessary and sufficient condition for the viability of such a model, and for the possibility of pricing by arbitrage any (square-integrable) contingent claim in it. In particular, the Corollary to Theorem 3 of Harrison and Kreps(1979, page 396) shows that $\pi'(x_1^n)$, the arbitrage price of x_1^n when embedded in the "normalized" economy, is given by

$$\pi'(x_1^n) = E\left(\max\left\{d\sum_{j=0}^{n-1}\frac{S^*(n)}{S^*(j)}\frac{1}{b_n(j)} - g_n,\ 0\right\}\right) \tag{A2.2}$$

with the process S^* defined in (2.9). Since we are interested in the price of x_1^n when embedded in the "original" economy, we note that the normalization has involved after all only a change in units of account, so that

$$\pi(x_1^n) = b_n(0)\pi'(x_1^n) = b_n(0)E\left(\max\left\{d\sum_{j=0}^{n-1}\frac{S^*(n)}{S^*(j)}\frac{1}{b_n(j)} - g_n,\ 0\right\}\right) \tag{A2.3}$$

We highlight now the main algebraic manipulations that lead from(A2.3) to (3.2.5). Observe first that substituing (2.9) and (2.5) into (A2.3), and recalling that the solution to the stochastic differential equation (2.2) that yields the process for the spot rate is (see Karatzas and Shreve(1988, page 354))

$$r(t) = r(0)e^{-at} + \theta(1-e^{-at}) - \eta\int_0^t e^{-a(t-s)}\,dW_2(s) \tag{A2.4}$$

one obtains, after some simple but otherwise tedious manipulations

$$\frac{S^*(n)}{S^*(j)}\frac{1}{b_n(j)} = \alpha(j,n)\exp\left\{\sigma_S(W_1(n) - W_1(j)) - \frac{\eta}{a}(W_2(n) - W_2(j))\right\}$$

$$\cdot \exp\left\{\frac{\eta}{a}\left[\int_0^n e^{-a(n-s)}\,dW_2(s) - \int_0^j e^{-a(j-s)}\,dW_2(s)\right]\right\} \tag{A2.5}$$

with $\alpha(j,n)$ as defined in the main text. Let now $X = (X_1, X_2)$ be a standard two-dimensional brownian motion, and $\alpha = \sqrt{\frac{1+\rho}{2}}$, $\beta = \sqrt{\frac{1-\rho}{2}}$. One has for all t in [0,n]

$$W_1(t) = \alpha X_1(t) + \beta X_2(t), \qquad W_2(t) = \alpha X_1(t) - \beta X_2(t) \tag{A2.6}$$

Substituting (A2.6) into (A2.5) we obtain, once again after some algebraic manipulations

$$\frac{S^*(n)}{S^*(j)} \frac{1}{b_n(j)} = \alpha(j,n) \exp\{\alpha (Y_1(n) - Y_1(j)) + \beta (Y_2(n) - Y_2(j)) \} \tag{A2.7}$$

where for all t in [0,n]

$$Y_1(t) = \int_0^t [(\sigma_S - \frac{\eta}{a}) + \frac{\eta}{a} e^{-a(t-s)}] \, dX_1(s) \tag{A2.8}$$

and

$$Y_2(t) = \int_0^t [(\sigma_S + \frac{\eta}{a}) - \frac{\eta}{a} e^{-a(t-s)}] \, dX_2(s) \tag{A2.9}$$

Formula (3.2.5) follows immediately upon substituting (A2.7) into (A2.3). Formula (3.2.6), the value of the contingent claim $x_2^n = \max\{ g_n - d\sum_{j=0}^{n-1} \frac{S(n)}{S(j)}, 0\}$, obtains by exactly the same steps followed to obtain (3.2.5).

The fact that the processes in (A2.8) and (A2.9) are jointly gaussian and independent from each other, i.e. cov ($Y_1(t)$, $Y_2(s)$) = 0 for all t,s in [0,n], follows from standard results concerning the solutions of linear systems of stochastic differential equations. In fact $E(Y_i(t)) = 0$ for all t in [0,n] , i=1,2 while for $s \le t$ we have

$$\operatorname{cov} \{Y_1(s), Y_1(t)\} = (\sigma_S - \frac{\eta}{a})^2 s + \frac{\eta}{a^2} (\sigma_S - \frac{\eta}{a}) (1 - e^{-as}) e^{-a(t-s)}$$

$$+ \frac{\eta}{a^2} (\sigma_S - \frac{\eta}{a}) (1 - e^{-as}) + \frac{1}{2} \frac{\eta^2}{a^3} (1 - e^{-2as}) e^{-a(t-s)} \tag{A2.10}$$

and

$$\operatorname{cov}\{Y_2(s), Y_2(t)\} = (\sigma_S + \frac{\eta}{a})^2 s - \frac{\eta}{a^2} (\sigma_S + \frac{\eta}{a}) (1 - e^{-as}) e^{-a(t-s)}$$

$$- \frac{\eta}{a^2} (\sigma_S + \frac{\eta}{a}) (1 - e^{-as}) + \frac{1}{2} \frac{\eta^2}{a^3} (1 - e^{-2as}) e^{-a(t-s)} \tag{A2.11}$$

depending, as claimed in the text, only on σ_S, η, and a.

References

Artzner, P. and F. Delbaen (1989), "Term Structure of Interest Rates: The Martingale Approach", *Advances in Applied Mathematics* 10 : 95-129.

Bacinello, A.R. and F. Ortu (1993a), "Pricing Equity-Linked Life Insurance with Endogenous Minimum Guarantees", *Insurance: Mathematics and Economics* 12: 245-257.

-------- and ---------- (1993b), "Pricing Guaranteed Securities-Linked Life Insurance under Interest-Rate Risk", *Actuarial Approach for Financial Risks*, Transactions of the 3rd AFIR International Colloquium, 1: 35-55.

Black, F. and M. Scholes (1973), "The Pricing of Options and Corporate Liabilities", *Journal of Political Economy* 81 : 637-659.

Brennan, M.J. and E.S. Schwartz (1976), "The Pricing of Equity-Linked Life Insurance Policies with an Asset Value Guarantee", *Journal of Financial Economics* 3: 195-213.

------------ and --------- (1979a), "Alternative Investment Strategies for the Issuers of Equity-Linked Life Insurance Policies with an Asset Value Guarantee", *Journal of Business*, 52: 63-93.

------------ and --------- (1979b), *Pricing and Investment Strategies for Guaranteed Equity-Linked Life Insurance*. Monograph n. 7, The S.S. Huebner Foundation for Insurance Education, Wharton School, University of Pennsylvania, Philadelphia.

Cheng, S.T. (1991), "On the Feasibility of Arbitrage-Based Option Pricing When Stochastic Bond Price Processes Are Involved", *Journal of Economic Theory* 53: 185-198.

Cox, J.C., Ingersoll, J.E. and S.A. Ross (1981), "A Re-examination of the Traditional Hypotheses about the Term Structure of Interest Rates", *Journal of Finance* 36: 769-799.

---------, ---------- and -------- (1985), "A Theory of the Term Structure of Interest Rates", *Econometrica* 53 : 385-407.

Delbaen, F. (1990), "Equity Linked Policies", *Bulletin Association Royal Actuaires Belges*, 33-52.

Delvaux, T. and M. Magnée (1991), *Les Nouveaux Produits d'Assurance-Vie*. Collection Actuariat, Editions de l'Université de Bruxelles.

Frigerio, A. , Ortu, F. and F. Pressacco (1992), "Contingent Claims Valuation under Interest Rate Risk with Applications to Portfolio Insurance", *Manuscript*.

Hadley, G. (1961), *Linear Algebra*. U.S.A.: Addison-Wesley Publishing Company.

Harrison, M.J. and D. Kreps (1979),"Martingales and Arbitrage in Multiperiod Securities Markets", *Journal of Economic Theory* 20 : 381-408.

Ingersoll, J.E. (1987), *Theory of Financial Decision Making* . Totowa, N.J.: Rownan and Littlefield.

Johnson, N.L. and S. Kotz (1970), *Continuous Univariate Distributions-1*. Boston, MA: Houghton Mifflin Company.

Karatzas, I. and S. Shreve (1988), *Brownian Motion and Stochastic Calculus* . New York: Springer-Verlag.

Rabinovitch, R. (1989), "Pricing Stock and Bond Options when the Default-Free Rate is Stochastic", *Journal of Financial and Quantitative Analysis*, 24 : 447-457.

Vasicek, O. A. (1977), "An Equilibrium Characterization of the Term Structure", *Journal of Financial Economics*, 5 : 177-188.

Solvency-Simulation in Non-Life Insurance

Bert Kramer
Faculty of Management and Organization
University of Groningen
P.O. Box 800, NL-9700 AV Groningen

Sytze Hobma
Department of System Development Non-Life
AEGON Nederland N.V.
P.O. Box 23000, NL-8900 MA Leeuwarden

This paper describes the development of a cash flow model that can be used to analyze the solvency-position of a non-life insurance company. The model can be used by the management of a company to analyze the consequences of different policies on the solvency-position in the coming years. The model is build up of 3 modules: a financial module where the value of and the profits on the investment portfolio are determined, an insurance-technical module where the loss-amount is determined, and the main model where the results of the first two modules are joined into a balance-sheet from which the solvency margin can be calculated. The model uses simulation to generate the needed values in the financial and insurance-technical modules. This research is partly based on and inspired by the management model of Daykin and Hey (see Daykin & Hey (1990)).[1]

---

[1]This paper is a summary of the master thesis of the authors for their Econometrics study at the University of Groningen, which is the result of a practice which they did with AMEV Nederland N.V., a large Dutch insurance company. The authors would like to thank H.J. Prins, C. Schweigman, K. Nevels, C.D. Daykin, J.H. von Eije, and two anonymous referees for very helpful comments on an earlier draft.

1. Introduction

The solvency is the most important gauge for the health of an insurance company. The principle of an insurance is that the insured pays a premium to the insurer, who in turn promises to the insured to pay a compensation when the insured suffers a loss/damage as specified in the insurance policy. In case of insolvency the insurer can not keep his promise so the principle of insurance will be undermined. The confidence in the insurance branch will be undermined when this situation occurs too often. Confidence is necessary to effect an insurance and it is therefore necessary for the branch as a whole that all insurance companies are sufficiently solvent.

To guarantee its solvency, an insurance company has at its disposal equity, free reserves, and possibly reinsurance. According to the current EC-laws the equity and the free reserves (defined as solvency margin[2]) have to obey certain requirements which get higher when gross received premiums rise and which get lower when more reinsurance cover is present.[3]

The legislation for solvency aims to be an early warning system: there should be enough time to take measures to prevent damage to the insured when a company fails to meet the legislation. There are, however, some criticizing comments to be made

---

[2]According to law the solvency margin is equal to the sum of:
- The paid-up authorised capital.
- Half of the not paid-up part of authorised capital, as soon as the paid-up part amounts to 25% of this capital.
- The statutory and free reserves not put against any obligation.
- The transferred surplus.

[3]The required solvency margin is the higher amount of the following two calculations (Kastelijn and Remmerswaal (1986)):
a) 18% of gross received premiums up to 10 million ECU plus 16% of gross received premiums in excess of 10 million ECU.
b) 26% of gross average incurred claims over the three last preceding years to 7 million ECU plus 23% of gross average incurred claims over the three last preceding years in excess of 7 million ECU.

In both cases the result is reduced by the ratio of net paid claims to gross paid claims in the last financial year, with maximum reduction of 50% (The difference between net and gross paid claims is paid by the reinsurer). In the above-mentioned formulae the ECU has to be converted against the prescribed rate (which is normally not equal to the market rate).

(Berkouwer (1992)):

- There are no rules for valuing technical reserves. This makes it possible to lower the technical reserves and thereby to increase the solvency margin.
- The solvency requirements do not have a theoretical basis. They originated in a political discussion.
- There is no specification of valuation standards for assets and liabilities. This makes it possible to flatter the numbers.
- Possible negative developments in the solvency margin are not taken into account as long as the minimum is not reached.
- There is not any allowance made for the solvency of possible reinsurers.
- The use of premiums as basis contains the danger, that when the premiums of a company are too low, the minimal solvency margin will also be too low.

The EC-standard can not be used as an internal standard within a company because it assumes a break-up situation, while you may expect from a company that it will go on (going concern situation). The EC-standard does not take into account the needed margin for new policies which are still to be effected.

In this paper we describe the development of a simulation model that can be used by the management of a non-life insurance company to analyze the development of the solvency margin of the company in the coming years. The model is built on two separated modules. The first, insurance-technical, module deals with the actuarial variables, while the second one, the financial module, is devoted to the analysis of the financial variables. The results of these two modules are integrated in the main model.

In the financial module we use the investment model put forward by Wilkie(1986). We extended this model with equations for property, in which the effect of the rent control mechanism present in the Dutch economy is taken into account. The approach taken in the insurance-technical module is a fairly standard one in the literature on solvency.

Our model is partly based on and inspired by the management model of Daykin & Hey (1990). There are, therefore, several resemblances between our solvency model and the management model of Daykin and Hey. Both are simulation models that look at the solvency margin in a dynamic framework that best fit the internal requirements of a non-life insurance company. There are, however, also some major differences between the models, some of which are: The management model only uses three reserves: the asset margin, the unearned premium reserve, and the outstanding claim reserve; while in our solvency model one can look at each existing (technical) reserve separately. The management model only generates the total claims amount in a year for each line of business (max. 6), while our solvency model separately generates each claim for all lines of business (max. 12). The management model is a long-term model (max. 20 years), while our solvency model is a medium-term model (3 years). Finally, the management model also look at the market position of the company, our solvency model does not do this.

Section 2 presents the problem definition, and section 3 specifies the model, with special attention to the insurance-technical module (3.1), the financial module (3.2), and the main model (3.3). Some numerical results of the model will be presented in section 4, and the paper will be closed by some final remarks in section 5.

2. Problem description

To develop a solvency-standard which is more suitable for internal use than the prevailing EC-standard, one first has to get insight into the factors influencing solvency. This can be done with the aid of a model which shows the development of the solvency position given the values of certain parameters. By varying the parameter-values one can get an idea of their influence on the solvency of the company. The results can then be used to develop a practical solvency-standard for internal use. The problem can thus be described as follows: develop a model to determine the dynamic solvency and to support the development of a suitable practical solvency-standard of a non-life insurance company.

To make the problem description operational it is necessary to define solvency as is most appropriate for our goals. Since one of the disadvantages of the EC-legislation was the static character, we want to formulate a dynamic definition. We will use the going-concern principle because the results will be for internal use. This leads us to the following definition: an insurance company is dynamic solvent, when its reserves are sufficient to enable it to continue writing business at the planned level in the future, with a very high probability that the equity capital and the free reserves stay above the legally required level. This definition is a slightly adapted version of the definition of dynamic solvency given by Campagne(1957).

From the definition it follows that solvency can not be measured objectively, because discussion is possible about what a "very high probability" is. This lack of objectivity is unavoidable. A disadvantage of the definition is, that it can not be used to develop a new legislative standard. However, the definition is important for the company, because it is important for the company to meet the requirements, not only now but also in the future.[4]

3. Specification of the model

From the first part of the problem definition it can be concluded that the model should be able to determine the solvency position of the company. According to the definition of dynamic solvency, the model should be able to determine the available and the legally required margins. A measure for the solvency is the probability that equity plus free reserves will drop below the legally required minimum.

Equity and free reserves are part of the balance sheet of the company. The size of these balance sheet items partly depends on the size and the development of other balance sheet items. Therefore, the best way to present equity and free reserves is with a balance sheet model. The model should be dynamic since we are interested in the dynamic solvency of the company. The dynamic property of our model is expressed by the fact that it is a multi-year model; the model estimates the (development of the) balance sheet items for the next three years.

The future amount of equity and free reserves is uncertain. The uncertainty is

[4]When the definition is used in a context where the legislation is put in question, then an adjusted version is necessary: an insurance company is dynamic solvent, when its reserves are sufficient to enable it to continue writing business at the planned level in the future, with a very high probability that it will be able to meet all liabilities in the future.

mainly caused by the uncertainty of the operating result. The operating result can be divided into the investment result, the insurance-technical result, and the expenses.

The investment result follows from the investment of the technical and free reserves in bonds, shares, loans, and property. The uncertainty of the result is caused by the uncertainty of the yield on the investments. The yield on investments consists of interest, dividend, rent, and price-changes.

The insurance-technical result is equal to the earned premiums minus incurred claims minus commission. The earned premiums partly depend on the competition at the insurance market, but a company does have some influence on these figures. The commission depends on earned premiums. Incurred claims, on the contrary, are fixed externally for the larger part. The insurer does have some influence, for instance by changing the level of the deductible, but it can not remove all but a small part of the uncertainty about the total amount of incurred claims.

The expenses consist of salaries and wages, social costs, other staff costs, housing, administration, telephone, advertisement, postage costs, etcetera. The expenses are normally quite well controllable.

Above-mentioned uncertainties will be considered as stochastic processes in the model. We use simulation as the model building technique. Simulation is a common, suitable, way to handle stochastics. When using simulation the model has to be run several times to get a good idea of the variability of the results.

Considering the above, we aimed at a simulation model that works according to the following principles:

1. As input should be given: the opening balance sheet, the expected premiums and reinsurance premiums given the policy intentions, and certain policy specific aspects (for example distribution policy: what percentage of profit will be distributed as dividend).
2. In addition to the input mentioned under point 1, the model also uses several statistical distributions. The parameters of the distributions can be given by the user.
3. As output will be given: an 'average', a 'best', and a 'worst' balance sheet. The legally required and the available solvency margins, and, for some balance sheet items and the solvency margins, the standard deviations and a correlation matrix will also be given.

The above-mentioned division of the result in investment and insurance-technical result can also be found in our model. The model is subdivided into three parts: an insurance-technical module, a financial module, and the main model.

The insurance-technical module determines the insurance-technical result. For each line of business the number of claims in a given year is determined stochastically, after which the claim size for each claim is determined (also stochastically). In this manner the total claims amount is estimated. Likewise, estimates are made for the claims reserves (i.e. reserve for outstanding claims) and for the amount paid by the reinsurers.

In the financial module the investment result is determined. Predictions are made for the yield on and the value of the different investment types.

The main model determines the remaining balance sheet items and combines them with the results of both other modules into a balance sheet. Finally, the available and required solvency margins are calculated from this balance sheet.

The model can be represented graphically in a schedule as follows:

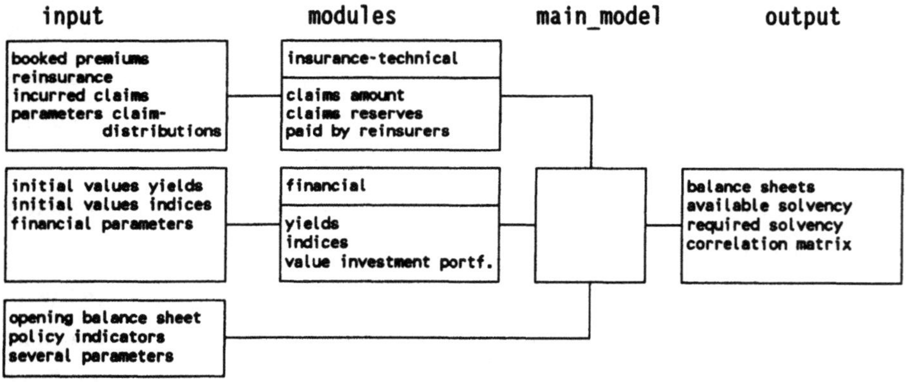

3.1 The insurance-technical module

The purpose of the insurance-technical module is to generate all the needed data for the main model in relation to the insurance-technical result. The main components are the booked claims, claims net of reinsurance, and changes in the claims reserves.

All these quantities are stochastic. To generate values for the future, we use probability distributions for which the parameters were estimated with the aid of realized values in the past. Obvious trends and/or cycles in the number of claims a year are included.

The determination of the above-mentioned quantities takes place in several steps. First the number of policies is calculated, then the number of claims, which depends on the number of policies, is estimated. A claim size is then determined for each claim. The claims reserves are determined in the final step of the module.

3.1.1 Calculation of the number of policies

The number of policies for a line of business is determined with the aid of the given total booked premiums. The total booked premiums are given as input by line of business. The number of policies is calculated as the quotient of the booked premiums and the average premium.

3.1.2 Estimation of the number of claims

The number of claims in a year is assumed to be negative-binomial distributed, where the parameters dependent on the number of policies. In the literature the Poisson-distribution is normally taken as statistical distribution for the number of claims. The Poisson-distribution was not adequate in our case since with a Poisson-distribution the average and the variance are equal, which was not the case here. The variance of the number of claims was much higher than the average for most lines of business. However, if the parameter of a Poisson-distribution is also stochastic, i.e. if the parameter has a statistical distribution, then variance and average do not have to be equal anymore. In that case, the distribution of the number of claims is case equal to a kind of generalized Poisson-distribution. The Gamma-distribution appears to be a good choice for the parameter-distribution. When a variable is Poisson distributed with a Gamma distributed parameter, then the variable is negative-binomial distributed (for derivation, see Nevels(1988)).

The parameters of the negative-binomial distribution are estimated from the average and the variance of the number of claims ('moment estimators'). The usual assumption is that the average number of claims depends on the number of policies, while the variance is assumed constant. Various authors (see for instance Pentikäinen(1982) or Beard, Pentikäinen & Pesonen(1984)) have found that the number of claims often follow cycles. Economical factors are the main course for this phenomenon. For a more extensive explanation of the cycles we refer to the literature.

In our case, the number of claims for most lines of business also showed cyclical behavior, so we decided to take these cycles into account.

The average number of claims is calculated as a fraction of the number of policies. This fraction is modelled as the sum of a constant and a sinus-function of time. The last part takes care of the cyclical behavior. The period and the amplitude of the cycles differ strongly between the different lines of business and for some lines of business cyclical behavior is not obvious.

So the number of claims (NCLA) is generated by line of business (....), depending on the number of policies (NPOL). For each line of business we assume:

....NCLA <- NEGBIN(p,s)

The parameters of the distribution are estimated with the aid of the moments-method. The moments are: $\mu = s \bullet (1 - p) / p$ and $\sigma^2 = s \bullet (1 - p) / p^2$. Rewriting gives:

$$p = \mu / \sigma^2$$
$$s = \mu^2 / (\sigma^2 - \mu)$$

$$\mu = \text{....NPOL} \bullet \{\alpha + \beta \bullet \sin(2 \bullet \pi \bullet t / \tau + 2 \bullet \pi \bullet f)\}$$

with α, β, τ, f and σ^2 estimated from data from the past.

In the equation for μ, α reflects the average number of claims per policy, β the amplitude of the cycle wave, τ the length of the period, and f the phase of the cycle wave at time $t=0$. σ^2 is the variance of the disturbance term, i.e. the difference between the observed number of claims and the average μ.

It can be deducted that a variable with a POISSON(θ) distribution, where the parameter θ is itself GAMMA(a,b) distributed, has a negative-binomial distribution with parameters $s = a$ and $p = b / (b + 1)$ (see Nevels(1988)).

It appeared that drawing from a negative-binomial or a Poisson distribution, with the claim numbers considered here, takes a lot of running time. Because of this we partly used a normal approximation (the size of θ justifies this). The procedure works as follows: after we have estimated the parameters of the negative-binomial distribution (see above), the estimations can be used to determine the parameters of the Gamma-distribution with the aid of the formulas given in the last paragraph; we now draw from the Gamma-distribution whereafter the outcome of the draw is used as parameter of the Poisson-distribution. When drawing from the Poisson-distribution we use the normal approximation, where the outcomes are rounded and outcomes less than 0 are thrown away. So we generate the number of claims as follows:

1. a = s
2. b = p / (1 - p)
3. θ <- GAMMA(a,b)
4. ....NCLA <- NORMAL(θ,θ) {Normal approximation of Poisson distribution with $\mu = \sigma^2 = \theta$}

3.1.3 Determination of the claim size

When generating a claim size, our model assumes a combined distribution which consists of three parts, namely a part that generates zero claims[5], a part that generates 'normal' claims (truncated Gamma-distribution) and a part that generates large claims (Pareto-distribution). The border between 'normal' claims and large claims is of course rather arbitrary. We especially looked at the shape of the distribution when choosing the border. Normally about 10% is taken as large claim.

The reason for this construction is as follows: firstly the zero claims are a considerable part of the total number of claims for several lines of business. That is why zero claims have to be considered separately. Secondly it appeared that the observed tail of the distribution does not fit the tail of a Gamma-distribution. Instead of using a complicated (and difficult to generate) alternative distribution, above-mentioned solution is chosen.

So we assume that the individual claim size (CLAI) by line of business (....) has a combined distribution:

---

[5]Zero claims are claims which are reported, but which have a payable amount of zero. This can be the case when the amount can be fully recovered, because there is no cover for the claim, or because of administrative procedures.

....CLAI <- COMBI(p,α,ß,M,θ)

COMBI is a combined distribution with distribution function:

$$F(x) = p1 + p2 \cdot GAMMA'(x;\alpha,\beta,M) + p3 \cdot PARETO(x;M,\theta)$$

with $p1 + p2 + p3 = 1$

so

$$P(X = 0) = p1$$

$$F(x \mid 0 < x \leq M) = p1 + p2 \cdot GAMMA'(x;\alpha,\beta,M)$$

$$F(x \mid M < x < \infty) = p1 + p2 + p3 \cdot PARETO(x;M,\theta)$$

The distribution GAMMA' is a truncated Gamma-distribution, and has as distribution function:

$GAMMA(x;\alpha,\beta) / F(M;\alpha,\beta)$	$x \leq M$
0	$x > M$

with $F(M;\alpha,\beta) = P(X < M)$. $P(X < M)$ is the probability that a GAMMA(α,ß) distributed variable X is less than M.

The fractions of the number of corresponding claims of the total number of claims were taken as estimators for p1, p2, and p3.

The normal claims are assumed to be Gamma distributed. A truncated Gamma-distribution is used here because there is put a maximum to normal claims. (I.e. a normal Gamma-distribution is taken, which is valid up to a maximum. The distribution is rescaled because otherwise the total probability would be less than 1.)

Because of the truncation the regular estimation procedures are not valid. That is why an iterative moment-estimator is used. To calculate the average and the variance of a truncated Gamma-distribution we need to determine the probability that a variable with a non-truncated Gamma-distribution with the same parameters (i.e. the same average and variance) exceeds the maximum. Since the parameters are unknown the probability is unknown. The probability can not be calculated analytically either. The method we used is to take initial values for the parameters, after which above-mentioned probability can be calculated. When the probability is known, it can be used to calculate new, better, moment-estimators for the parameters. For this new estimators we calculate above-mentioned probability again. The estimators are 'good' when the probability does not change significantly anymore. If the probability still changes significantly, then the last step will be followed once more. The moment-estimators of the normal/non-truncated Gamma-distribution can be taken as initial values. The (mathematical) formulation of this method will be given in the following paragraphs.

For a GAMMA(α,ß) distributed variable X it is valid that:

$$
\begin{aligned}
E[X \mid X < M] &= \{F(M;\alpha + 1,ß) / F(M;\alpha,ß)\} \bullet E[X] \\
&= \{F(M;\alpha + 1,ß) / F(M;\alpha,ß)\} \bullet \{\alpha / ß\} \\
E[X^2 \mid X < M] &= \{F(M;\alpha + 2,ß) / F(M;\alpha,ß)\} \bullet E[X^2] \\
&= \{F(M;\alpha + 2,ß) / F(M;\alpha,ß)\} \bullet \{\alpha(\alpha + 1) / ß^2\}
\end{aligned}
$$

It is now possible to derive iterative estimators of α and ß. The method works as follows:

1. A initial value for α and ß is chosen (here: the moment estimators of the complete Gamma-distribution).
2. Given α and ß F(M;α,ß), F(M;α + 1,ß) and F(M;α + 2,ß) can be calculated.
3. The values of F(M;α,ß), F(M;α + 1,ß) and F(M;α + 2,ß) calculated in step 2 are, together with the above-mentioned conditional moments, used to derive better estimators of α and ß.
4. Stop when the change in α and ß is not significant anymore; otherwise go to step 2.

The corresponding formulae are:

1. $\alpha(0) = \mu^2 / \sigma^2$

   $ß(0) = \mu / \sigma^2$
2. $t(n) = F(M;\alpha(n),ß(n))$

   $u(n) = F(M;\alpha(n) + 1,ß(n))$

   $v(n) = F(M;\alpha(n) + 2,ß(n))$
3. $\alpha(n + 1) = \{[(\sigma^2 + \mu^2) / \mu^2] \bullet [u(n)^2 / (v(n) \bullet t(n))] - 1\}^{-1}$

   $ß(n + 1) = [u(n) / t(n)] \bullet \alpha(n) / \mu$

with $n \in N$.

The Pareto-distribution is used as distribution for large claims. The Pareto-distribution normally has two parameters: a minimum value and a shape parameter. The minimum is fixed in advance and is equal to the maximum of the truncated Gamma-distribution. The remaining parameter can be estimated with the maximum-likelihood method.

Thus, the parameter M of the PARETO distribution is equal to the parameter M of the truncated GAMMA distribution, so M is known.

The parameter θ, however, still has to be estimated. This can be done with the Maximum-Likelihood method. Using this method leads us to the following estimator of θ:

$$\theta = 1 / [\Sigma_i \ln(x_i)/n - \ln(M)]$$

Here $\Sigma_i \ln(x_i)/n$ is the average of the natural logarithms of our observations and $\ln(M)$ is the natural logarithm of M.

The total claims amount is equal to the sum of all individual claims.

3.1.4 Determination of the claims reserves

A run-off scheme is used to determine the claims reserves and the booked claims. This scheme specifies the proportions of the incurred claims to be paid in the particular and the following years. The scheme is specified by line of business.

The booked claims are equal to the claims paid in a particular year. Which is equal to the total incurred claims amount minus the mutation in the claims reserves. The claims reserve is formed by the outstanding claims and the IBNR-claims (incurred but not reported). The IBNR-claims are not generated separately. Therefore the above-mentioned number of claims are including IBNR-claims. If necessary, this can be taken into account in the run-off scheme.

Besides the claims reserve, there are also other technical reserves. Each technical reserve is considered separately. For additions and withdrawals the internal procedures are used as much as possible. Since the specific kinds of premiums and claims used in the procedures are not always mentioned separately, estimations are sometimes required.

3.1.5 Reinsurance

In the model three different kinds of reinsurance are possible, namely: stop-loss, excess of loss, and proportional reinsurance. Stop-loss reinsurance insures that part of the total claims amount that exceeds the priority (deductible). Excess of loss reinsurance insures the amount exceeding the priority by event or by exposure unit. Proportional reinsurance insures a fixed percentage of the total claims amount. In the model, all different kinds of reinsurance have a maximum amount (dependent on the kind of reinsurance either by event or in total). The reinsurance aspect is currently still at a basic level.

3.1.6 The storm generator

In connection with their special character and the great influence of heavy storms, the model contains a separate 'storm generator'. The use of a storm generator can be defended by the fact that possible heavy storms are specified separately in the reports of the company, where the numbers of the claims directly caused by the storm are given and also the numbers corrected for storm. There is also a separate technical reserve for storm catastrophes.

The storm generator first generates the number of heavy storms in a year and after that the total claims amount caused by the storm. The number of heavy storms is assumed to be Poisson-distributed with parameter $\ln(1/p)$, with p equal to the probability on *no* heavy storm in a particular year (i.e. $p=0.9$ says that on average in one year out of ten at least one heavy storm occurs). The extent of the storm is assumed to be Beta-distributed; the Beta-distribution is recommended when few data is available (see for instance Law & Kelton (1982)), which was the case here.

3.2 The financial module

The financial module generates the different yields on and values of shares, bonds, loans, and property. Basis for the module is the investment model of Wilkie(1986). The model is extended with equations for property. The parameters of the investment model have been re-estimated for the Dutch market because the values given by Wilkie are for the British market.

3.2.1 The investment model of Wilkie

The investment model of Wilkie is a long-term model, i.e. it describes how certain investment variables (e.g. share price) develop over a longer period, without putting to much attention to short-term fluctuation. That is why factors which are important in the short run, but do not affect the long-term structure of the model, are left out for reasons of simplification.

The model considers regular shares and fixed interest stock. In an extension on the model, property is also taken into account (see Daykin & Hey (1990)). The extension for property appeared not to suffice for The Netherlands; we will return to the point later.

Wilkie postulates that inflation is the driving force for the other investment variables that have been investigated. Each is thus made dependent on inflation rather than vice versa.

Two series are considered for shares: dividend and dividend yield (dividend yield is received dividend as percentage of the share price), where share prices are defined as a function of both series.

Wilkie restricts himself to yields on long term Government securities, in fact represented by Consols, on the assumption that this one variable can be used to represent adequately the whole level of interest rates for varying terms. The conversion takes place with a risk-adjustment factor. He postulates a model in which the yield on Consols responds with a considerable time lag to changes in the rate of inflation.

The reader is referred to Wilkie(1986) for the explicit formulation of the original investment model.

3.2.2 The investment model of Wilkie including property

In 1988 Wilkie extended the investment model with equations for property. This extension can be found in Daykin & Hey (1990). The series which are used for property are: the index of property rents and the yield on the index of property rents (i.e. the rental index divided by the corresponding price index). The procedure is equivalent to the one used for shares. The equations implicitly assume a free market for rents. In The Netherlands, this assumption only holds for commercial and industrial premises, not for private houses. These rents are highly regulated in The

Netherlands. Since a 'normal' property portfolio includes both private houses and commercial and industrial premises, and since part of the property can be unoccupied, there is no completely free market, but neither is there a fixed, regulated rise in the rents. That is why new equations were developed for property in The Netherlands.

3.2.2.1 The property price index

Since the property price index is used in our main model, we first tried to develop an equation for the property price index. It appeared to be much easier to formulate an equation for the property price index directly instead of doing this via the index of property rents.

We assumed property to be an inflation resistant investment. That is why our first step was to link the rise in the property price index to the rise in the retail price index via a multiplicative model:

$$[V(t) \;/\; V(t-1)] = c(t) \bullet [Q(t) \;/\; Q(t-1)]^{\beta} \bullet \epsilon(t)$$

with V(t) the property price index, Q(t) the retail price index, ß a parameter independent of time, and $\epsilon(t)$ a white noise term.

The question now arises: what does c(t) look like? Since the left side of the equation consists of a function of the property price index and the right side of a function of the retail price index, it appears logical to take c(t) as a function of the property and the retail price indices. A good choice appears to be:

$$c(t) = [Q(t-1) \;/\; V(t-1)]^{\alpha}$$

While estimating the resulting equation it was found that α and ß do not differ significantly from each other. Rewriting thus gives:

$$[V(t) \;/\; V(t-1)] = [Q(t) \;/\; V(t-1)]^{\beta} \bullet \epsilon(t)$$

This can be linearized by taking the logarithm on both sides:

$$\nabla \ln V(t) = \beta \bullet (\ln Q(t) - \ln V(t-1)) + VE(t)$$

where $VE(t) = \ln\epsilon(t)$ is a white noise term.

With the estimation it appeared that the white noise term had both a simultaneous and a lagged effect:

$$VE(t) = VB \cdot VSD \cdot VZ(t-1) + VSD \cdot VZ(t)$$

with $VZ(t)$ a sequence of identically distributed unit normal variates and VSD the standard deviation.

The increase in the property price index can thus be modelled as follows:

$$\nabla \ln V(t) = \beta \cdot (\ln Q(t) - \ln V(t-1)) + VB \cdot VSD \cdot VZ(t-1) + VSD \cdot VZ(t)$$

3.2.2.2 The yield on the index of property rents

It is assumed that the yield on the index of property rents $YO(t)$ (i.e. yield from received rents, analogous to dividend yield on shares) only depends on the value of property (i.e. the property price index $V(t)$) and last year's yield. This leads us to the following equation:

$$YO(t) = [V(t) / V(t-1)]^{\tau} \cdot YO(t-1)^{(1-\tau)} \cdot \epsilon(t)$$

τ is a kind of distribution factor between the rise in the value of property and last year's yield.

When the equation is linearized and the terms are taken as deviations from the mean, the following equation results:

$$\ln YO(t) = \ln(YOMU) + YOW \cdot (\nabla \ln V(t) - VMU) + (1-YOW) \cdot [\ln YO(t-1) - \ln(YOMU)] + YOSD \cdot YOZ(t)$$

with $\ln(YOMU)$ equal to the mean of $\ln YO(t)$, VMU equal to the mean of $\nabla \ln V(t)$, YOW equal to $\ln\tau$, YOSD the standard deviation of the white noise term, and $YOZ(t)$ a sequence of independent identically distributed unit normal variates.

In comparison with the equation of Wilkie, the rise in the property price index in deviation from the mean is included as extra explanatory variable.

3.3 The main model

The connection between the insurance-technical module and the financial module, and the resulting available and required solvency margin is established in the main model. Here the cash-flow principle is used.

The main model consists of three parts: a part where the available solvency margin is determined, a part where the required solvency margin is determined, and a part where the remaining balance sheet items, which are not needed for the determination of the available or the required solvency margin, are determined.

The method on which the first two parts are based works as follows: first the definition equations of the available and of the required solvency margin (these are legally defined, see footnotes 2 and 3) are written out, after which the different components are written out until all parts are specified externally. This means that all the resulting variables either are given as exogenous input or are determined in the financial or insurance-technical module. The resulting equations are partly definition equations and partly estimated equations. Some equations are estimated because the definition equation is not practically feasible or because there is no definition equation available, and there is a good statistical relation with other variable(s). The equations are estimated with ordinary least squares (OLS).

A definition equation is not practically feasible if the equation contains variables which are difficult to determine. In that case strongly related variables are used which either are already available in the model or are easier to generate than the original variables.

When a particular variable can not be determined externally and when no definition equation is available, two options remain: either take the variable as exogenous input or estimate the variable with other variables which either are available already or are easier to determine.

The investments are the balancing item of the balance sheet. To achieve this, first the balance sheet will be drawn up with the value of the current investment portfolio, only. Thereafter, the resulting surplus/deficit is invested in the different types according to a given apportionment key. The investment portfolio is assumed to be changed once a year.

4. Some numerical results

We have run the model with imaginary data. The amount of reinsurance is put to zero. In this section we will present a summary of the results generated by the model. The number of simulation-runs is equal to ten. Table 1 gives the balance sheet and table 2 the profit and loss account of the company for the years 1993 to 1996. The amounts in these tables are the average values over all ten simulation-runs. The report file generated by the model also presents the results of the "worst" (i.e. lowest solvency over the years) and the "best" run, but those figures will not be shown here. An indication of the volatility of the results is given in table 4, which specifies the range of the ratio's of the available and the required solvency margins for the different runs.

The model predicts a loss for the company in 1993. This loss is mainly caused by a sharp rise in the (premiums and other technical) provisions. In the years after 1993, the company raises its premiums per policy. This causes a decline in the number of policies. This decline in the number of policies causes a decline in the total claims amount. At the same time, the premiums are quite stable, because the decline in the number of policies is compensated by a rise in the premiums per policy. Therefore, the model predicts that, on average, the profit and the solvency will rise in the years after 1993.

From the balance sheet and the profit and loss account, the available and required solvency margins can be deduced. The average margins are given in table 3. For a description of the range of the margins, see table 4. Table 3 and 4 also show a rise in the solvency of the company over the years. However, table 4 indicates that in one run the company almost became insolvent (i.e. the ratio got very close to 1) in 1994. In 1996, the solvency also worsens in, at least, one run: while in 1995 all ratio's were above 2.0, 1996 shows one ratio in the 1.5 to 2.0 range. Concluding, we can say that on average the company can expect a rise in its solvency, but also that bad times are always possible.

	1993	1994	1995	1996
Assets				
Investments:				
Private loans	106935	92010	87881	88977
Shares	21824	26286	39804	37016
Bonds	60064	75239	81269	85163
Property	26810	24623	23486	23669
Total:	215633	218159	232440	234825
Liabilities				
Capital	6000	6000	6000	6000
Reserves	8303	13760	27836	30559
Technical provisions:				
Premiums	36251	36030	35729	35208
Claims	12352	6757	4913	4276
Other	10250	10374	10439	10534
Other liabilities	142478	145238	147523	148249
Total:	215633	218159	232440	234825

Table 1: Balance sheet, average values, amounts in thousands.

	1993	1994	1995	1996
Premiums	68528	68937	69084	68425
Commission	-13810	-13892	-13922	-13789
Mov. in prem. prov.	-11251	221	301	522
(A)	43467	55265	55463	55158
Claims	29413	21581	14974	13077
Movem. in cl. prov.	-13427	- 5595	- 1844	- 637
(B)	15986	15986	13131	12440
(A)-(B)	27481	39279	42333	42718
Costs	-49398	-49437	-49450	-49389
Earned interest	6514	19081	21175	22357
Mov. in other prov.	- 3500	- 124	- 65	- 95
Profit before taxes	-18902	8801	13992	15591
Taxes	11760	- 2065	- 4240	- 5006
Net Profit	-7142	6735	9751	10586

Table 2: Profit and loss account, average values, amounts in thousands.

	1993	1994	1995	1996
available	15553	21010	35086	37809
required	11819	11886	11910	11803

Table 3: solvency margins, amounts in thousands.

range	1993	1994	1995	1996
-∞ - 0.0	0	0	0	0
0.0 - 0.5	0	0	0	0
0.5 - 0.8	0	0	0	0
0.8 - 0.9	0	0	0	0
0.9 - 1.0	0	0	0	0
1.0 - 1.1	0	1	0	0
1.1 - 1.2	2	0	0	0
1.2 - 1.5	8	1	0	0
1.5 - 2.0	0	6	0	1
2.0 - 3.0	0	2	6	3
3.0 - +∞	0	0	4	6

Table 4: Ratio of available and required solvency margin.

The results of the financial module are presented in table 5. The figures are the averages over the ten runs. These figures show very volatile financial markets in the years 1993 to 1994. Especially striking are the boom in share prices from 1993 to 1995, the fall in property prices, and the high yields on consols. However, we found quite different figures in other simulation-runs; some specific for a quiet, 'normal', financial market, but also some with very volatile markets. To really know the risks of your investments, it's best to see how they do in a volatile market.

	1993	1994	1995	1996
Dividend yield on shares	7.00%	6.96%	5.13%	6.35%
Share price index	1678	2000	2987	2718
Direct yield on consols	6.74%	7.43%	8.72%	8.87%
Direct yield on property	6.59%	7.33%	7.68%	7.60%
Property price index	155	142	132	127

Table 5: Results of the financial module.

5. Final remarks

We have described a model which predicts the development of the solvency of a non-life insurance company for the coming years. It has appeared to us that the solvency is influenced by many factors and that it is, therefore, very difficult, if not impossible, to represent this in a simple model. This becomes evident when looking at the size of the model. We are aware of the fact that the size and especially the large number of variables will not make the analysis of the model easy. But this is unavoidable if one wants to keep a model about solvency somewhat realistic.

The computer program is still in its test phases and is specially developed for and strongly based on AMEV Non-life. Because of this the program is not suitable for general use in its current form. Another Econometrics-student is currently continuing our work for his graduation-research. His aim is to further extend the model and to generalize it so the model can be used by other insurance companies, too.

6. References

Beard, R.E., Pentikäinen, T. & Pesonen, E. (1984). Risk Theory (3rd Edition). Chapman and Hall Ltd. London.

Berkouwer, H. (1992). Solvency Requirements in the EEC. Quaterly Letter from the Netherlands Reinsurance Group 129 (September): 3-7.

Campagne, C. (1956). Minimum Standards of Solvency for Insurance Firms. OEEC: TFD/PC/565.

Daykin, C.D. & Hey, G.B. (1990). Managing Uncertainty in a General Insurance Company. Institute of Actuaries. Oxford.

Kastelijn, W.M. & Remmerswaal, J.C.M. (1986). Solvency. Surveys of Actuarial Studies no.3. Nationale-Nederlanden N.V..

Law, A.M. & Kelton, W.D. (1982). Simulation Modeling and Analysis. McGraw-Hill. New York.

Nevels, K. (1988). Dictaat Actuariële Wiskunde. University of Groningen. Groningen

Pentikäinen, T.(ed.) (1982). Solvency of Insurers and Equalization Reserves Volume I. Insurance Publishing Company Ltd. Helsinki.

Wilkie, A.D. (1986). A Stochastic Investment Model for Actuarial Use. Transactions of the Faculty of Actuaries 39: 341-403.

A Multicriteria Classification:

An Application to Italian Mutual Funds

Luisa TIBILETTI
Istituto di Matematica Finanziaria
Facoltà di Economia e Commercio - Università
P.zza Arbarello, 8 I- 10122 Torino (Italy)
Tel. +39-11-54.68.05, Fax +39-11-54.40.04

1. Introduction[1]

The evaluation problem of the fund performance has been widely debated in the literature during the last twenty years (see for example, Treynor (1965), Levy-Sarnat (1984), Koury-Martel (1990)) and numerous performance measures have been proposed. Since each of them may take into account a different set of factors (such as the investment term, the safe return comparison,..) *discordant performance judgment* may be formulated by using different indicators. This fact has motivated the attempts to tackle the problem using multicriteria procedures in order to yield a *global* evaluation. An example in this direction is offered by Cardin *et al.* (1992), where a PROMETHEE multicriteria method has been employed. The crucial point of this method is the preference functions choice and although, that permits a proper fund classification, it may appear an "unfriendly" approach to users, who are not accustomed to deciding upon analytical expressions.

In order to meet users' requirements, we intend to propose a multicriteria procedure which appears to be a natural extension of the standard mono-criterion method based on the quantile notion.

If the classification procedure involves more than one performance measure, this notion requires a multidimensional formulation (for a sta-

[1] *Acknowledgments*

The Author wishes to thank M.F. Norese, L. Peccati and E. Volpe di Prignano for some valuable suggestions and comments. Obviously, she is completely responsible for any remaining error.

tistical approach see Tibiletti (1992) and for its use in multicriteria analysis see Tibiletti (1993)).

In this note, we investigate the performance of 35 Italian mutual funds during the triennium 1988-91. Since we have confined ourselves to an investigation of the fund performance from the investor's point of view, two factors play important roles: *(i)* the loads charged by the investor and *(ii)* the investment term. It follows that the global evaluation depends crucially on the investor's timing.

This paper is organized as follows. In the next section we discuss the standard methods of performance evaluation. In Sec. 3 we introduce the quantile multicriteria classification procedure. In Sec. 4 the results of the data processing are presented. Last session contains conclusions.

2. Some remarks on the performance measures

Among the numerous fund performance indicators proposed in literature, the simplest one is given by the *return on a share* over the period [0,T]

$$i = \frac{(Q_T + D) - Q_0}{Q_0} = \frac{Q_T + D}{Q_0} - 1 \qquad (1)$$

where Q_t stands for the net asset value (NAV) of the fund at epoch t and D is the sum of the capitalized dividends (per share) distributed over [0,T].

If the purpose of the classification is to compare funds in terms of *management efficiency* in running funds, then the index *i* proves an appropriate tool. Nevertheless, if the purpose is to offer a *supporting tool for investment decisions*, in other terms we consider the evaluation from the investor's point of view, then a more precise evaluation *must* take into account the loading charge which is added to the net asset value at the time of purchase[2].

It is well known that Italian mutual fund loads are not fixed, but:

- depend on the category, for example, bond funds charge lower loads than those imposed by stock funds;
- are proportional to the amount invested;

---

[2] A correct evaluation must also involve the redemption charges and the annual management fees, when established in the contract.

- load scaling differs from one investment company to another.

A more suitable performance indicator for our purpose is the *return on invested capital* referred to the period [0,T]

$$j = \frac{(Q_T + D)(1 - c) - Q_0}{Q_0} = (1+i)(1-c) - 1, \qquad (2)$$

where c is the loads charged at epoch 0 and it is expressed as a percentage of the amount invested (see Appendix for more details).
Since the loading charge penalizes the long term investment in a different manner from the short one, we will consider two performance indices:

x_1 = the value of j concerning a short-term investment
x_2 = the value of j concerning a long-term investment.

3. The Quantile Multicriteria Classification Procedure

3.1 The Multidimensional Quantile Notion

The problem of extending the concept of median and quantile into higher dimensions has been widely discussed in literature (for a rich critical survey of the numerous definitions introduced see Small (1990)). In line with this debate Tibiletti (1992) has proposed a notion which is consistent with their use in descriptive statistics. The definition is the following[3].

Definition 1. Let $X = (X_1,..,X_d)$ be a continuous random vector with cumulative function

$$F(x) = Pr[\{X_1 \le x_1\} \cap \{X_2 \le x_2\} \cap \ldots \cap \{X_d \le x_d\}],$$

and decumulative function

$$\bar{F}(x) = Pr[\{X_1 > x_1\} \cap \{X_2 > x_2\} \cap \ldots \cap \{X_d > x_d\}].$$

Each point of the sets

$$I_q = \{x \in \mathbb{R}^d : F(x) = q \},$$

[3] For a more rigorous definition the reader is referred to Tibiletti (1992).

$$\bar{I}_{1-q} = \{x \in \mathbb{R}^d : \bar{F}(x) = 1-q\}, \quad q \in [0,1]$$

is called a ***multidimensional q-th quantile*** of **X**.

Remark 1. If $d=1$, then[4] $F \equiv 1 - \bar{F}$. So I_q coincides with $\bar{I}_{1-q}$ and Definition 1 reduces to the usual notion of quantile.

Suppose now we want to evaluate the funds performance on the basis of d indicators. Therefore, each fund performance can be summed up in a d-dimensional vector. Clearly, each q-th quantile $x = (x_1,..,x_d)$ permits to divide the fund sample into two segments composed of, respectively, the q% and the $(1-q)$% of funds under discussion. In particular, if

- $x = (x_1,..,x_d) \in I_q$: funds with performance indices less than or equal to $x_1, x_2,..,x_d$ are the q% of the total. Consequently, the remaining funds are the $(1-q)$%;
- $x = (x_1,..,x_d) \in \bar{I}_{1-q}$: funds with performance indices greater than $x_1, x_2,..,x_d$ represent the $(1-q)$% of the total. Those such that at least one index is not greater than the respective x_i represent the q%.

3.2 A Multicriteria n-tomic Classification Procedure

After the pioneering work of Moscarola-Roy (1977), where a trichotomic classification procedure was introduced, a number of different ***multicriteria n-tomic segmentation procedures*** have been proposed in literature (see Roy (1981,1985), Massaglia-Ostanello (1989) and Yu (1992)). In line with this research, Tibiletti (1993) has suggested a multicriteria procedure based upon the quantile notion, which:

- is a classification procedure;
- permits the pre-determination of the segment sizes[5];
- has an *evolutive* decision rule:

  the judgment evaluation depends crucially on the fund sample, consequently the entrance of new funds may generate different evalua-

---

[4] It is known that this equality does not hold for d>1.

[5] In the usual segmentation procedures (see above references) segment sizes could not be pre-determinated. In fact, a fund belongs to a category, if its performance indexes vary into pre-fixed ranges, which are independent of the performance of the fund sample. Therefore, a segment may be empty. That is not the case of the quantile procedure.

tion thresholds.

3.2.1 The bidimensional dichotomic classification

Suppose that the decision maker wants to assign the judgment "*well-performed*" or "*badly-performed*" to the funds on the basis of the values (x_1, x_2) defined in Sec.2. This is a typical dichotomic classification that can be solved by *choosing* an *appropriate* bidimensional q-th quantile, denoted by (x_1^*, x_2^*).

- **Should (x_1^*, x_2^*) belonging to I_q or to $\bar{I}_{1-q}$ be chosen?**

The choice of (x_1^*, x_2^*) belonging to I_q or to $\bar{I}_{1-q}$ reflects the preference between a procedure based on *compensative* or *non-compensative procedure.* If $(x_1^*, x_2^*) \in I_q$, then the mutual fund f with performance indices (x_1, x_2) is assigned the qualification

- *well-performed*: if $x_1 > x_1^*$ and/or $x_2 > x_2^*$,
- *badly-performed:* if $x_1 \le x_1^*$ and $x_2 \le x_2^*$;

vice versa, if $(x_1^*, x_2^*) \in \bar{I}_{1-q}$, then f is assigned the qualification

- *well-performed*: if $x_1 > x_1^*$ and $x_2 > x_2^*$,
- *badly-performed:* if $x_1 \le x_1^*$ and/or $x_2 \le x_2^*$.

In conclusion, if the decision maker decides that opposite judgments based upon different performance indices may compensate for each other, then he must choose $(x_1^*, x_2^*) \in I_q$. On the contrary, if he decides that minimum requirements in *each* index are to be surpassed, then $(x_1^*, x_2^*) \in \bar{I}_{1-q}$.

- **How to choose (x_1^*, x_2^*) in the set I_q (or $\bar{I}_{1-q}$)**

The choice of (x_1^*, x_2^*) in I_q (or $\bar{I}_{1-q}$) depends on the weight assigned to each performance indicator, in other terms it reflects the decision maker's timing (short/long term). Denote by m_i a q-th unidimensional quantile of X_i, $i=1,2$. The shorter the investment planned by the decision marker, the "nearer" he will fix x_1^* to m_1, and vice versa.

Remark 2. Essentially, the appropriate quantile choice reflects the decision maker's opinion on *how* to classify funds with differing performance evaluations. *Note* that, two groups of funds, which are judged well-performed or badly-performed according *each* quantile choice, can be distinguished. They are

$$A_q = \{x \in \mathbb{R}^2 : F(x) > q\},$$

and

$$\bar{A}_{1-q} = \{x \in \mathbb{R}^2 : \bar{F}(x) > 1-q\},$$

respectively.

3.2.2 The bidimensional n-tomic classification

This previous procedure can be easily extended to the case of a *n*-tomic classification ($n>2$). Nevertheless, some remarks in order to avoid incoherent evaluations need to be added:

- the evaluation procedure (*compensative* or *non-compensative*) must be the same in each classification step;
- the choice of the *proper* quantile must be coherent: let us explain this concept with an example.
  Suppose that a trichotomic classification (good, medium, low performance) is desired.
  Let the compensative procedure be accepted. Denote by
  $$(a_1, b_1) \in I_{q_1} \quad \text{and} \quad (a_2, b_2) \in I_{q_2}, \; q_1 < q_2$$
  the fixed quantiles, then
  $$a_1 \le a_2 \text{ and } b_1 \le b_2.$$
  On the contrary, if the non-compensative procedure is chosen and
  $$(a_1, b_1) \in \bar{I}_{1-q_1} \text{ and } (a_2, b_2) \in \bar{I}_{1-q_2}, \; q_1 < q_2$$
  are the fixed quantiles, then
  $$a_1 \le a_2 \text{ and } b_1 \le b_2.$$

Remark 3. If there are more than two performance indicators, previous conditions can be extended in a natural way (see for a deeper treatment Tibiletti (1993)).

Remark 4. In this note the performance indices adopted present the *same preference direction* (the more is preferred to the less). On the contrary, (for example if a risk measure is chosen) then, the procedure must involve appropriate partially cumulative-decumulative functions (see Tibiletti (1992)).

4. Performance Analysis: Italian Mutual Funds

The data processing refers to a group of 35 Italian bond and preferred stock funds. The examined period covers the triennium 1988-1991. This temporal arc permits both a *short term* and a *long* term evaluations: these yield to multicriteria problems.

In Table[6] 1, for each fund the returns *on a share* and the returns *on invested capital* referred to a short period (the year 1988) and a long period (the triennium 1988-1991) are collected.

TABLE 1

Italian bond funds and preferred stocks funds

Funds	Loads	Return on a share		Return on invested capital	
		Short	Long	Short	Long
IMI 2000	4,00	11,7	10,9	7,2	9,4
GESTIRAS	4,00	11,0	9,8	6,6	8,4
RISP.REDD.	4,00	11,0	9,2	6,6	7,7
FONDIMPIEGO	4,00	8,3	10,8	4,0	9,3
MIDA OBBL.	3,50	13,3	10,5	9,3	9,2
VERDE	3,50	12,0	9,8	8,1	8,5
IMIREND	3,50	10,9	10,7	7,0	9,4
EUROANTARES	3,33	11,2	10,1	7,5	8,8
EUROMOB. REDD.	3,00	11,5	12,0	8,2	10,8
AUREO REND.	2,50	15,2	11,8	12,3	10,8
CENTRALE R.	2,50	13,1	10,7	10,3	9,7
RENDIFIT	2,50	11,5	10,7	8,7	9,8
NAGRAREND	2,50	10,8	9,7	8,0	8,7
CASHBOND	2,00	12,6	11,7	10,3	11,0
RENDICREDIT	1,75	12,0	10,3	10,0	9,7
GRIFOREND	1,75	11,0	11,2	9,1	10,5
NORDFONDO	1,75	10,4	10,1	8,5	9,5
ROLOGEST	1,75	8,6	9,0	6,7	8,3
FONDINVEST1	1,50	11,4	10,2	9,7	9,7
ALA	1,25	12,3	10,4	10,9	10,0
GEPOREND	1,25	12,1	9,6	10,7	9,1
FONDICRI1	1,25	11,7	10,0	10,3	9,5
EPTABOND	1,25	9,6	9,4	8,2	9,0
EUROVEGA	1,17	12,6	11,7	11,3	11,3
CISALPINO	1,00	12,8	12,1	11,7	11,7
SFORZESCO	1,00	12,0	10,3	10,9	10,0
PRIMECASH	1,00	11,9	11,2	10,8	10,9
FIDEURAM	0,83	10,6	10,1	9,7	9,8
ARCA RR	0,75	13,6	11,2	12,7	10,9
GENERCOMIT	0,75	12,1	11,4	11,3	11,1
AGRIFUTURA	0,75	12,0	11,1	11,2	10,8
BN RENDIFON.	0,75	11,8	9,6	11,0	9,3
GESTIELLE M.	0,75	11,0	10,4	10,2	10,1
INTERB. REN.	0,50	10,1	9,7	9,5	9,5
PROFESS. RED.	0,25	14,9	12,6	14,6	12,5

[6] The Author thanks Luigi Bollani for the help provided in the data processing.

As mentioned before, loads are not *fixed*, but decrease in percentage to the growth of the invested capital, so the following considerations hold for an initial investment of £. 30.000.000.
For the sake of clarity of expression, the triennium data are presented in terms of annual average rates.

Data show that the returns on a share are on average *higher* in the short term than in the long term: in fact, this happens for almost all the funds. On the contrary, the returns on the invested capital present the opposite trend. The significance of these differences is highlighted in Table 1, where the funds are listed according to decreasing loads (see for example IMI 2000, GESTIRAS e RISP. REDD. with load rated at 4%).
We have applied the classification procedure illustrated in Sec. 3 to the returns of the invested capital data.
In Fig. 1 a dichotomic classification example is reported.

FIGURE 1
Return on invested capital

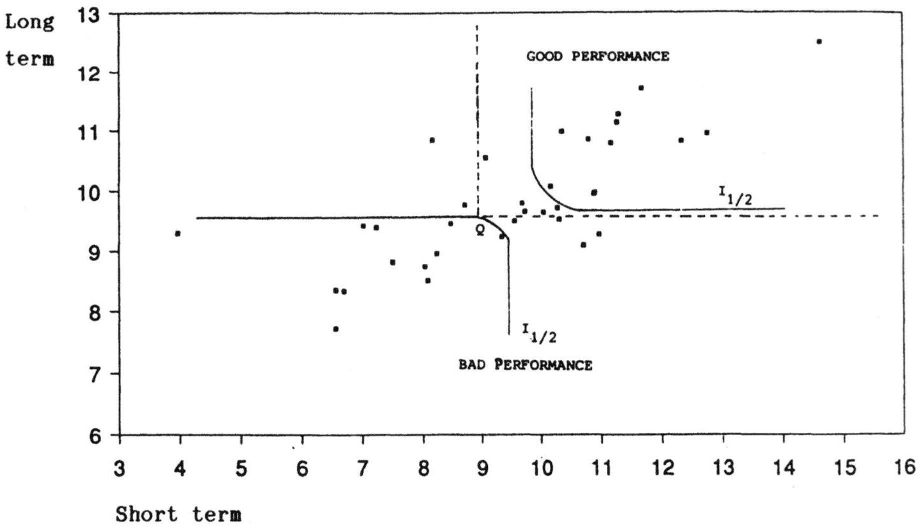

Sets $I_{1/2}$ and $\bar{I}_{1/2}$ permit to select the funds with "sure" performance:

(*i*) *well-performed* if they are placed over the curve $I_{1/2}$;

(*ii*) *badly-performed* if they are placed below the curve $\bar{I}_{1/2}$.

In order to decide on the remaining funds it was necessary to fix an appropriate median $Q(x_1^*, x_2^*)$.

• If the *non-compensative procedure* has been chosen, then Q belongs to $\bar{I}_{1/2}$ (see Fig. 1). Consequently, funds (x_1, x_2) such that

$$x_1 > x_1^* \text{ and } x_2 > x_2^*,$$

are evaluated well-performed. Vice versa, the remaining ones are judged badly-performed.

• If the *compensative procedure* has been fixed, then Q belongs to $I_{1/2}$. Consequently, funds (x_1, x_2) such that

$$x_1 > x_1^* \text{ or } x_2 > x_2^*,$$

are evaluated well-performed and the remaining ones are judged badly-performed.

A trichotomic classification is showed in Fig. 2, where the compensative procedure has been selected.

FIGURE 2

Return on invested capital

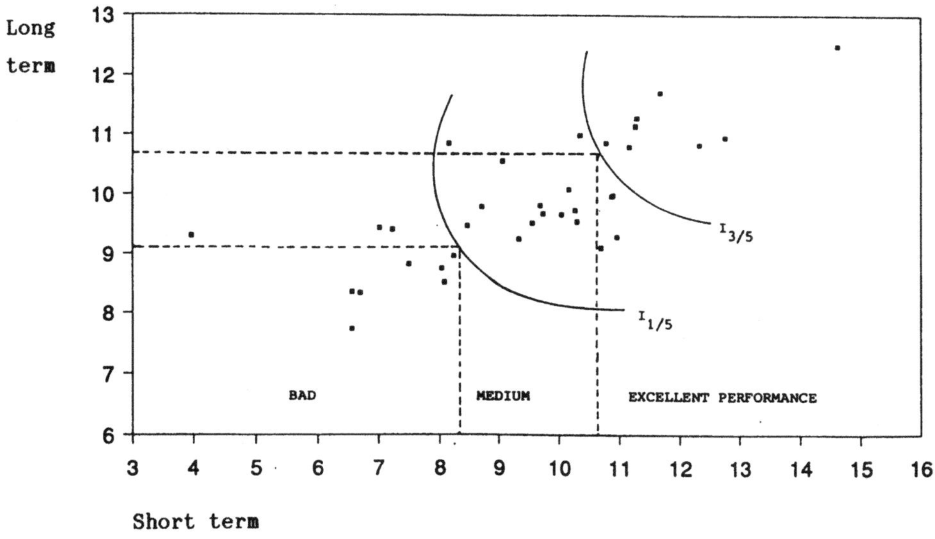

4. Conclusions

A group of Italian mutual funds is evaluated according more than one performance measure. A multicriteria procedure, which is user "friendly", has been proposed. Since the performance indicators adopted take into account the fund loads, the decision maker's investment timing plays an important role in the final judgment.

Appendix

Denote by A_t the capital amount available at epoch t. It follows that

1) the number of purchased shares at epoch 0 is

$$k = \frac{A_0 \,(1-c)}{Q_0}$$

2) the amount available at epoch T becomes $A_T = k\,(Q_T+D)$;

3) therefore, the return on invested capital A_0 becomes

$$j = \frac{A_T - A_0}{A_0} = \frac{(Q_T+D)(1-c) - Q_0}{Q_0} = (i+1)(1-c) - 1.$$

References

Cardin M., Decima G., Pianca P. (1992) Un metodo multicriterio per la valutazione della performance dei fondi d'investimento. *Il Risparmio.* 3: 623-632.

Khoury N.T., Martel J.M. (1990) The relation between risk-return characteristics of mutual funds and their size. *Finance.* 11: 67-82.

Levy H., Sarnat M. (1984) *Portfolio and investment selection: Theory and Practice.* Prentice Hall International Inc. London.

Massaglia R., Ostanello A. (1989) Un sistema di supporto alla valutazione di idoneità di candidati in un insieme evolutivo. *Atti delle Giornate di Lavoro* AIRO. Udine (Italy). 4-6 October.

Moscarola J., Roy B. (1977) Procédure automatique d'examen de dossiers fondée sur une segmentation trichotomique en présence de critères multiples. RAIRO. Recherche Opérationnelle. 2:145-173.

Roy, B. (1981) A Multicriteria Analysis for Trichotomic Segmentation Problems. in *Multiple Criteria Analysis and Applications* (Eds. P. Nijkamp - J. Spronk). Gower. Hampshire Gull:245-257.

Roy, B. (1985) Méthodologie Multicritère d'Aide à la Décision.

Economica. Paris.

Small, C. (1990) A Survey of Multidimensional Medians. *International Statistical Review*. Vol.58, 3:263-277.

Tibiletti, L. (1992) Some remarks on an extended notion of multidimensional quantile in connection with the partially cumulative-decumulative functions. *Atti del XVI Convegno* A.M.A.S.E.S.. Treviso (Italy). Sept., 9-12.

Tibiletti, L. (1993) A Multicriteria Procedure for a Closed-end Selection of Candidates. *Ricerca Operativa*. 65:61-74.

Treynor, J.L. (1965) How to rate management of the investment funds. *Harvard Business Review*. January-February.

Yu, W. (1992) Electre TRI. LAMSADE. Document n.74. April.

Abstract: The performance of an Italian mutual fund group is classified by means of a multicriteria procedure. Since the evaluations take into account the fund loads, the decision maker's investment timing plays a central role.

Key-words: Finance, Multicriteria Decision

ASSET LIABILITY MATCHING FOR PENSION FUNDS: A ONE-PERIOD MODEL

Paul C. van Aalst and C. Guus E. Boender
Department of Finance and Department of Management Science
Erasmus University Rotterdam
P.O. Box 1738, NL-3000 DR Rotterdam

1. Introduction

In recent years there has been a growing interest in the management of pension funds. The ageing population, new investment opportunities and closer monitoring by the plan sponsor and, in some countries, the government lead to the need for a more professional management of (the link between) the assets and liabilities of the pension fund. Besides the definition of risk[1] in an asset context, for example for the performance measurement of the portfolio manager, the risk of the whole fund should be taken into account. Risks of the liabilities that can be matched by an appropriate investment portfolio are not risks for the pension fund as a whole.

In this paper we will give an overview of the relevant risk factors of pension fund liabilities and present a one-period linear factor model, that can be used as a framework to estimate the influence of the risk factors and to describe the possibilities of matching.

This paper starts in paragraph 2 with an overview of the relevant risks of the liabilities of a pension fund. Essentially these are the inflation rate, the growth rate of real wages and changes in the (long) interest rate. Besides this, there is a stochastic uncertainty in the liabilities because the actuarial calculations use probability tables for the process of dying, promotion, resignation, etc. In paragraph 3 we will give an illustration of the relative importance of these risk factors using a simulation approach. In paragraph 4 we derive a linear factor model that summarizes the sensitivities of the liabilities for the mentioned economic risks. On the asset side a similar factor model has to be estimated: what are the

1 In this paper we will not make the distinction between risk and uncertainty as introduced by Knight [1921].

sensitivities of different investment returns for the inflation rate, the growth rate of real wages and changes in the long interest rate? The paper then describes in paragraph 5 a one-period model to match these sensitivities. Paragraph 6 summarizes the paper and concludes with some possibilities and difficulties of multi-period matching models.

2. Asset liability matching

2.1 Starting-points

Firstly we state that the primary function of a pension fund is insuring the pension rights of the (former) employees. The process of investing is – in a fully funded system – only a derived function. In other words: the liabilities are the *raison d'être* of the pension fund and the (long term) investment strategy should be matched to this. This starting-point implies that fluctuations in the value or the return of the assets cannot be considered a risk as long as the value or the return of the liabilities shows a comparable pattern.

The published year accounts of many pension funds apply different accounting procedures for the assets and for the liabilities. Assets can be valued at historical cost, nominal, taxation or market value, actuaries use different methods for calculating the present value of the liabilities. Conclusions about asset liability matching can only be useful when assets and liabilities are valued in the same way. This is our second starting-point.

Finally we define the liabilities of a pension fund as the present value of the accumulated rights of the present (active and non-active) participants. The asset liability matching process tries to immunize the risks in the present liabilities – which will be discussed in paragraph 2.2 – as good as possible by the well-considered selection of an asset mix. New years of service and new participants are new events, that will have to be financed by new contributions at the moment of origin. In this way we try to finance changes in the value of former pension liabilities by asset returns and new pension liabilities by new contributions.

2.2 *Liability risks*

If the risks in the liabilities of a pension fund are the starting-point for the selection of the strategic asset mix, we have to inventory what kind of risks are related to pension liabilities. Essentially the following risks can be distinguished.

Interest rate risk

In many, particularly Anglo-Saxon, countries a variable discount rate is used for calculating the present value of the liabilities. This discount rate is in some way related to the (long term) interest rate. In other countries a fixed discount rate is common. In the Netherlands, for example, a fixed discount rate of 4% is used since many years, regardless of the pension scheme.

Following the requirement that assets and liabilities should be valued in a comparable way, there are two possibilities. In a system with a fixed discount rate, the assets should be valued at the present value of the expected future cash flows on the basis of that same discount rate. If we want to value the assets at market value, a variable discount rate for the liabilities is necessary. Only in the latter case we can identify an interest rate risk in the liabilities, which may be absorbed by the investment portfolio.

Inflation and real wage growth risk

Also in this case we can distinguish two approaches. In many countries a legal view of the pension liabilities would imply a liquidation approach: suppose that all employees leave the company today, what would be the accumulated value of their rights? Firstly, in this way expected backservice liabilities because of future years of service are not taken into consideration. Secondly, the indexation of the rights of non-actives is in almost all countries conditional on the financial situation of the pension fund. The legal consequence of this is that the indexation is not part of the *liabilities* of the fund and the calculation of the expected liabilities cannot include the expected effect of the indexation.

From an economic point of view we consider the pension fund and the underlying company as a going concern. This implies an inflation and a real wage growth effect on the liabilities, resulting from the pension system (normally an final pay or an average pay system and affecting the rights of actives) and the indexation system (inflation or prosperity proof rights of non actives). Dependent on the exact pension and indexation system, the liabilities are more or less sensitive to changes in the inflation and real wage growth rate.

Actuarial risks

A pension fund applies several probability tables – related to death, marriage, resignation etc. – for the actuarial calculations. In general only the expected liabilities are presented. Implicitly it is assumed that the file of participants is large enough to neglect deviations from these expected values. Recently, doubt grows concerning this assumption. The deviations between the expected values and the realized values can be much larger than many pension fund managers expect. How can these risks be quantified and what is their role in the asset liability matching process?

If one is interested in quantifying these statistical uncertainties of the pension liabilities, one can try to find an analytical solution. As long as only one class of participants (say 35 year old female actives) and one transition probability (say dying) is taken into consideration, the solution is simple: the number of participants in the concerning transition follows a binomial distribution. For a complete pension fund with all kinds of participants and transitions and several interdependencies and conditions, an analytical solution appeared to be impossible up till now. In lack of such an analytical solution we will apply a simulation technique in this paper, see paragraph 3.

What is the use of quantifying these statistical/actuarial risks in the process of asset liability matching? It is not possible to absorb these risks by selecting a suitable asset mix! But it is possible to use the statistical risk in the process of determining upper or lower bounds of the funding level of the pension fund or a minimum rate of return on the assets.

Pension system risks

In all developing countries discussion grows about the fundamentals of the pension system. Equal treatment of males and females, a growing tendency towards individualization and flexibility in the pension system, the (uncertain) consequences of the ageing of the population and many other questions have an influence on the development of the (sensitivities of the) liabilities of pension funds. For example, more individualization means less solidarity in these schemes and more uncertainty in the outcomes of the liabilities. Changes from a final pay system to an average pay system affect the inflation and real wage growth sensitivities of the liabilities. It is rather questionable whether these (institutional) changes should play a role in the asset liability matching process. Because of this reason we will not address ourselves to this question in the underlying paper.

3. Relative importance of risk factors; a simulation model application

3.1 Liability model

The micro-simulation of the participants that is applied in this paper[2] tries to illustrate the uncertain development of the liabilities of a pension fund in a better way than the usual actuarial models do. The participants of the pension scheme are not classified by age and sex, but they are followed individually through time by means of simulation. Starting from the usual life-, promotion- and resignationtables a game of chance determines every year for every participant whether he dies, gets promotion, resigns, etc. By allowing new employees it is possible to control the size of the underlying company. For the process of getting promotion in the company we apply the pull approach: firstly the process of leaving the company, because of death, retirement or resignation, is simulated for all individual participants. After that an employee gets promotion (is pulled upwards in the organization) in case one of the positions in the organization is vacant. The promotion probabilities are therefore dependent on the situation of the other active participants. We refer to the appendix for further information about the file of participants and the way we simulated the economic series.

On the basis of a pension scheme and an economic scenario (inflation, real wage growth) the total liabilities[3] of the pension fund can be determined. By simulating the liability model, given a certain pension scheme and a certain file of participants, many times, the uncertainties of the liabilities of the pension fund are illustrated and quantified.

3.2 Results

The results in this section are presented as an illustration of the relative importance of the different risks of paragraph 2.2. We distinguish three variants:

I. In the base variant we consider a world without inflation or real wage growth. The discount rate for the actuarial calculations is fixed at 4%. The liabilities in this variant can vary only as a result of the unpredictable courses of lifes and careers of the participants. This variant quantifies the earlier mentioned actuarial risk of the pension fund.

---

2 See Van Aalst and Boender [1993] for an introduction of this technique.

3 We define the liabilities of a pension fund as the present value of the accumulated rights of the participants, as explained in paragraph 2.

II. In the second variant the inflation and real wage growth are simulated as described in the appendix. This has an influence on the rights of actives (because of general wage increases) and the rights of non-actives (because of the indexation system). The discount rate is still fixed at 4%.

III. In the third variant we introduce a variable discount rate, defined as the difference between the long interest rate and the inflation rate, with a minimum of 0%.

For all three variants simulations are executed 500 times for a period of 40 years from the fixed (present) starting file. We present the average liabilities (over 500 simulations) and the coefficient of variation (standard deviation divided by average) of the liabilities. We should emphasize the fact that the results are only meant as an illustration of the simulation principle. The outcomes depend very much on pension scheme, the file of participants and the chosen simulation method for the economic variables.

The figures 1 and 2 show the results for the liabilities of the original participants on basis of their original number of years of service. For the average liabilities we only present the variants I and II. Variant III is based on a variable discount rate, the difference between the long interest rate and the inflation rate, with an average of 2.9% (see table 1 in the appendix). Because of this the liabilities in variant III develop on a different level compared to variants I and II.

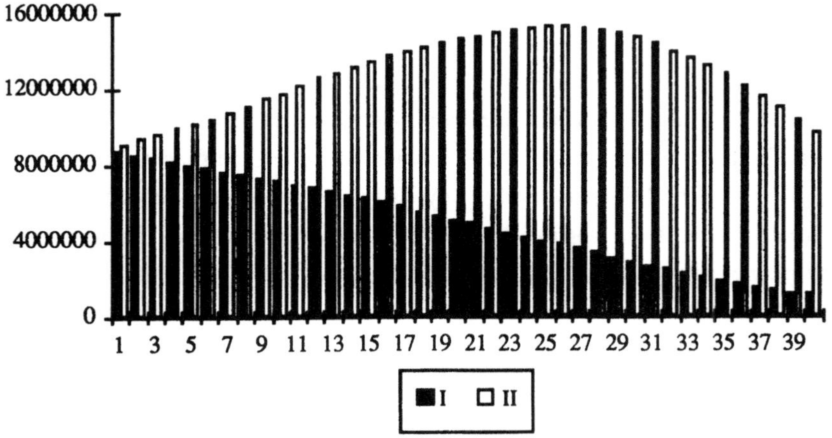

Figure 1: Average liabilities original participants

The liabilities increase as a result of inflation, wage growth, the career of the actives (backservice) and time (discount rate) and they decrease as a result of pension benefits and mortality. In variant I, without inflation and real wage growth, this results in monotonically decreasing average liabilities. In variant II we notice first increasing liabilities and later decreasing liabilities.

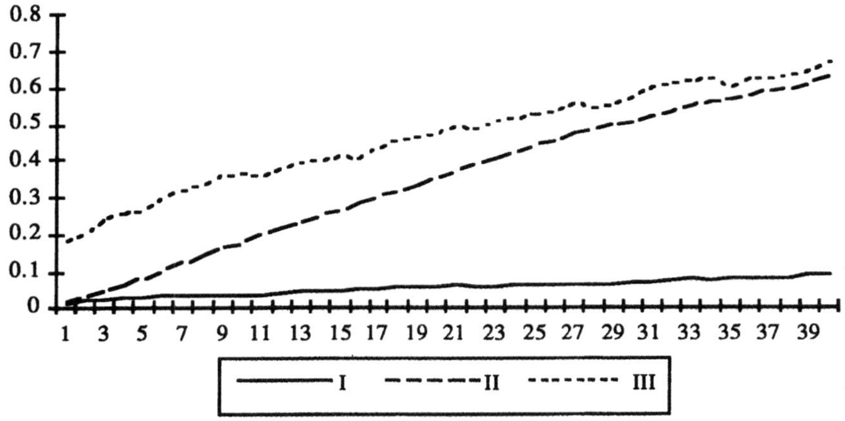

Figure 2: Coefficient of variation original participants

In the first year of the simulation period the coefficient of variation in variant I is 1.5% and in variant II 1.8%: in the short run the largest part of the uncertainty in the liabilities stems from statistical/actuarial risks and only a small part from the economic risk of indexation! Introduction of a variable discount rate leads to a coefficient of variation of 18.6% in the first year. In the last (40th) year of the simulation period the coefficients of variation are 9.5%, 62.5% and 66.5% respectively. Obviously, the uncertainty about the economic variables dominates in the long run. Notice the decreasing gap between II and III in figure 2. Because we only consider the original participants (in fact a file of participants that is dying out), the average age of the participants increases substantially during the simulation period. The effect of changes in the discount rate is smaller for older people.[4]

4 Or, stated otherwise, the duration of the liabilities decreases.

4. The liabilities of a pension fund: a one-period model

4.1 *Factor models*

In this paper we will present a factor model for the liabilities of a pension fund and use this model as a way of analyzing the possibilities of matching both sides of the pension fund balance sheet. This section gives a brief overview of (multi-)factor models. We refer to Haugen [1990] as an example of a more extensive introduction to factor models.

In general the growth rate of a stochastic variable can be described as:

$$g_t = E_{t-1}(g_t) + e_t \tag{4.1}$$

where:

E_{t-1} = the expectations operator, conditional on the information set at time t-1

The growth rate equals the expected growth rate plus a residual, describing the error process. This uni-dimensional error process can be refined to a linear multi-dimensional version, where the errors are related to unexpected changes in some general factors:

$$g_t = E_{t-1}(g_t) + b_1 \cdot f_{1,t} + b_2 \cdot f_{2,t} + \ldots + b_k \cdot f_{k,t} + \varepsilon_t \tag{4.2}$$

where:

b_i = the sensitivity of the growth rate to changes in factor i

$f_{i,t}$ = the *unexpected* change of factor i in period t

ε_t = the idiosyncratic growth rate in period t

Note that the expected changes in the factors are incorporated in the expected growth rate. The unexpected changes in the factors 1 to k are then the single sources of factor risk, because these unexpected changes account for the discrepancy between the actual growth rate and the expected growth rate. The sensitivities b_i determine the extent to which factor movements have an influence on the actual growth rate and can therefore be considered as factor risk measures. The idiosyncratic growth rate is the source of idiosyncratic risk. As the residual growth rates $\varepsilon_{i,t}$ are assumed to be mutually independent, the idiosyncratic risk can be diversified in a portfolio context.

In general it is possible to describe the growth rate of the liabilities and the growth rate of the assets (the return) as a one-period linear factor model like equation (4.2):

$$\text{(4.3)} \qquad \begin{aligned} \ln L_t - \ln L_{t-1} &= a_l + b_{l,1}\cdot f_{1,t} + b_{l,2}\cdot f_{2,t} + \dots + b_{l,k}\cdot f_{k,t} + \varepsilon_{l,t} \\ \ln A_t - \ln A_{t-1} &= a_a + b_{a,1}\cdot f_{1,t} + b_{a,2}\cdot f_{2,t} + \dots + b_{a,k}\cdot f_{k,t} + \varepsilon_{a,t} \end{aligned}$$

In the next section we will derive a linear factor model for the liabilities of a pension fund.

4.2 A one-period deterministic model

To illustrate the risks of a pension fund, we start with a simple one period model. Consider a fund with a single inflation proof pension benefit due in one period, say a year. B_1 is the expected real value of this benefit, i.e. the real value of the benefit, so excluding the (at the moment unknown) indexation, times the probability that the benefit will be paid.

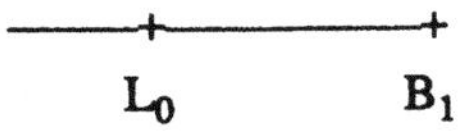

When using continuous discounting, the present value of this liability is:

$$\text{(4.4)} \qquad L_0 = B_1 \cdot \exp(E_0 infl_1 - {}_0r_1)$$

where:

$E_0 infl_1$ = the expected inflation rate for period 1 (t_0 to t_1) at t_0

${}_0r_1$ = the (certain) one year spot interest rate at t_0

If we define the real one year spot rate ${}_0rr_1$ as ${}_0r_1$ - $E_0 infl_1$ equation (4.4) can be rewritten as:

$$\text{(4.5)} \qquad L_0 = B_1 \cdot \exp(-{}_0rr_1)$$

At the end of period 1 the benefit B_1 plus the actual inflation rate are paid to the participants, so:

$$\text{(4.6)} \qquad L_1 = B_1 \cdot \exp(infl_1)$$

When the pension fund invests the present value L_0 and generates a total return on the asset mix of ret_1, the value of the assets will match the value of the liabilities if:

(4.7) $$L_0 \cdot \exp(ret_1) = L_1$$

Combining equations (4.5), (4.6) and (4.7) and taking natural logarithms, we get after rearranging:

(4.8) $$ret_1 = {}_0rr_1 + infl_1$$

(4.9) $$ret_1 = {}_0r_1 + UEinfl_1$$

where

$UEinfl_1$ = the unexpected inflation over period 1

= $infl_1 - E_0infl_1$

In words: the assets and the liabilities are matched if the return on the asset mix moves in line with the one period interest rate (the discount rate) and the unexpected inflation (the forecast error).

A multi-period example can be illustrated as follows:

——+————+————+————+—— .....

L_0 $\quad$ B_1 $\quad$ B_2 $\quad$ B_3

The liabilities of the pension fund consist of a set of expected future benefits $\{B_t\}$ (for t = 1, 2, ..., n), that, again, include real value of the benefits and the probability of payment but exclude the indexation. The present value of this liability is:

(4.10) $$L_0 = \sum_{t=1}^{n} B_t \cdot \exp\left(\sum_{i=1}^{t} E_0infl_i - t \cdot {}_0r_t\right)$$

where:

n = the year the last participant of the pension fund dies

E_0infl_i = the expected inflation rate for period i (t_{i-1} to t_i) at t_0

${}_0r_i$ = the (certain) i year spot interest rate at t_0

If we assume for simplicity a constant expected inflation rate for all future periods ($E_0 infl_i = E_0 infl$ for all i) and a flat term structure of interest rates (${}_0r_t = r_0$ for all t), equation (4.10) reduces to:

$$L_0 = \sum_{t=1}^{n} B_t \cdot \exp(t \cdot [E_0 infl - r_0]) \tag{4.11}$$

$$L_0 = \sum_{t=1}^{n} B_t \cdot \exp(-t \cdot rr_0) \tag{4.12}$$

where:

rr_0 = the real interest rate at t_0
$= r_0 - E_0 infl$

At t_1 the following happens: the indexed value of the first benefit is paid to the pensioners, a new expected level of future inflation rates $E_1 infl$ and a new level of the term structure of interest rates r_1 are defined.

$$L_1 = B_1 \cdot \exp(infl_1) + \sum_{t=2}^{n} B_t \cdot \exp(infl_1 + [t-1] \cdot [E_1 infl - r_1]) \tag{4.13}$$

$$L_1 = B_1 \cdot \exp(infl_1) + \exp(infl_1) \cdot \sum_{t=2}^{n} B_t \cdot \exp(-[t-1] \cdot rr_1) \tag{4.14}$$

If we define:

$$X = \sum_{t=2}^{n} B_t \cdot \exp(-[t-1] \cdot rr_0)$$

we can use the following first order approximation of the liabilities at t_1 on basis of realized value of $infl_1$, the new inflation expectation and the new discount rate:

$$L_1 \approx B_1 \cdot \exp(infl_1) + \exp(infl_1) \cdot \left[\sum_{t=2}^{n} B_t \cdot \exp(-[t-1] \cdot rr_0]) \right] \left[1 + \frac{\partial X / X}{\partial rr_0} \cdot \Delta rr_0 \right] \tag{4.15}$$

Notice that $-\frac{\partial X/X}{\partial rr_0}$ is the modified duration D_1 of the remaining liabilities at t_1. So equation (4.15) can be rewritten as follows:

(4.16) $$L_1 \approx B_1 \cdot \exp(infl_1) + \exp(infl_1) \cdot \left[\sum_{t=2}^{n} B_t \cdot \exp(-[t-1] \cdot rr_0)\right]\left[1 - D_1 \cdot \Delta rr_0\right]$$

Again there is a match between the assets and liabilities if equation (4.7) holds.

$$\exp(ret_1) \cdot \sum_{t=1}^{n} B_t \cdot \exp(-t \cdot rr_0) = \exp(infl_1) \cdot \left\{ B_1 + \left[\sum_{t=2}^{n} B_t \cdot \exp(-[t-1] \cdot rr_0)\right]\left[1 - D_1 \cdot \Delta rr_0\right] \right\}$$

(4.17)

Because $B_t = B_t \cdot \exp(-[t-1] \cdot rr_0)$ for t=1 we get:

(4.18) $$\exp(ret_1) \cdot \exp(-rr_0) \sum_{t=1}^{n} B_t \cdot \exp(-[t-1] \cdot rr_0) =$$

$$\exp(infl_1) \cdot \left\{ \left[\sum_{t=1}^{n} B_t \cdot \exp(-[t-1] \cdot rr_0)\right] - D_1 \cdot \Delta rr_0 \cdot \left[\sum_{t=2}^{n} B_t \cdot \exp(-[t-1] \cdot rr_0)\right] \right\}$$

After dividing by $\sum_{t=1}^{n} B_t \cdot \exp(-[t-1] \cdot rr_0)$ and taking logarithms, equation (4.19) results:

(4.19) $$ret_1 = rr_0 + infl_1 + \ln\left\{ 1 - D_1 \cdot \left[\frac{\sum_{t=2}^{n} B_t \cdot \exp(-[t-1] \cdot rr_0)}{\sum_{t=1}^{n} B_t \cdot \exp(-[t-1] \cdot rr_0)} \right] \cdot \Delta rr_0 \right\}$$

or:

(4.20) $$ret_1 = rr_0 + infl_1 + \ln\left\{ 1 - D_1 \cdot \alpha \cdot \Delta rr_0 \right\}$$

As a final step we take a first order approximation of the logarithmic term:

$$(4.21) \qquad ret_1 = rr_0 + infl_1 + \beta \cdot \Delta rr_0$$

or in terms of observable variables:

$$(4.22) \qquad ret_1 = r_0 + UEinfl_1 + \beta \cdot (\Delta r_0 - \Delta E_0 infl)$$

As the result of all this arithmetic, we have a factor model for this pension fund, which states that the assets and the liabilities match if the return on the assets moves in line with the one period interest rate (the discount rate) and the unexpected inflation (the forecast error) and the change in the interest rate and the expected inflation (affecting the change in the present value of the future liabilities). It is important to note that the sensitivity coefficient ($D_1 \cdot \alpha$ in (4.20) or its approximation β in (4.21)) is certain, i.e. can be calculated, at t_0.

Until now we have indexed all liabilities in the same way. In practice it is possible that different liabilities are indexed in different ways. For example: the rights of actives are prosperity proof, the rights of pensioners are inflation proof and the rights of sleepers are not indexed at all. In a general case the condition for asset liability matching can be summarized in the following factor model (where rwg = real wage growth):

$$(4.23) \qquad ret_t = r_0 + b_{1,1} \cdot \Delta r_0 + b_{1,2} \cdot UEinfl_t + b_{1,3} \cdot \Delta E_{t-1} infl + b_{1,4} \cdot UErwg_t + b_{1,5} \cdot \Delta E_{t-1} rwg$$

4.3 A one-period stochastic model

In section 4.2 we have only described the influence of the economic variables on the pension liabilities. Actuarial risks are not taken into consideration yet. A simulation model, as introduced in paragraph 2 and illustrated in paragraph 3, makes it possible to add (and quantify) a stochastic error term to equation (4.23), which measures the actuarial risk. In this way we can complete the one period multifactor model of the liabilities as:

$$(4.24) \qquad ret_t = r_0 + b_{1,1} \cdot \Delta r_0 + b_{1,2} \cdot UEinfl_t + b_{1,3} \cdot \Delta E_{t-1} infl + b_{1,4} \cdot UErwg_t + b_{1,5} \cdot \Delta E_{t-1} rwg + \varepsilon_t$$

This factor model gives the opportunity to quantify the in paragraph 2.2 mentioned risks and provides a framework for the matching of assets and liabilities, the problem we will address in paragraph 5.

5. Matching model

Equation (4.24) sets the goal for modelling investments. How well can returns on different assets be explained by the mentioned factors? Note that this implies that we are not interested in the set of factors that explain the returns of the assets as good as possible, we are only interested in the extent that the factors are 'translated' into asset returns.

In this paper we will not discuss the theory in this field. Besides dozens of other studies, we can refer to Fisher and Weil [1971], Cooper [1977] and Vasicek and Fong [1982] for some background of the interest rate sensitivity of bonds, to Joehnk and Petty [1980], Casabona, Fobozzi and Francis [1984] for the relation between interest rates and the return on common stocks and to Fama and Schwert [1977], Joehnk and Petty [1980] and Kaul [1990] for the effect of inflation on asset returns.

In the preceding paragraphs we described a way to estimate a linear factor model for the liabilities of a pension fund. This resulted in equation (4.24). In general we can describe the one-period growth rate of the liabilities as:

$$\text{(5.1)} \qquad \ln L_t - \ln L_{t-1} = ret_l = \sum_{k=1}^{K} b_{l,k} \cdot f_k + \varepsilon_l$$

When for different assets a similar factor model is estimated, we have:

$$\text{(5.2)} \qquad \ln A_t - \ln A_{t-1} = ret_a = \sum_{k=1}^{K} b_{a,k} \cdot f_k + \varepsilon_a, \text{ for } a = 1, \ldots, A$$

The growth rate of the surplus of the pension fund can then be described as:

$$\text{(5.3)} \qquad ret_s = \sum_{a=1}^{A} x_a \cdot ret_a - ret_l = \sum_{k=1}^{K} \left(\sum_{a=1}^{A} x_a \cdot b_{a,k} - b_{l,k} \right) \cdot f_k + \varepsilon_s$$

where:

x_a = fraction of total portfolio invested in asset a

If we can find an investment portfolio of which the term in brackets is zero, i.e. the weighted sensitivities b_a are the same as the b_l for all factors k, we have matched the assets and the liabilities of this pension fund. If it is not possible to find such an asset mix, the matching problem turns into a mean-variance framework: for each level of the growth rate of the surplus we are interested in the one with the least variation:

$$(5.4) \qquad \text{Min } E\left(\sum_{a=1}^{A} x_a \cdot ret_a - ret_l\right)^2$$

subject to:

$$\sum_{a=1}^{A} x_a \cdot ret_a - ret_l = ret^* \text{ and } \sum_{a=1}^{A} x_a = 1$$

In this way the factor model approach is not only an intuitively appealing approach to matching, but it also quantifies (in equation (5.4)) the possibilities of matching.

6. Conclusions and future research

In this paper we have investigated the financial position and risks of a pension fund. The essential function of a pension fund is insuring the rights of (former) employees. This starting-point leads to the following risks in the financial position of a fund: interest rate risk, inflation and real wage growth risk, actuarial risk and pension system risk. We derived a one-period linear factor model to describe these risks and proposed a simulation approach to estimate the third kind of risk. If a similar factor model is estimated for the different asset categories, that are available, we can try to match the assets with the liabilities on basis of a mean-variance approach.

For future research it is possible to extend the factor model to a multi-period one and to make an estimation of the relevant sensitivities for a particular pension fund. This multi-period case gives the opportunity to forecast changes in the file of participants, for example as a result of the ageing of the population, so giving the possibility to anticipate on those changes. It is also possible to look beyond short term fluctuations in the asset returns and to introduce lags between variables, for example between inflation and asset returns. On the other hand it should be stressed that the multi-period case becomes more difficult to estimate: the sensitivities $b_{l,k}$ at time t are dependent on both the history of the economic variables – inflation, wage growth and the discount rate – up till time t (economic risk) and the historic development in the file of participants up till time t (actuarial risk). But again simulation can give insight in the relative magnitude of the risks.

Appendix

In the simulation model of paragraph 3 we use a file of participants (generated by simulation) of a fictive pension fund. The relatively small file contains data of 100 actives, 58 sleepers, 65 pensioners and 40 widows/widowers. The 100 employees of the underlying company are divided over 5 function levels. Within every function level the employee starts at a basic wage and grows, not regarding promotion to the next function level, in 5 years to the maximum wage of that function level. The pension scheme includes an old age pension, based on a final pay system with a pension of 70% of the final wage in case of 40 active years. A correction for the State Pension, that every citizen receives, is built in. Apart from this the pension scheme offers a widow/widower pension for the partner of former employees. This pension is 70% of the old age pension. The accumulated rights of the non-actives are kept inflation proof. In other words they are indexed with the inflation rate.

For the determination of the liabilities of the pension fund we need time series describing the development of inflation, real wage growth and the interest rate during the simulation period. One possibility was to determine a set of fixed scenario's for these time series and to calculate the liabilities under these scenario's. Given the stochastic nature of the liability model the mentioned time series will be generated in a stochastic way in this paper. We did not choose a method that expresses a certain vision of the future (although this possibility can be built in), but a method that maintains the characteristics of the historic time series.

The method[5] estimates the means, (co)variances and auto(co)variances of the relevant time series during a certain (historic) period. Starting from the most recent values the method randomly extrapolates the time series such that the random future series converge to stationary time series with the same means, (co)variances and auto(co)variances as the historic estimates.

5 The method was introduced by Boender and Romeijn [1991].

We will use the following notation: the estimated vector of means is μ, the matrix of estimated (co)variances is V and the matrix of estimated auto(co)variances is W. Define Ω as WV^{-1} and the vector x_t as the random series at (the future) time t. It is possible to prove that the series:

$$\text{(A.1)} \quad x_t = \mu + \Omega(x_{t-1} - \mu) + \varepsilon_t$$

with

$$\text{(A.2)} \quad \varepsilon_t \sim N(0, V - \Omega V \Omega^T)$$

converge to series with the characteristics μ, V and W as described, from each vector with starting value x_0.

The method is not dependent on the vector μ. Assume that one wants to copy the volatility and mutual interdependence of the series from the historic data, but wants to use other expectations on the basis of an own vision. The Markov chain

$$\text{(A.3)} \quad x_t = \xi + \Omega(x_{t-1} - \xi) + \varepsilon_t$$

with e_t as in (A.2) converges to the self defined vector ξ preserving the characteristics as summarized in the matrices V and W.

Beside of this it is possible to simulate different investment scenario's within one simulation run of the liabilities, so with fixed series of inflation and real wage growth. Because of the mutual interdependence the return series, that will be generated, are conditioned on the already used inflation and real wage growth series.

Table 1 shows the input for the procedure used in this paper:

	average	st.dev.	correlationmatrix			autocorrelationmatrix		
			interest	wage	inflation	interest	wage	inflation
interest rate	7.41%	1.80%	1			0.911	-0.008	0.461
wage growth	6.21%	4.14%	-0.089	1		-0.190	0.734	0.661
inflation	4.53%	2.66%	0.469	0.708	1	0.352	0.724	0.826

Table 1: Interest rate, wage growth and inflation over the period 1960-1991 (Source: CBS)

References

Boender C.G.E. and H.E. Romeijn, 1991, The multidimensional Markov chain with prespecified asymptotic means and (auto)covariances, *Communications in Statistics*, pp. 345-359.

Casabona, P.A., F.J. Fabozzi and J.C. Francis, 1984, How to Apply Duration to Equity Analysis, *The Journal of Portfolio Management*, pp. 52-58.

Cooper, I., 1977, Asset Values, Interest Changes, and Duration, *The Journal of Financial and Quantitative Analysis*, 12/5, pp. 701-723.

Fama, E.F. and G.W. Schwert, 1977, Asset returns and inflation, *Journal of Financial Economics*, 5, pp. 115-146.

Fisher, L. and R.L. Weil, 1971, Coping with the Risk of Interest rate Fluctuations: Returns to Bondholders from Naive and Optimal Strategies, *Journal of Business*, pp. 408-431.

Haugen, R.A., 1990, *Modern Investment Theory*, Prentice-Hall, Englewood Cliffs, N.J.

Joehnk, M.D. and J.W. Petty, 1980, The Interest Sensitivity of Common Stock Prices, *The Journal of Portfolio Management*, pp. 19-25.

Kaul, G., 1990, Monetary Regimes and the Relation between Stock Returns and Inflationary Expectations, *The Journal of Financial and Quantitative Analysis*, 25/3, pp. 307-321.

Knight, F.H., 1921, *Risk, uncertainty, and profit*, Boston/New York.

Van Aalst, P.C. and C.G.E. Boender, 1993, A Micro-Simulation Model for Pension Funds, in: R. Flavell (ed.), Modelling Reality and Personal Modelling, Physica-Verlag pp. 327-341.

Vasicek, O.A. and H.G. Fong, 1982, Term structure Modelling Using Exponential Splines, *The Journal of Finance*, 37/2, pp. 339-348.

ASSET RISK IN A LIABILITY CONTEXT: AN EMPIRICAL STUDY FOR THE NETHERLANDS

Paul C. van Aalst, Winfried G. Hallerbach,
Margot E.T.A. van der Velden, Erwin A.C. van der Voort
Department of Finance, Erasmus University Rotterdam
P.O. Box 1738, NL-3000 DR Rotterdam

1. Introduction

We consider the position of an institutional investor, especially a pension fund. The investment process of a pension fund is a derived function: primarily it insures the pension rights of the (former) employees. Therefore the liabilities of the pension fund should guide the long term investment process. This implies that the analysis should not focus on absolute risk but on *relative risk*: to what degree does the value of the assets move in line with the value of the liabilities. Only the risks of the liabilities that cannot be matched by an appropriate asset mix are relevant. In short: when evaluating the financial position of a pension fund, one should concentrate on the value and the risks of the surplus, i.e. the value of the assets minus the value of the liabilities.

Starting point of our analysis are variables (factors) that have a pervasive influence on the liabilities of a pension fund. After an introduction to factor models in section 2, we present in section 3 a simple linear factor model that describes the relevant risk factors of pension liabilities. Section 4 gives a theoretical overview of how these factors may have an influence on asset returns. The next two sections are the heart of this paper: section 5 starts with an introduction of the data and section 6 gives some insight in the possibilities of matching inflation and interest rate risk in the Dutch stock and bond market. These possibilities appear to be very limited. Especially assets which provide some (short term) hedge to inflation are hard to find. Section 7 concludes the paper with a summary of our findings.

2. Factor models

In this paper we will present a factor model for both the liabilities and the assets of a pension fund and use this model as a way of analyzing the possibilities of matching both sides of the pension fund balance sheet. This section gives a brief overview of (multi-)factor models. We refer to Roll and Ross [1984], Rosenberg [1988] and Haugen [1990] as three examples of more extensive introductions of factor models.

In general the growth rate of a stochastic variable can be described as:

(2.1) $$g_t = E_{t-1}(g_t) + e_t$$

where:

E_{t-1} = the expectations operator, conditional on the information set at time t-1

The growth rate equals the expected growth rate plus a residual, describing the error process. This uni-dimensional error process can be refined to a linear multi-dimensional version, where the errors are related to unexpected changes in some general factors:

(2.2) $$g_t = E_{t-1}(g_t) + b_1 \cdot f_{1,t} + b_2 \cdot f_{2,t} + \dots + b_k \cdot f_{k,t} + \varepsilon_t$$

where:

b_i = the sensitivity of the growth rate to changes in factor i

$f_{i,t}$ = the *unexpected* change of factor i in period t

ε_t = the idiosyncratic growth rate in period t

Note that the expected changes of the factors are incorporated in the expected growth rate. The unexpected changes in the factors 1 to k are then the single sources of factor risk, because these unexpected changes account for the discrepancy between the actual growth rate and the expected growth rate. The sensitivities b_i determine the extent to which factor movements have an influence on the actual growth rate and can therefore be considered as factor risk measures. The idiosyncratic growth rate is the source of idiosyncratic risk. As the residual growth rates ε_t are assumed to be mutually independent, the idiosyncratic risk can be diversified in a portfolio context.

In general it is possible to describe the growth rate of the liabilities and the growth rate of the assets (the return) as a linear factor model like equation (2.2):[1]

$$
\begin{aligned}
(2.3)\qquad \ln L_t - \ln L_{t-1} &= a_L + b_{L,1}\cdot f_{1,t} + b_{L,2}\cdot f_{2,t} + \ldots + b_{L,k}\cdot f_{k,t} + \varepsilon_{L,t} \\
\ln A_t - \ln A_{t-1} &= a_A + b_{A,1}\cdot f_{1,t} + b_{A,2}\cdot f_{2,t} + \ldots + b_{A,k}\cdot f_{k,t} + \varepsilon_{A,t}
\end{aligned}
$$

If we can find an asset mix with sensitivities that are pairwise the same as the sensitivities of the liabilities, we have completely immunized the factor risks.

As stated in the introduction the asset liability management problem of pension funds focuses on *relative* risks: which asset mix hedges the risks of the liabilities in the best possible way? The liabilities represent the *raison d'être* of a pension fund and so they determine the risks that have to be matched. Therefore we will start in the next section with a one- and two-period model of pension liabilities. These simple models give a framework to inventory the essential risks of pension liabilities.

3. The liabilities of a pension fund

The first group of pension fund participants we consider are the active employees. In most European countries they build up pension rights following a final pay system or an indexed average pay system. In both cases the pension rights of the employee – and so the liabilities of the pension fund – are a function of his number of years of service and his wage, which increases with the inflation rate, the growth rate of the real wages and the individual career of the employee. The second group of participants consists of sleepers (former employees that are not yet retired) and pensioners. They do not build up new rights, but their pension benefits are frequently indexed with the inflation rate (inflation proof rights) or the nominal wage rate (prosperity proof rights).

A discount rate has to be defined for calculating the liabilities of a pension fund, the present value of the future pension benefits of all participants. Following the system in the United States and, more or less, the system in the United Kingdom, a growing number of European countries use a discount rate that is related to the long term interest rate on government bonds. This implies that changes in the interest rate change the value of the liabilities.

---

1 For simplicity we present the sensitivity coefficients here without a time index, thereby assuming that they are constant through time. This is probably is not true in practice.

To illustrate the risks of a pension fund, we start with a simple one-period model. Consider a fund with a single pension benefit due in one period, say a year. The real value of this benefit B_1 includes the probability that the benefit will be paid but excludes the indexation by the inflation rate.

$$\underset{L_0}{+}\qquad\qquad\underset{B_1}{+}$$

When using continuous discounting the present value of this liability is:

$$L_0 = B_1 \cdot \exp(E_0 infl_1 - {}_0r_1) \tag{3.1}$$

where:

$E_0 infl_1$ = the expected inflation rate for period 1 (t_0 to t_1) at t_0

${}_0r_1$ = the (certain) one year spot interest rate at t_0

At the end of period 1 the real benefit B_1 plus the actual inflation rate ($infl_1$) are paid to the participants. When the pension fund invests the present value L_0 at time t_0 and generates during period 1 a total return on the asset mix of ret_1, the value of the assets will match the value of the liabilities if:

$$L_0 \cdot \exp(ret_1) = B_1 \cdot \exp(infl_1) \tag{3.2}$$

Combining equations (3.1) and (3.2) and taking natural logarithms, we get after rearranging:

$$\begin{aligned} ret_1 &= {}_0r_1 + (infl_1 - E_0 infl_1) \\ ret_1 &= {}_0r_1 + UEinfl_1 \end{aligned} \tag{3.3}$$

where

$UEinfl_1$ = the unexpected inflation over period 1.

In words: the assets and the liabilities are matched if the return on the asset mix moves in line with the one-period interest rate (the time value of money) and the unexpected inflation (the estimation error).

A extended example with pension benefits in several periods, is described in Van Aalst and Boender [1993]. The main result of that paper is that the assets and the liabilities of a pension fund are matched if the return on the asset mix moves in line with the one-period interest rate (the time value of money), the unexpected inflation and real wage growth (the estimation error) and changes in the expected inflation, the expected real wage growth and the discount rate (the change in expectations). Equation (3.4) shows the result assuming a flat term structure of interest rates, inflationary and real wage growth expectations. For simplicity we present a first order approximation of the liability return. In practice this is not necessary. If needed, higher order approximations can be incorporated in the linear factor model.

$$(3.4) \qquad \ln L_t - \ln L_{t-1} = {}_{t-1}r_t + b_{L,1} \cdot UEinfl_t + b_{L,2} \cdot \Delta E_{t-1} infl + b_{L,3} \cdot UErwg_t + b_{L,4} \cdot \Delta E_{t-1} rwg + b_{L,5} \cdot \Delta r_{t-1} + \varepsilon_t$$

where:

rwg_t = real wage growth in period t

Equation (3.4) sets the (theoretical) goal for the asset liability matching problem. How well can returns on different assets be explained by the mentioned factors? This implies that we are not interested in the set of factors that explain the returns of the assets as good as possible, we are only interested in the extent that the factors are 'translated' into asset returns. In this paper we will restrict ourselves to the interest rate and the inflation variables. The next section gives some theoretical background for the relation between inflation, interest rates and asset returns.

4. Asset risk: theory

In this section we discuss theoretical aspects of interest rate risk of bonds and stocks and inflation risk of stocks.

4.1 Measuring interest rate sensitivities of bonds

The current (t=0) market value B of a straight default risk free bond equals the present value of the future (deterministic) payoffs:

$$(4.1) \qquad B = \sum_{t=1}^{T} CF_t \cdot (1 + {}_0r_t)^{-t} = \sum_{t=1}^{T} PV_t$$

where:

- T = the maturity of the bond
- CF_t = coupon of the bond for $0 < t < T$
- CF_T = coupon plus face value, to be received at time T
- ${}_0r_t$ = discretely compounded spot rate over the interval [0,t]
- PV_t = the present value of CF_t

The set $\{{}_0r_t\}_t$ denotes the term structure of interest rates (denoted as TSI).

Under these assumptions, changes in the TSI are the 'only' source of fluctuations in the bond price. The instantaneous bond return as a result of infinitesimally small changes in the TSI can be described as

$$(4.2) \qquad \frac{dB}{B} = \sum_t \frac{dPV_t}{B} = \sum_t \frac{dPV_t}{PV_t} \cdot \frac{PV_t}{B}$$

As several rates in the TSI can change, this interest rate risk has a multi-farious character. As

$$(4.3) \qquad \frac{dPV_t}{PV_t} = -t \cdot \frac{d\,{}_0r_t}{1 + {}_0r_t}$$

we can express the relation between the instantaneous bond return and small proportional changes in the spot rates as:

$$(4.4) \qquad \frac{dB}{B} = \sum_t -t \cdot \frac{PV_t}{B} \cdot \frac{d\,{}_0r_t}{1 + {}_0r_t}$$

The applicability of the analysis can be enhanced by specifying a factor model of the TSI. It is then assumed that there exist some reference rates that drive all other relevant spot rates. (For an overview of models to describe (changes in) the TSI, we refer to Dobson, Sutch & Vanderford [1976], Cooper [1977] and Vasicek & Fong [1982].) In case of a two-factor model, a perfect relation between (changes in) all interest rates and two reference rates (mostly a short rate and a long rate) is assumed:

$$(4.5) \qquad \frac{d\,{}_0r_t}{1 + {}_0r_t} = f(t) \cdot \frac{dr_S}{1 + r_S} + g(t) \cdot \frac{dr_L}{1 + r_L}$$

where:

r_S = short rate;

r_L = long rate

and where f(t) and g(t) are functions of time t.

Incorporating equation (4.5) in (4.4), we get:

$$(4.6) \qquad \frac{dB}{B} = -\left[\sum_t t \cdot \frac{PV_t}{B} \cdot f(t)\right] \cdot \frac{dr_S}{1+r_S} - \left[\sum_t t \cdot \frac{PV_t}{B} \cdot g(t)\right] \cdot \frac{dr_L}{1+r_L}$$

Equation (4.6) relates bond price variability to interest rate variability. The link between bond price variability and duration was developed by Hicks [1939] and Samuelson [1945], and rediscovered by Fisher [1966] (although in a different context), Hopewell & Kaufman [1973] and Weil [1973], who extended the role of duration as a proxy for interest rate risk. The terms between square brackets are denoted as 'partial duration measures' and represent the elasticity of the bond value for changes in the corresponding source of risk. Specific definitions of these durations depend on the specifications of the process that is assumed to drive interest rate changes. When proportional changes in all spot rates are equal, the partial durations collaps into the Fisher & Weil [1971] duration of the bond. Simplifying further by assuming a flat TSI (so ${}_0r_t = r$ for all t), the Macaulay [1938] duration results: the negative of the bond's point elasticity with respect to its internal yield to maturity.

In our empirical work, we use equation (4.6) as an approximation for bond returns as a function of changes in the long and the short rate. As this represents a first order approximation for the bond's return, we only expect a reasonable accurate approximation for small yield changes.

4.2 Interest rate risk of common stocks

Inspired by the bond analysis, a profound attention is paid in the literature to estimate 'equity duration', as a measure for the (negative of the) sensitivity of common stock returns to interest rate changes. An appropriately defined equity duration is the basis for an adequate analysis and possible control of interest rate risk of stock portfolios. Observing institutional investors (like pension funds) in many countries extending their bond portfolios with increasing investments in stocks, incorporating an equity duration measure into the calculation of portfolio duration would be a further step towards the effective management of their assets.

We review some work on gauging stocks' interest rate sensitivity, theoretically and empirically.

In empirical studies, several approaches are followed to estimate the interest rate sensitivity of stocks. Stone [1974], Chance & Lane [1980], Lynge & Zumwalt [1980] and Chance [1982] establish an indirect relationship between stock returns and interest rate changes by regressing security returns on both a stock and a bond index. Leibowitz [1986] extends this approach to a multi-step procedure in which the interest rate sensitivity is estimated by combining the univariate (regression) relations between the stocks, a stock market index, a 'representative' bond market index and changes in its yield to maturity. For the period 1980-1985, he estimates an implied duration (i.e. the negative of the interest sensitivity) for the S&P-Index of 2.2.

Aside from these indirect approaches, literature can be found in which a direct relation between stock returns and interest rate changes is estimated. Haugen, Stroyny & Wichern [1978] estimate the interest elasticity of utility stocks as measured by the arc-elasticity over a period of two months (December 1970-January 1971). For the utility industry, they estimated an elasticity of approximately -10. From the estimation results reported by Joehnk & Petty [1980], we can infer that interest rate sensitivities of various stocks (ranging from growth stocks to utilities) vary from approximately -1 to -13.

A different, frequently employed, approach for gauging equity duration starts from a PV-model of the stock. The present value (current price) of a share of common stock is equal to the appropriate discounted value of all future expected dividends (or free cash flows) accruing to the stockholder.

For default free straight bonds, changes in the term structure of interest rates are the 'only' sources of risk. Stocks, however, have an additional risk component, stemming from changes in the investors' expectations of the risky future dividends. After all, cash flow growth is the most outstanding feature separating bonds and common stocks. As risk averse investors will require compensation for this cash flow risk, a risk adjusted discount rate (RADR) must be used to discount the expected dividends. Both components of the RADR, the risk free interest rate and the risk premium, are in general assumed to be constant. Under this assumption, the current (i.e. at t=0) theoretical stock price can be expressed as:

$$(4.7) \qquad P_0 = \sum_{t=1}^{\infty} \frac{E_0(D_t)}{(1+k_t)^t} = \sum_{t=1}^{\infty} \frac{E_0(D_t)}{(1+k)^t}$$

where:

$E_0(D_t)$	= the current expectation for the dividend at time t
k	= $r + \pi$ = the RADR
r	= the risk free interest rate, reflecting time preference
π	= the risk premium, reflecting the risk of the dividend stream.

In theoretical analyses, we meet the same problems as in the case of bonds. Cooper's [1977] simulations show that returns on assets with longer remaining terms to maturity (> 7 years, e.g.) are sensitive to changes in the *level* of the TSI and almost not sensitive to changes in the *shape* of the TSI. As stocks have an infinite maturity, their returns will be predominantly affected by changes in the interest rate level and not by changes in the shape of the TSI.

The most simple closed-form PV-formula results if it is assumed that expected dividends grow at a constant rate g:

$$(4.8) \qquad P_0 = \sum_{t=1}^{\infty} \frac{D_0 \cdot (1+g)^t}{(1+k)^t} = \frac{D_0 \cdot (1+g)}{k-g} = \frac{E_0(D_1)}{k-g} \quad \text{for } k > g$$

where:

D_0	= the dividend received at time t=0

While the derivation of this formula is often attributed to Williams [1938] and is even widely identified as the Gordon & Shapiro [1956]-formula, its origin may go back as early as Makeham [1869].

Depending on the magnitude (and uncertainty) of the growth rate implied by the projected dividend stream, we can say that common stock can be situated in a continuum where at one side the common stock predominantly possesses the characteristics of a straight, default risk free bond and where at the other side its characteristics of earnings growth potential dominate. In case the expected growth rate equals zero (bond-like stocks, with more or less fixed dividends, such as preferred stocks), the common stock resembles a perpetual (risky) bond. The nature of interest rate risk of a bond-like stock mirrors the nature of a bond's interest rate risk; this risk can be attributed to the denominator of the PV-formula. When the common stock is issued by a corporation that can be characterized as a 'growth engine', the expected growth rate will be large. In that case, we expect the risks with respect to the growth rate of dividends to dominate (the numerator of the PV-formula).

Equity duration is now defined as the negative of the elasticity of the theoretical stock price with respect to a change in the risk adjusted discount rate k. Starting from the constant growth model equation (4.8), this elasticity can be computed as (cf. Durand [1957, p.358], Boquist, Racette & Schlarbaum [1975, p.1363] and Casabona, Fabozzi & Francis [1984]):

$$(4.9) \qquad \frac{dP_0/P_0}{dk/(1+k)} = -\frac{1+k}{k-g} = -\frac{P_0}{D_0} - 1$$

According to the latter equality (Williams & Pfeifer [1982]), the equity duration equals one plus the reciprocal of the dividend yield. Note that

$$\frac{dP/P}{dk/(1+k)} = \frac{dP/P}{dr/(1+r)}$$

for a constant risk premium π.

This approach to measure the interest elasticity of common stocks is a.o. employed by Haugen & Wichern [1974] and Casabona, Fabozzi & Francis [1984]. Typically, the values of this theoretical derived equity duration range from 20 to 50 or even 80 (Lanstein & Sharpe [1978]), much larger than the empirically estimated value of Leibowitz [1986]. From data provided by Farrell [1985, p.23], for example, and using equation (4.9), the duration of the S&P-Index ultimo 1984 can be estimated as 25!

This 'conventional' theoretical approach can be criticized on the facts that it treats the cash flow stream, accruing to the investor, as fixed coupons. The time pattern as well as the sensitivity of the expected dividend stream for interest rate changes is thus ignored. These 'dividend effects' could explain the large differences between theoretical durations and empirically estimated durations.[2]

We conclude that a theoretical present value model can only provide insights into the interest rate sensitivity when these 'dividend effects' are taken into account. Hence, the conventional

2 A growth pattern of dividends in which for the next years excess growth is expected, will decrease the theoretical duration. Haugen & Wichern [1974] consider a two-stage growth scenario, but their formulas become so complex that they can only be evaluated numerically. Also, when expected dividends are positively related to interest rates, the theoretical duration will decrease.

expression for equity duration is not adequate. As it will be very difficult (if not impossible) to estimate the influence of these dividend effects, we will confine ourselves to the empirical estimation of durations.

4.3 Inflation

The effects of inflation on common stock returns have been extensively investigated (Lintner [1975], Body [1976], Nelson [1976], Jaffe & Mandelker [1976], Fama & Schwert [1977], Fama [1981], Geske & Roll [1983], Gultekin [1983], Pindyck [1984] and Kaul [1990], to name a few)

The empirical research focuses on the relation between stock returns and expected inflation, unexpected inflation and/or changes in expected inflation. We agree with Kaul [1990, p.310] that a relation between stock returns and *the level* of expected inflation is anomalous. In the light of the efficient markets hypothesis, current expectations for future inflation rates are already incorporated in stock prices. *Unanticipated inflation* will cause investors to revise their expectations of this set of future inflation rates. This change in the 'term structure of inflation expectations' will in turn lead to changes in asset prices (cf. French, Ruback & Schwert [1983]). Whereas unexpected inflation provides information about an update of the whole term structure of expected inflation, a *change in expected inflation* by definition only reveals information about the update of next period expected inflation rate. For U.S. data however, the effect of changes in expected inflation on stock returns (usually) overshadows the effect of unexpected inflation (Fama & Schwert [1977]).

The general result that emerges from these analyses is that common stocks are "rather perverse as hedges against inflation" (Fama & Schwert [1977, p.144]). This is in contrast with the notion that stocks represent residual claims on cash flows, generated from real assets. Several explanations for this have been offered, but most hypotheses had to be rejected in empirical tests.

Fama [1981] explains the findings as a consequence of a negative relationship between inflation and real activity (a result from the money demand theory, given money supply). As real activity is a fundamental determinant of stock prices, the negative relation between stock returns and inflation is proxying a positive relation between stock returns and real activity. Geske & Roll [1983] establish a similar link: economic downturn is accompanied by lower tax receipts, monetization of the resulting deficit and finally inflation.

In the light of the PV-model of stock prices, we recognize the special feature of inflation: it does not only affect (part of) the discount rate, but can also affect the expected dividend growth rates. Depending on the degree in which the firm can increase the (expected) growth rate of its profits in line with (expected) inflation (the 'flow through'), the increased growth rates may (partially) offset the effect of the increased discount rate. This dual effect of inflation is recognized by Jahnke [1975] and Joehnk & Petty [1980] and analyzed by Estep, Hanson & Johnson [1983], Estep, Clayman, Johnson & McMahon [1984] and Leibowitz, Sorensen, Arnott & Hanson [1989]. The total effect of an unanticipated inflation shock on stock returns will thus be ambiguous.

The relationship between nominal interest rates and inflation expectations has been subject to extensive empirical analysis (see for example Fama [1975], Gultekin [1983] and Fama & Gibbons [1984]). According to the Fisher-hypothesis, the nominal interest rate consists of two (independent) components: the real interest rate and expected inflation. It will therefore be relevant whether a change in the nominal rate of interest can be attributed to a change in the real interest rate or to a change in inflation expectations. The sensitivities for these factors can differ very much. This is particularly relevant for empirical investigations on the basis of nominal interest rates, like we perform, but the question is how to decompose the real and inflation components of long term interest rates. This issue is left for further research.

5. The data

This section gives an overview of the data and basic transformations that are applied in describing the relationship between asset returns on the one hand and interest rates and inflation on the other hand. We consider the period 1970-1991 and use both monthly and quarterly data.

The consumer price index (CPI) of the Dutch Central Bureau of Statistics is used to estimate the inflation rate. The CPI series is published since the 1930s in a comparable way, so we have no problem for the 1970-1991 period. The inflation rate is defined as the change in the natural logarithm of the CPI:

$$(5.1) \qquad infl_t = \ln CPI_t - \ln CPI_{t-1}$$

For the long interest rate ($ilong_t$) and the short interest rate ($ishort_t$) we use end of month figures of the yield to maturity of long term government bonds and 3 months lower government paper ('kasgeld aan lagere overheden') respectively. Comparable to the other definitions we calculated the relative changes in the interest rates as:

(5.2a) $Dilong_t = \ln(1 + ilong_t) - \ln(1 + ilong_{t-1})$

(5.2b) $Dishort_t = \ln(1 + ishort_t) - \ln(1 + ishort_{t-1})$

There is a problem with these interest rates, because end of month figures are not available during the complete 1970-1991 period. Due to this fact we had to use monthly averages during the period 1970-1979 for the long rate and during the period 1970-1975 for the short rate. At first sight this may seem not so much a problem. Figure 5.1 shows the end of month and the average long rate for the years 1980-1990.

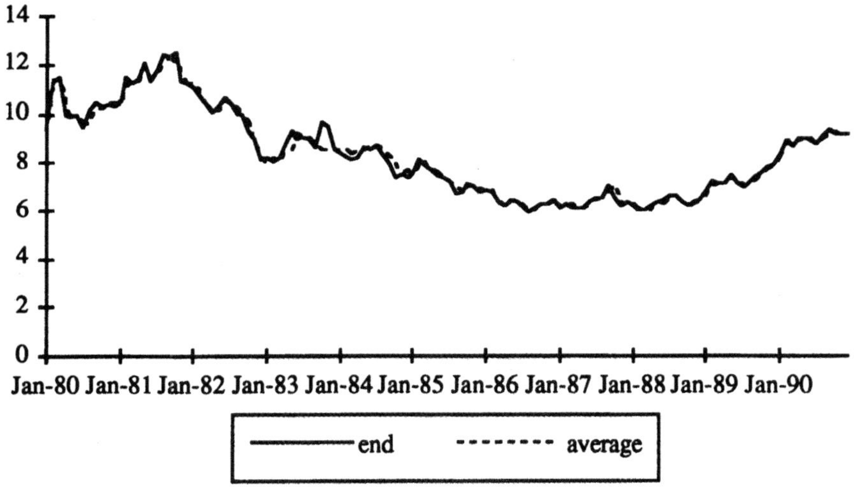

Figure 5.1 Long interest rate: end of month and monthly average

They look much alike: the coefficient of correlation between the two series is 0.99. But as explained in paragraph 3 we are not interested in the *level* of the interest rates, but in the *changes* in the interest rates. Figure 5.2 shows the changes in the long rate as defined above for the same period 1980-1990.

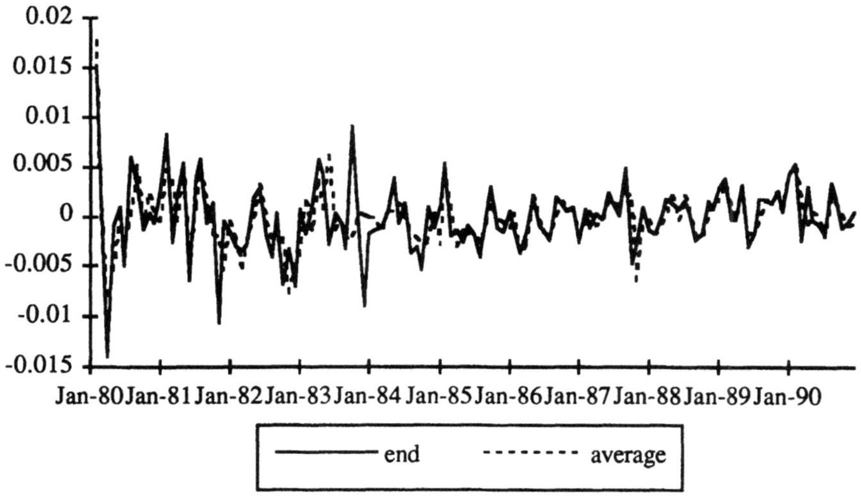

Figure 5.2 Changes in the long interest rate: end of month and monthly average

Although there is still a strong resemblance between the two series, the coefficient of correlation has dropped to 0.67. This implies that the information, contained in 55% of the variance of changes in the ultimo rate, is lost when average rates are used! In spite of these theoretical problems that arise from the lack of data, we have used the described mix of end of month and monthly average figures in the rest of this paper.

The total logarithmic returns on stocks ($TRstocks_t$) and bonds ($TRbonds_t$) for period t include the change in the price from t-1 to t and the dividends or coupons paid to the owner during this period. For Dutch stocks we used the Morgan Stanley Capital International (MSCI) data, which provide both capital gains and dividend return. The MSCI index for the Netherlands is a value-weighted index. It contains a set of stocks with a market value that accounts for over 90% of the market value of the Dutch stock exchange. The MSCI returns are available for the years 1970-1991. Total returns on Dutch long term government bonds are directly available from the Central Bureau of Statistics for the period January 1972 to March 1991. After this date the way of calculating the index changed significantly so that the results are no longer comparable.

Table 5.1 shows the statistical properties of the monthly data, i.e. the mean, standard deviation, skewness and the partial autocorrelations for 1, 2, 3, 4, 6 and 12 months.

Category	Mean	Standard Deviation	Skewness	ρ_1	ρ_2	ρ_3	ρ_4	ρ_6	ρ_{12}
infl	3.93E-3	4.66E-3	0.149	0.451	-0.112	-0.194	0.350	0.470	0.381
Dilong	1.70E-5	2.97E-3	0.017	0.105	-0.098	0.118	-0.171	-0.015	-0.016
Dishort	9.10E-5	8.40E-3	1.017	0.155	0.103	-0.036	-0.224	-0.052	0.047
TRstocks	1.05E-2	5.08E-2	-0.007	0.095	-0.012	0.032	-0.116	-0.087	0.090
TRbonds	6.73E-3	2.16E-2	0.513	0.246	0.064	-0.046	-0.080	-0.063	0.023

Table 5.1 Statistical sample properties of the data[3]

As explained in sections 3 and 4 the inflation rate itself is not so much of interest. To split the series into (changes in) expected inflation and unexpected inflation, we combined two approaches. First we made a correction for the autocorrelations in the inflation series. Table 5.1 shows the rather complex structure of the inflation series. For reasons of clearness and simplicity we decided to distinguish only between a short term autocorrelation (one month and one quarter for monthly and quarterly data respectively) and a long term autocorrelation (one year for monthly and quarterly data). Besides this it is possible that the short term or the long term interest rate contains some information about the expected inflation. For both the monthly and quarterly data the short term interest rate turned out to be the best inflation predictor. Combining these two ways we estimated the following equations:

(5.3a) $\quad infl_t = a + b \cdot infl_{t-1} + c \cdot infl_{t-12} + d \cdot ishort_{t-1}$ (monthly data)

(5.3b) $\quad infl_t = a + b \cdot infl_{t-1} + c \cdot infl_{t-4} + d \cdot ishort_{t-1}$ (quarterly data)

The estimates of these equations give the expected inflation for period t based on information available at time t-1 ($E_{t-1}infl_t$). The residuals of the equations (5.3a) and (5.3b) can be interpreted and will be used as the (ex post) unexpected inflation ($UEinfl_t$). The results and the correlations of the residuals are presented in table 5.2[4].

3 The standard error of the ρ's is 0.062.

4 In this and the following tables absolute t-values are presented in parentheses. The critical values for the monthly (n=264), quarterly (n=88) data are 1.96 and 1.99 at the 5% level of significance and 1.65 and 1.67 and the 10% level of significance (two sided).

Equation	a	b	c	d	R^2	ρ_1	ρ_2	ρ_3	ρ_4	ρ_6	ρ_{12}
(5.3a)	-0.002	0.211	0.552	0.017	0.51	-0.015	0.081	-0.186	0.074	0.358	0.038
	(0.48)	(4.62)	(13.06)	(2.17)							
(5.3b)	-0.009	0.152	0.613	0.047	0.57	-0.051	0.322	0.050	0.048	n.a.	n.a.
	(0.47)	(2.24)	(8.99)	(1.88)							

Table 5.2 Inflation equations

The year effect is the most clearly visible, although the short term autocorrelation in the inflation rates and the interest rates have also a significant effect in the inflation forecasts. A closer look at the correlations of the residuals tells us that there is a half year effect, that we did not take into account.

Parallel to the argument above only unexpected changes in the interest rates may have an influence on asset returns. Therefore we checked for an autoregressive or a mean reversion process in the long and short rate. For the mean reversion process, we have:

(5.4a) $\quad \text{Dilong}_t = a + b\cdot(\ln[1 + \text{ilong}_{t-1}] - \ln[1 + \overline{\text{ilong}}]) + \text{lres}_t$

(5.4b) $\quad \text{Dishort}_t = a + b\cdot(\ln[1 + \text{ishort}_{t-1}] - \ln[1 + \overline{\text{ishort}}]) + \text{sres}_t$

where:

$\overline{\text{ilong}}$ = average long term interest rate over complete period

$\overline{\text{ishort}}$ = average short term interest rate over complete period

The results in table 5.3 show a statistically significant, but small mean reversion effect in both the long and the short interest rate. As the residuals lres_t and sres_t are highly correlated we also constructed the series ssres_t in the following way:

(5.5) $\quad \text{sres}_t = a + b\cdot\text{lres}_t + \text{ssres}_t$

So ssres_t is the part of sres_t that is uncorrelated with lres_t.

Interest rate	Equation	Data	a	b	R^2	DW
Long	(5.4a)	monthly	0.000	-0.028	0.014	1.74
			(0.12)	(1.93)		
	(5.4a)	quarterly	0.001	-0.099	0.050	2.06
			(0.15)	(2.12)		
Short	(5.4b)	monthly	0.000	-0.070	0.034	1.80
			(0.00)	(3.05)		
	(5.4b)	quarterly	0.001	-0.271	0.134	1.86
			(0.08)	(3.65)		

Table 5.3 Interest rates

6. Asset risk: results

Combining the theory of sections 2, 3 and 4 and the data adjustments of section 5 we estimated the following equations for stocks:

(6.1a) $TRstocks_t = a + b \cdot UEinfl_{t-2} + c \cdot \Delta E_{t-3}\, infl_{t-2} + d \cdot lres_t + e \cdot ssres_t + \varepsilon 1_t$
(monthly data)

(6.1b) $TRstocks_t = a + b \cdot UEinfl_{t-1} + c \cdot \Delta E_{t-2}\, infl_{t-1} + d \cdot lres_t + e \cdot ssres_t + \varepsilon 2_t$
(quarterly data)

As we use changes in the logs for the total return indices as well as for the factors, we can interprete the sensitivities as elasticities of the stock prices with respect to the factors.

Two remarks:

- 1987 was a remarkable year! Because the results of the crash completely dominated the results, we have skipped respectively September to December 1987 and the last quarter of 1987 from our data set.
- The moment of publication is important for the inflation series. During the period 1970-1991 the CPI was published with a (decreasing) delay of 2.5 to 1.5 months. An unexpected inflation shock was therefore related to the inflation rate of about two

months before. Because of this publication delay we lagged the unexpected inflation and the change in the expected inflation two months and one quarter in the monthly and quarterly estimates respectively.

In both cases the coefficient of the short interest rate residual turned out to be insignificantly different from zero. The unexpected inflation and the change in the expected inflation are significantly correlated (as one could expect) so that only one of them would enter the regression. Again in both cases we got the same results: the unexpected inflation was selected and the residual of the change in the expected inflation (in a regression on unexpected inflation) had no explanatory power. We conclude that this finding is consistent with the notion that the term structure of inflation expectations is revised after unexpected inflation has occurred. The change in the expected inflation over the next period is only a small part of changes in this term structure. The results and the correlations of the residuals are presented in table 6.1.

Equation	a	b	d	R^2	DW	ρ_1	ρ_2	ρ_3	ρ_4	ρ_6	ρ_{12}
(6.1a)	0.011	-1.907	-3.590	0.068	1.96	0.008	-0.025	0.073	-0.087	-0.086	0.074
	(3.76)	(2.21)	(3.69)								
(6.1b)	0.026	-3.031	-5.845	0.206	1.91	0.054	-0.097	0.222	-0.054	n.a.	n.a.
	(3.18)	(2.29)	(3.90)								

Table 6.1 Results stocks

The average dividend yield on the stock index over 1970-1991 was 5.8%. According to equation (4.9) this would imply a theoretical interest rate sensitivity of about -18. Note that the effective duration is much lower, as one would expect.

For bonds we took a slightly different approach. The return on bonds should not only depend on the unexpected change in interest rates, but on the total change. Therefore we estimated the following equations:

(6.2a) $$TRbonds_t = a + b \cdot UEinfl_{t-2} + c \cdot \Delta E_{t-3}\, infl_{t-2} + d \cdot Dilong_t + e \cdot Dishort_t + \varepsilon 3_t$$
(monthly data)

(6.2b) $TRbonds_t = a + b \cdot UEinfl_{t-1} + c \cdot \Delta E_{t-2}\, infl_{t-1} + d \cdot Dilong_t + e \cdot Dishort_t + \varepsilon 4_t$ (quarterly data)

Table 6.2 shows the results of equations (6.2a) and (6.2b). We have corrected for a first order autocorrelation in the residuals using the Prais-Winsten method[5]. The inflation variables do not appear in the results because they were insignificantly different from zero. The change in the short term interest rates is only significant in the monthly case. Again we skipped the 1987 crash months c.q. quarter.

Equation	a	d	e	R^2	DW
(6.2a)	0.007	-6.774	-0.287	0.789	2.04
	(10.72)	(28.72)	(3.28)		
(6.2b)	0.064	-7.497		0.869	2.15
	(22.25)	(22.12)			

Table 6.2 Results bonds

To compare these results with table 6.1 we split the total change in the long interest rate into the residual after mean reversion (as was done before) and the expected change *because of* mean reversion.

(6.3a) $TRbonds_t = a + b \cdot UEinfl_{t-2} + c \cdot \Delta E_{t-3}\, infl_{t-2} + d \cdot lres_t + e \cdot Dilong_t|MR + f \cdot ssres_t + \varepsilon 5_t$ (monthly data)

(6.3b) $TRbonds_t = a + b \cdot UEinfl_{t-1} + c \cdot \Delta E_{t-2}\, infl_{t-1} + d \cdot lres_t + e \cdot Dilong_t|MR + f \cdot ssres_t + \varepsilon 6_t$ (quarterly data)

where:

$Dilong_t|MR$ = expected change in the long interest rate because of mean reversion (explained part of equation (5.4a))

$Dishort_t|MR$ = expected change in the short interest rate because of mean reversion (explained part of equation (5.4b))

5 This is the Cochrane-Orcutt method, which involves a special transformation of the first observation. See for example Maddala [1977].

Equation	a	d	e	f	R^2	DW
(6.3a)	0.007	-6.715	-11.283	-0.256	0.795	2.05
	(11.02)	(28.69)	(6.65)	(2.90)		
(6.3b)	0.064	-7.385	-17.047		0.932	2.05
	(52.21)	(27.61)	(17.97)			

Table 6.3 Results bonds

Although the coefficients d and e look much different, we have checked that for the monthly data their difference is not statistically significant from zero.

7. Conclusions

The paper is a first attempt to shape relative risk management of a pension fund. The key value is the extent to which there exists asset classes whose values move in line with the value of the liabilities.

We use a factor model to analyze risk in various dimensions; in this paper we focus on (nominal) interest rate risk and inflation risk of a stock market index and a bond market index. Over the period 1970 - 1991, we estimate the sensitivities of these indices for interest rate movements as well as unexpected inflation and changes in expected inflation. We combined a time series approach and Fisher's hypothesis to decompose the inflation rate in expected and unexpected inflation.

Stocks

After correction for mean reversion, we found that stocks exhibited a significant negative sensitivity for surprises in the long rate; unanticipated movements in the short rate did not have significant additional explanatory power. Although stock returns are significantly negatively correlated with both unexpected inflation and changes in expected inflation, the influence of unanticipated inflation dominated. In line with earlier results, we conclude that stocks in aggregate provide no hedge against inflation risk.

Bonds

For the bond index, we estimated effective partial durations with respect to the total changes in the long and the short rate. The short rate has only a marginal impact, as one could expect for a long term bond index. Comparing these results with the stock results before, bonds have a much higher (negative) interest rate sensitivity than stocks. We found no significant relation with the inflation variables. However, as we used nominal interest rates, a relation between bond returns and inflation cannot be ruled out. This will be a topic for future research.

References

Body, Z., 1976, Common Stocks as a Hedge Against Inflation, *The Journal of Finance* 31 May, pp. 459-470

Boquist, J.A., G.A. Racette & G.G. Schlarbaum, 1975, Duration and Risk Assessment for Bonds and Common Stocks, *The Journal of Finance* Dec., vol. 30/5, pp. 1360-1365

Casabona, P.A., F.J. Fabozzi & J.C. Francis, 1984, How to Apply Duration to Equity Analysis, *The Journal of Portfolio Management* Winter, pp. 52-58

Chance, D.M., 1982, Interest Sensitivity and Dividend Yields, *The Journal of Portfolio Management* Winter, pp. 69-75

Chance, D.M. & W.R. Lane, 1980, A Re-Examination of Interest Rate Sensitivity in the Common Stocks of Financial Institutions, *Journal of Financial Research* Spring, pp. 47-55

Cooper, I., 1977, Asset Values, Interest Changes, and Duration, *The Journal of Financial and Quantitative Analysis* Dec, vol.12/5, pp. 701-723

Dobson, S.W., R.C. Sutch & D.E. Vanderford, 1976, An Evaluation of Alternative Empirical Models of the Term Structure of Interest Rates, *The Journal of Finance* Sept, vol.31/4, pp. 1035-1065

Durand, D., 1957, Growth Stocks and the Petersburg Paradox, *The Journal of Finance* Sept., vol. 12, pp. 348-363

Estep, T., M. Clayman, C. Johnson & K. McMahon, 1984, *The Evolution of a New Approach to Investment Risk*, Salomon Bros Inc., May

Estep, T., N. Hanson & C. Johnson, 1983, Sources of Value and Risk in Common Stocks, *The Journal of Portfolio Management* Summer, pp.5-13

Fama, E.F., 1975, Short-Term Interest Rates as Predictors of Inflation, *The American Economic Review* June, vol.65/3, pp. 269-282

Fama, E.F., 1981, Stock returns, Real Activity, Inflation, and Money, *The American Economic Review* Sept., vol.71/4, pp. 545-565

Fama, E.F. & M.R. Gibbons, 1984, A Comparison of Inflation Forecasts, *Journal of Monetary Economics* vol.13, pp. 327-348

Fama, E.F. & G.W. Schwert, 1977, Asset Returns and Inflation, *Journal of Financial Economics* Nov., vol.5, pp. 115-146

Farrell, J.L., 1985, The Dividend Discount Model: A Primer, *Financial Analysts Journal* Nov/Dec, pp. 16-25

Fisher, L., 1966, An Algorithm for Finding Exact Rates of Return, *The Journal of Business* Jan, pp. 111-118

Fisher, L. & R.L. Weil, 1971, Coping with the Risk of Interest rate Fluctuations: Returns to Bondholders from Naive and Optimal Strategies, *Journal of Business* October, pp. 408-431

French, K.R., R.S. Ruback & G.W. Schwert, 1983, Effects of Nominal Contracting on Stock Returns, *Journal of Political Economy* 91/1, pp. 70-96

Geske, R. & R. Roll, 1983, The Fiscal and Monetary Linkage between Stock Returns and Inflation, *The Journal of Finance* March, vol.38, pp. 1-33
Gordon, M.J. & E. Shapiro, 1956, Capital Equipment Analysis: The Required Rate of Profit, *Management Science* 3 Oct., pp. 102-110
Gultekin, N.B., 1983, Stock Market Returns and Inflation Forecasts, *The Journal of Finance* June, vol.38/3, pp. 663-673
Haugen, R.A. & D.W. Wichern, 1974, The Elasticity of Financial Assets, *The Journal of Finance* Sept., vol.3/4, pp. 1229-1240
Haugen, R.A., A.L. Stroyny & D.W. Wichern, 1978, Rate Regulation, Capital Structure, and the Sharing of Interest Rate Risk in the Electric Utility Industry, *The Journal of Finance* June, vol.33/3, pp. 707-721
Haugen, R.A., 1990, *Modern Investment Theory*, Prentice-Hall, Englewood Cliffs, N.J.
Hicks, J.R., 1939, *Value and Capital*, Clarendon Press, Oxford
Hopewell, M.H. & G.G. Kaufman, 1973, Bond Price Volatility and Term to Maturity: A Generalized Respecification, *The American Economic Review* Sept, vol.63/4, pp. 749-753
Jaffe, J.F. & G. Mandelker, 1976, The 'Fisher Effect' for Risky Assets: An Empirical Investigation, *The Journal of Finance* 31 May, pp. 447- 458
Jahnke, W.W, 1975, What's Behind Stock Prices?, *Financial Analysts Journal* Sept/Oct, pp. 69-76
Joehnk, M.D. & J.W. Petty, 1980, The Interest Sensitivity of Common Stock Prices, *The Journal of Portfolio Management* Winter, pp. 19-25
Kaul, G., 1990, Monetary Regimes and the Relation between Stock Returns and Inflationary Expectations, *The Journal of Financial and Quantitative Analysis* 25/3 September, pp. 307-321
Lanstein, R. & W.F. Sharpe, 1978, Duration and Security Risk, *The Journal of Financial and Quantitative Analysis* Nov., vol. 13/4, pp. 653-668
Leibowitz, M.L., 1986, Total Portfolio Duration: A New Perspective on Asset Allocation, *Financial Analysts Journal* Sept/Oct, pp. 18-29, 77
Leibowitz, M.L., E.H. Sorensen, R.D. Arnott & H.N. Hanson, 1989, A Total Differential Approach to Equity Duration, *Financial Analysts Journal* Sept/Oct, pp. 30-37
Lintner, J., 1975, Inflation and Security Returns, *The Journal of Finance* May, vol.30/2, pp. 259-280
Macaulay, F., 1938, *Some Theoretical Problems Suggested by the Movement of Interest Rates, Bond Yields, and Stock Prices in the U.S. Since 1856*, National Bureau of Economic Research, New York N.Y.
Maddala, G.S., 1977, *Econometrics*, McGraw-Hill.
Makeham, W.M., 1869, On the Theory of Annuities Certain, *Journal of the Institute of Actuaries, and Insurance Magazine* 14, pp. 189-199
Nelson, C.R., 1976, Inflation and Rates of Return on Common Stocks, *The Journal of Finance* May, vol. 31/2, pp. 471-483
Pindyck, R.S., 1984, Risk, Inflation, and the Stock Market, *The American Economic Review* June, vol.74/3, pp. 335-349
Roll, R. & S.A. Ross, 1984, The Arbitrage Pricing Theory Approach to Strategic Portfolio Planning, *Financial Analysts Journal*, May-June, pp. 14-26.
Rosenberg, B., 1988, Choosing a Multiple Factor Model, *Investment Management Review*, Spring, pp. 55-67.
Samuelson, P., 1945, The Effect of Interest Rate Increases on the Banking System, *American Economic Review* 55, pp. 16-27
Stone, B.K., 1976, Systematic Interest Rate Risk in a Two-Index Model of Returns, *The Journal of Financial and Quantitative Analysis* Nov, vol.12/4, pp. 709-721
Van Aalst, P.C. van & C.G.E. Boender, 1993, Asset Liability Matching for Pension Funds: A One-Period Model, this volume
Vasicek, O.A. & H.G. Fong, 1982, Term structure Modelling Using Exponential Splines, *The Journal of Finance* May, vol.37/2, pp. 339-348
Weil, R.L., 1973, Macaulay's Duration: An Appreciation, *The Journal of Business* Oct, pp. 589-592

Williams, J.B., 1938, *The Theory of Investment Value*, Harvard University Press, Cambridge Mass.
Williams, A.O. & P.E. Pfeifer, 1982, Estimating Security Price Risk Using Duration and Price Elasticity, *The Journal of Finance* May, vol. 37/2, pp. 399-411

BANK STRATEGIC PLANNING PROCESS
A MULTIFACTOR ASSET AND LIABILITY RISK MANAGEMENT APPROACH

Mario Onorato[1]
Rotterdam Institute for Business Economic Studies
Erasmus University Rotterdam
P.O. Box 1738, NL-3000 DR Rotterdam

ABSTRACT

Bank Top Management, because of financial innovations, high volatility of interest rates and currency exchange rates, deregulation, internal organisational changes, mergers, take overs, high competition, needs *procedures* and *tools* that allow to make better-quality and faster strategic decisions. The purpose of this study is to examine and describe the main steps of *Bank Strategic Planning Process* and structure a procedure that allows to rationalise this process and to measure the ex ante and the ex post performance of strategic decision coherently.

1 MOTIVATION AND LITERATURE OVERVIEW

Despite the variety of financial planning, appropriate *Asset and Liability Management* (ALM) models for managing the whole banking are still rare. The first models in the field of bank financial management appeared in the late 19th century [Edg. 1888] and the 1920's and 1930's [Fis.1930]. During the 1940's and 1950's, banks had plentiful low-cost funds available in the form of demand and saving deposits. Hence the emphasis was mainly on asset management[Sam.1945] In this period the major works were the development of the Markowitz [Mar.1952] and Tobin [Tob.1958] model and the upcoming of portfolio theory

[1]The author wishes to thank Banca Popolare Santa Venera (Italy) for their financial support of this research and S. Lo Cascio, B. Matarazzo, J. Spronk, E. M. Vermeulen for stimulating discussions and critical remarks. Comments of an anonymous referee are also acknowledged. Of course, the responsibility for remaining errors is solely mine.

(for an overview see [Coh.1967]). From the sixties on, funds started to become less plentiful as corporate treasures began economising on cash balances. At the same time, the economy was prospering and therefore the loan demand increased rapidly. As a result, banks turned to manage their liabilities and researchers oriented their efforts towards strategic and operational planning models. Most of them had just one linear objective function [Bra. 1973] or only considered the asset side as being planable. During the 1970's, inflation, volatile interest rates, and a severe recession in the middle of the decade, caused banks to pay attention more on the management of both sides of their balance sheets (ALM). Researchers developed more sophisticated techniques to face this new reality coherently. Some included uncertainty within their models [Boo.1972], some others considered multiple objectives using goal programming (for an overview see [Spr. 1981]). Probably due to the increasing complexity of the financial world, in the 80's research almost lost interest to model ALM for the whole banking firm. Only at the end of the decade Langen [Lan.1989] developed a Multi-Objective Decision Support System for Strategic Bank ALM. There have been other quantitative attempts to steer the bank's business through ratios or indicators. The basic criticism is that "they are essentially measures of reaction and not for action and thereby planning"[2]. In the nineties, the timing and the quality of the procedures facing bank strategic problems will focus mainly on the risk management of assets and liabilities [Fab. 1991, Har. 1987]. We believe *Asset and Liability Risk Management* (ALRM) provides Top Management (TM) with a coherent framework to rationalise the Bank Strategic Planning Process (BSPP) within the new economic posture. The paper is organised as follows. In the next section the basic features of the BSPP will be analysed. The key phases of the BSPP will be outlined in section three. Section four is concerned with the description of the ALRM framework. Section five is devoted to the illustration of the theoretical model, the so called *Multifactor Asset and Liability Risk Management* approach (MFALRM), on the basis of which in section six a procedure aimed to rationalise the described BSPP and to measure the bank strategic performance is developed. Section seven is concerned with the operationalisation.

2 BASIC FEATURES OF THE BANK'S STRATEGIC PLANNING PROCESS

Bank strategic decisions, in general, are end products of steps of a *complex*, *dynamic* and *uncertain* process, the bank strategic planning process. Complex because of the number

[2] See [Lan. 1989], pag. 36.

and quality of relationship within the bank, outside the bank and connecting the bank with its environment; dynamic because most of these relationships change in number, quality and extent over time; uncertain because the process involves strategic decisions which cope with predictable, unpredictable and unknowable changes that may occur in the bank's environment.

We can think of *BSPP* as an ongoing, systematic and interactive process that tries to encompass and explain most of internal and external bank strategic interrelationships.

Generally, but not necessarily, the time horizon covered by a strategic decision is, at least, three years. The aim of strategic planning is to try to envisage the bank's position in the marketplace in the distant future. Strategic planning asks what the economy, the competition, regulations and technology will look like three or perhaps even more years into the future.

3 THE SIX KEY PHASES OF THE BANK'S STRATEGIC PLANNING PROCESS

In the analysis, we will distinguish six main steps in the BSPP.

Aim of first step is to provide a clear *description* of both the economic and organisational structure of the bank and the economic, social and political environment in which it operates. The description starts by defining the corporate mission, the first most challenging and important element in the planning process. Through an internal analysis it is possible to list the bank's strengths and weaknesses, opportunities and threats, available financial resources, recent developments of the financial positions and availability of personnel (paying also attention to first and second level managers' skill and expertise). To get insights into the surrounding economic, social and political environment an external analysis is needed. This encompasses a review of economic, social and political developments, competitive trends, customer characteristics, legal and regulatory changes, technological developments, etc.

Purpose of the second step is to *generate images of possible future positions of the bank*. TM can consider different scenarios to get insights about possible, reasonable, future economic evolutions. Future in fact is not always clear. We can't eliminate the uncertainty and the complexity characterising any strategic planning process, but we can look more carefully at the structural physical-economic interdependencies and, consequently, try to study which are the potential reactions of the bank to changes in important economic factors. This prospective way of dealing with strategic problems is one of the main targets of well structured planning process. We can, for example, introduce much more flexibility in our bank on basis of the results of a prospective analysis.

Next we have to introduce some *criteria*[3] *to evaluate the actual and the future position* of the bank. The crucial role played by clearly articulated sets of criteria is threefold:

a) to provide a yardstick to evaluate strategic decision ex ante.

b) to avoid ambiguity within the organisation as to what the financial institutions is attempting to achieve.

c) to provide managers guidelines to judge their performances (ex post control).

Generally, in the financial literature, the most important criterion is considered to be the maximisation of shareholder's wealth, defined as the present value of all future cash flows flowing to the shareholders. In reality some banks may use other good criteria as well. We remark that the maximisation of value is not always easy to operationalise because it is difficult to get a clear picture of the future and, consequently, how the future cash flows (CFs) will be generated. Obviously, this general remark is true for every prospective criterion. Besides, in reality, the set of criteria is not necessarily fixed. In fact, they are continuously updated (we can call them moving criteria) because of new insights coming from the decision process itself, changes in the economic environment and changes that can occur in the previously defined time horizon. Finally, although often the different criteria are treated and analysed separately, they can and will influence each other and therefore none of the criteria should be observed as a single criterion.

The fourth step concerns the *evaluation of the actual and future position* of the bank . If the bank is described in terms of criteria, evaluation of actual and comparison of (possible) future bank positions seems to be reasonably simple: manager chooses that plan with the best score. But, again we are confronted with a lot of complications. In fact, as said before, the description of the future position of the bank can be less clear than one wishes to be. Besides, some criteria are put in a more or less "fuzzy" way. In case of a multiplicity of criteria it is not always possible to rank them. In practice, we often have alternatives with a top score on some criteria and a low score on others.

In the fifth phase we illustrate which *alternatives*[4] (possible *actions*) or *combination of alternatives can be undertaken to improve the future position* of the bank. We remark that, in reality, it is not always possible to clearly identify and quantify the alternatives. This is because of the complexity of the economic environment and the inherent uncertainty. Therefore TM, to act coherently and prospectively, must study and develop actions take account for as many as possible consequences in each envisaged future. TM

---

[3]A *criterion* is a measure of effectiveness of performance.

[4]In general, through the *alternatives* how the results are to be achieved is stated.

can also search for (new) *instruments*[5] targeted to improve the envisaged position, in a continuous effort of reaching the previously determined criteria. The alternatives can also be proposed by the low level manager, whose practical experience of some aspects of specific problem is often one of the main and decisive elements on which the TM decision is based. In fact, the BSPP is not necessarily a "Top-Down" process, but, depending on the style of the organisation, there is a varying degree of participation of the lower level managers to the overall strategy.

In the sixth step, from a set of combination of feasible *projects*[6], *the strategic plan is selected.* Of course, given a set of feasible (combination of) projects, a lot of strategic plans can be extrapolated. Often at this point TM needs additional information to restrict and/or change this set of projects. Consequently the process restarts from the second step, until a bank strategic plan is selected. In practice, also this operation is not without problems. In fact, even if the feasible projects seem to be little in numbers, the economic interdependencies are so many, that is quite impossible to provide the manager with an exhaustive picture of "all possible consequences" related to the available (feasible) actions. Therefore, the final decision must take account of both the limitations of human mind to deal with this so complicated reality and the limitations of any decision support system as rough approximation of the real world. Obviously, in these steps a lot of feed-back and feed-forward loops do exist.

4 THE ASSET AND LIABILITY RISK MANAGEMENT FRAMEWORK

The business of banking has been, and is still, going through a period of rapid and profound changes. Bank strategic management and problems it copes with are also changing rapidly.

The timing and quality of the procedures facing bank strategic problems in the nineties will focus mainly on:

1) the capacity to anticipate structural and contingent changes;
2) the capacity to act so as to structure and restructure a bank's business;
3) the elaboration of a rational system;
4) the measurement of the ex ante and ex post performance of strategic decision;
5) the monitoring of risk exposure.

---

[5]Bank real and financial *instruments* (like options, futures, swaps etc.) are those that influence the impact of economic (factor) changes on bank performances.
[6]A *project* is defined as a set of independent compatible alternatives.

ALRM provides TM with a coherent framework to rationalise the BSPP within the new economic posture.

ALRM in fact is a systematic approach to a set of problems confronting bank managers: it is neither a set of hard and fast rules nor a set of static techniques offering specific solutions, rather it provides structured and integrated guidelines (way of thinking) both on strategic and operative level, the detailed formulation of which varies from bank to bank in line with changes in the criteria of bank managers and in the problems they face.

5 A MULTIFACTOR ASSET AND LIABILITY RISK MANAGEMENT APPROACH TO BANK STRATEGIC PLANNING PROCESS

Suppose, for simplicity, a one period model in which the analysis covers the period from t-1 to t. Consider the asset A_i. We define the stochastic future value of A_i, namely $\tilde{A}_{i,t}$, as the sum of the following two components:

$$\tilde{A}_i = E_{t-1}(\tilde{A}_i) + U\Delta(\tilde{A}_i)_{t-1,t} \tag{1}$$

$E_{t-1}(\tilde{A}_i)$ = Expected value, at the beginning of the period, of asset i at time t.

$U\Delta(\tilde{A}_i)_{t-1,t}$ = Un-expected changes in the value of asset i from time t-1 to t.

Let us define $\Delta(\tilde{F}_k)_{t-1,t}$ as the change of the exogenous factor k from time t-1 to t:

$$\Delta(\tilde{F}_k)_{t-1,t} = \tilde{F}_{k,t} - \overline{F}_{k,t-1} \tag{2}$$

where:

$\tilde{F}_{k,t}$ = stochastic future value of factor k at time t.

$\overline{F}_{k,t-1}$ = deterministic component, the value of which is known at time t-1.

Let consider $\Delta(\tilde{F}_k)_{t-1,t}$ as the sum of the following two elements:

$$\Delta(\tilde{F}_k)_{t-1,t} = E\Delta(\tilde{F}_k)_{t-1,t} + U\Delta(\tilde{F}_k)_{t-1,t} \tag{3}$$

where:

$E\Delta(\tilde{F}_k)_{t-1,t} = E_{t-1}(\tilde{F}_k) - \overline{F}_{k,t-1}$ = expected change of factor k from time t-1 to t.

$U\Delta(\tilde{F}_k)_{t-1,t} = \tilde{F}_{k,t} - E_{t-1}(\tilde{F}_k)$ = un-expected change of factor k from time t-1 to t.

with $E_{t-1}(\tilde{F}_k)$ defined as the expected value, at the beginning of the period, of factor k from time t-1 to t.

Assuming a linear (in parameters, namely the *sensitivities*, and in variables, namely the *un-expected factor changes*) CF outcome generating process between the un-expected changes in CFs of the generic asset i and the stochastic structure of the relevant, identified, un-expected factor changes, we get:

$$\tilde{A}_{i,t} = E_{t-1}(\tilde{A}_i) + \beta_{i,1} U\Delta(\tilde{F}_1)_{t-1,t} + \ldots + \beta_{i,k} U\Delta(\tilde{F}_k)_{t-1,t} + \tilde{\varepsilon}_{i,t} \quad i=1,\ldots,l; \quad k=1,\ldots,k. \qquad (4)$$

where:

$\beta_{i,k}$= sensitivity of $\tilde{A}_{i,t}$ for un-expected changes in factor k. This generic (conditional) risk measure component can be interpreted as the marginal influence of an un-expected change of factor k on the CF of asset i.

$\varepsilon_{i,t}$= error term representing potential un-expected asset CF movements which are not explained by the un-expected factor changes.

Let $\bar{b}_i = \left[\hat{b}_{i,1}, \ldots, \hat{b}_{i,k}\right]$ be the vector representing the estimated sensitivities of asset i. We define $\bar{b}_i$ as the *risk profile* of asset i. The estimation procedure of the expected values and of the sensitivities is a problem in itself, which is not addressed here.

6 MFALRM: A PROCEDURE TO EVALUATE THE EX ANTE AND EX POST BANK STRATEGIC PERFORMANCE

Assume that TM of a small medium sized bank is preparing the new strategic plan covering the next three years. An analyst supports TM during the strategic planning decision process by providing ex ante estimations of performance of strategic decisions.

The analysis starts by exploiting the *internal* (inside the bank) *structural economic relationships*, determining where possible, the direction and the entity of these connections. Examples of connections are: if the deposit interest rate increases, the deposits will increase too (direction of connection). If we specify the amount of increased deposit due to increasing interest rate deposit we are also specifying the entity. The bank relationships are dynamic. The direction and the entity of connections may change over time because of:

1) *external influences* (e.g., increasing degree of competition, changes in regulation, and so on) which are out of TM control;
2) *internal influences* (e.g., new TM performing new strategies focusing on different asset and liability mix) which are partially under TM control.

Through the connection exploitation procedure, we can assess the degree of co-ordination of existing assets and liabilities. We remark that a good co-ordination of asset and liability mix (e.g., perfect matching of maturities) may play a basic role in the selection of the projects of the strategic plan. For example, as less bank portfolio is exposed to interest rate movements, the inherent connections are more flexible. As a result new and costless financial resources can be addressed in other businesses. Co-ordination is one of the most challenging features of a well structured ALRM procedure and is an indicator of *efficiency of financial institutions organisation.*

In a second step we *connect the previously identified bank relationships with the surrounding economic environment* through the identification of the driving economic forces influencing the economic and financial on and off balance sheet items. We assume that some structure of the asset and liability (CF) outcome generating process can be captured by means of the previously described Multifactor model (MFM):

$$\tilde{A}_{i,t} = E_{t-1}(\tilde{A}_i) + \beta_{i,1} U\Delta(\tilde{F}_1)_{t-1,t} + \ldots + \beta_{i,k} U\Delta(\tilde{F}_k)_{t-1,t} + \tilde{\varepsilon}_{i,t} \quad i=1,\ldots,l; \quad k=1,\ldots,k. \quad (4)$$

The third step is concerned with the *measurement of the bank's and the projects' sensitivities*. Estimated sensitivities can be considered as conditional risk measures of the future inter temporal relationship (direction and entity) between un-expected changes of asset and liability CF and un-expected changes of the underlying sources of risk (factors). We assume *TM makes strategic decisions on the basis of the (estimated) asset and liability risk profile*.

The fourth step of the proposed procedure deals with the *evaluation of bank strategic performances*. These will be measured through the resulting strategic exposure defined as the vector of sensitivities of assets minus the vector of sensitivities of liabilities, i.e., the vector of capital risk profile. Let $\overline{A}_{rp}$, $\overline{L}_{rp}$ and $\overline{C}_{rp}$ be respectively the asset, liability and capital risk profile, we get: $\overline{A}_{rp} = [\overline{b}_1 + \ldots + \overline{b}_l]$ $\overline{L}_{rp} = [\overline{b}_{l+1} + \ldots + \overline{b}_{l+m}]$ $\overline{C}_{rp} = [\overline{b}_{l+m+1} + \ldots + \overline{b}_{l+n}]$ therefore,

$$\overline{A}_{rp} = \overline{L}_{rp} + \overline{C}_{rp} \quad (5)$$

This additivity property of sensitivities holds under specific assumptions with respect to the stochastic structure of the error process. The theorem, the proof and related results are shown in appendix 1. The $\overline{A}_{rp}$, $\overline{L}_{rp}$ and $\overline{C}_{rp}$ provide TM with a cardinal ranking of asset, liability and capital exposure to a single, specific, factor through the inherent sensitivities.

In this MFM we are implicitly assuming that the sensitivity remain the same for every possible un-expected change in factor, i.e.: $\beta_{i,k} = c_k \beta_{j,k}$, with $c_k \in R$, $\forall \; U\Delta(\tilde{F}_k)_{t-1,t} \in R$.

In this context we define asset i to be more exposed to (un-expected movements of) factor k than asset j[7] if $\beta_{i,k} > \beta_{j,k} > 0$ or $\beta_{i,k} < \beta_{j,k} < 0$, $\forall\ U\Delta\left(\tilde{F}_k\right)_{t-1,t} \in R$. If for instance, one or more of these risk exposures are considered to be too high, TM may decide to use (financial) instruments as futures, options and the like, to change their value. New risk profiles are then re-estimated as: $\overline{A}^{\bullet}_{rp}$, $\overline{L}^{\bullet}_{rp}$ and $\overline{C}^{\bullet}_{rp}$.

The last step concerns the *selection of the strategic plan*.

Even in the most simplest case of compatible independent alternatives and assuming that the decisions concerning the alternatives will be taken at the same time, a lot of interdependencies do exist. If, for example, TM has to analyse ten projects, the number of (potential) strategic plans is $2^{10} = 1024$. Moreover, if we consider how many different future values the factors influencing the bank performances can have, we get quite a clear idea of the complexity inherent in the strategic decision process. In reality TM will consider only a very small subset P of the space of feasible projects and only some of the potential strategic plans that can be extrapolated through P. We assume TM will select a strategic plan on basis of resulting, re-estimated, risk profiles. In the analysis each strategic plan is confronted with some possible future economic structures represented by the un-expected factor changes. The procedure provides TM with the following information:

SCENARIOS

$$
\begin{array}{lccc}
 & U\Delta\overline{F}_1 & \cdots & U\Delta\overline{F}_g \\
PLAN\ 1 & \left\{\begin{array}{c} \overline{A}^{\bullet}_{rp1\,1} \\ \overline{L}^{\bullet}_{rp1\,1} \\ \overline{C}^{\bullet}_{rp1\,1} \end{array}\right. & \begin{array}{c} \cdots \\ \cdots \\ \cdots \end{array} & \begin{array}{c} \overline{A}^{\bullet}_{rp1g} \\ \overline{L}^{\bullet}_{rp1g} \\ \overline{C}^{\bullet}_{rp1g} \end{array} \\
\vdots & \vdots & \vdots & \vdots \\
PLAN\ s & \left\{\begin{array}{c} \overline{A}^{\bullet}_{rps1} \\ \overline{L}^{\bullet}_{rps1} \\ \overline{C}^{\bullet}_{rps1} \end{array}\right. & \begin{array}{c} \cdots \\ \cdots \\ \cdots \end{array} & \begin{array}{c} \overline{A}^{\bullet}_{rpsg} \\ \overline{L}^{\bullet}_{rpsg} \\ \overline{C}^{\bullet}_{rpsg} \end{array}
\end{array}
$$

---

[7]It is technically possible, through coefficient standardisation, compare sensitivities among different factors, but because both correlations among and spacings of the observations on independent variables, their magnitude may be significantly affected.

where $\overline{A}_{rpsg}$, $\overline{L}_{rpsg}$ and $\overline{C}_{rpsg}$ respectively denote the re-estimated asset, liability and capital risk profile of sth combination of projects (strategic plans) under the gth scenario, which is spanned by $U\Delta\overline{F}_g$, where the latter stands for the vector of the un-expected factor changes considered in the gth scenario.

7 OPERATIONALISATION AND CONCLUSIONS

With respect to the operationalisation of MFALRM a series of problems arise, among others:

1) Identification of the most relevant factors.
2) Identification and specification of projects.
3) Calculation of expected values.
4) Estimation of sensitivities.

There are many ways to attack these problems [Spr. 1989], but none has been experimented in the bank strategic planning context.

Moreover some assumptions of the theoretical model might be reconsidered. For example, the assumption that β will not change no matter the value of the un-expected factor change, might be modelled through a more general multifactor framework.

REFERENCES

Booth G: (1972) Programming Bank Portfolios under Uncertainty: an Extension. Journal of Bank Research. Winter, pp. 28-40.

Bradley S.P., Crane D.B. (1973) Management of Commercial Bank Management Security Portfolios:. An Optimisation Approach under Uncertainty. Journal of Bank Research. Spring, pp. 18-30.

Cohen K.J., Hammer F.S. (1967) Applications of Financial Theory - Linear Programming and Optimal Bank Asset Management Decisions. Journal of Finance. Vol. 22 No. 2, pp.147-165

Edgeworth F.Y. (1888) Mathematical Theory of Banking. Journal of the Royal Statistical Society. March, pp. 113-127.

Fisher I. (1930) The Theory of Interest. Augustus M. Kelley, Bookseller (1965) reprint of the original edition. New York.

Fabozzi F.J., Konishi A (1991) Asset and Liability Management. Probus.

Harrington R. (1987) Asset and Liability Management by Banks. OECD. Paris.
Langen D. (1989) An (Interactive) Decision Support System for Bank Asset and Liability Management. Decision Support System, pp. 389-401.
Langen D. (1989) Strategic Bank Asset and Liability Management Peter Lang Verlag. Frankfurt-Genf.
Markowitz H.M. (1952) Portfolio Selection. Journal of Finance. March, pp 77-91.
Samuelson P.A. (1945) The effect of Interest Rate Increases on the Banking System. American Economic Review. March pp. 16-27.
Santomero A.M. (1984) Modelling the Banking Firm- A Survey. Journal of Money, Credit and Banking. November, Vol. 16, No. 4, part 2, pp. 576-602.
Spronk J. (1981) Interactive Multiple Goal Programming. Applications to Financial Planning. International Series in Management/Operations Research ed. Ignizio J.P., Nijhoff M. Publications. Boston.
Spronk J. (1989) Multi Factorial Financial Planning. In Improving Decision Making in Organisation ed. Lockett A.G., Islei G..Springer-Verlag. Berlin.
Tobin J. (1958) Liquidity Preference as Behaviour Towards Risk. Review of Economic Studies 25.

APPENDIX 1

Theorem

Let l be the number of considered assets.

If

$U\Delta\tilde{F}_{ik}$, with k=1,...,k (i.e. finite set of factors), are independent, randomly distributed, stochastic variables, with k<l;

$\tilde{\varepsilon}_{i,t} \sim N(0,\sigma_i^2)$ i=1,...,l; t=1,...,T.

$E(\tilde{\varepsilon}_{i,t-1},\tilde{\varepsilon}_{i,t}) = 0$ i=1,...,l; t=1,...,T.

$E(\tilde{\varepsilon}_{i,t},\tilde{\varepsilon}_{j,t}) = 0$ with i≠j i=1,...,l; j=1,...l; t=1,...,T.

$E\left(U\Delta(\tilde{F}_k)_{t-1,t}, U\Delta(\tilde{F}_h)_{t-1,t}\right) = 0$ with k≠h h=1,...,k; k=1,...,k; t=1,...,T.

The asset cash flow outcome generating process is linear, i.e.:

$$\tilde{A}_{i,t} = E_{t-1}(\tilde{A}_i) + \beta_{i,1} U\Delta(\tilde{F}_1)_{t-1,t} + \ldots + \beta_{i,k} U\Delta(\tilde{F}_k)_{t-1,t} + \tilde{\varepsilon}_{i,t} \quad i=1,\ldots,l; \quad k=1,\ldots,k. \quad (4)$$

The stochastic factor structure remain the same for each asset.

Let define $F_{U\Delta}$ the lxk matrix, the generic element of which, $f_{i,k}$, represents $U\Delta\left(\tilde{F}_k\right)_{t-1,t}$.

We assume that the rank $F_{U\Delta}$ is k<l.

Then

the estimated sensitivity of each considered asset to a specific factor is *additive*. Therefore:

$$\sum_{i=1}^{l} U\Delta\left(\hat{A}_i\right)_{t-1,t} = \sum_{i=1}^{l}\sum_{k=1}^{k} \hat{\beta}_{i,k} U\Delta\left(\tilde{F}_k\right)_{t-1,t} \tag{6}$$

Proof

By, separately, minimising the residuals of this general, multiple regression model, we get,

$$\left[\hat{\beta}_{i,1},\ldots,\hat{\beta}_{i,k}\right]^T = \left(F_{U\Delta}^T F_{U\Delta}\right)^{-1}\left(F_{U\Delta}^T U\Delta\left(\tilde{A}_i\right)_{t-1,t}\right) \qquad i=1,\ldots,l \quad k=1,\ldots,k \quad t=1,\ldots,T.$$

The matrix $\left(F_{U\Delta}^T F_{U\Delta}\right)$ is guaranteed to have an inverse because of our assumption that $F_{U\Delta}$ as rank k and the second order conditions for the minimisation follows from the fact $\left(F_{U\Delta}^T F_{U\Delta}\right)$ is a positive definite matrix.

Summing up for i=1,...,l the foregoing relationship, we get:

$$\left[\left(\hat{\beta}_{1,1},\ldots,\hat{\beta}_{1,l}\right),\ldots,\left(\hat{\beta}_{1,k},\ldots,\hat{\beta}_{l,k}\right)\right]^T = \left(F_{U\Delta}^T F_{U\Delta}\right)^{-1}\left[F_{U\Delta}^T\left(\sum_{i=1}^{l} U\Delta\left(\tilde{A}_i\right)_{t-1,t}\right)\right]$$

consequently:

$$\sum_{i=1}^{l} U\Delta\left(\hat{A}_i\right)_{t-1,t} = \sum_{i=1}^{l}\sum_{k=1}^{k} \hat{\beta}_{i,k} U\Delta\left(\tilde{F}_k\right)_{t-1,t}$$

of course, if we make aggregate estimates, and therefore we consider the following equation

$$\sum_{i=1}^{p} U\Delta\left(\hat{A}_i\right)_{t-1,t} = \sum_{i=1}^{p}\sum_{k=1}^{k} \hat{\beta}_{i,k} U\Delta\left(\tilde{F}_k\right)_{t-1,t} + \tilde{\mu}_t \tag{7}$$

In general, R^2 of equation (2), is different from the sum of R^2 of single estimates, because

$\tilde{\mu}_t \sim N\left(\sum_{i=1}^{l} \sigma_i^2\right)$, with p<l, where p represents the sum of the considered assets, and with

$\tilde{\mu}_t \sim N\left(\sum_{i=1}^{l} \sigma_i^2\right)$, because $\tilde{\varepsilon}_{i,t} \sim N(0,\sigma_i^2)$ and $E\left(\tilde{\varepsilon}_{i,t},\tilde{\varepsilon}_{j,t}\right) = 0$.

INDEX TRACKING: SOME TECHNIQUES AND RESULTS

Winfried G. Hallerbach
Dept of Finance, Erasmus University Rotterdam
POB 1738, NL-3000 DR Rotterdam, The Netherlands

1. INTRODUCTION

An index fund is a portfolio designed to mimic the behavior of a stock market index. These broad stock market indexes are recognized benchmarks for institutional portfolios. Also, the growing acceptance of efficient market theory legitimized indexing as an investment strategy for institutional investors. By the late 1980s, for example, the surge in indexing to the S&P 500 turned the incorporated stocks into the *"Nifty 500"* (Jacques [1988]).

In this paper, we do not discuss the first set of questions that arise: what is a target index to match?, is matching to stock indexes desirable?, are index funds efficient investments?, what are the market implications of large scale indexing? and so on. For these aspects, we refer to the large and growing body of literature (Good, Ferguson & Treynor [1976], Calderwood [1977], Burgess & O'Dell [1978], Ferguson [1978], Frankfurter [1978], Frankfurter & Phillips [1980], Ryan & Kritzman [1980a,b], Brealey [1986], Rubinstein [1989], Samuelson [1989], Haugen & Baker [1991] and O'Barr & Conley [1992], e.g.).

Instead, we focus on the question of how to construct a portfolio that mimics a stock portfolio index. In this matter, one could *replicate* the target index by buying all the stocks that are comprised in the index in the right proportions. The obvious advantage of this strategy is that the return of the replicating portfolio will in principle match the index return exactly[1]. On the negative side, one must commit a large amount of capital to form the index and one faces high costs (administration, operational and custodial costs).

An alternative strategy is to *track* the index. When following this

---

1) Although this also depends on the nature of the index. For a description of biases that can occur from computational procedures, we refer to Latané, Tuttle & Young [1971], Kantor [1972] and Brennan & Schwarz [1985].

strategy, one buys only a subset of stocks and aims to achieve returns close to index returns. Aside from the question of how much capital to commit, one faces questions as: what is the tracking criterion?, which stocks to incorporate in the tracking portfolio?, what are the optimal investment fractions?, how close to track the target index?, how often to revise the tracking portfolio?, and so on. As the target index returns are not perfectly matched by the tracking portfolio but approximated to some degree, there will be a tracking error. The problem then is to find an optimal balance between tracking error and the transaction costs, needed for periodically revising the tracking portfolio.

In essence, there are two ways to track a target (cf. Meade & Salkin [1989]). The first is to stratify the tracking portfolio. This means that the tracker has the same sector representation and proportional capitalization as the index, but consists only of stocks above some level of capitalization. The second is to select a relatively small number of stocks and combine them into a portfolio on the basis of statistically estimated portfolio weights. Also, the two approaches can be combined (see Meade & Salkin [1989] and Toy & Zurack [1989], e.g.).

We will focus on the second approach. Section 2 discusses some tracking criteria and procedures to form a tracking portfolio. In Section 3, we present a regression approach to maximum correlation tracking. A crucial assumption underlying all of these statistical models is *stationarity*: the persistence of historical relationships between stock returns and target index returns. Section 4 deals with the implied turnover effect, that is important for evaluating (tracking) portfolio stability and for computing the transaction costs of a strategy. In section 5, we present empirical results of our efforts to track a Dutch stock market index by following two strategies. Section 6 contains some thoughts on tilted index tracking and another application of maximum correlation tracking: forming factor portfolios. Section 7 summarizes the paper.

2. TRACKING CRITERIA & PROCEDURES

Before discussing some tracking criteria, we define the tracking error and briefly review the so-called market model. We will use this model to compare various tracking procedures. This is especially relevant when components of the objective function are reformulated in terms of restrictions.

The return on a tracking portfolio T over period t (from time t to t+1) is defined as:

$$r_{T,t} \equiv \sum_{i=1}^{M} X_i r_{i,t} \tag{2.1}$$

with:

$$\sum_i X_i = 1 \tag{2.2}$$

where: $r_{i,t}$ = the return on stock i in period t;

X_i = the fraction of total investment capital, invested in stock i;

M = the number of stocks in the opportunity set.

We define the tracking error TE_t in period t as the difference between the return on the tracking portfolio $r_{T,t}$ and the return on the target index $r_{I,t}$:

$$TE_t \equiv r_{T,t} - r_{I,t} \tag{2.3}$$

The relation between the tracker return and the index return can be described by the market model (cf. Fama [1973; 1976 Ch.3]):

$$r_{T,t} = \alpha + \beta r_{I,t} + \epsilon_t \quad , \quad t \in N \tag{2.4}$$

In terms of linear algebra, this model represents an orthogonal projection of the N-vector with returns on the tracker on the space that is spanned by the N-vector with returns on the target index; the N-vector with the error terms ϵ_t represents the orthogonal complement. In statistical terms, eq. (2.4) is an ordinary regression (OLS) model in which the intercept α and the slope β are choosen to minimize the mean square error of the residual ϵ. It has the following properties:

$$Cov(r_{I,t}, \epsilon_t) = 0 \tag{2.5}$$

$$\beta = Cov(r_{T,t}, r_{I,t}) \;/\; Var(r_{I,t}) \tag{2.6}$$

$$E(\epsilon_t) = 0 \tag{2.7}$$

$$\alpha = E(r_{T,t}) - \beta E(r_{I,t}) \tag{2.8}$$

where E, Cov and Var denote the expectations, covariance and variance operator, respectively.

In the next subsections, we discuss three tracking criteria: minimize the (root) mean square tracking error, minimize the variance of the tracking error and maximize the correlation between the tracker returns and the index returns.

2.1 Minimize RMSTE

The root mean square tracking error RMSTE over a sample of N return observations is defined as:

$$RMSTE = \left[\frac{1}{N} \sum_{t=1}^{N} (r_{T,t} - r_{I,t})^2 \right]^{\frac{1}{2}} \tag{2.9}$$

This criterion is, among others, employed by Meade & Salkin [1989, 1990]. Incorporating eq. (2.1) in (2.9), the quadratic optimization problem can be stated as:

$$\min_{X_i} \ RMSTE \qquad , i \in M \tag{2.10}$$

subject to the full investment condition $\sum_i X_i = 1$ and the no short sale restrictions $X_i \geq 0 \ \forall \ i \in M$. Stratification and capitalization restrictions are added by Meade & Salkin [1989].

Substituting the market model (2.4) in (2.9) and squaring, we get:

$$MSTE = \alpha^2 + (\beta-1)^2\sigma^2{}_I + \sigma^2{}_\epsilon \tag{2.11}$$

where $\sigma^2{}_I$ and $\sigma^2{}_\epsilon$ denote the variance of the target index return and the residual variance, respectively. In terms of the market model, minimizing (R)MSTE thus implies the minimization of excess return α, differential systematic 'risk' $|\beta-1|$ and unsystematic 'risk' $\sigma^2{}_\epsilon$ in a particular way[2]. The implied goal of forcing β to 1 can be made

---

[2] Actually, the term 'risk' is unwarranted, since we do not make any assumptions about the preferences of the investor.

explicit by adding the β-restriction $\sum_i X_i\beta_i = 1$ to the optimization problem (as do Meade & Salkin [1990]). A drawback of the latter formulation is that a trade-off between differential systematic risk $(\beta-1)^2$ and unsystematic risk σ^2_ϵ is no longer possible. The shadow price of the β-restriction may be large!

Rudd & Rosenberg [1979] follow a somewhat different route by reformulating the objective function (2.11) as

$$\lambda_1\alpha + \lambda_2(\beta-1)^2 + \lambda_3\sigma^2_\epsilon \tag{2.12}$$

possibly extended with terms reflecting transaction costs and other portfolio attributes. Two things are worth noting. First, each term in the objective function is weighted individually by the parameters λ, thus allowing great flexibility with regard to specifying trade-offs among portfolio attributes. Second, not α^2 but α enters the objective function. The Rudd & Rosenberg-model can therefore be considered as a special case of the next set of tracking models.

2.2 Minimize Var(TE)

Using eq. (2.3), the MSTE can also be decomposed as:

$$\text{MSTE} = \text{Var(TE)} + [\text{E(TE)}]^2 \tag{2.13}$$

Minimization of the tracking error variance Var(TE) thus ignores the bias component $[\text{E(TE)}]^2$ of the MSTE. The optimization problem is:

$$\text{Min Var}\left(\textstyle\sum_i X_i r_{i,t} - r_{I,t} \right) \qquad , \; i \in M \tag{2.14}$$

subject to the full investment and the no short sale restrictions.

Haugen & Baker [1990] and Haugen [1993, Ch.10] provide an elegant way in which this problem can be solved with standard Markowitz optimization programs[3]. To see this, we rewrite eq. (2.14) as:

$$\text{Min Var}\left[\textstyle\sum_i X_i (r_{i,t} - r_{I,t}) \right] \tag{2.15}$$

3) Markowitz [1987, p. 50] provides an alternative formulation in the framework of the general portfolio selection problem. The drawback of his formulation is that it extends over the whole set of stocks that are comprised in the target index.

When the adjusted stock return series (i.e. the return differentials between brackets) are used as input for the quadratic portfolio optimization program, the minimum variance set appears in E(TE)-Var(TE)-space. Points on this minimum variance set indicate portfolios that minimize tracking error variance, given a level of mean tracking error. The global minimum variance portfolio is the portfolio that minimizes tracking error variance. Although the mean tracking error is no instrumental variable in this optimization problem, the MSTE can be computed using eq. (2.13).

Substituting the market model eq. (2.4) in (2.14) or (2.15), we get:

$$Var(TE) = (\beta-1)^2\sigma^2_I + \sigma^2_\epsilon \qquad (2.16)$$

Therefore, minimizing the tracking error variance entails the minimization of $|\beta-1|$ and σ^2_ϵ in a particular way. Rudd [1980] makes the implied goal of forcing β to 1 explicit by reformulating the optimization problem as:

$$\text{Min } \sigma^2_\epsilon \qquad \text{s.t. } \beta = \textstyle\sum_i X_i\beta_i = 1 \qquad (2.17)$$

and subject to the full investment and the no short sale restrictions.

This approach can be expanded by modelling the covariance structure of stock returns by means of index models or factor models[4]. However, the problem of these approaches, according to which the market model beta or the factor/index model beta's are matched between the tracker and the target index, is that the shadow prices of these constraints are likely to be ignored. The ideal form of a tracking optimization problem, therefore, is a *multi-criteria* one, especially when transaction (revision) costs are incorporated into the optimization.

Haugen & Baker [1990] provide an approach to circumvent the problem that is attached to the formulation in eq. (2.17). The standard Markowitz portfolio optimization program is fed with the covariance matrix of the return differentials $(r_{i,t} - r_{I,t})$ and the vector with mean return differentials per stock, $E(r_{i,t} - r_{I,t})$, is replaced by the

---

4) These models assume that stock returns respond to the pull of one or more indexes or factors (Elton & Gruber [1991, Ch.6]; Haugen [1993, pp.293-294]). In the context of index tracking, Meade [1991] focused on the modelling of covariance structures of international stock returns.

vector with stock beta's $\{\beta_i\}_{i\in M}$. The minimum variance set now appears in β-Var(TE)-space. Points on this minimum variance set indicate portfolios that minimize tracking error variance, given a specific beta β for the tracking portfolio. In this way, the trade-off between differential systematic risk $|\beta-1|$ and tracking error variance is made explicit. Note that the tracking portfolio's β is no instrumental variable in this optimization problem; instead, it can only be monitored. As shown by Roll [1992], beta-constrained strategies have some undesirable properties.

2.3 Maximize tracker - target correlation

The last tracking criterion we discuss entails maximizing the correlation between the tracking portfolio returns and the target index returns. When we transform the minimum variance set in β-Var(TE)-space (as described above) into the minimum standard deviation set in β-σ(TE)-space, the maximum correlation tracking portfolio will be the one maximizing the slope of the radial (i.e. a line extended from the origin) that touches the minimum standard deviation set (Haugen & Baker [1990] and Haugen [1993, p.295-296]). This procedure is valid, regardless of the restrictions placed on the investment fractions $\{X_i\}_i$. In section 3, we present an alternative procedure to estimate the composition of a maximum correlation tracking portfolio.

An obvious problem with this tracking criterion is that correlation does not measure the congruence, but the strength of a linear relationship. It is quite possible that the beta-differential $|\beta-1|$ of the maximum correlation tracking portfolio is large. So, considering eqs. (2.11) and (2.16), a high degree of correlation is a necessary but not a sufficient condition for minimizing (R)MSTE or minimizing tracking error variance. The omission of this beta-differential in the objective function (or in the set of restrictions) implies that the maximum correlation tracker can be different from the minimum variance tracker.

3. A REGRESSION APPROACH TO MAXIMUM CORRELATION TRACKING

We present a simple procedure to estimate the composition of a maximum correlation tracking portfolio. Section 3.1 deals with the general case where short sales are allowed. Section 3.2 presents the derivation of some statistics that are relevant in the context of the market model. The short sales restriction is introduced in section 3.3 and section 3.4 contains some remarks on estimation risk.

3.1 Short sales allowed

The correlation R between the tracking portfolio return and the target index return is:

$$R = \mathrm{Cov}(r_T, r_I) \;/\; \sigma_T \sigma_I \tag{3.1}$$

Using eq. (2.1), the most simple tracking optimization problem is:

$$\max_{X_i} \; R \quad , \; i \in M \tag{3.2}$$

subject to the full investment condition eq. (2.2).
Note that the correlation R is homogeneous of degree zero in r_T and r_I. This is obvious since correlation is the covariance between standardized variates. This implies that we do not have to incorporate the full investment condition into the optimization procedure. We can simply perform an unconstrained optimization and scale the solution afterwards to satisfy (2.2). To compute the optimum, a set of M simultaneous linear equations need to be solved.

The computations can be simplified by using standard multiple regression programs. In essence, the calculations required to fit a regression equation to a given set of data are those of solving a set of simultaneous linear (normal) equations. We formulate the following regression model:

$$r_{I,t} = a + b r_{T,t} + e_t \quad , \; t \in N \tag{3.3}$$

Using eq. (2.1), this can be expanded into:

$$r_{I,t} = a + \textstyle\sum_{i \in M} bX_i r_{i,t} + e_t \tag{3.4}$$

or

$$r_{I,t} = a + \textstyle\sum_{i \in M} c_i r_{i,t} + e_t \tag{3.5}$$

Considering eq. (2.4), we can label the model (3.3) - (3.5) as a *'reversed market model'*. Performing the regression (3.5), the coefficients $\{c_i\}_{i\in M}$ will be choosen such that the residual variance σ^2_e is minimized. As there are no constraints on the coefficients, this implies the maximization of the R^2 of the regression.

After running the regression (3.5), each of the estimated coefficients c_i can be decomposed into b and X_i. From eqs (3.4), (3.5) and (2.2) it follows that:

$$\sum_i c_i = \sum_i bX_i = b \tag{3.6}$$

which is the regression coefficient of eq. (3.3). Dividing each c_i by b yields an estimate of the optimal investment fraction X_i:

$$X^*_i = c_i \,/\, (\sum_j c_j) = c_i/b \quad , \quad i,j \in M \tag{3.7}$$

A tracking portfolio T with this composition $\{X^*_i\}_{i\in M}$ will maximize the correlation with the target index I. The correlation R trivially follows from the R^2 of the regression:

$$R = \mathrm{sgn}(b)\cdot\sqrt{(R^2)} \tag{3.8}$$

The residual variance σ^2_e of the reverse market model equals the residual sum of squares $\sum_t e^2_t$ divided by the number of observations N:

$$\sigma^2_e = \sum_t e^2_t/N \tag{3.9}$$

For computing the sample estimate of the residual variance, we must correct for the degrees of freedom (dgf):

$$s^2_e = \sigma^2_e\cdot N/(N-M-1) \tag{3.10}$$

3.2 Relevant statistics

From b and the statistics R^2 and s^2_e of the multiple regression (3.5), we can compute all relevant numbers. From the definition of R^2, the sample estimate of the target index variance (corrected for dgf) is:

$$s^2_I = \frac{(N-M-1)}{(N-1)}\cdot\frac{s^2_e}{(1-R^2)} \tag{3.11}$$

From eq. (3.3) we have $\sigma^2_I = b^2\sigma^2_T + \sigma^2_e$ and $\sigma^2_e = (1-R^2)\sigma^2_I$, hence the sample estimate of the target index standard deviation is:

$$s_T = (R/b)\cdot s_I \tag{3.12}$$

The R^2's of the market model eq. (2.4) and the reverse market model (3.3) are of course identical. From the definition of R^2 and the estimated b from the reverse market model, the estimated beta β of the market model eq. (2.4) can then be computed as:

$$\beta = R^2/b \tag{3.13}$$

The market model's residual variance σ^2_ϵ satisfies

$$\sigma^2_\epsilon = (1-R^2)\sigma^2_T \tag{3.14}$$

Using eqs. (3.12) & (3.11) and correcting for dgf, the sample estimate of the residual standard deviation in the market model (2.4) is:

$$s_\epsilon = \frac{R}{b}\cdot s_e\left[\frac{N-M-1}{N-2}\right]^{\frac{1}{2}} \tag{3.15}$$

Of special importance are the standard deviations of the parameters α and β in the market model eq. (2.4). Assuming spherical disturbances $\{\epsilon_t\}_{t\in N}$, these can be used to test the significance of excess return α and the significance of the beta differential $|\beta-1|$. The sample estimate of the variance of slope β is defined as:

$$s^2(\beta) = \frac{s^2_\epsilon}{\sum_t\ [r_{I,t} - E(r_{I,t})]^2} = s^2_\epsilon/(N\cdot\sigma^2_I) \tag{3.16}$$

Using (3.14) and then (3.12) (adjusting the latter for dgf), we get

$$s^2(\beta) = \frac{(1-R^2)}{(N-2)}\cdot\frac{R^2}{b^2} \tag{3.17}$$

From (3.13), we have $b^2 = R^4/\beta^2$. Plugging this into eq. (3.17) yields

$$s^2(\beta) = \frac{R^{-2} - 1}{(N-2)} \beta^2 \tag{3.18}$$

The t-value for testing β against unity then follows as:

$$t(\beta=1) = \frac{\beta - 1}{s(\beta)} = \frac{\beta - 1}{\beta} \left[\frac{N - 2}{R^{-2} - 1} \right]^{\frac{1}{2}} \tag{3.19}$$

The sample estimate of the variance of intercept α is defined as:

$$s^2(\alpha) = \frac{\sum_t (r_{T,t})^2}{N(N \cdot \sigma^2_I)} s^2_\epsilon = [\sigma^2_I + E(r_I)^2] \frac{s^2_\epsilon}{N \cdot \sigma^2_I} \tag{3.20}$$

Using (3.16) and (3.18), this simplifies to

$$s^2(\alpha) = [\sigma^2_I + E(r_I)^2]\, s^2(\beta) = [\sigma^2_I + E(r_I)^2] \frac{R^{-2} - 1}{(N-2)} \beta^2 \tag{3.21}$$

The t-value for testing α against zero then readily follows as:

$$t(\alpha=0) = \frac{\alpha}{|\beta|} \left[\frac{N - 2}{[\sigma^2_I + E(r_I)^2](R^{-2} - 1)} \right]^{\frac{1}{2}} \tag{3.22}$$

Although the tracking criterion is not to minimize MSTE, the MSTE can be computed from eqs. (2.11) or (2.13), or equivalently (using eqs. 3.12 and 3.13) as:

$$\begin{aligned} MSTE &= Var(r_T - r_I) = \sigma^2_T + \sigma^2_I - 2R\sigma_T\sigma_I \\ &= \sigma^2_I \; [\; 1 + \beta(\beta R^{-2} - 2) \;] \end{aligned} \tag{3.23}$$

3.3 Short sales restriction

An obvious problem with the regression approach sketched above is that there is no short sale restriction. However, we can use Waterman's [1974] procedure to solve the *restricted least squares problem*. In broad lines, the procedure is as follows. When one or more of the coefficients c_i in unrestricted regression eq. (3.5) is negative, the solution to the restricted problem $c_i > 0$ must be a boundary point. Therefore, at least one coefficient must be zero. Next, subsets of the M stocks are formed and the residual variance for the regressions with all coefficients $c_i \geq 0$ are computed. The regression equation with the lowest residual variance is then selected. In most index tracking cases, the number of initial negative coefficients c_i will be very small. As a short cut to Waterman's procedure, we found in our sample that it suffices to delete the stock with a negative c_i from the opportunity set and rerun the unconstrained regression on the remaining stocks.

3.4 Estimation risk

It is crucial to remember that the investment fractions in a portfolio optimization problem are statistically estimated and consequently surrounded by estimation error. In a Markowitz formulation of the tracking problem, results derived by Jobson & Korkie [1980, 1983] can be helpful to evaluate the estimated vector of investment fractions.

The estimated standard deviations or t-values of the estimated coefficients $\{c_i\}_i$ that result from regression (3.5) can be also used to evaluate this estimation risk. The standard deviation of any estimated c_i is the standard deviation of $(X_i b)$. This standard deviation may be interpreted as the standard deviation of the estimated X_i, *conditional* on the estimated b. This argument is equivalent to the case of two variates, y and x, with the regression equation $y_t = bx_t + u_t$. The variance of the estimated slope b equals $E(\sigma^2_u/\sum_t x^2_t)$, but is in practice evaluated as $\sigma^2_u/\sum_t x^2_t$, i.e. conditional on the observed x_t's (cf. Maddala [1977, p.152].

In case of selecting the number of stocks in the opportunity set to construct the tracking portfolio, a stepwise regression procedure (forward selection or backward elimination) can be employed to incorporate only those stocks that provide a significant contribution to the explanatory power of the regression (i.e. to maximizing the correlation between tracker and target index). This contribution can be gauged by the t-values (partial $\sqrt{F}$'s) of the coefficients c_i. Also, the standard deviations of the investment fractions can be used in evaluating the need to revise the tracking portfolio.

4. PORTFOLIO STABILITY: THE IMPLIED TURNOVER EFFECT

Before turning to the application of some tracking procedures to the Dutch stock market, we discuss an effect that we have labeled 'implied turnover'. When applying tracking strategies over time, it will be necessary to rebalance the portfolio from time to time. Turnover is a measure for the resulting portfolio instability. Because of transaction costs, the tracking portfolio strategy with the lowest turnover will be favored, ceteris paribus. In evaluating the stability of tracking portfolios, recognition of the 'implied turnover' effect is essential.

Over the period [t,t+1], the return on a 'buy-&-hold' investment portfolio p, composed from the opportunity set of M stocks, equals:

$$1+r_{p,t} = V_{t+1}/V_t = \sum_i X_{i,t}\,(1+r_{i,t}) \qquad (4.1)$$

$X_{i,t}$ denotes the relative proportion of initial capital V_t invested in stock i at time t:

$$X_{i,t} = \frac{n_i P_{i,t}}{\sum_j n_j P_{j,t}}, \qquad i,j \in M \qquad (4.2)$$

n_i is the number of shares of stock i and $P_{i,t}$ is the value of one share of stock i on time t. So, at the beginning of period t (i.e. at time t), the relative composition of portfolio p is characterized by the vector $\{X_{i,t}\}_{i\in M}$ of investment fractions.

When the returns on the M stocks in the portfolio over period t are not equal, the composition of this 'buy-&-hold' portfolio in terms of the 'absolute' proportions $\{n_i\}_{i\in M}$ is unchanged. The investment fractions $\{X_i\}_{i\in M}$ in contrast, are changed. At the end of period t (i.e. at time t+1), the investment fractions equal:

$$X_{i,t+1} = \frac{n_i P_{i,t+1}}{\sum_j n_j P_{j,t+1}} = \frac{n_i P_{i,t}\,(1+r_{i,t})}{V_{t+1}} = \frac{\dfrac{n_i P_{i,t}}{V_t}\,(1+r_{i,t})}{V_{t+1}\,/\,V_t} \qquad (4.3)$$

Incorporating eq. (4.2) in (4.3) gives:

$$X_{i,t+1} = X_{i,t} \left[\frac{1 + r_{i,t}}{1 + r_{p,t}} \right] \tag{4.4}$$

$X_{i,t+1}$ denotes the investment fraction of stock i that is implied by a difference between the return on stock i and the portfolio return, given a 'buy-&-hold' strategy over period t. The larger the difference between the return on an individual stock and the portfolio return, the larger the relative change in the corresponding investment fraction. In fact, it is obvious that the investment fraction increases (decreases) when the individual return is higher (lower) than the portfolio return.

The outcome of a portfolio optimization procedure with respect to period t is the vector $\{X^*_{i,t}\}_{i\in M}$ with *optimal* investment fractions. Over different consecutive periods, different vectors $\{X^*_{i,t}\}_t$ result. In addition, however, cross sectional differences between the realized stock returns are responsible for part of the changes in the *actual* investment fractions. In evaluating the stability in portfolio composition, one should therefore at any time compare the optimal investment fractions with the actual fractions that are implied for that time.

We define the *explicit portfolio turnover* from time t to time t+1 as the sum of the absolute changes in the optimal investment fractions:

$$\sum_i |X^*_{i,t+1} - X^*_{i,t}| \tag{4.5}$$

Considering eq. (4.5), the *implied portfolio turnover* over this period t is defined as:

$$\sum_i |X^*_{i,t} - X^*_{i,t}(1+r_{i,t})/(1+r_{p,t})| \tag{4.6}$$

Finally, the *net portfolio turnover* equals:

$$\sum_i |X^*_{i,t+1} - X^*_{i,t}(1+r_{i,t})/(1+r_{p,t})| \tag{4.7}$$

Net portfolio turnover is the only relevant turnover measure as it adequately states the fraction of invested capital that is needed for buy as well as sell transactions. Multiplying net turnover with percentage transaction costs gives the actual costs of revising the former optimal portfolio into the new optimal portfolio. Using explicit portfolio turnover for computing revision costs can result in gross over- or understatements of actual transaction costs. Meade & Salkin

[1990] for example, measure transaction costs for index tracking as proportional to explicit turnover, as defined by eq. (4.6); this is a source of possible bias. Also, when following a turnover-constrained approach to portfolio revision (as developed by Schreiner [1980] and used by Perold [1984] e.g.), recognition of the implied turnover effect is of paramount importance.

5. TRACKING A DUTCH STOCK MARKET INDEX

We applied two tracking techniques to the Dutch stock market. The target portfolio is the CBS-All Share Price Index. This chain index is capitalization weighted and includes the price relatives of all common stocks listed on the Amsterdam Stock Exchange (real estate funds and investment funds excluded). The opportunity set of stocks for forming the tracker portfolio consists of 15 stocks. The stocks are listed in Table 1. The stocks belong to the largest capitalizations on the ASE (on all stocks, options are traded on the European Option Exchange). We also applied some sort of stratification criterion by selecting the stocks over different sectors. We used weekly (Wednesday) closing prices, starting from 2/1/1985 to 27/3/1991. From these prices we computed log price relatives for the index and the 15 stocks. This gives us 325 weekly returns over 25 quarters.

TABLE 1: The opportunity set of stocks, grouped by sector.

Finance & Insurance:	1. AEGON	:	Aegon
	2. AMEV	:	AMEV
	3. NMB-P	:	NMB-Postbank
Energy:	4. RD	:	Royal Dutch/Shell
Transportation:	5. KLM	:	KLM
Food & Beverages:	6. HEI	:	Heineken
	7. UNI	:	Unilever
Basic Industries:	8. AKZO	:	Akzo
	9. HOOG	:	Hoogovens
Trade:	10. AHOLD	:	Ahold
	11. B-TET	:	Bührmann-Tetterode
Electronics:	12. PHIL	:	Philips
Publishing:	13. ELS	:	Elsevier
	14. VNU	:	VNU
Capital Goods:	15. STORK	:	VMF-Stork

TABLE 2A: In-sample statistics of Minimum Variance of Tracking Error Portfolio T1 (52-week windows rolling 13 weeks).

	α (%)	s(α)	t(α=0)	β	s(β)	t(β=1)	R^2	s(TE)%	RMSTE%
1	-0.007	0.026	-0.266	0.994	0.017	-0.348	.9863	0.1825	0.1827
2	0.034	0.033	1.060	0.971	0.019	-1.497	.9806	0.2335	0.2349
3	0.002	0.032	0.067	0.994	0.018	-0.321	.9836	0.2287	0.2287
4	0.004	0.035	0.130	1.016	0.017	0.895	.9856	0.2465	0.2467
5	0.015	0.033	0.460	1.021	0.016	1.311	.9875	0.2367	0.2373
6	0.057	0.027	2.124	1.023	0.014	1.629	.9904	0.1977	0.2065
7	0.072	0.027	2.660	1.043	0.013	3.258	.9922	0.2101	0.2252
8	0.050	0.027	1.832	1.050	0.013	3.761	.9919	0.2184	0.2272
9	0.028	0.038	0.734	1.020	0.010	1.879	.9947	0.2755	0.2761
10	0.028	0.041	0.679	1.024	0.011	2.293	.9946	0.3036	0.3043
11	-0.014	0.039	-0.370	1.017	0.010	1.628	.9949	0.2812	0.2818
12	-0.036	0.037	-0.973	1.013	0.010	1.286	.9950	0.2690	0.2720
13	-0.022	0.029	-0.757	1.035	0.014	2.456	.9908	0.2158	0.2159
14	-0.003	0.025	-0.108	1.023	0.015	1.506	.9891	0.1753	0.1754
15	-0.024	0.022	-1.107	1.010	0.016	0.652	.9883	0.1468	0.1481
16	0.017	0.022	0.781	1.019	0.015	1.263	.9888	0.1513	0.1537
17	0.043	0.021	2.075	1.026	0.013	1.971	.9916	0.1473	0.1565
18	0.044	0.025	1.766	1.035	0.015	2.315	.9894	0.1858	0.1923
19	0.066	0.031	2.133	1.048	0.019	2.552	.9841	0.2342	0.2435
20	0.048	0.032	1.502	1.037	0.016	2.255	.9877	0.2337	0.2362
21	0.041	0.032	1.290	1.043	0.017	2.498	.9865	0.2346	0.2360
Average R:		.9946	(Avge R)^2:		.9892		average:	0.2194	0.2229

TABLE 2B: In-sample statistics of Maximum Correlation Portfolio T2 (52-week windows rolling 13 weeks).

	α (%)	s(α)	t(α=0)	β	s(β)	t(β=1)	R^2	s(TE)%	RMSTE%
1	-0.011	0.026	-0.407	0.997	0.016	-0.161	.9863	0.1827	0.1831
2	0.037	0.033	1.130	0.969	0.020	-1.608	.9806	0.2337	0.2354
3	-0.001	0.032	-0.029	0.998	0.018	-0.136	.9837	0.2291	0.2291
4	0.024	0.031	0.764	1.014	0.015	0.902	.9879	0.2251	0.2269
5	0.007	0.031	0.220	1.039	0.015	2.546	.9881	0.2445	0.2448
6	0.047	0.025	1.848	1.046	0.013	3.452	.9911	0.2090	0.2153
7	0.065	0.024	2.664	1.062	0.012	5.292	.9931	0.2234	0.2368
8	0.042	0.024	1.723	1.070	0.012	5.923	.9930	0.2325	0.2400
9	0.026	0.035	0.751	1.043	0.010	4.394	.9953	0.2999	0.3000
10	0.024	0.037	0.662	1.053	0.010	5.565	.9954	0.3416	0.3417
11	-0.003	0.036	-0.097	1.043	0.010	4.465	.9954	0.3104	0.3109
12	-0.025	0.035	-0.712	1.035	0.010	3.621	.9954	0.2896	0.2919
13	-0.042	0.027	-1.575	1.068	0.013	5.404	.9919	0.2418	0.2419
14	-0.010	0.023	-0.420	1.046	0.014	3.238	.9898	0.1845	0.1848
15	-0.021	0.021	-1.003	1.027	0.015	1.825	.9887	0.1508	0.1511
16	0.006	0.021	0.289	1.036	0.015	2.499	.9893	0.1563	0.1582
17	0.036	0.019	1.840	1.043	0.013	3.396	.9921	0.1535	0.1620
18	0.025	0.023	1.086	1.058	0.014	4.194	.9903	0.1969	0.1998
19	0.052	0.028	1.847	1.070	0.017	4.117	.9852	0.2457	0.2513
20	0.058	0.028	2.036	1.077	0.014	5.332	.9894	0.2604	0.2622
21	0.048	0.028	1.723	1.084	0.015	5.543	.9885	0.2604	0.2611
Average R :		.9950	(Avge R)^2 :		.9900		average:	0.2320	0.2347

We use the 52 sample points over the first 4 quarters to estimate the composition of the first tracker portfolio. In quarter 5, we combine this composition with the actual returns on the 15 stocks to obtain 13 out-of-sample returns on the tracker. Then, we move the estimation window by 13 weeks and repeat the procedure. In total, we have 21 rolling (partly overlapping) estimation intervals, from which follow 273 out-of-sample tracker returns over 21 quarters.

We followed two tracking strategies:[5)]

T1: minimization of the tracking error variance according to Haugen & Baker's [1990] full covariance procedure (section 2.2 eq. (2.15));

T2: maximization of correlation between target and tracker (section 3, eqs. (3.5 - 3.7)).

No short sales were allowed.

Table 2A presents in-sample statistics for T1. The average (sample) standard deviation of the tracking error, s(TE), is almost 1.6% per year and only marginally lower than the RMSTE. This implies that the mean return differential between the index and the tracker (the bias) is very small. The average correlation is almost 99.5%. The tracker's β significantly exceeds unity in 8 out of 21 cases. This is an illustration of the result stated by Roll [1992]: the minimum-s^2(TE)-tracking portfolio's β will always exceed unity when the average target index return exceeds the return on the global minimum variance portfolio. The composition of the tracking portfolios is given in Table 3A. The dominance of Royal Dutch in the tracker is not surprising as Royal Dutch, together with the Japanese NTT, forms the world top-2 capitalization stocks. The net turnover over the 21 periods is about 325% or on average 16% per quarter. The difference between explicit and net turnover varies per period, but is in total only 25 %-points.

The in-sample statistics for T2 are in Table 2B. The s(TE) is about 1.67% per year and slightly larger than for T1. Here also, the difference between s(TE) and RMSTE is only marginal. The average correlation is 99.50% and about the same as for T1. Note that in 16 out of 21 cases the tracker's β significantly exceeds unity. This is the obvious drawback of a relative tracking criterion, in contrast with an

5) We also performed the strategy of minimizing the tracking error variance with the restriction that the in-sample OLS-β with respect to the index equals unity. Due to limited space and the problems attached to this procedure (Roll [1992]), we do not report the results.

TABLE 3A: In-sample portfolio composition of tracker T1 (52-week windows rolling 13 weeks).

	AEGON	AMEV	NMB-P	RD	KLM	HEI	UNI	AKZO	HOOG	AHOLD	B-TET	PHIL	ELS	VNU	STORK	%-TURNOVER Expl	Impl	Net
1-4	4.91	2.10	5.49	42.14	1.21	2.93	9.49	4.98	2.21	4.40	1.99	9.49	1.59	4.71	2.36			
2-5	5.58	2.44	5.27	38.54	3.09	3.34	9.10	5.90	2.18	5.84	1.00	10.54	2.11	2.71	2.35	14.48	6.89	18.09
3-6	4.36	3.47	6.26	37.75	2.81	3.54	10.39	2.62	2.71	5.43	1.94	11.10	2.04	2.19	3.40	13.17	7.24	15.15
4-7	0.58	6.69	6.45	36.57	2.07	5.41	11.62	3.76	3.75	4.92	1.43	10.88	2.53	1.26	2.09	18.36	6.09	21.90
5-8	1.79	7.10	4.25	37.00	2.38	5.84	13.36	5.65	1.55	4.06	0.98	8.37	2.28	2.79	2.59	16.91	9.15	14.04
6-9	0.87	5.92	5.57	39.50	2.88	2.79	18.75	3.55	1.35	1.52	1.67	7.45	3.48	2.39	2.30	23.18	9.60	19.30
7-10	2.52	5.31	4.62	38.88	3.05	3.62	15.77	4.79	1.02	2.75	1.82	7.58	2.39	3.71	2.16	13.44	5.08	15.97
8-11	3.98	5.18	5.00	39.91	2.08	3.78	16.15	4.89	0.79	1.36	2.96	7.67	0.95	4.25	1.06	10.54	4.41	11.76
9-12	5.04	4.78	7.2	40.35	1.51	4.33	16.70	2.58	1.28	1.10	2.87	8.34	0	2.79	1.14	12.08	10.79	14.10
10-13	2.40	4.43	4.95	42.59	0.89	6.15	16.99	3.89	0	1.81	4.09	6.93	0	3.81	1.05	17.24	6.07	21.08
11-14	3.31	3.74	6.21	43.30	1.53	2.96	16.98	3.44	0	1.92	5.36	7.91	0.23	2.30	0.83	12.20	5.94	15.47
12-15	2.83	2.92	6.27	44.11	2.87	4.96	14.52	2.66	0	1.43	5.71	8.80	0.47	2.05	0.40	11.40	4.03	14.41
13-16	3.16	1.97	5.40	44.40	2.91	4.08	12.64	6.91	0	1.87	3.22	6.97	3.11	2.70	0.65	17.79	1.96	18.38
14-17	3.94	4.28	5.39	42.83	3.09	4.94	10.52	6.96	0.01	2.89	3.74	6.17	2.62	1.33	1.32	12.76	5.64	16.89
15-18	4.38	4.04	4.53	40.62	3.17	5.90	9.88	6.12	0.06	2.57	5.29	6.84	2.26	2.61	1.74	10.93	2.53	10.33
16-19	4.06	3.89	2.61	40.39	2.47	5.63	9.68	7.22	2.07	3.7	5.92	7.54	2.05	1.48	1.29	11.16	4.99	13.45
17-20	3.86	3.35	1.16	40.78	1.82	6.44	9.68	6.56	2.62	2.93	4.37	9.08	4.37	1.40	1.57	11.80	3.53	12.34
18-21	5.00	3.67	2.07	39.61	0.27	3.40	10.53	9.42	1.74	1.53	1.96	9.09	8.15	1.56	2.00	20.89	4.51	21.54
19-22	8.31	4.10	2.63	39.37	0	2.84	11.94	7.22	1.48	0	3.66	7.44	7.82	0	3.19	17.21	7.15	15.35
20-23	9.15	1.84	4.15	41.12	0	2.12	14.34	8.84	0.20	1.10	2.15	6.91	5.35	0.31	2.42	19.08	11.49	21.71
21-24	6.98	0.29	6.64	40.73	0	1.67	16.89	6.19	0.87	2.28	2.00	5.08	6.00	0	4.38	18.99	5.29	15.99
average:	4.14	3.88	4.86	40.50	1.91	4.13	13.14	5.44	1.23	2.64	3.05	8.11	2.85	2.21	1.92	15.18	6.12	16.36
total:																303.60	122.38	327.24

TABLE 3B: In-sample portfolio composition of tracker T2 (52-week windows rolling 13 weeks).

	AEGON	AMEV	NMB-P	RD	KLM	HEI	UNI	AKZO	HOOG	AHOLD	B-TET	PHIL	ELS	VNU	STORK	%-TURNOVER Expl	Impl	Net
1-4	4.98	2.10	5.48	42.29	1.24	2.69	9.36	4.84	2.24	4.45	1.97	9.67	1.64	4.79	2.24			
2-5	5.40	2.43	5.26	38.47	3.17	3.37	8.96	5.92	2.12	5.98	1.10	10.54	2.17	2.68	2.44	15.11	6.92	18.45
3-6	4.67	3.49	6.35	37.74	2.80	3.69	10.49	2.62	2.69	5.27	1.86	10.96	2.01	2.22	3.16	12.95	7.26	14.58
4-7	0.79	5.70	6.10	36.70	1.62	4.43	12.65	4.93	2.60	3.51	1.43	10.34	3.52	2.47	3.21	18.48	6.08	22.83
5-8	1.91	7.05	4.57	36.55	2.22	6.19	14.89	6.21	1.43	2.75	0.28	8.72	2.87	2.12	2.22	16.71	8.48	15.16
6-9	1.14	5.85	5.45	38.75	2.52	3.45	18.74	4.87	1.20	0.77	1.01	8.03	4.48	1.67	2.07	19.11	9.35	15.74
7-10	3.60	5.47	4.61	39.14	2.87	3.39	14.40	6.01	0.64	1.62	1.32	8.63	3.72	2.91	1.70	14.66	5.07	16.11
8-11	4.63	5.76	4.20	40.15	1.76	4.14	15.17	6.30	0.03	0.71	2.63	8.31	1.23	3.61	1.36	12.37	4.50	13.66
9-12	5.76	5.19	5.02	39.86	1.77	4.12	15.85	4.05	0.36	1.53	4.02	7.84	0	3.15	1.49	10.60	11.09	13.78
10-13	4.52	5.45	2.66	41.53	1.19	3.71	15.65	3.85	0	2.51	5.75	7.05	0	4.09	2.06	12.29	5.87	14.01
11-14	5.91	4.05	4.09	41.59	1.29	2.23	16.32	3.55	0	2.14	6.57	7.99	0	2.80	1.46	10.87	6.32	14.10
12-15	4.68	3.56	4.90	42.56	2.62	4.28	14.00	3.50	0	1.87	6.39	8.29	0	2.37	0.99	10.89	3.96	13.56
13-16	3.02	2.95	4.86	42.87	2.35	4.91	16.03	5.90	1.03	0.51	2.26	6.10	4.93	2.06	0.22	22.65	2.09	24.50
14-17	2.65	3.23	4.65	42.75	3.25	5.09	12.94	5.90	0.94	2.14	3.70	6.38	3.22	2.32	0.83	11.20	5.65	15.03
15-18	3.13	3.70	4.04	41.16	3.32	5.36	10.30	6.00	0.61	2.06	5.68	7.18	3.02	2.62	1.83	10.90	2.76	10.76
16-19	2.93	3.68	2.23	41.67	3.00	4.79	9.63	7.29	2.41	2.89	5.97	7.76	3.25	1.43	1.06	11.12	4.98	14.33
17-20	4.15	2.63	1.08	41.69	3.09	5.75	9.45	6.31	2.88	2.63	3.93	9.19	4.33	1.50	1.38	11.30	3.48	12.99
18-21	5.34	3.38	1.99	40.24	2.11	2.37	10.18	8.60	2.24	1.31	3.02	9.22	7.19	1.33	1.47	17.72	4.73	18.63
19-22	8.12	3.40	1.93	40.47	0.70	1.68	12.21	7.73	1.70	1.75	4.24	7.26	5.48	0.37	2.96	16.43	7.09	13.34
20-23	7.44	2.36	2.99	39.00	0.10	0.60	15.39	8.13	1.30	2.56	3.41	6.56	5.34	0	4.81	14.59	11.66	21.47
21-24	4.70	1.79	4.90	40.07	0	0.67	17.74	6.04	0.86	3.72	3.28	4.99	5.12	0	6.13	15.74	5.30	13.32
average:	4.26	3.96	4.16	40.25	2.05	3.66	13.35	5.65	1.30	2.51	3.32	8.14	3.03	2.21	2.15	14.28	6.13	15.82
total:																285.67	122.67	316.38

TABLE 4: Out-of-sample summary statistics of tracking portfolios:
T1: MVTE = Minimum Variance of Tracking Error Tracker
T2: MaxCorr = Maximum Correlation Tracker

	Index	T1: MVTE		T2: MaxCorr	
	I	T1	TE(T1)	T2	TE(T2)
E(r)	.08446	.07647	-.00799	.07790	-.00655
s(r)	2.32228	2.45075	.32004	2.45829	.32105
RMSTE*)		.32014		.32105	
regression:					
α		-0.01199		-.01084	
$s(\alpha)$		0.01824		.01812	
$t(\alpha=0)$		-0.6576		-.5983	
β		1.0474		1.0507	
$s(\beta)/100$		.7861		.7812	
$t(\beta=1)$		6.0231		6.4929	
R		.9925		.9926	
R^2		.9850		.9852	
$s(\epsilon)$		.30222		.30031	
# obs for which $r_T > r_I$:		135		141	
# obs for which $r_T \leq r_I$:		138		132	
Transaction costs:		.04908		.04746	
Net average weekly returns:		.07269		.07425	

All figures on basis of *weekly* logarithmic returns *in percentages*.
Total number of observations: N = 273
E(r) = average return ; s(r) = sample standard deviation of return
TE(T#) = tracking error ($r_T - r_I$) of tracker #
RMSTE = sample Root Mean Square Tracking Error *)
The regression statistics refer to a out-of-sample regression of the tracker on the index: (2.4) $r_{T,t} = \alpha + \beta r_{I,t} + \epsilon_t$
Dgf for sample standard deviations & tracking error: 272
Dgf for regressions: 271
Transaction costs: *quarterly average* transaction costs in percentages, computed @ .3% (.6% for round trip) over quarterly average net turnover, as specified in Tables 3A & 3B.

*) The population RMSTE is defined as $\sqrt{(\sum |r_T - r_I|^2/N)}$. As this measure has a variance component and a bias component, we computed the sample RMSTE as $\sqrt{\{Var(r_T-r_I)\cdot 273/272 + [E(r_T-r_I)]^2\}}$.

absolute criterion like minimum RMSTE or minimum s(TE). From Table 3B we see that the average composition of the portfolio much resembles that of T1. Total net turnover is now about 316% (on average almost 16% per quarter) and lower than that of T1. The lower net turnover is mostly due to smaller portfolio revisions.

The interesting and crucial part is evaluating out-of-sample tracking performance, as given in Table 4. On a yearly basis, the target index return is on average 4.39% with a standard deviation of 16.75%. T1 and T2 underperform the index on average with .42% and .34% per year. Their tracking error variance s^2(TE) and RMSTE differ only slightly. Looking to the results of the market model estimation, we see that the out-of-sample β's of both trackers significantly exceed unity; we already expected this from the in-sample results. The difference in performance in terms of average tracker returns slightly increases after adjusting for transaction costs. We assumed proportional transaction costs of .3% over net turnover. On a yearly basis, the transaction costs for the trackers are .20% and .19%, implying net yearly average portfolio returns of 3.8% and 3.9%, respectively. Finally, we note that for both trackers the out-of-sample correlation R with the target index is almost identical and only slightly lower than the average in-sample correlation. With quarterly rebalancing of the holdings of a relatively small number of 15 stocks, the historical relationships between index and tracker returns seem to persist.

6. SOME ADDITIONAL ISSUES

In this section, we discuss two issues that are closely related to index tracking: tilted index tracking and factor tracking. The application of these two variations on pure index tracking (as discussed above) is also important in practical portfolio management.

Instead of tracking a target index as close as possible, an investor could want to tilt the tracking portfolio in some dimension. Tilting implies increasing or decreasing the score of the tracking portfolio on some attribute relative to the target index. As a result, the tracking error is deliberately increased. Tilted index tracking is a less passive strategy than pure index tracking; its application depends on the degree to which the investor possesses information on the dimension in which the tracker is tilted.

In the *return dimension*, one could strive for an increase of the dividend yield on the tracker above the dividend yield on the target, or to increase the expected return on the tracker above the expected return on the target. We could label these strategies as 'enhanced index tracking'. Fong [1978], for example, suggests enhanced index tracking by applying stratification: he starts from an opportunity set of M stocks that are identified as undervalued. Of course, the success of an expected return-tilt depends on the degree to which an investor can estimate expected returns.

In the *risk dimension*, we have the example of a beta-tilt. In that case, a tracking portfolio is formed whose beta is higher or lower than unity. By manipulating the tracker's beta, the 'systematic' component $(\beta-1)^2\sigma^2_I$ of the mean square tracking error in eq. (2.11) is deliberately increased. This strategy makes sense when an investor can specify expectations with respect to bull or bear markets.

In the framework of a multifarious risk concept, it is assumed that stock returns respond to some degree to the pull of various pervasive economic factors (cf. footnote 4 and Chen, Roll & Ross [1986]). In this context, an investor could wish to increase or decrease the sensitivity of the tracker with respect to movements in a factor, relative to the target index. The return behavior of the target is thus mimiced, except that the tracker's exposure to factor risk is modified in a particular dimension. For example, a tracking portfolio can be tilted towards a higher (lower) sensitivity for changes in the exchange rate against the dollar. This strategy makes sense when the investor expects that the exchange rate will increase (decrease) in the near future. Of course, the persistence of historical relationships between stock returns and factor movements is crucial (cf. section 2). Hallerbach [1993] provides an example of tilted index tracking.

An obvious advantage of tilted tracking, and especially of factor-tilted tracking, is that the reference portfolio (i.e. the target) performs the role of a benchmark. The pure tracking portfolio is therefore the basis portfolio. In addition to this passive component of the strategy, the tilting leaves room for active components of portfolio management. Research into the possibilities to construct factor-tilted tracking portfolios is in progress.

Tracking procedures cannot only be used for tracking a stock index or some other reference portfolio, but also for tracking economic factors. Haugen & Baker [1990] employ their procedure to track the U.S. inflation rate by a stock portfolio. Factor tracking can also be used as an alternative to Chen's [1983] methodology for forming factor portfolios for the Arbitrage Pricing Theory from factor analysis. In this context, a maximum correlation procedure is also suited. The procedure we presented in section 3 is tailored for constructing factor portfolios. The portfolio composition is readily obtained from regressing the factor returns on the returns on the stocks in the opportunity set (preferably without the short sale restriction; eq. 3.5). The sensitivity of the factor portfolio with respect to the factor then follows from eq. (3.13). When the return series on the factor portfolio is corrected for the intercept (eq. 2.8) and is rescaled for its factor sensitivity, we finally obtain a series of stock portfolio returns that exhibits maximum correlation with the factor as well as a factor sensitivity of unity. This corrected return series can take the place of the actual factor return series in a (multiple) factor model.

7. SUMMARY AND CONCLUSIONS

In this paper, we highlighted some aspects of index tracking strategies and presented a simple and practical procedure for maximum correlation tracking. By using the market model, we discussed several tracking procedures in a unified framework. In setting up a tracking problem, we warned for the translation of components of the objective function into restrictions. In doing so, the shadow prices of these constraints are likely to be ignored. The ideal form of a tracking optimization problem therefore is a *multi-criteria* one, especially when transaction (revision) costs are incorporated into the optimization. In evaluating (tracking) portfolio stability and analyzing portfolio revisions, we stressed the effects of *implied turnover*. We applied two tracking strategies to the Dutch stock market. The out-of-sample results are comforting and imply that the historical relationships between index returns and tracker returns seem to persist over time. In applying statistical procedures for index tracking, however, estimation risk is of paramount importance and needs further attention.

We finally mentioned two variations on pure index tracking. *Tilted index tracking* (in risk and/or return dimensions) can be characterized as a compromise between active portfolio management and passive index tracking. *Factor tracking* is relevant in practical applications of factor models (or the Arbitrage Pricing Theory) in portfolio management. Especially the presented maximum correlation procedure is useful for constructing factor portfolios.

Topics for further research include the role of estimation risk, coupled to alternative estimation procedures for betas and factor sensitivities to control systematic risks, as well as the design of effectively (factor-) tilted index tracking portfolios. The management of investment risks with respect to some reference portfolio deserves more interest.

REFERENCES:

Brealey, R.A., 1986, How to Combine Active Management with Index Funds, *The Journal of Portfolio Management* Winter, pp. 4-10

Brennan, M.J. & E.S. Schwarz, 1985, On the Geometric Mean Index: A Note, *The Journal of Financial & Quantitative Analysis* 20/1 March, pp. 119-122

Burgess, R.C. & B.T. O'Dell, 1978, An Empirical Examination of Index Efficiency: Implications for Index Funds, *The Journal of Financial & Quantitative Analysis* March, pp. 93-100

Calderwood, S., 1977, The Truth About Index Funds, *Financial Analysts Journal* July/Aug, pp. 36-47

Chen, N.-F., 1983, Some Empirical Tests of the Theory of Arbitrage Pricing, *The Journal of Finance* 38/5 Dec, pp. 1393-1414

Chen, N.-F., R. Roll & S.A. Ross, 1986, Economic Forces and the Stock Market, *The Journal of Business* 59/3, pp. 383-403

Elton, E.J. & M.J. Gruber, 1991, *Modern Portfolio Theory and Investment Analysis*, John Wiley, New York N.Y.

Fama, E.F., 1973, A Note on the Market Model and the Two-Parameter Model, *The Journal of Finance* 28/5, pp. 1181-1185

Fama, E.F., 1976, *Foundations of Finance*, Basic Books, New York

Ferguson, R., 1978, Do Market Inventory Funds Really Make Sense?, *Financial Analysts Journal* May/June, pp. 38-45

Fong, H.G., 1978, An Alternative to Indexing, *The Journal of Portfolio Management* Fall, pp. 33-37

Frankfurter, G.M., 1978, Index Funds: Fad or Foe?, *Journal of Accounting, Auditing & Finance* 1/2, pp. 116-123

Frankfurter, G.M. & H.M. Phillips, 1980, Catch 500: The Irony of Indexing, Comment, *The Journal of Portfolio Management* Fall, pp. 80-81

Good, W.R., R. Ferguson & J. Treynor, 1976, An Investor's Guide to the Index Fund Controversy, *Financial Analysts Journal* Nov/Dec, pp.27-36

Hallerbach, W.G., 1993, Financial Factors and the Dutch Stock Market: Some Empirical Results, in: R. Flavell (ed.), *Modelling Reality and Personal Modelling*, Physica/Springer Verlag, Heidelberg, pp. 145-168

Haugen, R.A., 1993, *Modern Investment Theory*, Prentice-Hall, Englewood Cliffs N.J.

Haugen, R.A. & N.L. Baker, 1990, Dedicated Stock Portfolios, *The Journal of Portfolio Management* Summer, pp. 17-22

Haugen, R.A. & N.L. Baker, 1991, The Efficient Market Inefficiency of Capitalization-Weighted Stock Portfolios, *The Journal of Portfolio*

Management Spring, pp. 35-40
Jacques, W.E., 1988, The S&P 500 Membership Anomaly, or Would You Join this Club?, *Financial Analysts Journal* Nov/Dec, pp. 73-75
Jobson, J.D. & B. Korkie, 1980, Estimation for Markowitz Efficient Portfolios, *Journal of the American Statistical Association* 75/371 Sept, pp. 544-554
Jobson, J.D. & B. Korkie, 1983, Statistical Inference in Two-Parameter Portfolio Theory with Multiple Regression Software, *Journal of Financial & Quantitative Analysis* 18/2 June, pp. 189-197
Kantor, M., 1972, On Market Indexes, in: G.P. Szegö & K. Shell (eds), *Mathematical Methods in Investment and Finance*, North-Holland, Amsterdam, pp. 620-632
Latané, H.A., D.L. Tuttle & W.E. Young, 1971, Market Indexes and their Implications for Portfolio Management, *Financial Analysts Journal* Sept/Oct, pp. 75-85
Maddala, G.S., 1977, *Econometrics*, McGraw-Hill, Auckland
Markowitz, H.M., 1987, *Mean-Variance Analysis in Portfolio Choice and Capital Markets*, Basil Blackwell, Cambridge MA
Meade, N., 1991, Developing an International Index Fund, *Proceedings of the Xth Meeting of the EURO Working Group on Financial Modelling*, November, London U.K.
Meade, N. & G.R. Salkin, 1989, Index Funds - Construction and Performance Measurement, *Journal of the Operational Research Society* 40/10, pp. 871-879
Meade, N. & G.R. Salkin, 1990, Developing and Maintaining an Equity Index Fund, *Journal of the Operational Research Society* 41/7, pp. 599-607
O'Barr, W.M. & J.M. Conley, 1992, Managing Relationships: The Culture of Institutional Investing, *Financial Analysts Journal* Sept/Oct, pp. 21-27
Perold, A.F., 1984, Large-Scale Portfolio Optimization, *Management Science* 30/10 Oct, pp. 1143-1160
Roll, R., 1992, A Mean-Variance Analysis of Tracking Error, *The Journal of Portfolio Management* Summer, pp. 13-22
Rubinstein, M., 1989, Market Basket Alternatives, *Financial Analysts Journal* Sept/Oct, pp. 20-29, 61
Rudd, A., 1980, Optimal Selection of Passive Portfolios, *Financial Management* Spring, pp. 57-66
Rudd, A. & B. Rosenberg, 1979, Realistic Portfolio Optimization, *TIMS Studies in the Management Sciences* 11, pp. 21-46
Ryan, J.C. & M. Kritzman, 1980a, Catch 500: The Irony of Indexing, *The Journal of Portfolio Management* Winter, pp. 30-32
Ryan, J.C. & M. Kritzman, 1980b, Reply, *The Journal of Portfolio Management* Fall, p. 82
Samuelson, P.A., 1989, The Judgment of Economic Science on Rational Portfolio Management: Indexing, Timing, and Long-Horizon Effects, *The Journal of Portfolio Management* Fall, pp. 4-12
Schreiner, J., 1980, Portfolio Revision: A Turnover-Constrained Approach, *Financial Management* Spring, pp.67-75
Toy, W.W. & M.A. Zurack, 1989, Tracking the Euro-Pac Index, *The Journal of Portfolio Management* Winter, pp. 55-58
Waterman, M.S., 1974, A Restricted Least Squares Problem, *Technometrics* 16/1 Febr, pp. 135-136

Acknowledgement: The author is indebted to Andrew Pollock and two anonymous referees for their comments on an earlier draft.

Expectations and News in an Imitative Stock-Market[1]

Egidio Battistini
Politecnico di Milano
P.le Leonardo da Vinci 24, I-20133 Milano
Luigi Ferrari and Lorenzo Peccati
Università di Torino, Fac. Ec. Comm.
C.so Unione Sovietica 218bis, I-10134 Torino

1 Introduction

A basic starting point, in describing the literature about the causes of stock market prices movements, is the trivial evidence that the analysis is roughly split in two main parts: the theoretical and the empirical one, with clear problems of communication.

On the one hand, the bedrock belief of a host of academics and scholars, the efficient market hypothesis (EMH), assumes that a stock-market is (almost) always efficient and rational, even if a growing part of the same contemporary theoretical analysis is devoted to discuss the realism of this hypothesis. On the other hand, the literature counts on a bulk of empirical works on the irrationality and on the difficulties in finding the rationale of the behaviour of the agents.

The EMH is usually presented in three versions: the weak, the semistrong, the strong versions are based on the common assumption that it is impossible to beat the market, regularly, by using information, because the prices, immediately incorporate process at best all the available information.

The only differences between the three version concern the quantity and quality of information processed:

> "a weak form which considers only information gathered from historical price movements; a semistrong form, in which prices reflect all information that is public; a strong form, in which both private and public information is supposed to be reflected in the market price." See PHLIPS (1988) p. 244.

[1]The Authors are deeply indebted with an anonymous referee for useful remarks and suggestions that have improved this research. The responsibility of the authors for the remaining mistakes is full and exclusive.

The EMH hypothesis lays the emphasis on information, on signals, which can modify the expectations about the fundamental value of the stocks and on the aftermaths on their prices.

A common view within the EMH wing is centered around the assumed rationality of all the agents in processing signals and news. By contrast, at the other extreme, many analysts, economists, investment advisors, or journalists, who are expected to predict the financial market, stress on the psychological dimension in processing the available information, particularly during the market's crises and crashes, or, on the other side, in the manic phase. We think that it is worthwhile to overcome the shortcomings of the two wings, trying to integrate both empirical and theoretical results.

More in details, our approach rests on:

(a) the rejection of the EMH's view of the stock market as a community of almost similar agents as concerns the access to information, and the capability to process it. Our contention is that agents are very different. Information is a commodity (see ARROW (1984), p. 138):

> "I will think rather of information as a general descriptive term for an economically interesting category of goods which has not hitherto been accorded much attention by economic theorists.".

Some agents can use far and wide all information available, other can only seize the signals represented by the investment behaviour of the smart-money investors. Imitation in the marketplace is the behavioural consequence of the information shortage, both of the availability of signals and of the capability to process them correctly;

(b) the hypothesis of the immediate discount by the professional traders of any change in expectations of the price of the stocks, brought about by news;

(c) the rejection of the too simple equations:

(I) difficulties to understand the behaviour of the agents in the marketplace = irrationality, "madness" of the market

(II) psychological variables = irrationality

(III) irrationality = incomprehensible, inscrutable issue;

(d) the interdisciplinary analysis, where the cognitive psychology, supported by empirical inquiries, has a role in finding some typical aspects of the cognitive behaviour of the agents in processing news and in modifying their expectations. We have recently had the possibility to find a substantial agreement between our approach and two non formalized monographies in psychological economics of the beginning of the Eighties: see MAITAL (1982) and SMITH (1981).

In light of our own beliefs, we are now approaching a core problem: the modelling of the impact of news on an imitative stock-market. Under some simplifying assumptions, a particular attention will be dedicated to the formalization of some fundamental psychological features of the issue.

The sketch of the paper is the following.

In sec. 2 we shall briefly remind the main points behind the framework of the imitative approach (FERRARI, LUCIANO AND PECCATI (1993)), with an equation describing the endogenous formation of the call epochs sequence, that we shall adopt as departure point. Sec. 3 is devoted to introduce the main hypotheses of the present model as concerns the arrival of signals to the agents. Sec. 4 recalls the main results from psychology concerning the way human beings react to the stimuli they receive. Sec. 5 offers an overview of a general model incorporating the signalling process introduced before. Owing to the fac that this general model appears to be untreatable with analytical tools, in sec. 6 we describe a special version and give account of the results of some numerical simulations we have made on it. Sec. 7 gathers the main conclusions stemming from the simulations.

Paper concerning partially related problems with reference to different market model are: KYLE (1989), where rational informed and uninformed agents interact, HALTIWANGER WALDMAN (1985), where the utility of the result for informed and uninformed agents turns down to depend (negatively) on the nummer of agents that choose similarly and irreversibly and the more recent VIVES (1992) where the speed of revelation of information is focused. In our framework,

1. not necessarily the agents act on the basis of strict standard rules of rationality, but follow schemes described in GOTA PECCATI (1993),
2. what is irreversible is the structure of behaviour but not the behaviour in itself
3. we emphasize the effect of a random process of information arrival instead of studying the revelation process.

2 The imitative approach

The general framework of the model is, in essence, the same of the paper FERRARI LUCIANO PECCATI (1993) (see also FERRARI PECCATI (1989), LUCIANO (1989), CORNAGLIA (1993), LUCIANO (1993), CORNAGLIA (1991), an GOTA PECCATI (1993)), characterized by institutionally different kinds of agents: smart investors (P.T.: "professional traders" in the model), and nonprofessional ones (N.P.T.), who imitate the P.T.'s in their investment decisions, and a neuter agent (S.: the "specialist" in the model), whose aim is to clear the market making a price on the stock.

In that model the only relevant piece of news for the agents was the initial price, inherited at the beginning of a trading day from the previous session. Starting from this initial price, the market mechanism determines a sequence of prices at which a sequence of transactions is made. All the P.T.'s observe these prices and assume their decisions. The information coming from the prices is processed through a comparison with the personal opinion about the fundamental value (f.v.) of the asset. The difference between the current price and f.v., assumed *constant during the trading day*, is one of the key variables for the order placing policy of the agents. We assumed no other signal during the negotiations.

Summarizing and more in details, in the previous model there are only three types of agents:

(i) The Specialist (S.) who is obliged to make a price on the stock, his aim is to clear the market, not to make profits.

(ii) The Professional Traders (P.T.); this kind of agent continuously negotiates with the specialist to make profits every time there is a difference between the current price of the security and his opinion on its fundamental value (f.v.). The professional trader pays constant attention to the information flow arriving to the market, he has a good capability to process all the news relevant for the market. Precisely he is able to transform heterogeneous signals into adequate stock prices revisions induced by the incoming news. Because of that he continuously changes his expectations on the dynamics of the fundamental value of the stock. This does not imply that his position is always that of the "winner"; we simply assume that these habilities are present in a P.T. with a larger extent than in the trades we shall shortly describe in the next item.

(iii) The Non-Professional Traders (N.P.T.), who haven't the availability of information and the capability, by processing it, to change their expectations on the f.v.. The non-professional traders, aware of their weak position in the market, can only, rationally, try to imitate the professional investor's decisions to trade. Eventually the non-professional traders, far from the continuous negotiations and quotations of the market, enter the market, buying or selling, before the beginning of the trading day (t.d.), placing irrevocable orders.

The fundamental equations of the model are the following:

$$B_n - B_{n-1} = -\beta\,[p_{n-1} - h] \tag{1}$$

$$p_n = k + \eta\,[Q + B_{n-1}] \tag{2}$$

$$p_0 = p \tag{3}$$

$$q_m = -\alpha_m[p - r] + \gamma_m B^* \qquad (m = 1, 2, 3, \ldots, M) \tag{4}$$

$$Q = -A[p - r] + \Gamma B^* \ ; \ A = \sum_{m=1}^{n} \alpha_m \ ; \ \Gamma = \sum_{m=1}^{n} \gamma_m \tag{5}$$

In equation 1, describing the behaviour of the P.T., B_n is the total amount of orders placed in the n-th epoch of the trading day, β is the positive reaction parameter to the difference between the last price, in the epoch t_{n-1}, made by the S. and h, namely the f.v. in the opinion of the P.T. The total amount of transactions by the P.T. in the t.d. is:

$$B^* \stackrel{d}{=} \lim_{n\to+\infty} B_n \text{ (if this limit exists).}$$

In equation (2) we formalize the behaviour of the S., where η is a positive parameter and k represents the value of the F.V. in the opinion of this agent. In equation (2) there is also the variable Q, which can be described (in equation (5)) as the summation of the q_m from equation 4.

In our hypotheses there are M N.P.T., labelled with $m = 1, 2, 3, \ldots, M$, each of them enters the market by an order whose value, q_m, on one hand, is function result of the difference between the f.v., in the opinion of this agent, and the listed price of the previous t.d. and on the other hand is a fraction of the total transactions of the P.T. in the last trading day. The parameters α, γ and Γ are positive.

The starting price p_0 of the t. d. is the listed price of the previous negotiations.

The equilibrium values of B_n and p_n are:

$$B^* = \frac{h-k}{\eta} - Q \tag{6}$$

$$p^* = h \tag{7}$$

The equilibrium is stable iff (FERRARI LUCIANO PECCATI (1993)) $|1 - \eta\beta| < 1$.

Some results, obtained in this oversimplified framework, deserve interest, but this approach can be sophisticated to get: a large part of the empirical evidence suggests that trading days without impact on the negotiations of relevant news are rare.

Because of this, our concern, in the present paper, is with the effect of the arrival of news in an imitative stock-market. Our aim is to elaborate the framework of a more general model, which comprises the previous, no-signals one, as a special case. For the sake of the simplicity in this model (and in the previous one) only the dynamics of a single stock is analysed. In the previous model of an imitative stock-market we drew attention both on the short-run equilibrium price (the listed price for a single trading day), and on the long-run price. In this model the long-run equilibrium will remain out of view.

3 The basic hypotheses of the model

We define a "signal" as the unit of information available by the P.T. The representative agent changes his expectations on the dynamics of the f.v. according to the signals, as soon as possible. We assume that there is no setback in processing signals. In other words, the financial market must be seen as a place where an incessant stream of news changes continuously expectations for returns and capital gains.

Signals and, generally speaking, information differ under many aspects. The most important is the tremendous qualitative heterogeneity, signals can concern all kind of events. In the first place data regularly supplied on macroeconomic variables should be considered. See LOISTL LANDES at p. 136. They also write at p. 157:

> ... the variation of a company's quotations is explained 45 to 75 per cent by the data of the annual report of that company.

Other relevant signals come from one-off events like wars, riots, political shocks, tax cuts, etc., both, chains of different, but related events, or other single very different and idiosyncratic contingencies.

In the model we overlook all these qualitative aspects, in fact we assume the capability of the agents for integrating all these aspects of information into their judgement. Let h be the f.v. at the arrival of a signal. The agent processes it and updates his opinion about the f.v. from h to $h + \Delta h$.

In the model the only relevant aspects of signals are:

(a) the *sign* of each information, namely if the signal implies a positive or negative Δh;

(b) the *intensity* or the market impact of news, namely their effect on $|\Delta h|$;

(c) the effect of the whole set of signals on the *expectation* of a *trend*;

(d) related to the previous point, the *timing* of signals, namely the reciprocal position in time of the news.

We assume that the third and the fourth points are important for the psychological climate of the market, particularly for understanding phenomena as the investor's jitters, panic, depressed mood, mania, etc.

More in details, in the present model, only the P.T. has access to the news, relevant for the market. Another line of attack can be discerned: only the P.T., mainly in comparison with the N.P.T.'s, has the scientific tools for integrating information into a judgement on f.v.. In our model, these views do coincide.

Similar problems have been studied recently in CENCI CERQUETTI (1991) and (1992). These interesting results are obtained with the assumption of an exogenous deterministic process of evolution for the f.v.. With this paper we try to study the case of a random process influencing this evolution.

During the daily stock-market negotiations, the P.T. changes his opinion about the f.v. $(h + \Delta h)$ according to the variations of his expectations, brought about by signals. A sequence of calls is made at times $t_1, t_2, \ldots, t_n, \ldots$ and in the occasion of each call t_n the S. fixes the market price p_n. The difference between the last equilibrium price (p_{n-1}) and the updated opinion about the f.v. presses the P.T. to trade.

During the trading day there can be: $s = 0, 1, 2, 3, 4, \ldots$ signals, different in their sign and in their intensity. They arrive at epochs $z_1, z_2, \ldots, z_s, \ldots$. We can also assume that s has a finite maximum value. In fact there can be little if any room for doubting that the informative channels have a maximum capacity, and the capability to process the information is bounded. Anyway the possibility of an infinity of signals could be accepted in some cases to get approximations easy to handle.

We assume that the number of signals per trading day is a random variable. We assume also that the arrival time of *each* signal, during the fixed time span of the t.d., is a random variable. Each signal, as previously stressed, generates an expectation and consequently a Δh, different in sign and intensity. We assume that the Δh's are independent random variables. Obviously the values $\Delta h < -h$ are absurd. To avoid this setback and to avoid to change the normal probability distribution in another distribution, difficult to handle, we assume a sufficiently small variance.

Many types of distributions appear to be interesting. This point is touched tentatively in the conclusions section.

In the numerical simulations we made normality for Δh was assumed, although densities like the one portrayed in the figure 1 appears to be interesting to grasp the non-neutral randomness of the sequence of signals during — say — the downswing phase of the economic cycle, when values $\Delta h < 0$ are more probable.

4 Further hypotheses on signals

It is well known that, at present, there is no specific psychological study on the impact of news in a marketplace, except for the phenomena of the "rumor". Nevertheless it seems worthy and reasonable to make some informed guesses. We think that it is important, at this stage of evolution of the theory, to suggest some new hypotheses also as a starting point for further empirical researches.

It is important to outline that signals cannot be interpreted as "atomic" stimuli without any mutual interference. It is intuitive that there can be a difference in reacting to the same (sign and intensity) stimuli between the case of separate and far in time signals, that appear to be disposed in a neuter and well balanced sequence, and the case where the same stimuli are disposed in a non-neuter sequence. For instance, at the beginning of the negotiations two negative signals, very close each other, can strengthen a pessimistic mood in the formation of the following expectations.

It is necessary to keep in mind that the quality and the quantity of information, in comparison with the role it plays in the financial markets, are always scarce. Because of this fact, the agents, under the continuous stress represented by their role of decision makers, in very short lapses of time, try always to foresee beyond the simple "atomic" events. The "hunger" of news in financial markets is particularly glaring in rumor phenomena. We cite from KOENIG (1985), p. 157:

> What does play a big part on Wall Street is rumor as a substitute for news. In a population where information is essential what is not available is often invented. Because information is critical everyone is operating with a high-power antenna. In this tense atmosphere the population is sensitized to a bit of news here, a piece of report there. People under stress need closure, order, a feeling of completion; they need to put pieces together so that they can make a sense of the whole.

In other words, what is called the mood of the market can be interpreted as a sort of mutual reinforcement of the signals, maybe different in quality and intensity, but homogeneous in the sign. We think that this attitude about the sequences of news affecting the expectations and the same processing of the further signals, far beyond the content of each event, can be captured and formalized in some important aspects. As a basis of every further analysis on this issue, may be worth to lay emphasis on two remarkable achievements of the cognitive psychology:

(a) the empirical and experimental evidence of a judgement mechanism, consisting in the spontaneous comparison of the new cognitive stimuli with an adaptation level, a sort of "anchor" cognitive content, resulting from the average of the intensities of the previous similar stimuli. See HELSON (1947) and (1964).

    This author analysed the phenomena consisting in the difference of sensations brought about by the same cognitive stimuli in different conditions. Helson observed in his experiments a spontaneous comparison of the new stimuli with an adaptation level, namely a sort of average of previous similar stimuli, changing with the accruing of similar experiences. This "anchor" estimate represents a sort of neuter point, like the zero point in the centigrade scale.

For instance if an individual, who must valuate the height of some other persons, has a continuous and durable experience, prior the valuation, of short persons (for instance, 1.65 meters in average height) will valuate a 1.70 meter person as tall. To the contrary, he will valuate the same person short, if he had an experience, of long duration, of taller persons.

See also EISER (1980).

(b) the empirical and experimental evidence of a misconception of chance, not limited to naive subjects, according to which (KAHNEMAN TVERSKY (1982))

> "People expect a sequence of events generated by a random process will represent the essential characteristics of that process even when the sequence is short".

Kahneman and Tversky immediately further write:

> In considering tosses of a coin for heads or tails, for example, people regard the sequence H-T-H-T-T-H to be more likely than the sequence H-H-H-T-T-T, which does not appear random, and also more likely than the sequence H-H-H-H-T-H, which does not represent the fairness of the coin. Thus, people expect that the essential characteristics of the process will be represented not only globally in the entire sequence, but also locally in each of its parts.

and also (at p. 7):

> Another consequence of the belief in local representativeness is the well-known gambler's fallacy. After observing a long run of red on the roulette wheel, for example, most people erroneously believe that black is now due, presumably because the occurrence of black will result in a more representative sequence than the occurrence of an additional red.

Thus it is reasonable, assuming that agents (P.T.), after a sequence, dense of signals, have the spontaneous tendency

(a) to interpret the sequence of signals, consistent in sign, as nonrandom, even if it is very short and actually random.

(b) to evaluate cognitively (and emotionally) all the new signals on the basis of the previous, measuring the new Δh_{j+1} under the influence of the last Δh_j's ($j = 1, 2 \ldots n$), as a sort of "anchor" value. An investor, pressed by time and compelled to decide, somewhat intuitively could find a "trend", namely the expectation of future events of the same sign, even if the events are merely random. As concerns the emotional attitude, this "trend" can be seen as the pessimistic/optimistic mood. Eventually, we draw the reader's attention on the enormous advantage that the early finding of an actual trend can offer versus the simple processing of each single signal. A large evidence suggests that this mechanism is in a tight relationship with time. The less the time to process the information and to decide how to trade, the less the capability to react in a non-emotional, non-spontaneous way. The less the time between signals, the more perceivable are the relationship between them.

The formalization of this functional relationship with time can be drawn from a lot of experimental studies in related topics (See BORING (1950) and HILGARD BOWER (1987).

5 The general theoretic model

It is time to formalize all the focal points on the variations of the f.v. and their effect on the negotiations of the stock, after the occurrence of a signal. We shall stress, mainly, on the modifications, brought about by the news, on the f.v. of the P.T.. The most general equation, on the P.T.'s behaviour, (the key equation of the previous and present model) is now the following:

$$B_n - B_{n-1} = b[p_{n-1}, G(t_n)]. \tag{8}$$

We assume B_n as the total amount of orders placed within the n-th epoch of the trading day, $b : \mathbb{R}^2 \to \mathbb{R}$ as an appropriate function and $G(t_n)$ as a stochastic process, whose realizations give the time evolution of the values.

Needless to say that equation 8 has its initial conditions. A general set of models, consistent with this equation, can be explicitly dealt with by considering the generic process $G(t_n)$ in the following way:

1. by defining the signal arrival's instant z_j as a random variable (the number of signals per day is also a random variable);
2. by associating, given the instants z_j, the random values Δh_j's.

The value of $G(t_n)$ at t_n will be: $G(t_n) = H_{\hat{j}}$; where $\hat{j} = \max\left\{j | z_j < t_n\right\}$.

H_j is recursively defined by the equation:

$$H_j = L(H_{j-1}, \Delta h_j, z_j - z_{j-1}) \tag{9}$$

If in the time lapse (t_{n-1}, t_n) don't fall z_j values, it follows that: $G(t_n) = G(t_{n-1})$.

The realizations of the stochastic process $G(t_n)$ are piecewise constant with "jumps" at the epochs z_j. The amount of these variations is brought about by the Δh_j with a correction, which is a function of the length of the time lapse between two consecutive "jumps". The time instants t_n are functionally related by the equation:

$$t_n = \Phi(\tau - t_{n-1}, z_{\hat{j}}, \Delta h_{\hat{j}}) \tag{10}$$

where τ denotes the t.d. length.

Moreover we (obviously) assume that: $\lim_{n \to +\infty} t_n = \tau$.

Summarizing, equation 1 can be written as:

$$B_n - B_{n-1} = b[p_{n-1}, \Delta h_{\hat{j}}] \tag{11}$$

where $\hat{j} = \max\left\{j | z_j < t\right\}$ and the z_j's are the epochs of the random occurrence of the signals (also their amount is a random variable) during the trading day. Focusing on the term H_j (see the equation 9), the function L is assumed monotone, decreasing and convex with respect to its last argument.

6 Special cases and numerical simulations

In the present paper our concern is with a some special cases. Tipically they result from specializing and itemizing the general model, portrayed by equation 8.

The framework of these models follows:

$$B_n - B_{n-1} = -\beta\left[p_{n-1} - (h + H_j)\right]; \beta > 0 \tag{12}$$

$$H_j = \Delta h_j + H_{j-1}\phi\left(z_j - z_{j-1}\right) \tag{13}$$

with ϕ monotone, decreasing, convex and such that $\phi(0) = 1$.

$$H_0 = 0, \Delta h_0 = 0 \tag{14}$$

$$\Delta h \sim N(0, \sigma^2) \tag{15}$$

$$p_n = k + \eta\left[Q + B_n\right]; k > 0; h \geq 0; Q \geq 0 \tag{16}$$

$$q_m = -\alpha_m.(p - r) + \gamma_m B^*; m = 1, 2, 3, \ldots, M \tag{17}$$

$$Q = -A(p - r) + \Gamma B^*; A = \sum_{m=1}^{M} \alpha_m; \Gamma = \sum_{m=1}^{M} \gamma_m \tag{18}$$

$$p_0 = p \tag{19}$$

$$t_n = t_{n-1} + \left[\frac{1}{1 + D_{n-1}}\right](\tau - t_{n-1}) \tag{20}$$

$$D_{n-1} = \theta.\left|p_n - p_{n-1}\right|; \theta > 0 \tag{21}$$

Equation 16 describes the behaviour of the S.. For more details and for the meaning of the constants Q and q (equations: 17, 18) see the appendix.

The initial condition $p_0 = p$ equates the starting price of the trading day to the listed price of the previous trading day.

The equations 20 and 21 determine the reaction time of agents after each call and, therefore, the distance between one call and the ensuing one. A general analysis of this topic is available in FERRARI LUCIANO PECCATI (1993).

On the other side of the model, there can be two alternative lines of attack to the z_j's:

(a) given the maximum s, *i.e.*, the maximum finite number of signals per trading day and given the random value s for the specific trading day, s numbers z_j $(1 \leq j \leq s)$ are drawn in independent trials, as independent random variables with probability density function (p.d.f.) $f(z_j) = 1/\tau$ $(0 \leq z_j \leq \tau)$;

(b) the lengths of the time spans $z_j - z_{j-1}$ are assumed to be independent random variables with the same exponential p.d.f..

An important result is common for all the realizations of $G(t_n)$ in the subset of models, previously outlined: $G(t_n)$ can be interpreted as a sum of at random number of dependent random variables:

$$G(t_n) = h + \Delta h_{\hat{j}} + \sum_{j=1}^{\hat{j}} \Delta h_j \prod_{i=j-1}^{\hat{j}} \phi\left(z_i - z_{i-1}\right); \hat{j} = \max j \mid z_j < t_n \tag{22}$$

An important step forward, up to this point, seems to show the frequencies of the different final equilibrium values of p_n, by numerical simulation. Our goal is to enquire on the qualitative shape of the p.d.f. of the equilibrium value for p_{t_n}.

The simulation actually was performed by software tools which simulated, several thousand times, the stochastic path of all the variables of the model (12) — (21), by choosing the option (a) for the z_j's and with appropriate initial conditions.

In particular, in figure 2.1 are graphed the different percentages of the equilibrium prices, given the following initial conditions and parameters:

$p_0 = 50$
$B_0 = 0$
$0 \leq s \leq 5$
$k = 50$
$h = 50$
$Q = 20$
$\sigma^2 = 1$
$\beta = .3$
$\eta = .4$
$\theta = 1.5$
total number of simulations $= 80607$

In figure 2.2 are graphed the results of the same kind of numerical simulation, with only one different parameter:

$$1 \leq s \leq 2$$

and with total number of simulations $= 12794$.

Caution must be exercised in the interpretation of the results, but it seems plausible that the p.d.f. of the equilibrium price appears to be nearly normal with σ^2 directly functionally related to the maximum capacity of the information channels.

Another exploration we have made concerns the way the prices at subsequent epochs are related. We have computed the standard autocorrelation coefficients between prices with lags of 1,2,3,4,...,10 periods. We got declining values starting from approx. .9 for the lag 1 till to approx. .38 in the case of 10 periods lag. This can give a rough idea about the effect on prices paths of the random flow of information.

7 Conclusions and further research

The purpose of this paper is to analyze the listed price for a single trading day, under the random pressure and influence of news. Commenting on this set of highly simplified models, in our opinion, the most important conclusions are four.

1. The erratic fluctuations of the day to day movements in prices of the stocks, similar, in the opinion of many scholars, to the Brownian motion, can be interpreted as the partial result of the stream of all the news into the marketplace. Caution must be exercised, but this approach provides an interesting and even fascinating window on further empirical and theoretical inquiries

about the fundamental characteristics of the mechanisms of using information in the marketplace and on their influence on prices, until now poorly known.

2. The approach, based on signals, supplies some interesting improvements with respect to the previous formalizations of imitation in the stock market. In the original models the N.P.I.'s clearly entered the market always "irrationally", because only the P.T. could make profits. Indeed the f.v. of the N.P.I.'s was irrelevant in the equilibrium price determination, except in the extreme situation of equality with the f.v. of the P.T. In the present model, instead, the equilibrium price is a random variable, thus neither the P.T., nor the N.P.T. can a priori beat the market in the medium term (few trading days).

3. In the present model the closeness between the stock market and the economic cycle can be, partially, formalized by different shapes of the normal p.d.f. of the random variable Δh, as previously outlined.

4. One place where the model surely applies is the microanalysis of the behaviour of agents during negotiations. Undoubtedly it seems worthwhile an empirical verification of some interesting results of the models:

   (a) Commenting on these results, an important point is that, in the sequences the first Δh's have, by far, the most important impact on the final variation of the F. V. and on the equilibrium price. The more the signals, the more important are the first news in the trading day. The first signals influence the mood of the further negotiations, unless the following signals are, by far, outstanding in their effect on Δh's.

   (b) If the first signals have an high intensity, they have an interesting asymmetric effect: if the last news have the same sign, then they brought about volatility of prices; on the contrary if the last signals have a different sign then prices are sticky in their moving to the previous equilibrium price. There is an interesting debate on the volatility of the stock market. Current debate often falls on the measures of the variance of speculative stock prices, against simple models of market efficiency. Some alternative models have been provided, involving, for example, the economic culture of people as a key variable to allow, in models, more variation in prices, see SHILLER (1990). Underlying this position there is the opinion that the signals processed during negotiations are exactly those necessary to forecast dividends of the next epochs, processed by perfectly rational agents, without distortions. Our contention is that, in light of these beliefs, the a posteriori measures of volatility confute the "naive" view of the role of information, not the possibility to refer the volatility to the random stream of information. In our opinion it is important to overcome the too simple opinion about the mechanisms of processing information, we mean the "atomic" view of signals. A more realistic view of the role and mechanisms of processing news in the market can overcome the interpretation of the measures of volatility "as implying that prices show too much variation to be explained in terms of the random arrival of new information about the fundamental determinants of price" (SHILLER (1990), p. 131)

(c) In general, the more the signals in the trading day the less probable the values of the equilibrium price close to h.

Under the simple hypothesis that the signals have non-positive expected values it is easy to prove that $G(t_n)$ is a supermartingale. Further resarch is needed to try the application of limit theorems for (super)martingales. See, for instance HALL HEYDE (1980).

References

ARROW K. J. (1984), *The economics of information*, Oxford, Basil Blackwell.

BORING E. G. (1950), *A History of Experimental Psychology*, Appleton Century-Crofts, New York.

CENCI M. CERQUETTI A. (1991), 'Modelli evolutivi per un mercato azionario con valori fondamentali variabili nel tempo e asimmetria di informazioni', *Atti del XV Convegno AMASES*, Grado.

CENCI M. CERQUETTI A. (1992), 'Chi muove i fili del mercato azionario?', *Atti del XVI Convegno AMASES*, Treviso.

CORNAGLIA A. (1993), 'A non-linear model of stock market with istitutionally different agents and imitation', in J. STOKKING AND G. ZAMBRUNO (eds.) *Recent Research in Financial Modelling*, Physica-Verlag, Heidelberg.

CORNAGLIA A. (1991), 'A non-linear model of stock-market behaviour and imitation', *Quaderni dell'Istituto di Matematica Finanziaria dell'Università di Torino*, Serie III, N. 62.

EISER J. R. (1984), *Cognitive Social Psychology*, McGraw-Hill Book Co., Maidenhead (Berkshire), UK.

FERRARI L. PECCATI L. (1989), 'Stock market behaviour and imitation: a simple model' 6th Meeting of the EURO Working Group on Financial Modelling, Liège. *Quaderni dell'Istituto di Matematica Finanziaria dell'Universita' di Torino*, Serie III, N. 62.

FERRARI L., LUCIANO E. AND PECCATI L. (1993) 'Institutionally different agents in an imitative stock-market with asymmetric information', in J. STOKKING AND G. ZAMBRUNO (eds.) *Recent Research in Financial Modelling*, Physica-Verlag, Heidelberg.

GOTA M.L. PECCATI L. (1993), 'On imitation', in FLAVELL R. (ed.): *Modelling Reality and Personal Modelling*, Physica-Verlag, Heidelberg.

HALL P. HEYDE C.C. (1980), *Martingale limit theory and its applications*, Academic Press, New York.

HELSON H. (1947) 'Adaptation-level as frame of reference for prediction of psychophysical data', *American Journal of Psychology*, **60**, 1-29.

HELSON H. (1964), 'Adaptation-level theory', Harper & Row, New York.

HILGARD E.R. BOWER G.H. (1966): *Theories of Learning*, Appleton Century-Crofts, New York.

KAHNEMAN D. SLOVIC P. TVERSKY A. (1982), *Judgment under uncertainty: heuristics and biases*, Cambridge University Press, Cambridge.

KYLE A.S. (1989), 'Informed Speculation with Imperfect Competition', *Review of Economic Studies*, 56, pp. 317-356.

KOENIG F. (1985) *Rumor in the marketplace, the social psychology of commercial hearsay*, Auburn House Publishing Company, Dover.

LOISTL O. LANDES T. (1989), *The dynamic pricing of financial assets*, McGraw-Hill Book Company, Hamburg.

LUCIANO E. (1989), 'Equilibrium in a financial market with asymmetric information', 6th Meeting of the EURO Working Group on Financial Modelling, Liège. *Quaderni dell'Istituto di Matematica Finanziaria dell'Universita' di Torino*, Serie III, n. 62.

LUCIANO E. (1993), 'Market making with irrationalities; the case of a specialist financial market with heterogeneous traders'. in J. STOKKING AND G. ZAMBRUNO (eds.), *Recent Research in Financial Modelling*, Physica-Verlag, Heidelberg.

MAITAL S. (1982), *Minds, Markets and Money — Psychological Foundations of Economic Behavior*, Basic Books, Inc., Publishers, New York.

PHLIPS L. (1988), *The economics of imperfect information*, Cambridge University Press, Cambridge.

SHILLER R. J. (1990), *Market volatility*, The MIT Press, Cambridge.

Smith C.W. (1981), *The Mind of The Market — A Study of Stock Market Philosophies, Their Uses, and Their Implications*, Croom Helm, London.

WERNER F. M., DE BONDT M. AND THALER R. (1985), 'Does the stock market overreact ?', *The Journal of Finance*, **XL**, 3, 793-808.

VIVES X. (1992), 'The Speed of Information Revelation in a Financial Market Mechanism', *Working Paper Series of the Network in Financial Markets*, #16, September.

APPENDIX

We consider the process generating the sequence of the call epochs $\{t_n\}$. We specialize slightly equation(3) by dropping the direct dependence of the inter-call time lapse on the signal process.

We assume that two consecutive call epochs t_n and t_{n+1} are related by a difference equation of the type:

$$t_{n+1} - t_n = \psi(\delta_n, \tau - t_n) \tag{23}$$

where $\delta_n = |p_n - p_{n-1}|$. This equation states that:

A. 1 *the generic time span between calls h depends only on the (absolute) value of the two last stock prices and on the residual time of the market session;*

or, in symbols, and omitting the indices:

$$h = \psi(\delta, \tau - t)$$

A further assumption concerns the type of dependence of h on the most recent price variation:

A. 2 *h'_δ/h depends only on δ, and it is the same whatever the residual time of the session $\tau - t$.*

This assumption allows us to write:

$$h = \psi_1(\delta)\psi_2(\tau - t)$$

Qualitative properties of ψ_1 that appear to be acceptable are:

A. 3 *ψ_1 is positive, decreasing, convex and equal to 1 in the origin*

In our simulation model we adopted the specification:

$$\psi_1(\delta) = \frac{1}{1+\delta}$$

Now we turn to the dependence on $\tau - t$. A reasonable assumption could be:

A. 4 *the relative variation of h is inversely proportional to the residual time:*

$$h'_t \propto \frac{h}{\tau - t}$$

this implies $\psi_2(\tau - t) = (\tau - t)^m$ or:

$$h = \psi_1(\delta)(\tau - t)^m \tag{24}$$

with $m > 0$.

Another reasonable requirement is that

A. 5 *if the price is in equilibrium then no more transaction is made:*

$$\delta = 0 \Rightarrow h = \tau - t \tag{25}$$

In this case $\psi_1(0) = 1$ and consequently from (24) we get $h = (\tau - t)^m$. This is compatible with 25 iff $m = 1$ or:

$$h = \psi_1(\delta)(\tau - t)$$

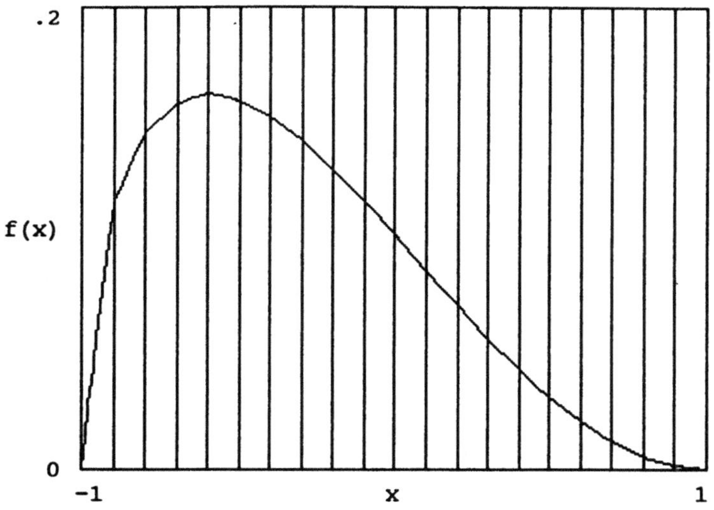

Figure 1

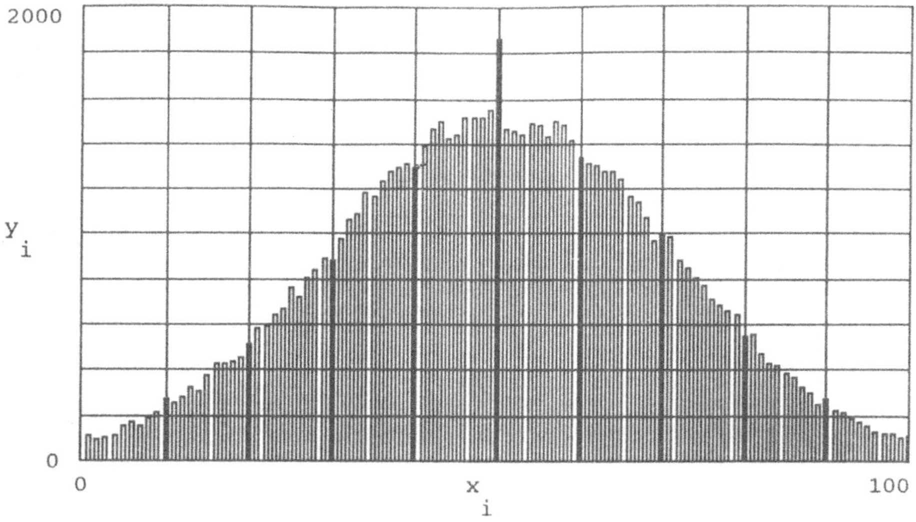

Figure 2.1

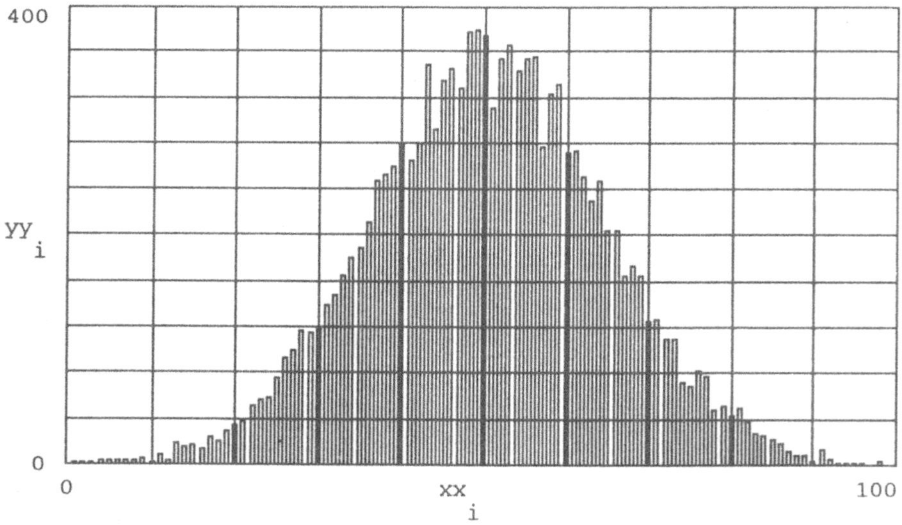

Figure 2.2

An Artificial Adaptive Speculative Stock Market

Andrea Beltratti[a] and Sergio Margarita[b]

[a]Istituto di Economia Politica G. Prato, Università di Torino
Piazza Arbarello 8, 10122 Torino, Italy

[b]Istituto di Matematica Finanziaria, Università di Torino
Piazza Arbarello 8, 10122 Torino, Italy

The model presented in this paper considers the interaction among traders acting in a financial market. Each agent bases her evaluation of the asset on an (agent-specific) interpretation of an (partially agent-specific) information set. The evaluation process of an agent is simulated by a neural network, which can be interpreted as a nonlinear way to process the available information. It is shown in the paper that, given our assumptions on the structure of the market, each agent learns from her experience and updates her "model of the world" according to the distance between the actual average opinion of the market and her forecast of the same variable. We study the long-run distribution of the behavior of the market, and show the importance that history may have in determining the long-run equilibrium. We also study the performances of various agents in terms of wealth, and show the importance of learning ability. The market shows long periods of calm followed by sudden burst of volatility, when the agents revise their average opinion.

1. Introduction

This paper builds upon the consideration that the availability of powerful computers coupled with the discovery of new computational models and methods (some of which, like neural networks, will be described later on) now allows researchers to explicitly use models based on interactions among heterogeneous agents. This is particularly useful since often technical problems force economists to adopt the representative agent fiction to study situations which, in practice, can only be understood by considering many interacting agents. For example the debate about the relationship between stock prices and the present value of fundamentals originated by the work of Shiller (1981) may be interpreted as an attempt to understand financial markets on the basis of the valuation given by a single representative agents.

The strong assumptions shared by representative agent models contrast deeply with our intuition and our informal knowledge of the way markets work in practice, see for example the surveys contained in Shiller (1987), which show that agents differ as to a number of factors among which are: (i) the information set, which contains some private information (ii) the interpretation of the public information set (iii) personal characteristics like wealth and risk aversion. Many empirical regularities which cannot be explained by over-simplified single-agent models are an indication that more general models should be used to understand financial markets.

In this paper we use a different approach, based on letting many agents interact and give rise to a (possibly) complex aggregate outcome. We consider a set of rational agents who can carry their wealth to the future by holding money or shares; our assumption of risk-neutrality implies that the share will be held only if its expected return is larger than 0. Agents go to the market without a precommitment to buying as opposed to selling, they only want to exploit available opportunities. The interaction between demand and supply determines the market equilibrium and the price, and this in turn helps agents to decide whether the forecasting power of a given rule is good or not. This learning process generates new rules and induces new behaviors.

It is an important point of our model that the market price is endogenously determined by the social interaction of the agents, which differ among each other with respect to the information set and the interpretation of the information; agents have different models of the world. We are interested in seeing whether it is possible to generate complex dynamics from a model based on agents behaving simply but rationally. Interactions and learning are the basic reasons why the aggregate equilibrium of our model may be qualitatively different from the actions of each single agent. We will consider questions like: what is the evolution of equilibrium prices? what is at each point in time the heterogeneity of the forecasts of the agents? what is the long run evolution of the best strategies?

Our approach is related to previous work by Arthur (1991), Margarita (1991, 1992), Nottola et al. (1992), Cecconi and Parisi (1991) and Terna (1991). Arthur and Terna show that simple algorithms may generate behavior which is similar to the one adopted by humans, pointing out the attitude of these methods to simulate human behavior. Margarita also analyzes the strategies of agents in a stock market, but he considers the price as an exogenous factor. Nottola et al. consider a set of questions which are related to ours, but differ considerably as to methodology. Similarities and differences with previous works will become clear during the exposition of this paper.

The plan of the paper is the following: section 2 describes the behavior of the agents and their interaction in the market place; section 3 provides a general description of artificial neural networks, while section 4 describes their application to our model, with a description of the learning of the agents. Section 5 presents the equations which describe the dynamics of the system, and section 6 the results of the simulations. Section 7 concludes. All the notation is reported in an Appendix at the end of the paper.

2. The model with risk-neutrality

2.1 The behavior of the agents

Agent i enters the early morning of day t with a given amount of money $M_{i,t}$, a stock of shares $S_{i,t}$ and an information set $I_{i,t}$. We will shortly be more specific about the content of the latter. She has two choices for carrying her wealth to the following morning: money and shares, about which she will have to make a decision at noon of day t. Each day t shares can be bought or sold against money in a stock market opening at noon, at a price $P_{ij,t}$ which depends on the value assigned to shares by the agent j who will be (randomly) met in the marketplace (see section 2.2). We also assume that: (i) agents are risk-neutral (ii) each transaction involves buying or selling K shares, where K is exogenous (iii) actions of day t are based on expectations formed in the morning of time t before the market opens. The relevant expectation is the price at which the share may be sold in period t+1 (i.e. $P_{ij,t}$ not the market price π_t, due to our assumptions about the structure of the market, see section 2.2); we denote the expectation of agent i with $E_{i,t}P_{t+1}$, a general symbol to underscore that agent i does not know the identity of agent j with whom she will transact. These expectations are formed on the basis of an information set containing the previous history of market prices and transaction prices. Given these assumptions the optimal action is the following:

buy K shares if $P_{ij,t}$ is such that $(E_{i,t}P_{t+1} - P_{ij,t}) > 0$
sell K shares if $P_{ij,t}$ is such that $(E_{i,t}P_{t+1} - P_{ij,t}) < 0$
indifference if $P_{ij,t}$ is such that $(E_{i,t}P_{t+1} - P_{ij,t}) = 0$

where $E_{i,t}P_{t+1} - P_{ij,t}$ is the expectation of agent i about the change in stock prices between the morning of day t and the morning of day t+1.

The behavior of the agent is simple to interpret: the anticipation of a growth in prices induces the agent to demand shares since this is more convenient than holding money. An agent who on average makes few mistakes in forecasting the change in prices will tend to buy low and sell high, and to increase her total amount of wealth more than an agent who on average make mistakes by buying high and selling low. Also note that imposing on each transaction an amount of K shares is always binding, since risk-neutral agents would not diversify and would tend to keep their wealth either in the form of money or in the form of shares.

These assumptions imply that once we know the expectations of agent i (about the formation of which we will be more specific in the next section), we immediately know her demand schedule: she is willing to buy K units of the stock at any price below $E_{i,t}P_{t+1}$, sell K units at any price above $E_{i,t}P_{t+1}$, and is indifferent if the price is equal to $E_{i,t}P_{t+1}$. Note that each agent in general takes a position; everybody wants to either sell or buy since the alternative is money, which can be interpreted as a bond which pays no interest. We impose no constraint on buying or selling, in that an agent can go short in either money or shares.

2.2 The marketplace

After forming their reservation prices agents meet randomly in a decentralized marketplace which contains no auctioneer. From the sample of J agents we randomly select two agents and match them. Given the assumptions we have made about the demand schedule, a transaction always occurs in our model, unless the two reservation prices are the same, in which case agents are indifferent between transacting or not. The transaction between i and j may be described as follows:

$$P_{ij,t} = 0.5\,(E_{i,t}P_{t+1} + E_{j,t}P_{t+1}) \tag{1}$$
$$\text{if } E_{i,t}P_{t+1} < E_{j,t}P_{t+1},\ \text{j buys K units at } P_{ij,t}$$
$$\text{if } E_{i,t}P_{t+1} > E_{j,t}P_{t+1},\ \text{i buys K units at } P_{ij,t}$$

which means that each transaction takes place at a price which is the simple average of the two expectations. After the transaction is completed we exclude agents i and j and sample from the remaining agents, obtaining another transaction and another price. When all the agents have been selected and all the transactions have been performed we have J/2 prices, whose simple average is considered for determining the market price at time t, π_t. Note that the market price π_t is not directly relevant to the transaction which took place during day t, since this was carried out at a price which is the simple average of the two reservation prices. The market price is however a useful piece of information, being a signal of the average opinion of the agents.

Note that all the transactions take place because agents differ in their expectation of the future. The interest of this simple model lies precisely in the fact that we can analyze a complex environment where each agent is trying to forecast the forecast of others (section 4 will make this more clear from a formal point of view). There is no "objective" centre of attraction in this system, since the different evaluations depend on differences in the information set and on different ways to interpret a given set of signals.

3. Artificial neural networks

To model the expectations of the agents we use artificial neural networks. This section gives a general introduction to the topic, while section 4 describes the application to the specific problem we are considering.

3.1 The general properties of neural networks

Artificial neural networks are biologically inspired devices used for mapping a set of inputs into a set of outputs. The mapping is carried out by the processing elements, called artificial neurons, that are interconnected to form a network divided into some (usually three) layers: the input layer receiving inputs from outside (for example, as in our work, from the environment in which it operates), the output layer sending outputs to the outside and one or more hidden layers connecting the input and output layers. The basic properties of neural networks, which are independent of the specific structure (number of layers, numbers of neurons . . .), are the following:

(i) *learning*: the capability of the network to adapt its behavior to the environment, in other words to build autonomously a representation of the map from inputs to outputs on the basis of a set of examples;

(ii) *generalization*: the possibility to react in a coherent way to imperfect inputs or to inputs not seen during the training;

(iii) *soft degradation*: the alteration or elimination of some elements of the network does not prevent it to work but induce only a smooth degradation of the performance.

In our model we consider one of the most widely used architecture, known as three-layer, fully interconnected, feed-forward network with back-propagation learning.

3.2 A specific structure

In this structure, described in Figure 1, the neurons are grouped in three layers: input, hidden and output. In the example there are 4 input neurons (denoted with 1, 2, 3, 4), 3 intermediate neurons (5, 6, 7) and 2 output neurons (8, 9). The structure is fully interconnected because each neuron in the input layer is connected with each neuron in the hidden layer, which in turn communicates directly with each neuron in the output layer. Each connection has an associated weight (w_{ij} is the weight from neuron i to neuron j) that defines the strength of the communication. The information received by the neurons flows only in the forward direction, from input to hidden to output, without feedback.

The processing performed by each neuron is the following: each input signal is multiplied by its weight, all these products are summed and the output of the neuron results from the application of an activation function to this weighted sum. The logistic function is often used as activation for its biological plausibility. For example, if at a given time t the four inputs receive signals X_{1t}, X_{2t}, X_{3t}, X_{4t}, the overall signal passed to neuron 5 is equal to:

$$net_{5t} = w_{15}X_{1t} + w_{25}X_{2t} + w_{35}X_{3t} + w_{45}X_{4t} \qquad (2)$$

where net_{it} denotes the input going to the i-th neuron. Neuron 5 then transforms this linear combination of inputs by means of the logistic activation function:

$$[1 + \exp(-net_{5t})]^{-1}$$

This output is then considered, together with the output of neurons 6 and 7, to form a linear combination which is passed on to neurons 8 and 9. These neurons make a new pass through a logistic to obtain the final output of the neural network. If A and B are matrices that collect the values of the weights respectively from inputs to hidden and from hidden to output (for the example in Figure 1, A is a (4, 4) matrix, while B is a (3, 2) matrix), o_t is the output of the network at time t, x_t is the input vector at time t and f is the activation function, then the network can be described in the following way:

$$o_t = f(Bf(Ax_t))$$

The weights of the network, that is the strength of the connections between neurons, are the devices encoding the information into the network.

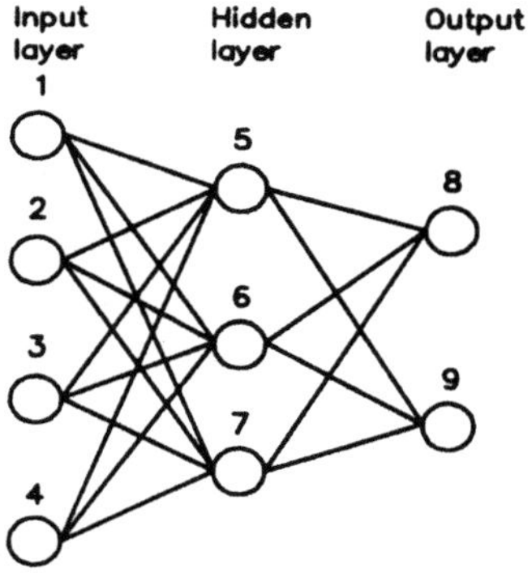

Figure 1. An example of artificial neural network.

So, for a given structure, the behavior of the network strictly depends on the set of weights. The aim of the learning process is to choose the value of these weights so as to realize the desired mapping from input to output; as White (1991) notes, even in the network learning one is trying to minimize a nonlinear function with respect to a set of parameters (the weights). The simplest way to do it is by means of an algorithm called back-propagation, described in the next section.

3.3 The back-propagation algorithm

The back-propagation algorithm (Rumelhart and McClelland, 1986) has the goal of minimizing:

$$E(w) = 0.5 \sum_{t=1}^{T} E_t = 0.5 \sum_{t=1}^{T} \sum_{z=1}^{Z} (g_{tz} - o_{tz})^2 \qquad (3)$$

where E is the total error, a function of the vector of weights w connecting the neurons (18 in our previous example), Z is the number of outputs (2 in our example), T is the number of examples used to train the network (in a time series T is the total number of observations, in a cross-section the number of units), o_{tj} is the value of output neuron j for the t-th example, g_{tj} is the target value of neuron j for example t.

Like in a standard nonlinear least squares problem, the goal is the minimization of the sum of error squares with respect to a set of coefficients. In principle this goal could be achieved with any computational methods (Judge et al., 1985). In practice the largest part of the neural network literature uses the back-propagation algorithm, which can be interpreted (White, 1989) as a form of gradient descent of the type:

$$w_{k+1} = w_k - \alpha \nabla E_t \qquad (4)$$

where α is the learning rate, and ∇ denotes the gradient of the subsequent vector. To describe the details of the application of this general rule to the problem at hand we use the following section-specific notation:

net_{tj}	the weighted sum of the inputs of neuron j resulting from the propagation of input vector t
i_{ti}	value of input neuron i in input vector t
f	activation function (logistic function)
f'	first derivative of the activation function; for the logistic function $f'(\cdot) = f(\cdot)[1-f(\cdot)]$
$h_{tj} = f(net_{tj})$	value of hidden neuron j resulting from the propagation of input vector t

$\delta_{tj} = g_{tj} - o_{tj}$ error of output neuron j resulting from the propagation of input vector t

$\Delta_t w_{ij}$ change to apply to the connection weight from neuron i to neuron j resulting from propagation of input vector t

The learning algorithm is made of the following steps:

(i) All the weights of the network are initialized randomly;

(ii) The input vector for one example is presented, propagated through the network and the output vector of the network is computed;

(iii) The difference between the output and the target vectors is calculated to compute the error for the example at hand;

(iv) The error is fed backward through the network and weights are modified according to the gradient descent function previously described;

(v) The process is repeated many times for all the examples used in the training (called training set), until the total error E(w) reaches a sufficiently low level.

The equations for actually changing the weights involve the derivatives of the objective function in the way described in Rumelhart and McClelland (1986):

Weights from hidden to output layer

$$\Delta_t w_{ij} = \alpha \cdot h_{tj} \cdot \delta_{ti} \tag{5}$$

$$\delta_{ti} = \alpha \cdot (g_{ti} - o_{ti}) \cdot f'(net_{ti})$$

$$= \alpha \cdot (g_{ti} - o_{ti}) \cdot o_{ti} \cdot (1 - o_{ti})$$

Weights from input to hidden layer

$$\Delta_t w_{ij} = \alpha \cdot i_{tj} \cdot \delta_{ti} \tag{6}$$

$$\delta_{ti} = \alpha \cdot f'(net_{ti}) \cdot \sum_{z=1}^{Z} \delta_{tz} \cdot w_z i$$

$$= \alpha \cdot i_{tj} \cdot h_{ti} \cdot (1 - h_{ti}) \cdot \sum_{z=1}^{Z} \delta_{tz} \cdot w_{zi}$$

The larger α, the faster the learning but the higher the risk of oscillations. To improve the learning speed and avoid oscillations, a *momentum* term β is added, that make depend the actual change in a weight from its change in the previous cycle. So, using v as an index referring to the number of learning cycles, the rule becomes

$$\Delta_t w_{ij}(v+1) = \alpha \cdot x_{tj} \cdot \delta_{ti} + \beta \cdot \Delta_t w_{ij}(v) \tag{7}$$

Finally, one can distinguish two kinds of learning with the generalized delta rule: *on-line back-propagation* in which weights are changed after the presentation of every example; *off-line back-propagation* in which changes deriving from individual patterns are summed and the correction of weights occurs only once for every presentation of the entire training set.

4. Learning of artificial agents

4.1 Learning to forecast market prices

We can now describe how the expectations are formed on the basis of the available information. We model agent i by means of a neural network (Figure 2); note that in our application there is only one output (Z=1). We restrict the information set to the following inputs of the network: π_t, $\Delta\pi_t$, $P_{ij,t}$, $\Delta P_{ij,t}$ (for the way π_t is computed see the next section). In general we can therefore write:

$$E_{i,t}P_{t+1} = f_{i,t}(\pi_t, \Delta\pi_t, P_{ij,t}, \Delta P_{ij,t}) \qquad (8)$$

where the functional form is equal for each network, but the weights vary from one to the other and from one time period to the other. Note that the network only considers private and public information known the early morning of day t. On the basis of the weights connecting the three layers the network forecasts the price at t+1.

To understand how agents learn to forecast note that at the end of each day agents know the market price π_t, and can therefore update their "view of the world", that is the weights of the network. The forecast made at the beginning of day t cannot be compared to anything which is known at the end of the same day, since the forecast is about variables which will be known during day t+1. At the end of day t the network can use newly available information to find a proper term of comparison for the forecast made at t-1.

This can be done by noting that the transaction at time t was executed at price given by equation (1), which is exactly what the network was trying to forecast at t-1.

If it were known that the transaction would be conducted with agent j the output of network i at t-1 would be the simple average between the forecast of the output of the same network i at t and the forecast of the output of network j at t. But the network does not know which agent will be met in the marketplace at t. The random matching procedure that is used implies that there are equal probabilities of meeting any of the remaining J-1 agents.

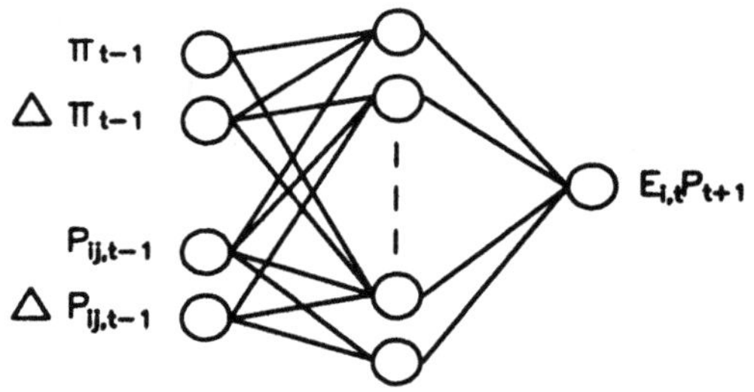

Figure 2. The structure of the artificial agent.

Therefore we can write:

$$E_{i,t-1}P_t = 0.5\ [E_{i,t}P_{t+1} + (J-1)^{-1} \sum_{\substack{j=1 \\ j\neq i}}^{J} E_{j,t}P_{t+1}] \tag{9}$$

Equation (9) can be reformulated in a more interpretable way by noting that:

$$\pi_t = J^{-1} \sum_{j=1}^{J} E_{j,t}P_{t+1} \tag{10}$$

so that the second term on the right-hand-side of equation (9) can be written as:

$$(J-1)^{-1} (\sum_{\substack{j=1 \\ j\neq i}}^{J} E_{j,t}P_{t+1} + E_{i,t}P_{t+1} - E_{i,t}P_{t+1}) =$$

$$= (J-1)^{-1} (J\pi_t - E_{i,t}P_{t+1}) \tag{11}$$

Substituting (11) in (9) we have:

$$\begin{aligned} E_{i,t-1}P_t &= 0.5\ [E_{i,t}P_{t+1}+(J-1)^{-1}(J\pi_t-E_{i,t}P_{t+1})] = \\ &= 0.5\ (J-1)^{-1}[(J-2)E_{i,t}P_{t+1} + J\pi_t] \end{aligned} \tag{12}$$

This shows that at t network i modifies her weights by comparing her output at t-1 with the simple average between her output at t and a function of the market price. Note that as long as J is high the network is basically comparing her forecast with the average opinion of the market. This is similar to the Keynesian "beauty context" interpretation of the stock market (Keynes, 1936), reformulated by Townsend (1983) as "forecasting the forecasts of others".

Given the previous parameters, the learning process allows agents to enter the morning of day t+1 with a new way of interpreting the information set and using it to predict the price at time t+2.

4.2 Degenerate learning

We showed in the previous section how we used our theoretical model to define both o_{ti}, the output value of the network (the expectations of the price) and g_{ti}, the target value of the learning process (see (12)). We now want to remark that the learning process implemented by back-propagation may sometimes lead to form of non-learning. To see this, consider the rule for modifying the weights given in (6) and (7), and note that the derivative of the logistic function is present in the (multiplicative) form $x_{tj}(1-x_{tj})$, where x is o or h, depending on the layer we consider, and x varies from 0 to 1. Recalling that α is constant and less than 1, we have

$$\lim_{x_{ti} \to 0} \Delta_t w_{ij} = \lim_{x_{ti} \to 1} \Delta_t w_{ij} = 0$$

So while this activation function implements a form of automatic gain control (small signals correspond to high gain and large signals produce a gain decrease), it is worth noting that in conditions of low number of learning cycles, this characteristic leads to forms of non-learning: the change in the weights is so small it has no practical effect and the initial weights assignment remains essentially the same.

How does this aspect influence our model of stock trader? Some networks, because of a particular initial configuration of weights, tend to exhibit a binary behavior, that is they tend to output values very close either to 0 or 1. Although the forecasting error is high, the term $\Delta_t w_{ij}$ tends to 0 and learning does not occur significantly during the limited number of cycles.

Since the coexistence of learning and non-learning agents has an important influence on price dynamics, we want to describe more formally the learning ability of the networks. We define *dumb* networks, those networks whose output is greater than 0.95 or lower than 0.05 in the first time period, since these are the networks which learn very slowly. The occurrence of such extreme forecasts depends on the slope of the activation function over the relevant interval of the inputs. We can control for the slope of the logistic function by the parameter G of the modified logistic function:

$$y = [1 + \exp(-Gx)]^{-1}.$$

We report in Figure 3 a plot of the average proportion of dumb networks, as previously defined, as a function of the G parameter. The average is based on 100 random generations of the population for each value of G. In our simulations we use G=1 as a situation with a high number of non-learning agents, and G=0.3 to consider cases where most of the agents learn quickly.

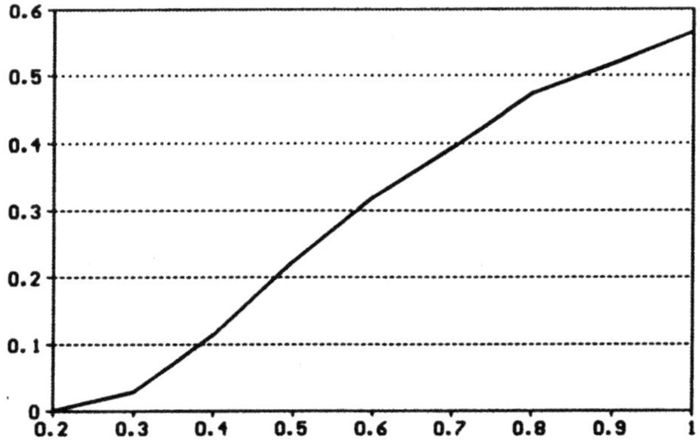

Figure 3. Proportion of dumb agents as a function of the parameter G

Given the previous parameters, the learning process allows agents to enter the morning of day t+1 with a new way of interpreting the information set and using it to predict the price at time t+2.

5. The dynamics of the system

We return now to the model, and consider the implications in terms of market price dynamics. Is it possible to forecast, for given initial conditions, the long-run evolution of the market? To answer the question one needs to study the equations of motion of the system:

$$\pi_t = J^{-1} \sum_{j=1}^{J} E_{j,t}P_{t+1}$$

$$E_{i,t}P_{t+1} = f_{i,t}(\pi_{t-1}, \Delta\pi_{t-1}, P_{ij,t-1}, \Delta P_{ij,t-1})$$

$$P_{ij,t} = 0.5\ (E_{i,t}P_{t+1} + E_{j,t}P_{t+1})$$

This system of equations shows how the information at the beginning of day t is processed into a market price, which is a new input for the future evaluations. The nonlinear structure of the difference equation, due to the nonlinear structure of the networks, seems to prevent the application of the methods proposed by Marcet and Sargent (1989) to analyze the long-run dynamics of systems with agents that learn and

affect the equilibrium values of the variables, though this is an issue that we still have to consider carefully.
However a knowledge of the long-run behavior of the system is clearly important for judging the different results we obtain from the simulations. We use the computer to characterize the solutions provided by the equations of motion. We calculate a sort of asymptotic distribution of the market price by letting the model (with 50 agents) run until time T (where T is alternatively equal to 200, 1000 and 2000) and recording the market price at T. We repeat the exercise 100 times to get a frequency distribution which can be used to evaluate the statistical "significance" of our results.

6. Results

We use feedforward, three-layer neural networks with 4 inputs, 5 hidden and 1 output. The population is composed of 100 networks. The starting values of the weights and the number of time periods on which learning is performed depend on the specific application and will be described later. In all cases K (the number of shares which can be transacted) is equal to 1. The learning rate is 0.6 and the momentum is 0.9. Share prices are normalized between 0 and 1. We discuss the results in different groups, according to the specific question we are trying to answer, the general goal of our simulations is to interpret the market behavior emerging from the simple trading rules we have given to the agents. The figures reporting the results of the simulations are presented at the end of each subsection.

6.1 Heterogeneity of the agents

We start the description of the results by studying the importance of heterogeneity of agents' models on the dynamics of market prices. More precisely, we consider the effects of different interpretations of the information sets on the part of the agents. Figure 4 shows the evolution of the market price and of the dispersion of the forecasts of the various agents (standard deviation of the forecasts of the agents at each time t) when the initial values of the weights are uniformly randomly distributed between -0.5 and 0.5. The variability of the market price is low, and the standard deviation of the forecasts quickly tends to 0. We interpret these results as saying that the market converges to an equilibrium fairly quickly when the agents are very similar in the first place.
In Figure 5 we increase the heterogeneity of the agents (initial weights go from -5 to 5), and obtain that the market price is more volatile than before; the standard deviation decreases from 0.4 to about 0.2, but is still considerable. Even when considering a longer

period of time (see Figure 6, where T=2000), divergences of opinions do not disappear. Especially at the beginning the market price shows some quite interesting dynamics, with sudden booms and collapses which can sometimes be found in actual data.

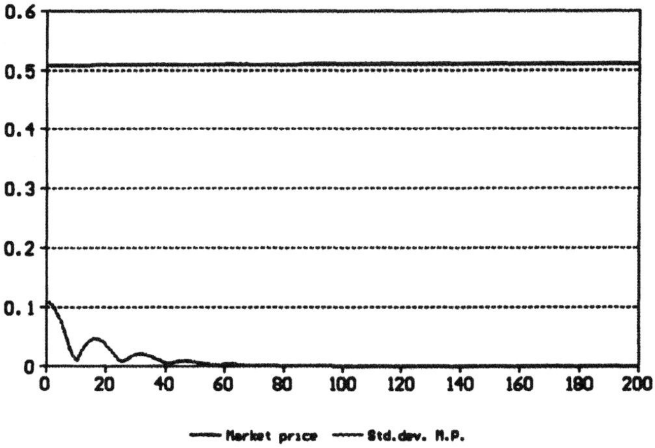

Figure 4. Market price evolution and dispersion
(-0.5 < w_{ij} <0.5, G=1, T=200)

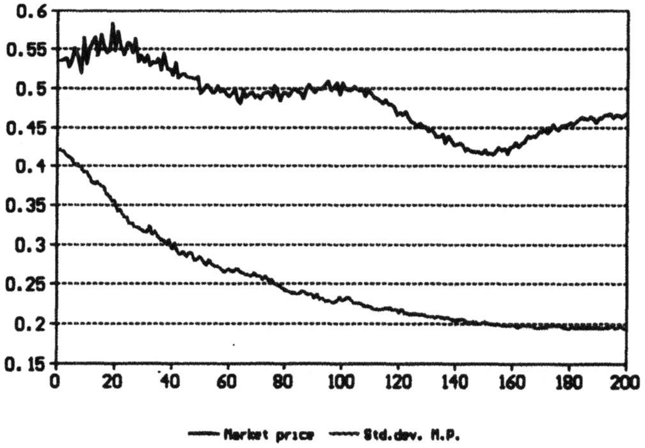

Figure 5. Market price evolution and dispersion
(-5 < w_{ij} < 5, G=1, T=200)

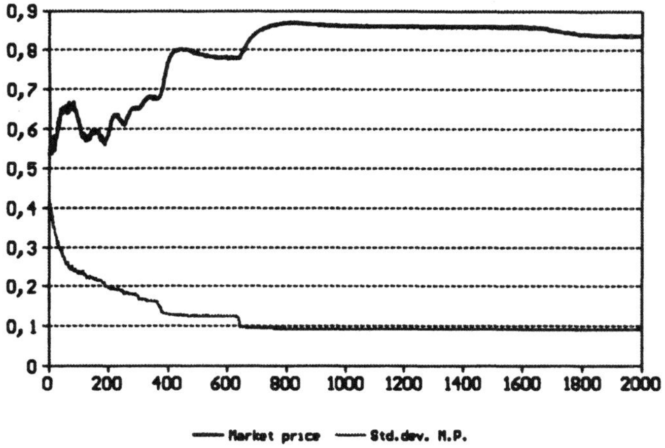

Figure 6. Market price evolution and dispersion
($-5 < w_{ij} < 5$, G=1, T=2000)

6.2 Smart and dumb agents

The speed of learning of the agents may be an important parameter for the dynamics of the market (in the previous simulations G was set to 1, therefore allowing for a substantial number of dumb agents). We now perform a simulation with G=0.3, therefore reducing the initial number of dumb to about 10% of the population. The results are in Figure 7; we used the same initial conditions as those used in the previous simulations, so that the only difference is due to the speed of learning. The figure shows that the price is more stable and the standard deviation decreases substantially. More speed in learning eliminates stubborn agents and make forecasting the forecasts of others an easier task.
We now turn to the goal of understanding more deeply the possible dynamics generated by our model, and the importance of the learning speed, by studying the individual behavior of the agents.

6.3 Speed of learning and initial forecasts

To understand the evolution we have to start from the initial conditions. Figures 8a and 8b show frequency distributions of the initial forecasts of the market price, i.e. the first output of each network, for a given initial (random) configuration of weights and for a homogeneous (across agents) information set given by π_t=0.5, $\Delta\pi_t$=0, $P_{ij,t}$=0.5, $\Delta P_{ij,t}$=0.
When G=0.3 there are no dumb agents, in the sense that only a small percentage forecasts values equal to either 0 or 1. When G=1 instead a relevant proportion of agents forecasts

values close to the extremes. In both cases the average, and therefore the market price at time 1, is about 0.5. At the end of day 1 there is still no learning, which starts at the end of day 2, when each agent compares her own forecast for t=1 with an average of the market price at 2 and her forecast at 2 (equation 12). If the agent is dumb we know that this mistake will not make any difference as to the structure of the future forecasts.

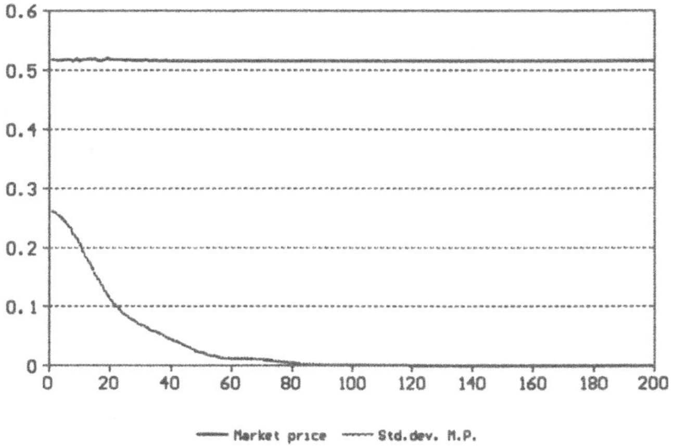

Figure 7. Market price evolution and dispersion
($-5 < w_{ij} < 5$, G=0.3, T=200)

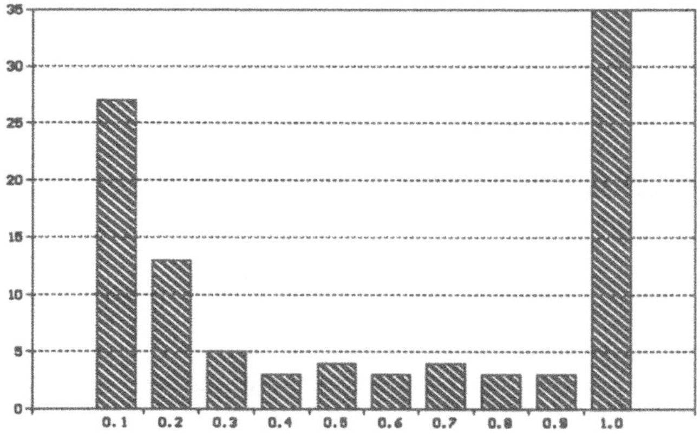

Figure 8a. Initial forecasts (G=1)

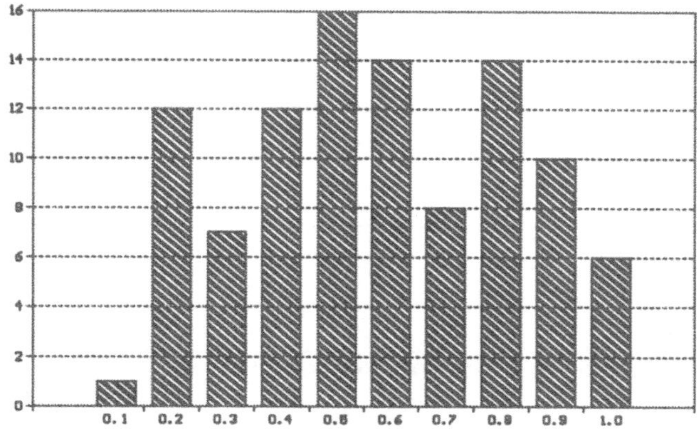

Figure 8b. Initial forecasts (G=0.3)

6.4 The performance of the best and of the worst agents

To consider the history of forecasts, forecast errors and wealth of the best and the worst performers in a given simulation we consider a dynamics of wealth defined in the following way:

$W_{i,t+1} = (M_{i,t} - K\,P_{ij,t}) + \pi_t(S_{i,t} + K)$ for a buyer

$W_{i,t+1} = (M_{i,t} + K\,P_{ij,t}) + \pi_t(S_{i,t} - K)$ for a seller

Figure 9a and 9b show the forecast and the forecast error of the best agent; the forecasting performance is good, especially when compared to that of the worst (Figure 10a), who always forecasts 0 and make a stable mistake. These different forecasting abilities have consequences in terms of the value of the wealth which is accumulated during the simulations. The smart get richer and some of the dumb get poorer (Figures 9c and 10b).

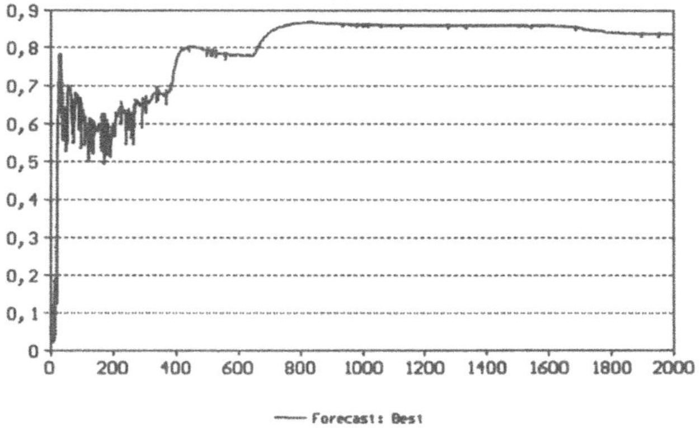

Figure 9a. Forecast of the best agent

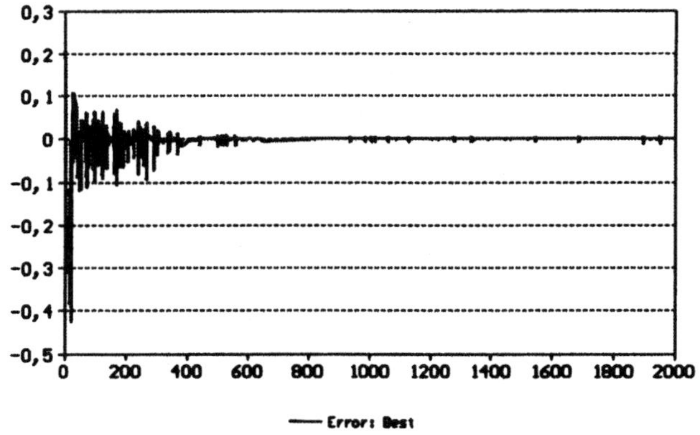

Figure 9b. Forecast error of the best agent

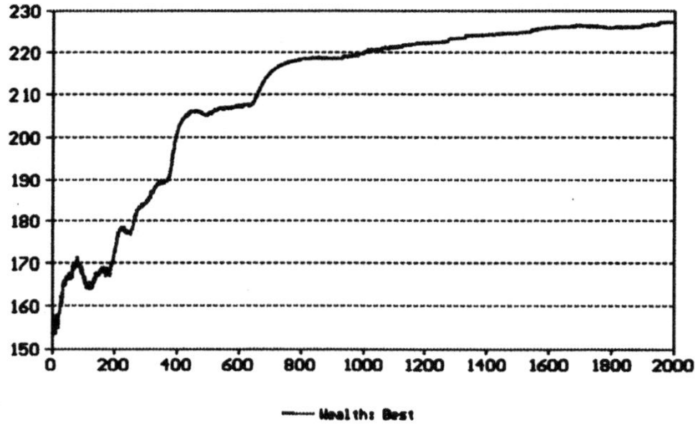

Figure 9c. Wealth of the best agent

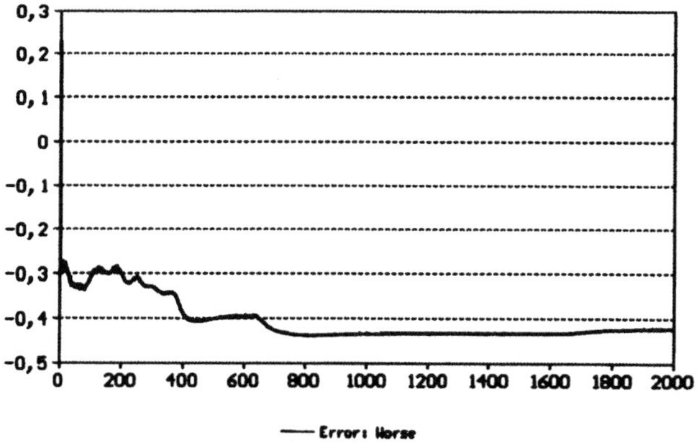

Figure 10a. Forecast error of the worst agent

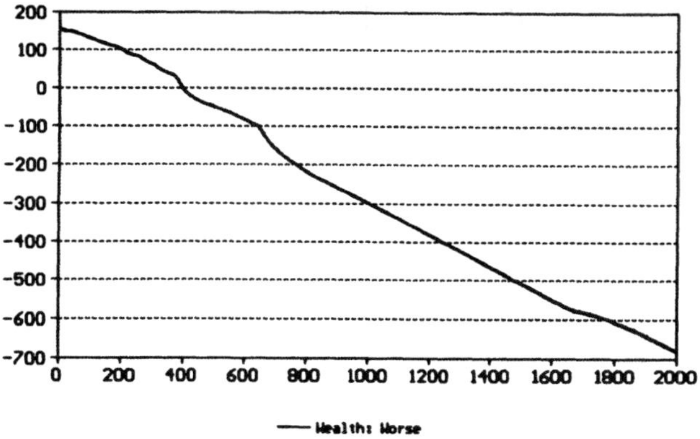

Figure 10b. Wealth of the worst agent

6.5 Asymptotic distribution of the market price

After analyzing some examples, we now ask ourselves a more general question about the long-run evolution of the system. To answer this question we computed the "asymptotic distribution" of the market price. We present in Figure 11a the histogram of the frequency distribution for G=1, which is wildly dispersed. The average across simulations is 0.49 and the standard deviation, always across simulations, is 0.33. This shows that this system does not converge to a definite equilibrium, at least within the time period of 200 epochs that we consider. We repeated the exercise with G=0.3, and obtained a distribution which is less dispersed than before.

When T=1000 (Figures 12) and T=2000 (Figures 13) these features are even more clear. This shows the permanent and important effects of the presence of dumb agents on the evolution of the price. When they are in sufficient proportion they actually drive the long run evolution of the market price, since the smart agents learns that a large number of traders keep believing that the market price will keep going up or going down. The final outcome depends therefore on the proportion of dumb agents, on the proportion of dumb agents forecasting 0 or 1, and probably on the history of the meetings among traders. If smart agents keep meeting people that forecast 1, while those forecasting 0 keep meeting among themselves, they will move their beliefs towards 1, giving a tendency to the rise of the market price.

Of course this evolution has precise consequences in terms of wealth. Dumb agents on the "wrong side of the forecast" lose their wealth, while smart agents accumulate the wealth lost by the dumb. Being dumb is however not necessarily bad for wealth, as long as one is following the same direction taken by the majority of the dumb. When the price starts rising towards 1, the dumb who are forecasting 1 increase their wealth at the expense of those who, because of their forecasting 0, keep selling in the expectation of a decrease in price. However it is likely that at the end of the story the wealthiest agent is a smart one, who can profit not only from the general trend of the price, but also from the various shorter cycles which take place. For example, a dumb always forecasting 1 will keep choosing stocks even when the downward movement in the price would make cash a more attractive asset, while a smart trader would move to the right asset at the right times, therefore increasing wealth at a fastest rate.

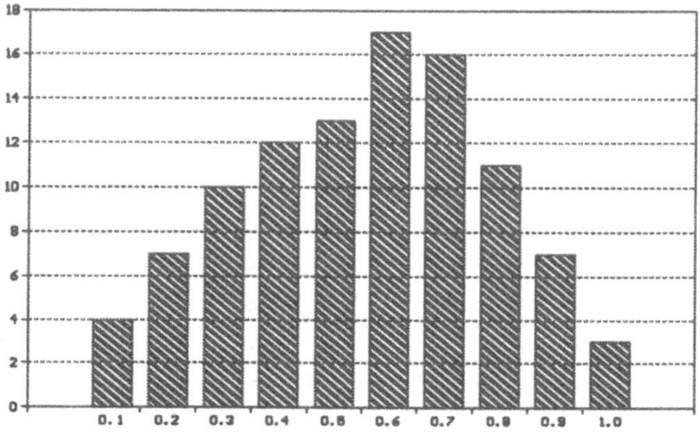

Figure. 11a. Asymptotic distribution of market price
(J=50, G=1, T=200)

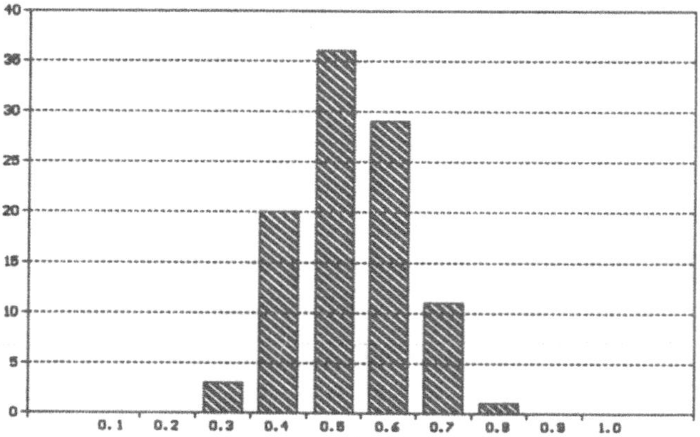

Figure 11b. Asymptotic distribution of market price
(J=50, G=0.3, T=200)

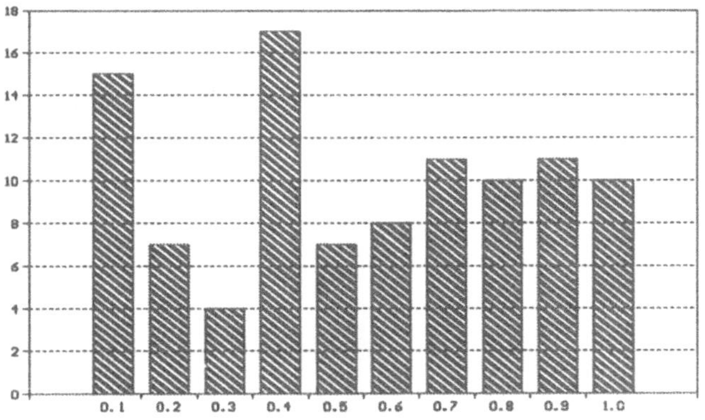

Figure 12a. Asymptotic distribution of market price
(J=50, G=1, T=1000)

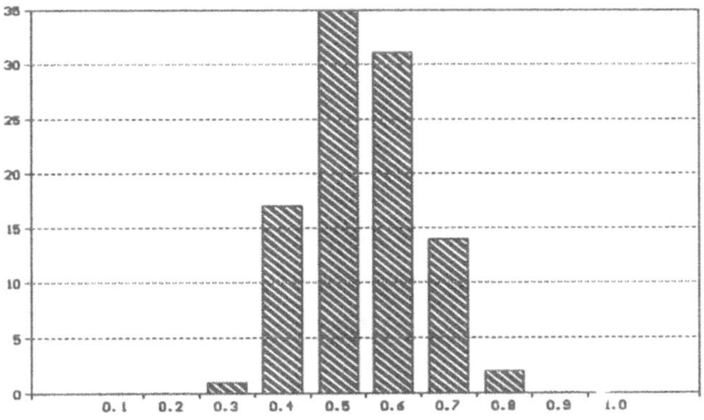

Figure 12b. Asymptotic distribution of market price
(J=50, G=0.3, T=1000)

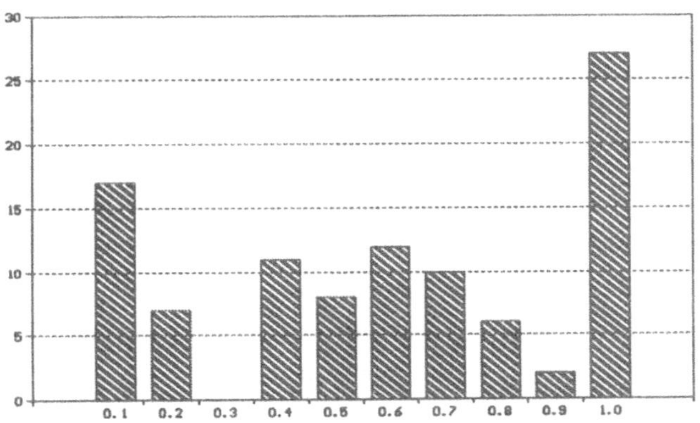

Figure 13a. Asymptotic distribution of market price
(J=50, G=1, T=2000)

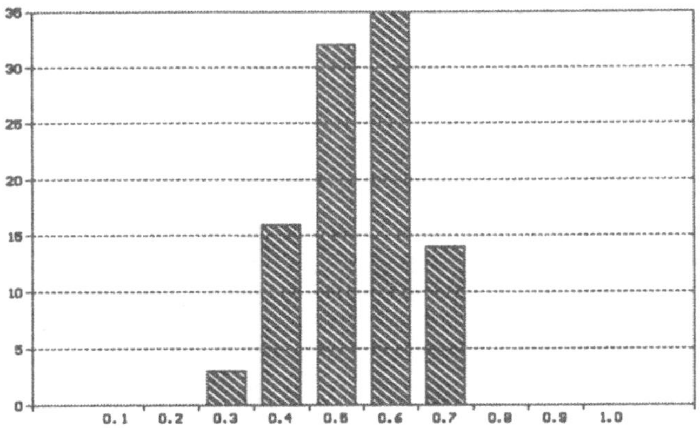

Figure 13b. Asymptotic distribution of market price
(J=50, G=0.3, T=2000)

7. Conclusions

This paper can be considered as a starting point for a research project trying to simulate the behavior of financial markets by means of neural networks and other new computational devices. We have shown that a market populated by agents acting according to some simple rules, and forecasting according to specific models, can generate rich dynamics in market price. The final outcome of the market depends on the characteristics of the agents and on the history of the market. Agents make or lose money according to their forecasting ability.

In these conclusions we describe some directions for future research:

(i) risk-neutrality is a useful assumption as it allows an easy derivation of the demand schedule of each agent. We plan to extend the model to consider risk-averse agents who endogenously determine the demand and supply at given prices, and therefore choose the quantity to trade

(ii) the market we have considered has no fundamentals. We plan to extend the model to consider the payment of dividends. This would be useful to compare our artificial market to a market where agents have rational expectations and price the asset in order to make it equal to the expected discounted value of dividends

(iii) finally we plan to consider agents who follow rules that mimic some of the strategies used by technical analysts. The interactions of such agents with the ones described in this paper may generate richer dynamics.

Appendix: Notation

The notation is the following:

J	denotes the number of agents;
π_t	the stock market price in terms of money;
$E_{i,t}P_{t+1}$	the output of network i at time t, to be interpreted as i-th agent's forecast of the price at which a transaction involving shares against money will be executed at t+1; given the structure of the model, explained in the following sections, this turns out to be also her reservation price;
$I_{i,t}$	the information set available at the beginning of period t, used to form the expectation;
$P_{ij,t}$	the price at which the actual transaction between agents i and j is executed during period t;
$M_{i,t}$	the stock of money of agent i available at the beginning of day t, equal to the stock available at the end of t-1, after the markets closed;
$S_{i,t}$	the number of shares held at the beginning of day t by agent i, equal to those at the end of t-1;
K	the number of shares which can be bought or sold at each transaction;
$W_{i,t}$	the stock of wealth of agent i at the beginning of t;
G	a parameter of the logistic function, $y=[1+\exp(-Gx)]^{-1}$.

References

Arthur W.B. (1991) Designing economic agents that act like human agents: a behavioral approach to bounded rationality, American Economic Review 81/2: 353-359

Cecconi F., D. Parisi (1990) Evolving organisms that can reach for objects, in J.A. Meyer and S.W. Wilson (Eds.), From animals to animats, MIT Press, Cambridge, Mass.

Judge G.G., W.E. Griffiths, R.C. Hill, T. Lee (1985) The theory and practice of econometrics, John Wiley & Sons, New York

Keynes, J.M. (1936) The general theory of Employment, Interest and Money, MacMillan, London

Marcet A., T.J. Sargent (1989) Convergence of least-squares learning in environments with hidden state variables and private information, Journal of Political Economy 97/6: 1306-1322

Margarita S. (1991) Neural networks, genetic algorithms and stock trading, in T. Kohonen, K. Mäkisara, O. Simula and J. Kangas (Eds.), Artificial neural networks, Elsevier Science Publishers B.V. (North-Holland), Amsterdam

Margarita S. (1992) Genetic neural networks for financial markets: some results, in B. Neumann (Ed.), Proceedings of ECAI 92, 10th European Conference on Artificial Intelligence, John Wiley & Sons, Chichester

Nottola C., F. Leroy, F. Davalo (1992) Dynamics of artificial markets, in F.J. Varela, P. Bourgine (Eds.), Toward a practice of autonomous systems, MIT Press, Cambridge, Mass.

Rumelhart D.E., McClelland J.L. (1986) Parallel Distributed Processing, Explorations in the Microstructure of Cognition, MIT Press, Cambridge, Mass.

Shiller, R.J. (1981) Do stock market prices move too much to be justified by subsequent changes in dividends?, in Shiller, 1989

Shiller, R.J. (1987) Investor behavior in the October 1987 stock market crash: survey evidence, chapter 23 of Shiller, 1989

Shiller, R.J. (1989) Market volatility, MIT Press, Cambridge, Mass.

Terna P. (1991) Labor, consumption and family assets: a neural network learning from its own cross-targets, in T. Kohonen, K. Mäkisara, O. Simula and J. Kangas (Eds.), Artificial neural networks, Elsevier Science Publishers B.V. (North-Holland), Amsterdam

Townsend D. (1983) Forecasting the forecasts of others, Journal of Political Economy 91/4: 546-588

White A. (1991) Learning in artificial neural networks: a statistical perspective, Neural Computation 1: 425-464

Valuation of the Embedded Prepayment Option
of Mortgage-Backed Securities [1]

Rita L. D'Ecclesia
Department of Economic Sciences
University of Urbino
Piazza Repubblica, 3
61029 Urbino, ITALY.

Stavros A. Zenios
Decision Sciences Department
The Wharton School
University of Pennsylvania
Philadelphia, PA 19104 USA.

1 Introduction

Mortgage-backed securities (MBS for short) combine features of both bonds and options. The investor in the MBS has purchased a fully amortizing bond, with known coupon rate and maturity date. However, at the same time the investor has written a call option to the mortgage borrower. The homowner's privilage to refinance his or her mortgage at any point in time complicates attempts to price the MBS. Further complications arise due to the homowners' propensity to prepay their mortgage, even if this decision may not appear to be economically desirable. For example, a homeowner may sell or refinance the house in an unfavorable interest rate environment. Reasons for this decision include, for example, family dynamics (birth, death, divorce) and employment opportunites (relocation).

Traditionally, the pricing of MBS has concentrated on two key aspects of the problem. First, in estimating the prepayment activity of homeowners based on historical observations. Second, in coupling the payout function implied by the prepayment model with appropriate assumptions about the shape of the term structure of interest rate to obtain a fair price for the MBS. Green and Shoven [1986], Richard and Roll [1989] and Kang and Zenios [1992a] are some of the recent publications in the first direction. (See also references therein.) Dunn and McConnell [1981], Brennan and Schwartz [1985], Schwartz and Torous [1989], McConnel and Singh [1990]

[1] Special tanks to prof. Marida Bertocchi for her contribution with thwe solutiion methodology of the differential equation

are some of the publications in the second direction. Recent pricing literature explicitly recognizes that prepayments are exercised in a "suboptimal" fashion, but it does so by assuming some idealistic *proportional hazards* model to describe prepayment. In contrast, practical applications of MBS pricing utilize elaborate forecasting models for capturing the prepayment activity as a factor of economic factors, seasonality, history of interest rates, demographic considerations, housing activity and so on. See, for example, Hayre [1990] and Hutchinson and Zenios [1991]. Furthermore, practical applications realize the limitations of the prepayment models and the markets desire to be compensated for the additional risk, and resort to *option adjusted analysis* to compile a rich/cheap profile of MBS in comparison to the Treasuries market. See, again, Hayre and Hutchinson and Zenios.

The prepayment feature of mortgage backed security has always been considered as an essential component for the valuation of MBS. The influence that the prepayment option exerts on MBS pricing has been analyzed by Dunn and McConnel [1981], the prepayment function has been estimated by Schwartz and Torous [1989] and integrated in the MBS valuation, in this paper we try to valuate the prepayment option embedded in the MBS according to specified assumptions.

With the recent interest in the development of analytic models for managing portfolios of MBS — see Hiller and Eckstein [1991] and Zenios [1991] — the temporal variation of the price of the embedded option becomes particularly important. When viewed in the context of a multi-period, dynamic portfolio management problem, one needs to place a price on the MBS at some future time periods, and under different interest rate scenarios. Zenios and McKendall [1991] have developed such models that were subsequently used in constructing mean-absolute deviation efficient portfolios by Kang and Zenios [1992b]. The pricing model of Zenios and McKendall requires the estimation of the option adjusted spread at future points in time. Unfortunately, this spread is obtained empirically based on market data, and hence the pricing model is rather circular. However, if we can obtain the temporal variation of the price of the embedded option (assuming it is exercised optimally) then we can calculate a spread due to the suboptimal exercise of the option. This spread will presumably remain constant accross time, and can be calibrated based on today's prices. It can then be used to price the MBS at some point in the future. In essence, we are separating the MBS into a fully amortizing bond, a call option with optimal exercise policies, and a spread due to the additional risks created by the stylized behavior of homeowners. The last component is constant accross time, and for the first two we can obtain pricing equations based on standard financial theories.

The purpose of this paper is precisely to develop a pricing model for the embedded prepayment option. The theory of option pricing has had extensive applications to different contingent claims, as well as the pricing of callable warrants, see Merton [1973], or the pricing of convertible saving bonds, Brennan and Schwartz [1979a,1982] and callable bonds. We apply options pricing theory to value the prepayment option embedded in a MBS due to changes in interest rates, ignoring the influence exerted by other factors. We use the seminal model of Black and Scholes [1973] as extended by Merton [1973], and couple those with the interest rate model of Brennan and Schwartz [1983]. Hence we derive the stochastic differential equation that governs the temporal variation of the option under different short-term and long-term interest rates. An algorithm based on the Alternating Directions Implicit method is used to solve the resutling equation. Numerical results with the application of our model are presented.

The plan of the paper is as follows: Section 2 introduces the problem. Section 3 develops the pricing model: It introduces the assumptions, specifies and calibrates the stochastic processes for the interest rates, and derives the pricing equation. Section 4 presents numerical results, and a final section offers some concluding remarks.

2 Preliminaries

The main characteristics of a mortgage can be summarized by the following variables:

1. The age of the mortgage t,
2. The month of the year m,
3. The mortgage contract rate R_c.

All mortgage loans approved by the Federal Housing Administration can be prepaid (i.e. called by the mortgagor) at any time without a prepayment penalty. The key factor that affects the mortgagors' call strategies when markets are frictionless is the "difference" between his or her mortgage contract rate R_c and the prevailing market rate R at which a new mortgage can be obtained. A homeowner will never let the market value of his existing loan exceeding its outstanding principal balance. When this condition is violated the loan could be refinanced with an otherwise identical loan which has a lower effective rate of interest than the rate on the existing loan.

The balance of mortgage loan with T months to maturity, at a given point in time, t, per unit of monthly payment, is given by

$$B(t) = \frac{1-(1+R_c)^{t-T}}{R_c}. \tag{1}$$

Tipically $T = 360$, and in this paper we deal exclusively with 30-year fixed rate mortgages without any loss of generality. The market value of a T months new mortgage is given by:

$$\Delta(t) = \frac{1-(1+R)^{t-T}}{R} X = V(t)X. \tag{2}$$

where X denotes the monthly payment and the interest rate R is assumed to follow a continuous stationary stochastic process according to the theory of the term structures of interest rates derived by Brennan and Schwartz [1987, 1989].

When markets are frictionless mortgagors will exercise their prepayment option only when they can refinance their existing loan with a similar loan that has a lower contract interest rate, that is when R is lower Than R_c. This implies a value of the annuity $V(t)$ larger than $B(t)$. Note that the relation of $V(t)$ to $B(t)$ is uniquely determined by the mortgage contractual rate R_c and the prevailing refinancing rate R: at time t if $R \leq R_c$ then $V(t) \geq B(t)$ and the homeowner has an incentive to prepay the mortgage.

One of the notable characteristics of mortgagors is that they often call their loans suboptimally. The prepayments are suboptimal in the sense that the amount of the prepayment (the outstanding balance of the loan) exceeds the market value of the debt ($B(t) > V(t)$), this occurs when $R > R_c$. These prepayments usually occur in presence of one of the following events:
1) a mortgagor moves out and the obligation for the existing mortgages is not assumed by the purchaser of his house;
2) the present house is refinanced so that the owner can withdraw his equity;
3) the mortgagor defaults on his loan.

3 The Pricing Model

3.1 Basic Assumptions

The mortgagor's option to call a piece of the pool away from the investor anytime during the life of the mortgage can be compared to an American call option with an exercise price equal to the mortgage balance $B(t)$ and a time to maturity, $\tau = T - t$, where t denotes time since issuance of the mortgage, and T is the original maturity of the mortgage. The value of the mortgage balance decreases as t approaches maturity. At maturity, $\tau = 0$, the remaining principal balance $B(R_c, T) = 0$.

The model for valuing prepayment of mortgage backed securities is based on the generic model for pricing contingent securities developed by Brennan and Schwartz. The main assumptions are :

1. The value of a default free fixed interest rate security, $P(r, \tau)$, is a function only of the current value of the instantaneously risk-free rate r, the consol rate l and its term to maturity;

2. All information about the term structure of short-term and long-term interest rates on default free securities is summarized, at any point in time, by the current value of the instantaneously riskless rate r, and the consol rate l;

3. The instantaneously riskless rate and the consol rate follow a joint stochastic process of the general type:

$$dr = [a_1 + b_1(l - r)]dt + \sigma_1 r dz_1 \tag{3}$$

$$dl = l[a_2 + b_2 r + c_2 l]dt + \sigma_2 l dz_2 \tag{4}$$

   Here t denotes calendar time and z_1 and z_2 follow a standard Wiener processes with $E[dz_1] = E[dz_2] = 0$, $E[dz_1^2] = E[dz_2^2] = dt$ and $E[dz_1 dz_2] = \rho dt$, where ρ is the instantaneous correlation between the short-term and the long-term rates. The coefficients $a_1, a_2, b_1, b_2 and c_2$ are assumed to be constant;

4. mortgagors are non satiated and agree on the specification of 3;

5. the capital market, including the market for individual junior and senior mortgage loans, is perfect and competitive, trading takes place continuously;
6. the cash flows from mortgages are paid continuously.

Assumptions 1,2 and 3 of the Brennan-Schwartz model imply that the whole term structure of interest rates is determined by the yields on the shortest and longest maturity instruments. The value of a riskless bond of any maturity may be written as a function of three state variables r, l and t. Furthermore, the major restrictions on the interest rate dynamics is that the instantaneous change in each interest rate depends only on the current values of the two interest rates and the two correlated stochastic processes. According to (3) and (4) the scale of the unanticipated change in each of the interest rates is proportional to the current value of that rate. This system of equations also allows the unanticipated changes in the two interest rates to be correlated with each other. Assumptions 4 and 5 ensure that a borrower will prepay his loan according to the optimal call strategy. Assumption 6 is a convenient means of approximating the way in which mortgage backed securities are actually traded.

The fundamental assumption of the model to value the prepayment option is that the homeowner decides to exercise his or her right to prepay the mortgage if the present value of the mortgage balance $V(t)$ is higher then the balance of the existing mortgage, $B(t)$. (A constant threshold above B_t can easily be introduced to account for the fixed costs in obtaining a new mortgage.) At each time t there is an optimal exercise boundary point, $V^*(t)$, above which the prepayment option will be exercised. We assume that when a prepayment occurs the homeowner will pay back the whole mortgage balance.

In the following sections we denote the value of the prepayment option by F. This definition refers to a MBS with monthly balance $B(t)$, when the prevailing mortgage rate is R, which corresponds to a present value of the mortgage balance equal to $V(t)$, and with $\tau = T - t$ years before expiration. For an optimal exercise policy the prepayment option value F must satisfy:

$$F(V(t), \tau, B(t)) \geq 0 \tag{5}$$
$$F(V(t), \tau = 0, 0) = 0 \tag{6}$$
$$F(V(t), \tau, B(t)) \geq \max[0, V(t) - B(t)] \tag{7}$$

Given two mortgages with the same fixed coupon rate R_c, under the same prevailing mortgage rate R, but with different maturities $\tau_1 \geq \tau_2$ we have

$$F(V(t), \tau_2, B(t)) \geq F(V(t), \tau_1, B(t)). \tag{8}$$

Furthermore, two mortgages with the same time to maturity and the same prevailing mortgage rate R, but with different coupon rates $R_{c1} \leq R_{c2}$ — this implies $B(1t) \geq B(2t)$ — must satisfy

$$F[V(t), \tau, B(1t)] \leq F[V(t), \tau, B(2t)] \tag{9}$$

In order to apply option based methodologies to value the prepayment option linked to a MBS a few specifications are required. The underlying security in this case is represented by the mortgage balance which is a deterministic function of the mortgage rate R. The exercise price is represented by the monthly mortgage balance $B(t)$, computed on the basis of the mortgage contract rate R_c. The mortgage rate R is strongly related to the long-term interest rate, defined as the consol rate in Brennan and Schwartz [1982]. According to data collected from the U.S. markets in the period 1975–1991 the monthly long-term spot rates and the monthly mortgage rates are highly correlated with correlation coefficient greater than 0.95. Hence, we assume that the mortgage rates can be very well approximated by the consol rates of interest. Further discussion on modeling the current mortgage coupon yield is given by Golub and Pohlman [1991]. The precise specification of the stochastic process for the interest rates is left for the next section.

In order to introduce the stochastic interest rates in pricing the prepayment option we consider the price of a riskless discount loan $P(\tau)$ which pays one dollar τ years from now. With positive interest rates we have

$$P(0) = 1 > P(\tau_1) > P(\tau_2) > \cdots > P(\tau_n).$$

We assume that at any point in time the mortgagor, after having fulfilled his obligation to pay the monthly installments, $B(t)$, may choose between two different investments, (A1) and (A2). Those are defined as follows:

Investment (A1):

- Keep the prepayment option involved in the MBS whose value is $F[V(t), \tau, B(t)]$.
- At the same time invest the amount corresponding to the monthly mortgage balance due at time $t+1$, $B(t+1)$, in a riskless bond and paying $B(t+1)P(1)$ in order to receive $B(t+1)$ at time $t+1$ and pay the next monthly payment. $P(1)B(t+1)$ is the present value of $B(t+1)$ at time t discounted at the riskless interest rate r.

The value of this investment strategy at time t is: $F[V(t), \tau, B(t)] + B(t+1)P(1)$.

Investment (A2):

- Invest the present value of the mortgage balance $V(t)$, which is a function of the prevailing mortgage rate $R(t)$. In this case the mortgagor will be covered if he, at time $t+1$ decided to exercise the prepayment option and get a new mortgage at the new prevailing mortgage rate, $R(t+1)$.

The value of this investment strategy is equal to $V(t)$.

At time $t+1$ investment (A1) will be worth the value of the option plus the value of the mortgage balance, i.e., $F[V(t+1), \tau, B(t+1)] + B(t+1)$. The option is going to be worthless only if there is no incentive to exercise the prepayment option, (i.e., when $R(t+1) > R_c$):

1. If $V(t+1) \geq B(t+1)$ then $F[V(t+1), \tau, B(t+1)] = V(t+1) - B(t+1)$. Investment (A1) is therefore worth $V(t+1) - B(t+1) + B(t+1) = V(t+1)$.
2. If $V(t+1) \leq B(t+1)$ then $F(V(t+1), \tau, B(t+1)) = 0$. Investment (A1) is worth $0 + B(t+1) = B(t+1)$.

On the other hand, at time $t+1$ investment (A2) will be worth $V(t+1)$. Investment (A1) and investment (A2) are going to be equal if $V(t+1) > B(t+1)$. However, when $V(t+1) < B(t+1)$ investment (A1) will be worth more than investment (A2). Hence, investment (A1) dominates (A2) [1]. In order to avoid dominant investments in this market we have to assume that the current value of (A1) is at least as large as (A2). This implies that at time t:

$$\begin{aligned} F(V(t),\tau,B_t) + B(t+1)P(1) &> V(t) \\ \Rightarrow F[V(t),\tau,B(t)] &> \max[0,V(t)-B(t+1)P(1)] \\ \Rightarrow F[V(t),\tau,B(t)] &> \max[0,V(t)-B(t)] \end{aligned} \tag{10}$$

We have thus defined a relationship for the value of the prepayment option on the basis of the new mortgage balance $V(t)$and the existing mortgage balance $B(t+1)P(1)$.

In the case of an equity option we refer to $\max[0,S-E]$ as the intrinsic value of the option. In the case of a prepayment option linked to a MBS we have to consider $\max[0,V(t+1)P(t)-B(t+1)P(t)]$ as the intrinsic value.

From (10) we formally deduce that the price of the prepayment option is a function of the following variables:

1. $P(1)$, and hence the short-term riskless rate r.
2. The new mortgage balance $V(t)$ which is determined on the basis of the new prevailing rate R, and therefore of the consol rate l.
3. The time to maturity τ.
4. The existing mortgage balance B_t.

We will denote the price of the option merely by F, and it is understood to be a function of these variables.

The price of the option is a decreasing function of the new mortgage rate, R. If the mortgage rate increases the homeowner has no incentive to prepay. The present value $V(t)$ of the new mortgage balance would be lower then the existing mortgage balance B_t. In this case the option will be worthless, i.e., F=0: $\frac{\partial F}{\partial R} < 0$. The option to prepay the mortgage is equivalent to borrowing the present value of the mortgage balance $B(t+1)$ and paying it back at time $t+1$. The present value of such a loan is a decreasing function of the interest rates, so for a fixed new mortgage rate the option price will be a decreasing function of the short-term interest rate, i.e., $\frac{\partial F}{\partial r} < 0$.

3.2 Calibration of the interest rate processes

According to (3)–(4) the scale of the unanticipated change in each of the interest rates is proportional to the current value of that rate. This system of equations also

[2]Security A is dominates security B, if on some known date in the future the return on A will exceed the return of B for some possible states of the world and it will be at least as large as B for all other possible states. But the existence of a dominant security would be equivalent to the existence of an arbitrage situation.

	7-year T-Bond	10-year T-Bond	Mortgage Rate	30-day CD
7-year	1.000000			
10-year	0.993292	1.000000		
Mort. rate	0.950959	0.950367	1.000000	
30-day	0.831865	0.818206	0.805345	1.000000

Table 1: Correlation coefficients of US Government rates of different maturities with the mortgage rate.

allows the unanticipated changes in the two interest rates to be correlated with each other. The estimation of the parameters of the interest rate processes requires data on r and l. The instantaneous risk free rate was approximated by the annualized 30-day CD-rate, while the long term rate was approximated by the annualized yield on 10-year US Government T-Bonds. Monthly data on r and l were collected from January 1979 to November 1991, for a total of 154 observations. The data were collected from the Federal Reserve Monthly bulletin.

In order to choose the proper consol rate to represent the mortgage refinancing rates we analyzed the rates of US Government T-Bonds of different maturities. According to our data the annualized yield to maturity on the 10-year T-Bond has a correlation of 0.9504 with the monthly mortgage rate [3]. Hence, for the purpose of this paper we considered the stochastic process for the long term rate on the basis of the 10-year US T-Bond rates. Furthermore, the 10-year rate shows a significant correlation with the 30-day interest rate, see Table 1.

The parameters of the interest rate process were estimated using the following discrete approximations:

$$\frac{r_t - r_{t-1}}{r_{t-1}} = \frac{a_1}{r_{t-1}} + b_1 \frac{l_{t-1} - r_{t-1}}{r_{t-1}} + \epsilon_{1t} \tag{11}$$

$$\frac{l_t - l_{t-1}}{l_{t-1}} = a_2 + b_2 r_{t-1} + c_2 l_{t-1} + \epsilon_{2t} \tag{12}$$

ϵ_{1t} and ϵ_{2t} are errors in the model. A least-squares approach was employed to estimate the parameters of the stochastic process, that minimize the square of these error terms. A standard nonlinear programming package (GAMS, Brooke, Kendrick and Meeraus [1988]) was used for the estimation. The calibrated interest rate processes are as follows:

$$dr = [-0.106 + 0.022(l - r)]dt + 0.021 r dz_1 \tag{13}$$

$$dl = l[0.073 + 0.002r - 0.004l]dt + 0.003 l dz_2 \tag{14}$$

The estimated values of the parameters a_1 and b_1 from the drift of the short-term interest rate process and the parameters a_2, b_2, c_2, for the drift of the long term

[3] Although the prevailing mortgage rates have historically been highly correlated with the 10-year T-Bond rates the spread between the two has not been constant. This spread averages about 150 basis points. For further modeling of the mortgage refinancing rates see Golub and Pohlman [1991].

process are similar to the parameters obtained by Brennan and Schwartz [1983]. The estimated standard deviation of changes in short term interest rates exceeds the estimated standard deviation of changes in long term rates, $\sigma_1 = 0.01$ and $\sigma_2 = 0.02$. Short term interest rates were more volatile than long term interest rates over our sample period.

3.3 The Pricing Equation

We are now ready to develop the basic pricing equation. Our development proceeds in three steps. First, we develop the stochastic partial differential equation followed by $V(t)$. Second, we develop the stochastic partial differential equation followed by $P(t)$. Third, we develop the stochastic partial differential equation followed by F, based on the assumptions we imposed on F in section (3.1). The coefficients of the first two equations are determined by the calibrated parameters of the interest rate processes. The coefficients of the equation for F can be determined by invoking standard arbitrage arguments, and this, together with the appropriate boundary conditions, will completely specify the pricing equation for F. At maturity, $\tau = 0$, the value of the remaining principal balance $V(R,0) = 0$ and in this case the prepayment option is worthless: $F(0,0,0) = 0$.

The value of an interest dependent security goes to zero as the interest rate approaches infinity. This implies:

$$\lim_{R\to\infty} V(R,\tau) = 0 \tag{15}$$

and therefore

$$\lim_{R\to\infty} F(V,\tau,B) = 0 \tag{16}$$

Finally optimal calls occur according to the change of the risk free interest rate. For each maturity there is some level of the risk free interest rate, say R_e for which the market value

$$V[R_e,\tau] = V^*, \rightarrow V* > B(R_c,\tau)$$

and the call option will be exercised. Risk free interest rates above $R_c(\tau)$ are not relevant for pricing the prepayment option. This implies that:

$$F[V*(t),\tau,B(t)] \geq \max 0, V*(t) - B(t)$$

3.3.1 Stochastic Partial Differential Equation for $V(t)$

According to (2) the present value of a new mortgage $V(t)$ is a continuous non-random function of the mortgage rate R. This rate is taken to be the consol rate l of our calibrated Brennan-Schwartz model. Applying Ito's Lemma and using the stochastic processes (3)–(4) for r and l we obtain the following diffusion process for $V(t)$:

$$dV = \left[\frac{\partial V}{\partial t} + \frac{\partial V}{\partial l} l(a_2 + b_2 r + c_2 l) + \frac{\partial^2 V}{\partial l^2}\sigma_2^2 l^2\right] dt + \frac{\partial V}{\partial l}\sigma_2 l dz_2 \tag{17}$$

where :

$$\begin{aligned}
\frac{\partial V}{\partial t} &= -\frac{(1+l)^{t-360}}{l}\log(1+l) \\
\frac{\partial V}{\partial r} &= \frac{\partial^2 V}{\partial r^2} = \frac{\partial^2 V}{\partial r \partial l} = 0 \\
\frac{\partial V}{\partial l} &= -\frac{(t-360)(1+l)^{t-361}}{l} + \frac{(1+l)^{t-360}-1}{l^2} \\
\frac{\partial^2 V}{\partial l^2} &= \left[2 - \frac{l(t-361)}{(1+l)}\right]\frac{(t-360)(1+l)^{t-361}}{l^2} \\
&\quad + \frac{2}{l^3}\left[1-(1+l)^{t-360}\right]
\end{aligned} \tag{18}$$

Applying the standard multiplication rules and introducing simple substitutions:

$$\begin{aligned}
\mu V &= \frac{-(1+l)^{t-360}}{l}\log(1+l) + \sigma_2^2\Big[(t-360)(1+l)^{t-361} \\
&\quad \left(2-\frac{l(t-361)}{(1+l)}\right) + \frac{2}{l}\left(1-(1+l)^{t-360}\right)\Big] \\
&\quad - \left[(t-360)(1+l)^{t-361} - \frac{(1+l)^{t-360}-1}{l}\right](a_2+b_2 r+c_2 l) \\
\varphi V(t) &= -\sigma_2\left[(t-360)(1+l)^{t-361} - \frac{(1+l)^{t-360}-1}{l}\right]
\end{aligned} \tag{19}$$

we obtain:

$$\frac{dV}{V} = \mu dt + \varphi dz_2 \tag{20}$$

$\mu(r,l,t)$ and $\varphi^2(r,l,t)$ are the mean and variance, respectively, of the instantaneous value of the mortgage payment at time t given that the mortgage rate is l.

3.3.2 Stochastic Partial Differential Equation for $P(t)$

As pointed out by several authors, see, e.g., Cox, Ingersoll and Ross [1985] or Brennan and Schwartz [1979b,1980,1982], bond prices can be expressed as a deterministic function of the two interest rate state variables. The value of any default free bond can then be written as $P(r,l,t,c)$, where t is the time to maturity and c is the coupon rate. For our purposes, since we consider a pure discount bond we may suppress the coupon rate argument and write the bond value simply as $P(r,l,t)$.

The diffusion process for the bond price P, according to Brennan and Schwartz [1989] is defined by

$$\frac{dP(t)}{P(t)} = \beta(r,l,t)dt + \eta_1(r,l,t)dz_1 + \eta_2(r,l,t)dz_2 \tag{21}$$

where

$$\beta(r,l,t) = \left[a_1\frac{\partial P}{\partial r} + a_2\frac{\partial P}{\partial l} + \frac{1}{2}\frac{\partial^2 P}{\partial r^2}\sigma_1^2 + \frac{1}{2}\frac{\partial^2 P}{\partial l^2}\sigma_2^2 + \frac{1}{2}\frac{\partial^2 P}{\partial r \partial l}\sigma_1\sigma_2\rho + \frac{\partial P}{\partial t}\right] / P \tag{22}$$

$$\eta_1(r,l,t) = \frac{\partial P}{\partial r}\frac{\sigma_1}{P} \tag{23}$$

$$\eta_2(r,l,t) = \frac{\partial P}{\partial l}\frac{\sigma_2}{P} \tag{24}$$

where $\beta(r,l,t)$, $\eta_1^2(r,l,t)$ and $\eta_2^2(r,l,t)$ are the mean and variance respectively of the instantaneous rate of return on a bond with maturity date t given that the current spot rate is r.

3.3.3 Stochastic Partial Differential Equation for F

According to the basic assumptions of section (3.1) the price of the prepayment option is a function of time to expiration τ, the monthly mortgage balance, $V(t)$, the price of a riskless bond which pay one dollar in τ months from now, $P(\tau)$, and the monthly contract mortgage balance $B(t)$. The change in the option price over time could be expressed, by applying Ito's lemma to the distributional assumption made on $V(t)$, and $P(t)$:

$$dF = \frac{\partial F}{\partial t}d\tau + \frac{\partial F}{\partial P}dP + \frac{\partial F}{\partial V}dV + \frac{1}{2}\left[\frac{\partial^2 F}{\partial V^2}(dV)^2 + \frac{\partial^2 F}{\partial V \partial P}dV\,dP + \frac{\partial^2 F}{\partial P^2}(dP)^2\right] \tag{25}$$

where:

$$\begin{aligned} d\tau &= -dt \\ dP &= P(\beta dt + \eta_1 dz_1 + \eta_2 dz_2) \\ dV &= V(\mu dt + \varphi dz_2) \\ dP^2 &= P^2(\eta_1^2 dt + \eta_2^2 + 2\eta_1\eta_2\rho)dt \\ dV^2 &= V^2\varphi^2 dt \\ dV\,dP &= PV(\eta_1\varphi\rho + \eta_2\varphi\rho)\,dt \end{aligned} \tag{26}$$

Substituting and rearranging terms we may write (25) as:

$$\begin{aligned} dF = {} & \left[-\frac{\partial F}{\partial t} + P\frac{\partial F}{\partial P}\beta + V\frac{\partial F}{\partial V}\mu + \frac{1}{2}\frac{\partial^2 F}{\partial P^2}P^2(\eta_1^2 + \eta_2^2 + 2\eta_1\eta_2\rho)\right. \\ & \left. + \frac{1}{2}\frac{\partial^2 F}{\partial V^2}V^2\varphi^2 + \frac{1}{2}\frac{\partial^2 F}{\partial P \partial V}PV\varphi\rho(\eta_1 + \eta_2)\right] dt \\ & + P\frac{\partial F}{\partial P}\eta_1 dz_1 + V\frac{\partial F}{\partial V}\varphi dz_2 + \frac{\partial F}{\partial P}P\eta_2 dz_2 \end{aligned} \tag{27}$$

or, equivalently, as

$$\frac{dF}{F} = \pi dt + \delta_1 dz_1 + \delta_2 dz_2 \tag{28}$$

where:

$$\begin{aligned}
\pi &= \frac{1}{F}\left[-\frac{\partial F}{\partial t} + P\frac{\partial F}{\partial P}\beta + V\frac{\partial F}{\partial V}\mu + \frac{1}{2}\frac{\partial^2 F}{\partial P^2}P^2(\eta_1^2 + \eta_2^2 + 2\eta_1\eta_2\rho)\right. &(29)\\
&\left. + \frac{1}{2}\frac{\partial^2 F}{\partial V^2}V^2\varphi^2 + \frac{1}{2}\frac{\partial^2 F}{\partial P \partial V}PV\varphi\rho(\eta_1 + \eta_2)\right]\\
\delta_1 &= \frac{P\eta_1}{F}\frac{\partial F}{\partial P}\\
\delta_2 &= \frac{V\varphi}{F}\frac{\partial F}{\partial V} + \frac{P\eta_2}{F}\frac{\partial F}{\partial P} &(30)
\end{aligned}$$

3.3.4 The arbitrage argument

We consider now a portfolio containing the prepayment option, the present value of the mortgage $V(t+1)$ and the riskless bond with maturity equal to the expiration of the option. We might be able to combine the three securities in order to get an initial investment equal to zero. Let H_1 be the amount invested in the option, H_2 the amount invested in the riskless bond and H_3 the amount invested in the new mortgage $V(t)$. The condition of zero initial investment could be written as :

$$H_1 + H_2 - H_3 = 0 \tag{31}$$

This portfolio could be realized by using the proceeds of short sales and borrowing to finance long positions. If dY is the instantaneous dollar return of the portfolio we have:

$$dY = H_1\frac{dF}{F} + H_2\frac{dP}{P} - H_3\frac{dV}{V} \tag{32}$$

Substituting from expressions (20),(21) and (28) we have:

$$\begin{aligned}
dY &= H_1(\pi dt + \delta_1 dz_1 + \delta_2 dz_2) + H_2(\beta dt + \eta_1 dz_1 + \eta_2 dz_2) &(33)\\
&+ H_3(\mu dt + \varphi dz_2)
\end{aligned}$$

Since $H_3 = -(H_1 + H_2)$ we can rewrite (33) as:

$$\begin{aligned}
dY &= H_1(\pi - \mu)dt + H_2(\beta - \mu)dt + (H_1\delta_1 + H_2\eta_1)dz_1 + &(34)\\
&+ (H_1\delta_2 - H_1\varphi - H_2\varphi + H_2\eta_2)dz_2
\end{aligned}$$

Let us define a strategy H_j^*, $j = 1, 2$, such that the coefficients of dz_1 and dz_2 are always zero. In this case the dollar return on the portfolio dY^* would be non-stochastic. The portfolio requires zero initial investment, and in order to avoid arbitrage profits the expected return on the portfolio should also be zero. Hence, we impose the following equilibrium conditions:

$$\left\{\begin{array}{lll}
H_1(\delta_2 - \varphi) & -H_2\varphi - \eta_2 & = 0\\
H_1\delta_1 & +H_2\eta_1 & = 0\\
H_1(\pi - \mu) & +H_2(\beta - \mu) & = 0
\end{array}\right. \tag{35}$$

This system will provide a non trivial solution $H_j^* \neq 0$, $j = 1,2$, if and only if:

$$\frac{\pi - \mu}{\beta - \mu} = \frac{\delta_1}{\eta_1} = \frac{\delta_2 - \varphi}{\eta_2 - \varphi} \tag{36}$$

In expression (36) $\mu, \beta, \eta_1 \eta_2$ and φ can be estimated from the calibrated parameters of the stochastic processes of the interest rates. π, δ_1 and δ_2 have to be determined in order to guarantee the absence of arbitrage. From the first two equilibrium conditions in (35) we get:

$$\frac{\delta_1}{\eta_1} = \frac{\delta_2 - \varphi}{\eta_2 - \varphi} \tag{37}$$

Substituting for δ_1 and δ_2 we obtain:

$$F = P\frac{\partial F}{\partial P} - \frac{\varphi}{\eta_2 - \varphi}(\frac{\partial F}{\partial V}V - 1) - \frac{\eta_2}{\eta_2 - \varphi}\frac{\partial F}{\partial P}P \tag{38}$$

From the second and third equilibrium conditions in (35) we get:

$$\frac{\pi - \mu}{\beta - \mu} = \frac{\delta_1}{\eta_1} \tag{39}$$

From the definition of δ_1 we get:

$$P(\beta - \mu)\frac{\partial F}{\partial P} = (\pi - \mu)F \tag{40}$$

Using now the definition of π and substituting equation (38) into (40) we obtain the following second order, linear, parabolic partial differential equation for F:

$$\begin{aligned} \frac{\partial F}{\partial t} &= \frac{1}{2}\left[\frac{\partial^2 F}{\partial P^2}P^2(\eta_1^2 + \eta_2^2 + 2\eta_1\eta_2\rho) + \frac{1}{2}\frac{\partial^2 F}{\partial V^2}V^2\varphi^2 \right. \\ &\left. \frac{1}{2}\frac{\partial^2 F}{\partial V \partial P}PV\varphi\rho(\eta_1 + \eta_2)\right] + \frac{\eta_2 V \mu}{\eta_2 - \varphi}\frac{\partial F}{\partial V} + \frac{P\mu\eta_2}{\eta_2 - \varphi}\frac{\partial F}{\partial P} - \frac{\mu\varphi}{\eta_2 - \varphi} \end{aligned} \tag{41}$$

The price of the embedded prepayment option F must satisfy this differential equation, subject to the following boundary conditions:

$$\begin{cases} F[V(t), \tau = 0, P(t)] & = 0 \\ F[V(t), \tau, P(t)] & \geq \max[0, V(t) - B(t)] \end{cases} \tag{42}$$

4 Numerical Results

We employed the Alternating Directions Implicit (ADI) method in order to solve the parabolic partial differential equation (41). See, for example, Lapidus and Pinder [1982], for a general discussion of ADI. The various constants of the equation are obtained from the calibrated interest rate stochastic processes of section (3.2).

In the first experiment we solved the parabolic PDE making a simplified assumption concerning the price of a discounted loan with no risk of default $P(\tau)$. $P(0) = 1$

with certainty and in the special case when the interest rate is non-stochastic and constant over time we have that $P(\tau) = e^{-r\tau}$.

According to this assumption the partial differential equation (41) becomes the following:

$$\frac{\partial F}{\partial t} = \frac{1}{2}\left[\frac{\partial^2 F}{\partial P^2}P^2\eta_1^2 + \frac{\partial^2 F}{\partial V^2}V^2\varphi^2 + \frac{\partial^2 F}{\partial V \partial P}PV\eta_1\varphi\rho\right] \tag{43}$$

For a given coupon rate ($R_c = 7\%$) we obtained a three dimensional surface of the price of the option at discrete values of R and r. Both the short term and long term rates were discretized in step sizes of 0.01 in the range 4% to 15%. Figure 1 illustrates the value of the option for different, constant, values of R together with the appropriate boundary conditions. We observe that the value of the option is lower for higher mortgage refinancing rates. Similar results are obtained if we display the value of the option for fixed values of the short term rate.

Assuming a higher volatility of the long term rate, that is instead of using $\sigma_1 = 0.021$ and $\sigma_2 = 0.003$ as obtained from the calibration of the interest rate processes with historical data, we use $\sigma_1 = 0.025$ and $\sigma_2 = 0.1$. Figure 2 illustrates the difference between the option value calculated with the two volatility assumptions. As expected, the option has a higher price for higher volatility parameters.

Finally, we point out that it is possible to modify the boundary conditions to reflects the homeowner's inertia in refinancing new mortgages, even if the refinancing rates are favorable. This behaviour is captured in all prepayment models, that want prepayment activity being very low for new mortgages, and increasing gradually as the mortgage seasons. The well known PSA (i.e. Public Securities Association) standard, for example, has prepayment activity increasing from 0 to 6% within the first 30 months of the life of the mortgage, and remaining constant thereafter. This behavior can be explained if we assume that homeowners will incur some overhead cost in refinancing their mortgage, which we denote by $L(t)$. This cost is large for new mortgages, and is gradually reduced. The boundary condition (42) has to be modified to reflect tha fact that $V(t)$ must exceed $B(t)$ by more than the overhead cost $L(t)$ before the option is exercised. Hence, we have

$$\begin{cases} F[V(t), \tau = 0, P(t)] & = 0 \\ F[V(t), \tau, P(t)] & \geq \max[0, V(t) - B(t) - L(t)] \end{cases} \tag{44}$$

Figure 3 illustrates the boundary condition assuming an overhead cost function that decreases linealry from a large starting value to 3% within the first 30 months of the mortgage life.

5 Conclusion

We have developed a model for pricing the embedded option of a fixed rate martgage backed securities. The results of the model are intuitively appealing. Furthermore, the model captures the effect of different refinancing rates and interest rate volatilities, on the price of the option. The model is idealistic, i.e., it only takes into account the pure economic incentives for mortgage refinancing. Neverthless, the economic

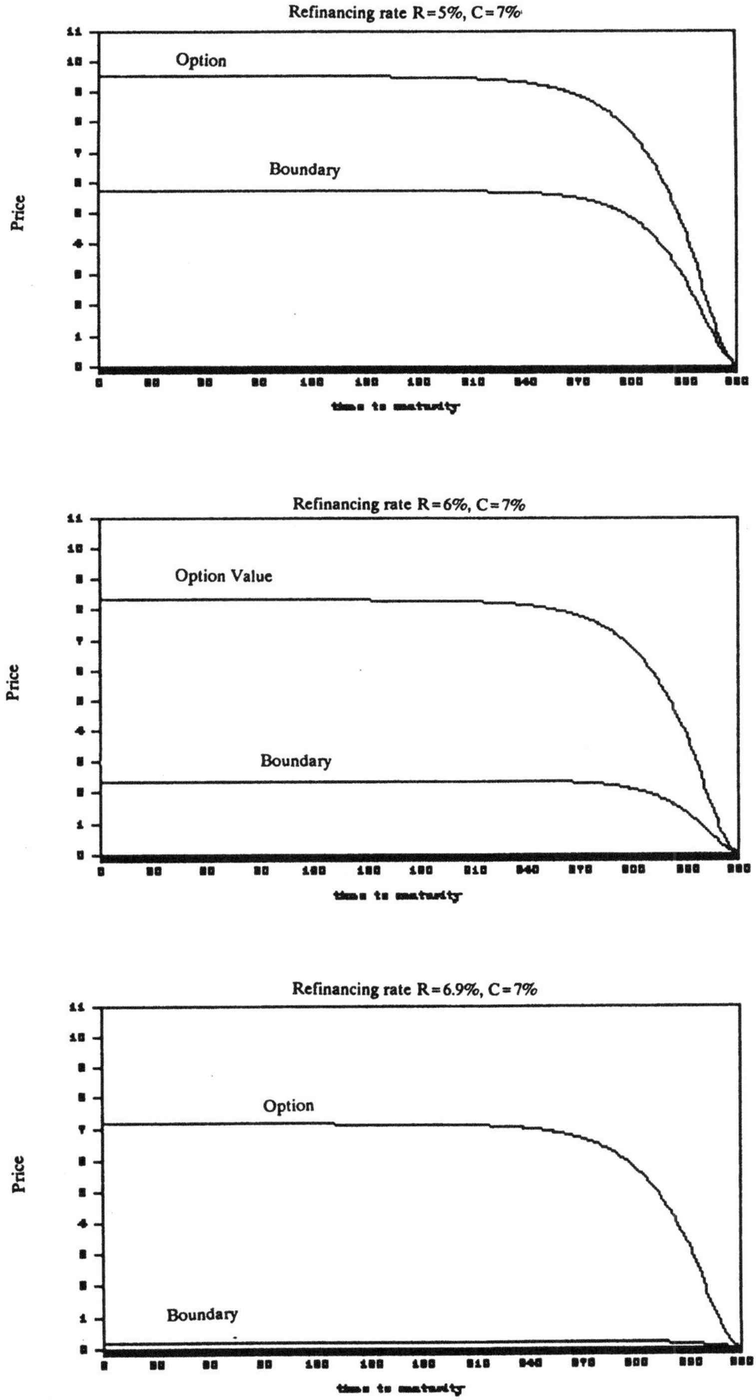

Figure 1: Value of the option and boundary conditions for different constant refinancing rates R_t, and $C = 7\%$

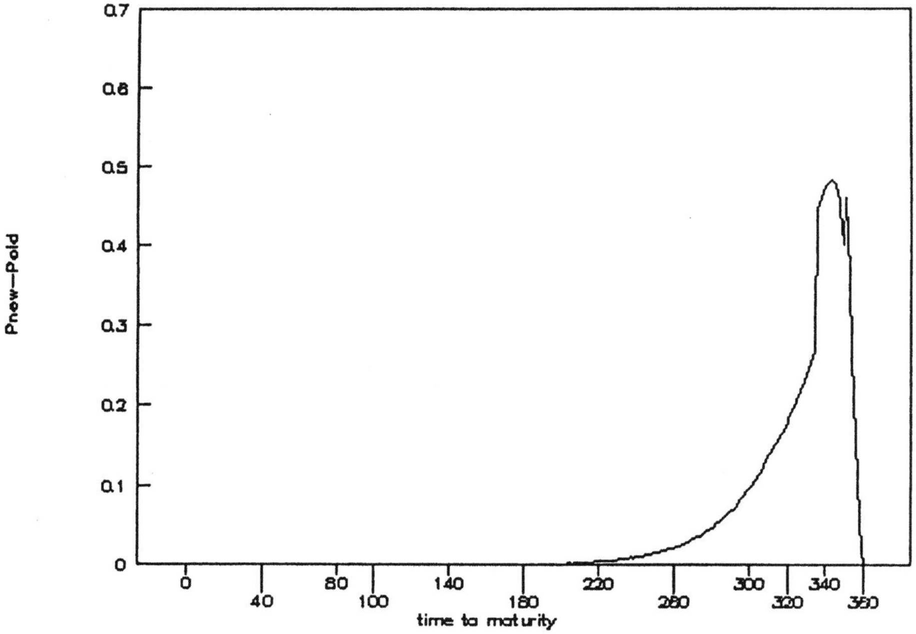

Figure 2: Difference between the value of the option for different volatility parameters. (Value of the option under high volatility, $\sigma_1 = 0.025, \sigma_2 = 0.1$ - Value of the option under low volatility $\sigma_1 = 0.021$, $\sigma_2 = 0.003$)

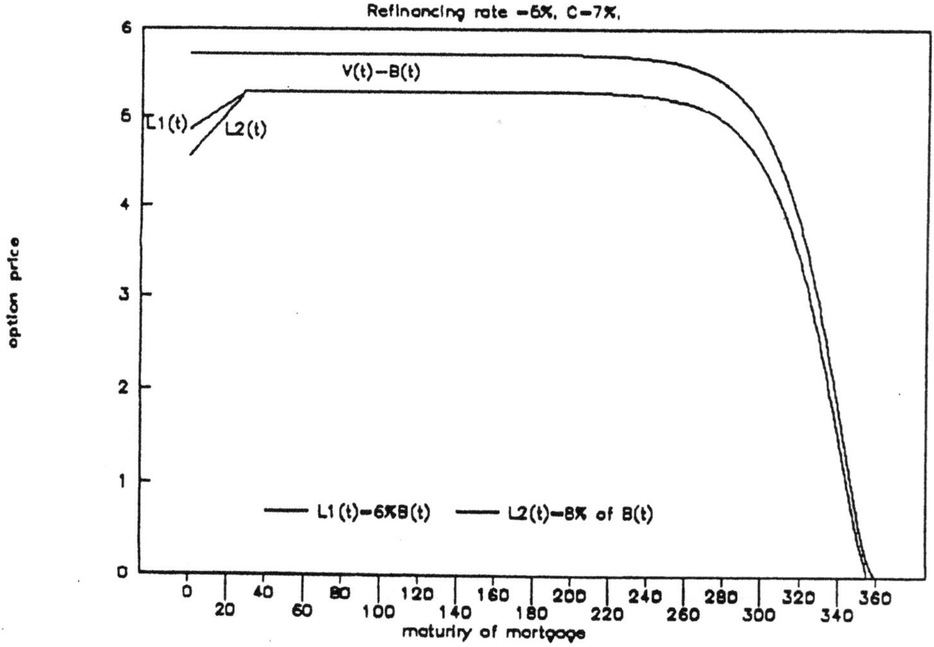

Figure 3: Value of the boundary conditions assuming a linearly decreasing overhead cost function, L_t, for different constant refinincing rates R_t and $C = 7\%$.

incentive is the strongest factor that affects refinancing decisions. Furthermore, non-economic factors can be captured by a suitable overhead cost function included in the boundary conditions.

References

Babbel D.F.(1988) Interest Rate dynamics and the term structure. Journal of Banking and Finance, 12.

Babbel, D.F. amd Zenios, S.A. (1992) Pitfall in the analysis of option- adjusted spreads. Financial Analysts Journal, (to appear).

Black F.J. and Scholes M.J. (1973) The pricing of options and corporate liabilities. Journal of Political Economy, 81:637–659.

Brennan, M.J. and Schwartz, E.S.(1979) A continuous time approach to the pricing of bonds. Journal of Banking and Finance, 3:133–155.

Brennan, M.J. and Schwartz, E.S. (1991) Convertible bonds: valuation and optimal strategies for call and conversions. The Journal of Finance, XXXII:1699–1715, Dec.

Brennan M.J. and Schwartz, E.S.(1985) Determinants of GNMA mortgage prices. AREUEA Journal, 13(3)(4687):210–228, Feb.

Brennan, M.J. and Schwartz, E.S.(1982) An equilibrium model of bond pricing and a test of the market efficiency. Journal of Financial and Quantitative Analysis, XVII:301–329, Sept.

Brennan, M.J. and Schwartz, E.S.(1979) Savings Bonds: Theory and Empirical Evidence. Monograph Series in Finance and Economics, Salomon Brothers Centers, New York.

Brooke, A. Kendrick, D. and Meeraus, A.(1988) GAMS: A User's Guide.

Cox, J.C. ,Ingersoll, J.E., and Ross, S.A.(1985) A theory of the term structure of interest rates. Econometrica, 53(2):385–407, March.

Golub, B. and Pohlman, L.(1991) Modelling the Current Coupon Mortgage Yield. Working Paper, Blackstone Financial Management.

Green, J. and Shoven, J.B.(1986) The effects of interest rates on mortgage payments. Journal of Money, Credit, and Banking, 41–59, February.

Hayre, L.S.(1990) Understanding option-adjusted spreads and their use. The Journal of Portfolio Management, Summer.

Hiller, R.S. and Eckstein, J.. Stochastic dedication: designing fixed income portfolios using massively parallel benders decomposition. Management Science. (to appear).

Hutchinson, J.M. and Zenios, S.A.(1991) Financial simulations on a massively parallel. Connection Machine. International Journal of Supercomputer Applications, 5(2):27–45.

Kang, P. and Zenios, S.A.(1992) Mean-Absolute Deviation Portfolio Optimization for Mortgage Backed Securities. Working Paper, Decision Sciences Department, The Wharton School, University of Pennsylvania, Philadelphia.

Kang, P. and Zenios, S.A.(1992) Complete prepayment models for mortgage backed securities. Management Science. (to appear).

Lapidus, L. and Pinder, G.F.(1982) Numerical Solution of Partial Differential Equations in Science and Engineering. John Wiley and Sons, New York, NY.

McConnel, J.J. and Singh, M.J.(1990) Prepayments and the Valuation of Adjustable Rate Mortgage Backed Securities. Technical Report, Krannert School of Management, Purdue University, Oct.

Merton, R.C.(1973) Theory of rational option pricing. Bell Journal of Economics and Management Science, 4:141–183.

Richard, S.F. and Roll, R.(1989) Prepayments on fixed rate mortgage backed securities. Journal of Portfolio Management, 73–82, Spring.

Schwartz, E.S. and Torous, W.(1989) Prepayment and the valuation of mortgage backed securities. The Journal of Finance, XLIV:375–392.

Zenios, S.A.(1991) Massively parallel computations for financial modeling under uncertainty. In J. Mesirov, editor, Very Large Scale Computing in the 21-st Century, pages 273–294, SIAM, Philadelphia.

Zenios, S.A. and McKendall, R.A.(1991) Pricing and Re-Pricing Mortgage-Backed Securities using Massively Parallel Computing. Report 91–12–01, Decision Sciences Department, The Wharton School, University of Pennsylvania, Philadelphia.

The Effects on Optimal Portfolios of Shifts on a Risky Asset: The Case of Dependent Risky Returns

Luisa Tibiletti
Istituto di Matematica Finanziaria
Facoltà di Economia e Commercio - Università
Piazza Arbarello, 8 I-10122 Torino (Italy)
Tel. +39-11-546805, Fax +39-11-544004

1. Introduction[1]

Many financial market factors may determine fluctuations in asset prices and force investors to change their evaluations on the random returns of their portfolios.

The aim of this note is to investigate how a risk-averse investor adjusts the proportions of the assets in his optimal portfolio, when he judges that the distribution of one asset return has undergone a stochastically dominating shift.

This problem, which is essentially one of comparative statics, has been widely explored in recent years. In working out the details of these changes for expected utility maximizing investors most research has been confined to portfolios consisting of one risky and one safe asset (see, for example, Arrow (1971), Fishburn and Porter (1976), Cheng *et al.* (1987), Landsberger and Meilijson (1990)). Recently, Hadar and Seo (1990) have generalized this literature by considering more than one risky asset. They assume, however, that the risky returns are independently distributed. Unfortunately, this assumption appears inconsistent with almost all real asset portfolios. Attempts have been made to remove this condition and some results have been yielded under rather complex restrictions on the investor's utility function and the return distributions (Kira and Ziemba (1980)) and in a special type of dependence (Meyer and Ormiston (1992)).

[1] *Acknowledgments*

I thank Lorenzo Peccati for his helpful comments and valuable suggestions. Obviously, I am completely responsible for any remaining errors.

In this note we enlighten the fact that the crucial point *is not the independence* among assets, but rather *the type of change in their dependence structure,* in the sense that will be specified.
We analyse the effects of two types of shifts in the distribution of one asset: shifts in the sense of the first-degree stochastic dominance (FSD) and second-degree stochastic dominance (SSD). We show that, under invariance of the dependence structure, sufficient conditions that guarantee non decreasing optimal investment proportion in the shifted asset are the same as those provided in the single risky asset case by Fishburn and Porter (1976), and in the independent case by Hadar and Seo (1990) and in the "deterministic" dependence case by Meyer and Ormiston (1992). Vice versa, if *the dependence structure is also modified,* then further conditions on the concordance between the new assets need to be added.

This paper is organized as follows. In the next section, the notation and assumptions of the two risky asset portfolio decision model are presented. In Sec. 4 and 5, we explore the effects of FSD and SSD shifts on a risky return in the cases of invariance and variance of the dependence structure. In the last section conclusions are provided and the directions of further research are suggested. An Appendix contains the proofs of the theorems stated in Sec. 4.

2. The Portfolio Allocation Problem with two risky assets

Consider a portfolio composed of a mixture of two assets, whose random returns are denoted by X and Y, respectively. Thus, the investor's final wealth is given by

$$Z = kX + (1-k)Y, \quad k \in [0,1] \tag{1}$$

with k being the proportion of the investor's funds invested in the asset with return X. The realizations of Z depend on those of X and Y and the selected value for k. Let H be the joint distribution function of (X,Y) and F and G the distributions of X and Y (called marginals). Let all the returns lie in the interval [0,A], so that Ran(F) = Ran(G) = [0,A].

The investor is assumed to choose k acting according to the von Neumann-Morgenstern criterion of maximization of the expected utility u

of the final wealth

$$E(u(Z)) = \int_{\mathbb{R}^2} u(z)dH(x,y), \tag{2}$$

where $z = kx + (1-k)y$.

Following Hadar and Seo (1990) and Meyer and Ormiston (1992), the distribution function of returns is assumed to be such that the agent attains a unique, regular, interior maximum[2] at k^*. This is defined by the first order condition

$$\int_0^A \int_0^A \psi(x,y;k^*)dH(x,y) = 0, \tag{3}$$

where $\psi(x,y;k^*) = u'(z^*).(x-y)$ and $z^* = k^*x + (1-k^*)y$ and u is assumed continuously differentiable on $[0,A]$.

Suppose that the distribution of returns H undergoes a change. If the distribution of one return is subject to a stochastically dominant shift, the abovementioned investor *may not necessarily increase the investment in that asset*. Our purpose is to provide restrictions on the distribution shifts and the investor's utility function which are sufficient to bring about no decrease in the investment in that asset.

In order to investigate them, it could be useful to represent the joint distribution in a way that emphasizes the separate role of the marginals and of the dependence structure. This statement is made more precise by the following lemma.

Lemma 1 (Sklar, 1959). *Let H be a two-dimensional distribution function with marginals F and G. Then, there exists a function $C:[0,1]^2 \to [0,1]$ such that*

(i) $C(a,b) = 0$, if $a=0$ or $b=0$ *and*
$C(1,b) = b$; $C(a,1) = a$ for all a, $b \in [0,1]$;

(ii) $C(a_2,b_2) - C(a_1,b_2) - C(a_2,b_1) + C(a_1,b_1) \geq 0$, whenever

[2] This simplification may possibly eliminate some cases that are of some interest.

$a_1 \leq a_2,\ b_1 \leq b_2;$

(iii) $\quad H(x,y) = C(F(x),G(y))$.

The function C (called copula) is unique on Ran(F) X Ran(G). *Therefore C is unique on* $[0,1]^2$ *iff F and G are continuous.*

It is worth mentioning that the copula can be regarded as a distribution function with uniform maginals.

Note. In this paper, in order to keep the main ideas in focus and for the sake of brevity, we restrict our attention to continuous marginals[3].

All the information about the dependence structure of a joint distribution function is therefore contained in the copula C. Moreover, the copula is independent of the individual distribution functions F and G. This property is crucial for our purpose, since it guarantees that *a distribution shift of a return does not modify the dependence structure between the returns.*

Let us explain this statement.
Suppose that the distribution of the first asset changes from F_0 to F_1. Denote by X_0 and X_1 the respective returns. We have that X_1 may be obtained from X_0 by means of a strictly increasing transformation, *i.e.*,

$$X_1 = h(X_0), \text{ where } h = F_1^{-1}(F_0)$$

where F_1^{-1} stands for the inverse[4] of F_1. Clearly, h is strictly increasing on Ran(F_0). Since C is invariant under strictly increasing transformations of its components (Schweizer and Wolff (1981)), it turns out that (X_0,Y) and (X_1,Y) have the same copula.

---

[3] For more details on the copula and its historical overview the reader is referred to Schweizer (1991).

[4] The inverse of F_1 is defined by

$$F_1^{-1}(t) = \sup\{x: F_1(x)<t\},\ t\in\mathbb{R}.$$

Note that

$$F_1(x) = P[h(X_0) \leq x] = P[X_0 \leq h^{-1}(x)] = F_0[h^{-1}(x)], \text{ for all } x\in\mathbb{R}.$$

Therefore $F_1(x) = F_0[h^{-1}(x)]$. Thus $F_1(h) = F_0$ and $h = F_1^{-1}(F_0)$. That proves our statement.

That suggests to distinguish between two types of shifts:

- a *simple* shift of one return distribution (consequently the return dependence structure is unaltered); or

- a shift of one return distribution and in addition a *change* of the return dependence structure.

3. Marginal shifts and fixed dependence structure

The following analysis applies to situations where an asset return distribution changes, but the dependence structure between the assets in the portfolio remains unaltered. For instance, these circumstances may occur if:

- the assets are independently distributed;

- the assets are dependently distributed (for instance, they are common stocks of two corporations in the same industry) but one asset may depend on further random factors, which are independent of the other asset;

- finally, the assets are dependent on one another, but some special changes may involve only one asset. An example is when one firm acquires another whose return is independent of the other asset in the portfolio. Or when a specific event such as a change in management in one firm, and this can modify the return of one asset without effecting the other.

Theorem 1. *Assume that*

- *The utility function u is twice (thrice for* SSD *only) continuously differentiable on* $[0,A]$ *and satisfies* $u'>0$, $u''\leq 0$, ($u'''\geq 0$ *for* SSD *only);*
- (X_i,Y), $i=0,1$ *have the same copula C and marginals* F_i, G;
- $\mathrm{Ran}(F_i) = \mathrm{Ran}(G) = [0,A]$;
- $E[u(kX_i + (1-k)Y)]$ *is maximized at* k_i^* *(and* k_i^* *is unique).*

If X_1 FSD X_0 *and* $u'(z)z$ *is nondecreasing then* $k_1^* \geq k_0^*$.
If X_1 SSD X_0 *and* $u'(z)z$ *is nondecreasing and weakly concave then* $k_1^* \geq k_0^*$

The proof of Theorem 1 is given in the Appendix.

Note. The above conditions on utility are the same as those found: (i) in the single risky asset case, by Fishburn and Porter (1976) for FSD shifts and by Rothschild and Stiglitz (1971) for mean preserving contraction shifts; (ii) in the independent case, by Hadar and Seo (1990) and (iii) in the "deterministic" dependent case by Meyer and Ormiston (1992).

The above conditions on u can be rewritten in differential terms.

- $u'(z)z$ *nondecreasing* means $R \leq 1$, where R is the *relative risk aversion coefficient,*
- $u'(z)z$ *weakly concave* means $u'''(z)z \geq -2u''(z)$.

Let us examine them for some common utility functions.

- **Quadratic utility**: $u(z) = z - z^2/(2B)$, where $z<B$. Since $R = z/(B-z)$, then
  $u'(z)z$ is *nondecreasing* iff $z \leq B/2$ or $B \geq 2A$;
  $u'(z)z$ is *weakly concave*: always.

- **Exponential utility**: $u(z) = -\exp(-\alpha z)$, $\alpha > 0$.
  $u'(z)z$ is *nondecreasing* iff $z \leq \alpha^{-1}$ or $\alpha \leq A^{-1}$;
  $u'(z)z$ is *weakly concave* iff $z \leq 2\alpha^{-1}$ or $\alpha \leq 2A^{-1}$.

- **HARA utility**: $u(z) = z^\gamma$, $0 \leq \gamma \leq 1$.
  $u'(z)z$ is *nondecreasing*: always;
  $u'(z)z$ is *weakly concave*: always.

- **Logarithmic utility**: $u(z) = Log(1+z)$.
  $u'(z)z$ is *nondecreasing*: always;
  $u'(z)z$ is *weakly concave*: always.

Theorem 1 shows *how* the optimal asset proportions *vary* due to a marginal shift. In the following we examine *how* the expected utility *varies*, because of a FSD marginal shift.

Theorem 2. *Assume that*

- *u is a nondecreasing utility function;*
- (X_i, Y), *i=0,1 have the same copula C.*

If X_1 FSD X_0 *then* $E[u(kX_1+(1-k)Y)] \geq E[u(kX_0+(1-k)Y)]$, *for all* $k \in [0,1]$.

The proof of Theorem 2 is given in the Appendix.

Remark 1. Theorem 2 shows that if X_1 FSD X_0, the investor's expected utility does not decrease if the asset proportions remain unaltered. Consequently, even the maximum expected utility does not decrease.

Remark 2. Note that the copula invariance *does not guarantee Pearson's correlation coefficient*[5] invariance. In fact, Pearson's correlation coefficient admits the following representation (Whitt (1976)):

$$r(X,Y) = \frac{1}{D(X)D(Y)} \int_0^1 \int_0^1 [C(a,b) - ab]\, dF^{-1}(a)\, dG^{-1}(b),$$

where *D* stands for the standard deviation. Clearly, *r* depends *both* on the copula and on the marginals.

On the other hand, copula invariance guarantees the invariance of the *measures of concordance*. Among the most familiar of these are Spearman's ρ and Kendall's τ and Gini's *G* coefficients (see the next section).

Remark 3. Note that the random vector $(g(X_0),Y)$ may differ from (X_0,Y) for *both* marginals and copula, if *g* is *not strictly increasing.* For example, for strictly decreasing transformations *g*, Schweizer and Wolff (1981) provide the copula transformation formulas.

Meyer and Ormiston (1992) called X_1 a *deterministic transformation* of X_0 if the representation

$$X_1 = h(X_0)$$

holds for *any* function *h*. Their results (see Corollary 1) do not hold in general. Nevertheless, they hold if *h* is *strictly increasing.* In this

---

[5] Meyer and Ormiston (1992) report two examples in order to show that, but they do not explain the motive.

hypothesis the copula is invariant and Theorem 1 guarantees their claim.

4. Marginal and dependence structure shifts

In the following, we explore the general case where the dependence structure between the portfolio assets is altered, too. That may occur, for example, when the assets under discussion are common stocks of two corporations of the same industry and one of these corporations decides to expand its production in a different industrial sector: consequently, the original association between the portfolio assets diminuishes.

A useful way to evaluate a dependence structure shift is to investigate its effects on the *concordance* between the random returns. The intuitive idea that underlies the concept of concordance is this: X and Y are concordant when large values of X go with large values of Y. Some attempts have been made to formulate this concept precisely (see Tchen (1980), Consonni and Scarsini (1982)). Since it is desirable that the definition is consistent with the idea of invariance with respect to monotone increasing transformations[6] of X and Y, a general notion has been introduced by using the concept of copula.

Definition 1. (Scarsini, 1984) Let (X_0,Y_0) and (X_1,Y_1) be two pairs of random variables with copulas C_0 and C_1, respectively. Then (X_1,Y_1) is *less concordant* than (X_0,Y_0) if $C_1(a,b) \le C_0(a,b)$, for all a, $b \in[0,1]$.

Now, we can state the following

Theorem 3. *Assume that*

- *The utility function u is twice (thrice for* SSD *only) continuously differentiable on* [0,A] *and satisfies* $u'>0$, $u''\le 0$, *(*$u'''\ge 0$ *for* SSD *only);*
- (X_1,Y) *is less concordant than* (X_0,Y)*;*

[6] Concordance is a matter of association of X and Y along a (strictly) monotone function and takes into account the kind of monotonicity, i.e., the more X and Y tend to cluster around the graph of a monotone function y=f(x). If f is increasing, the more they are concordant, vice versa, if f is decreasing the less they are concordant.
On the contrary, dependence is a matter of association along any function, i.e., the more X and Y tend to cluster around the graph of any function y=f(x), the more they are dependent.

- $\operatorname{supp}(F_i) = \operatorname{supp}(G) = [0,A]$;
- $E[u(k_iX_i + (1-k)Y)]$ *is maximized at* k_i^* (*and* k_i^* *is unique*).

If X_1 FSD X_0 *and* $u'(z)z$ *is nondecreasing then* $k_1^* \geq k_0^*$.
If X_1 SSD X_0 *and* $u'(z)z$ *is nondecreasing and weakly concave then* $k_1^* \geq k_0^*$

We omit the proof of Theorem 3 because it is quite similar to that of Theorem 1.

Remark 4. An intuitive explanation of the above less concordance condition is the one that guarantees non decrease of the favourable portfolio diversification effect.
Imagine, for example, the extreme case, in which the perfect discordance between X and Y holds. Let X be stochastically dominated by Y. In order to reduce the portfolio risk, a risk-averse investor may prefer to invest a portion of his wealth in the dominated asset X rather than in Y. Suppose, now, that the concordance between the two assets increases. Consequently, the *insurance effect* provided by X may appear reduced. So, even if X_1 "dominates" X_0 the investor may prefer not to increase the investment in this asset.

5. Conclusions and further research

In this paper we have extended the analysis of the optimal investment strategy for a two-asset portfolio to the case of the dependence structure changes and stochastically dominated shifts in one of the assets. Sufficient conditions for no decrease of the investment in the shifted asset are provided.
The main directions of further research seem to be

- the generalization of our results to portfolios with more than two assets and more than one stochastically dominating shift;

- the extension of the model studied by Ormiston (1992), where a firm is assumed to choose its output rate in order to maximize expected utility of profit. We intend to explore the case in which the profit is determined by multiple dependent random factors.

Appendix

Proof of Theorem 1

Denote by $\eta(k)$ the difference between the derivatives with respect to k of the expected utility under the two distributions of X; that is

$$\eta(k) = \frac{d}{dk} \mathrm{E}[u(kX_1+(1-k)Y)] - \frac{d}{dk} \mathrm{E}[u(kX_0+(1-k)Y)].$$

Denote by $H_i(x|y)$ the conditional distribution of X_i, given $Y = y$, then $H_i(x,y) = H_i(x|y)G(y)$, i=0,1. From the continuity of u', the above relation can be rewritten as

$$\eta(k) = \int_0^A \int_0^A (x-y)\ u'(z)\ d[H_1(x|y) - H_0(x|y)]\ dG(y),$$

where $z = kx + (1-k)y$. Integrating by parts, $\eta(k)$ results equal to

$$-\int_0^A \int_0^A [k(x-y)\ u''(z)+ u'(z)]\ [H_1(x|y) - H_0(x|y)]\ dx\ \ dG(y) \qquad (4)$$

Since $u'(z)z$ is nondecreasing and $u''\leq 0$, it follows that[7]

$$k(x-y)u''(z)+u'(z) \geq 0.$$

- Let X_1 FSD X_0. Since $F_1 \leq F_0$, it follows that
$$C(F_1(x),G(y)) - C(F_0(x),G(y)) \leq 0.$$

Therefore

$$H_1(x|y) - H_0(x|y) \leq 0, \text{ for all } x,\ y.$$

Consequently, $\eta(k) \geq 0$ for all $k\in[0,1]$. Evaluating

$$\eta(k_0^*) = \frac{d}{dk} \mathrm{E}[u(kX_1+(1-k)Y)]\Big|_{k=k_0^*} \geq 0 .$$

For the concavity of u implies $k_1^* \geq k_0^*$.

- Let X_1 SSD X_0. Thus

$$\int_0^x F_1(t)\ dt \leq \int_0^x F_0(t)\ dt \quad \text{for all } x\in[0,A].$$

Since C is continuously nondecreasing in each argument separately we have

$$\int_0^x C[F_1(t),G(y)]\ dt \leq \int_0^x C[F_0(t),G(y)]\ dt$$

---

[7] It suffices to note that

$$k(x-y)u'' + u' = u''kx - u''ky + u' = u''z - u''y + u',$$

where $u''z + u'\geq 0$ and $u''\leq 0$,

for all $x \in [0,A]$ and $G(y)$ fixed.

Since $C[F_i(t), G(y)] = H_i(t|y).G(y)$, it follows that

$$\int_0^x [H_1(t|y) - H_0(t|y)]\,dt \le 0 \quad \text{for all } x \in [0,A].$$

Integrating (4) by parts, it results

$$\eta(k) = \int_0^A \left(\int_0^x [H_1(t|y) - H_0(t|y)]\,dt \right) k\,[u''(z) + k(x-y)u'''(z) + u''(z)]\,dx\,dG(y)$$

where $z = kx + (1-k)y$. By concavity of $u'(z)z$ and $u''' \ge 0$, it follows that $\eta(k) \ge 0$ for all $k \in [0,1]$. Thus, $\eta(k_0^*) \ge 0$. For the concavity of u, it results $k_1^* \ge k_0^*$ and our claim comes out. □

Proof of Theorem 2. If X_1 FSD X_0, then (X_1,Y) dominates (X_0,Y),, *i.e.*,

$$E[u(X_1,Y)] \ge E[u(X_0,Y)], \text{ for all } u \in \mathcal{U}_2,$$

where $\mathcal{U}_2$ is the class of nondecreasing utility functions $u: \mathbb{R}^2 \to \mathbb{R}$ (see Scarsini (1988)). Imposing $u(x,y) = u(kx + (1-k)y)$ we have the desired result. □

References

ARROW K. (1971) *Essays in the Theory of Risk Bearing*. Markham. Chicago.

CHENG H.C., MAGILL M.J.P., SHAFER W.J. (1987) Some Results on Comparative Statics Under Uncertainty. *International Economic Review*. 28: 493-507.

CONSONNI G., SCARSINI M. (1982) Lo studio della concordanza nel contesto della teoria della variabilità superficiale. *Statistica*. 42: 69-77.

FISHBURN P.C., PORTER R.B. (1976) Optimal Portfolios With One Safe and One Risky Asset. *Management Science*. 22: 1064-1073.

HADAR J., SEO T.K. (1990) The Effects of Shifts in a Return Distribution on Optimal Portfolios. *International Economic Review*. 31, n.3: 721-736.

KIRA D., ZIEMBA W.T. (1980) The Demand for a Risky Asset. *Management Science*. 26: 1158-1165.

LANDSBERGER M., MEILIJSON I. (1990) Demand for Risky Financial Assets: A Portfolio Analysis. *Journal of Economic Theory*. 50: 204-213.

MEYER J., ORMISTON M.B. (1992) The Effect on Optimal Portfolios of Changing the Return to a Risky Asset: The Case of Dependent Risky Returns. presented at *Sixth International Conference on the Foundations and*

Applications of Utility, Risk, and Decision Theory, 16 June. Paris.

ORMISTON M.B. (1992) First and Second Degree Transformations and Comparative Statics Under Uncertainty. *International Economic Review*. 33: 33-44.

SCARSINI M. (1984) On Measures of Concordance. *Stochastica*. vol. VIII. 3: 201-218.

SCARSINI M. (1988) Multivariate Stochastic Dominance with fixed dependence structure. *Operations Research Letters*. 7, n.5: 237-240.

SCHWEIZER B. (1991) Thirty years of copulas. in G. Dall'Aglio, S. Kotz and G. Salinetti (eds.) *Advances in Probability Distributions with Given Marginals*. Kluwer Academic Publishers. Dordrecht.

SCHWEIZER B., WOLFF E.F. (1981) On nonparametric measures of dependence for random variables. *The Annals of Statistics*. 9, n.4: 879-885.

SKLAR A. (1959) Fonctions de répartitions à *n* dimensions et leur marges. *Publications de l'Institut de Statistique de l'Université de Paris*. 8: 229-231.

TCHEN A. (1980) Inequalities for distributions with given marginals. *Annals of Probability*. 8: 814-827.

WHITT W. (1976) Bivariate distributions with given marginals. *Annals of Statistics*. 4: 1280-1289.

Abstract: When the distribution of the return of a risky asset undergoes a stochastically dominating shift, a risk-averse investor may not necessarily increase the investment in that asset. The note provides conditions on the investor's utility function and on the change in the dependence structure among assets, that guarantee non decreasing demand for the abovementioned asset.

Key words: Finance-Portfolio; Stochastic Dominance

CORPORATE INVESTMENT AND DIVIDEND DECISIONS UNDER DIFFERENTIAL PERSONAL TAXATION: A NOTE TO MASULIS AND TRUEMAN'S MODEL

Bosco Stefano
Istituto di Matematica Finanziaria
Facoltà di Economia e Commercio
Università di Torino
10122 Torino, Italy

ABSTRACT

In this paper we consider Masulis and Trueman's model and introduce additional hypotheses as for taxation. We study the effects on the model of:

- differential personal tax rate at different dates,
- taxable bonds,
- tax credits on dividend income according to the Italian Tax Code,
- taxation on dividend income at all dates.

The contributions of the modified model are:

- dividend deferral is costly as in Masulis and Trueman's model and shareholders may prefer cash payments to the increase in the value of the firm determined by investment in real assets,
- investment in real assets depends on the method of financing, but it cannot be stated ex-ante that investment in real assets is always higher when the firm may avail of internal funds than when it is externally financed.

I. INTRODUCTION

The relationships between dividend policy, investment decisions and the value of the firm has been long debated in the finance theory.
In a word without taxes, transaction costs and information asymmetry [Miller and Modigliani (1961)] - but also when corporate and personal taxes are considered [Farrar and Selwyn (1967), Miller and Scholes

(1978)] - dividend payout policies do not affect the value of the firm and shareholders are either indifferent between dividend and stock repurchases or prefer stock repurchases as capital gains are taxed at a lower rate than dividends.

Empirical analysis shows that in the real world companies pay cash dividends to shareholders. Brennan (1970) suggests that dividend payouts should be considered as a datum in the CAPM: this means that dividend policy is relevant in determining the value of the firm. Ross (1977), Bhattacharya (1979), Hakansson (1982), Miller and Rock (1985) present theories based on the informativeness of dividend payouts. In a world with asymmetric informations, dividends are considered by investors as a signal of higher future cash flows (and profitability). That is why firms pay dividends despite the tax disadvantage of doing so. Rozeff (1982) suggests that a trade-off exists between the cost of external financing and the reduced agency costs when the firm increases dividend payouts: an optimal dividend policy may exist even though tax considerations are ignored.

Masulis and Trueman (1988) base their framework on the complexity of the individual and corporate tax system in the US and on diminishing returns to scale technology. An optimal dividend policy may exist because dividend deferral is costly for the firm. In fact, profitable investment opportunities in real assets may be less than the total internal funds available in the firm and security purchases may not be profitable from the shareholders' point of view. In this case cash dividends would be preferred by the shareholders.

Another consequence of the model is that the method of financing is relevant in determining corporate investment decisions. When the firm has internal funds, investment in the production process and in securities is higher than when new shares are issued and sold on the market to finance the investment. This means that from the shareholders' point of view external financing is more costly than internal financing (cash flows).

In Section II we consider additional hypotheses to Masulis and Trueman's model and verify the results.

II. MODIFICATIONS INTRODUCED AND NEW RESULTS

In addition to Masulis and Trueman's hypotheses we introduced in the model:

- differential personal tax rate at different dates (not only does the dividend tax rate differ across individuals according to their income, but it may change in time for an individual as he may move from one tax bracket to another),
- taxable bonds (municipal bond claims are not tax-exempt),
- tax credits on dividend income according to the Italian Tax Code (see Appendix B),
- taxation on dividend income at all dates.

A. INVESTORS' CONSUMPTION-PORTFOLIO DECISIONS

The investor's decision problem at date 0 becomes

$$\max_{c_0^i, x_i(s), m_i(s)} \quad U_i = u_i(c_0^i) + \sum_s \beta_i \pi_s u_i(c_1^i(s)) \quad , \tag{1}$$

subject to

$$\bar{c}_0^i + \sum_j \bar{x}_{ij}\left[(1-\delta_j)(v_j-q_j(1-\alpha t_c)) + \delta_j\left(v_j+(\bar{q}_j-q_j(1-\alpha t_c))\frac{1-t_{0d}^i}{1-t_c}\right)\right]$$
$$+ \sum_s \bar{m}_i(s)p_b(s) = c_0^i + \sum_s x_i(s)p_e(s) + \sum_s m_i(s)p_b(s) \quad , \tag{2}$$

$$c_1^i(s) = x_i(s)\frac{1-t_{1d}^i}{1-t_c} + m_i(s)(1-t_b) \quad , \forall\, s \tag{3}$$

$$x_i(s), m_i(s) \geq 0 \quad , \forall\, s \qquad s=1,2,\ldots,S.$$

Note that in the date 0 budget constraint (2) and in the date 1 consumption constraint (3), tax credits make the after-tax dividend be greater than in the hypotheses of Masulis and Trueman's paper (see Appendix A for notation).

The date 0 market value of each firm j is the after-tax present value of its state-contingent date 1 output

$$v_j = \sum_s p_e(s) f_j(q_j;s)(1-t_c) \quad . \tag{4}$$

In an externally-financed firm shareholders maximize the date 0 net market value of the firm before any shares are sold

$$v_j - q_j(1-\alpha t_c) \quad , \tag{5}$$

whereas in an internally-financed firm they maximize their personal cum-dividend valuation of the firm

$$v_j + (\bar{q}_j - q_j(1-\alpha t_c))\frac{1-t^i_{0d}}{1-t_c} \quad . \tag{6}$$

Investor i must choose between consumption at date 0 and investment in the security market so that to consume his endowment at date 1.
If investor i holds a one-unit equity claim, his marginal valuation of it is equal to its market price. The pricing relation is

$$p_e(s) = \frac{\beta_i \pi_s u_{is}}{u_{i0}} \frac{1-t^i_{1d}}{1-t_c} \equiv p^i_e(s) \tag{7}$$

whereas if he holds a one-unit debt claim, his marginal valuation of it is equal to its market price. The pricing relation is

$$p_b(s) = \frac{\beta_i \pi_s u_{is}}{u_{i0}}(1-t_b) \equiv p^i_b(s) \ . \tag{8}$$

The purchase of bond and equity claims is indifferent only for the investors in one tax bracket, denoted here as $t^w_{1d}(s)$, for which (7) and (8) both can be satisfied. Investors whose tax rate is less than $t^w_{1d}(s)$ would prefer the investment in the equity, as the after-tax profit is higher, whereas investors whose tax rate is more than $t^w_{1d}(s)$ would purchase bond claims.
It can be seen from (7) and (8) that $p_b(s)$ and $p_e(s)$ are related to $t^w_{1d}(s)$ by the following condition

$$p_e(s)\frac{1-t_c}{1-t^w_{1d}(s)} = p_b(s)\frac{1}{1-t_b} \tag{9}$$

and that shareholders are only the investors in the lower tax brackets (note that corporate control purposes are not considered in the model).

B. INVESTORS' PREFERENCES OVER THE PRODUCTION LEVEL OF THE FIRM WHEN SECURITY PURCHASES ARE PRECLUDED

When the firm is externally financed, shareholder i favours a unit increase in investment until

$$\bar{x}_{ij}\left(\frac{\partial v_j}{\partial q_j} - (1-\alpha t_c)\right) = 0 \quad , \tag{10}$$

that is as long as the resulting increase in the market value of the firm is greater than the cost of its financing. Expression (10) is consistent with the shareholder's maximization of the net market value of the firm.
When the firm is internally financed, shareholder i compares the increase in the market value with the dividend foregone at date 0 to finance the unit of investment, that is, he is favourable until

$$\bar{x}_{ij}\left(\frac{\partial v_j}{\partial q_j} - (1-\alpha t_c)\frac{1-t^i_{0d}}{1-t_c}\right) = 0 \quad . \tag{11}$$

Condition (11) maximizes the shareholder's personal cum-dividend valuation of the firm.
Note that shareholder i's valuation of the cost of financing - *i.e.*, the dividend foregone at date 0 - may be lower or higher than the effective cost paid by the firm for a unit increase in investment. Whether it is or not depends on his tax rate. It is lower when his tax rate is greater than the firm's tax rate on income, it is higher when his tax rate is less. In Masulis and Trueman's model the valuation was always lower, as there were no tax credits on dividends.
In conclusion, the effect of tax credits is that the level of investment in production under internal financing may be higher or lower than under

external financing. Whether it is or not depends on which shareholders are in the majority (those with a higher tax rate than the rate of the firm or those with a lower tax rate).
It follows that it cannot be stated ex-ante that an internally-financed firm would invest more in production than an externally-financed one which is identical as for structure of costs, shareholders and investment opportunities.

C. INVESTORS' PREFERENCES OVER THE FIRM PRODUCTION LEVEL AND SECURITY PURCHASES

1. THE CASE OF EXTERNAL FINANCING

The externally-financed purchase of bonds is profitable if and only if

$$\left[p_e(s)\frac{1-t_b}{p_b(s)} - 1\right] > 0 \quad . \tag{12}$$

Shareholders will favour the purchase if the increase in the net market value of the firm at date 0 is positive. From (9) it follows that it should be

$$t^w_{1d}(s) < t_c \quad . \tag{13}$$

When condition (13) is verified the purchase is profitable for all shareholders whereas when $t^w_{1d}(s) > t_c$ conflict will arise between the shareholders whose tax rate t^i_{1d} is less than t_c (they favour the purchase) and those whose tax rate is more than t_c (they do not favour the purchase).
The externally-financed purchase of shares is profitable if and only if

$$\left[p_e(s)\frac{1}{p_e(s)} - 1\right] > 0 \quad . \tag{14}$$

Shareholders are indifferent as they will get neither a profit nor a loss from the purchase.

In conclusion, an externally-financed firm may invest in bonds. Shareholders for whom the purchase of bonds is profitable would like the firm to invest in the production process until the present value of the after-corporate tax marginal product equals 1, with the remaining funds invested in the security. On the contrary, for investors whose tax rate at date 1 is less than t_c, the increase in the net market value of the firm at date 0 is negative: only the investment in the production process will be profitable. The firm will buy bonds if the first group of shareholders is in the majority.

2. THE CASE OF INTERNAL FINANCING

Under internal financing funds are limited and shareholders have to decide how to distribute them among dividends, investment in the production process and in securities.
The internally-financed purchase of bonds is profitable if and only if

$$p_e(s)\frac{1-t_b}{p_b(s)}\,\frac{1-t^i_{1d}}{1-t_c} - \frac{1-t^i_{0d}}{1-t_c} > 0 \quad . \qquad (15)$$

Shareholders will favour the purchase if the after-personal tax present value of the increase in the date 1 dividend is greater than the after-personal tax date 0 dividend foregone. For shareholders who do not predict they will change bracket - *i.e.*, for whom it will be $t^i_{0d}=t^i_{1d}$ -, from (9) it follows that (15) is equivalent to

$$t^w_{1d}(s) < t_c \quad , \qquad (16)$$

which is equal to expression (13) in the case of external financing - *i.e.*, there may be shareholders favourable to the purchase of bonds.
For shareholders who predict they will change bracket - *i.e.* for whom it would be $t^i_{0d}\neq t^i_{1d}$ -, (15) is equivalent to

$$t^w_{1d}(s) < \frac{-t^i_{1d}+t^i_{0d}+t_c-t^i_{0d}t_c}{1-t^i_{1d}} \quad . \qquad (17)$$

The left-hand side of (17) is the tax rate of indifference, the right-hand side is a function of shareholder i's tax rates at date 0 and at

date 1. Shareholders for whom condition (17) is verified want the firm to purchase bonds whereas the others do not find bonds profitable.
The internally-financed purchase of shares is profitable if and only if

$$p_e(s)\left(\frac{1}{p_e(s)}\right)\frac{1-t^i_{1d}}{1-t_c} - \frac{1-t^i_{0d}}{1-t_c} > 0 \quad . \tag{18}$$

The left-hand side of (18) is the after-personal tax present value of the increase in the date 1 dividend determined by the purchase of one share minus the after-personal tax value of the date 0 dividend foregone.
Shareholders who do not predict a change in their bracket will be indifferent whereas shareholders who predict that they will change bracket will favour the purchase if for them

$$t^i_{1d} < t^i_{0d} \quad , \tag{19}$$

that is, if their tax rate at date 1 is less than the tax rate at date 0.
In conclusion, the purchase of securities may be profitable for some shareholders. Whether the firm purchases securities or not depends on which shareholders are in the majority. There may be firms which buy bonds, firms which buy shares and firms which buy neither. If for shareholders both shares and bonds were profitable, they would choose the most profitable. They would want the firm to invest in the production process until the internal rate of return were greater than the profit given by securities and to invest the remaining funds in the security they find more profitable. The level of investment depends on the shareholders who are in the majority.

III. SUMMARY

In this paper we show that the method of financing is relevant in determining shareholders' decisions both with regard to the production process and with regard to the capital market, but it cannot be stated ex-ante that investment in real assets is greater in an internally-financed firm than in an externally-financed firm which has the same structure of costs, shareholders and investment opportunities. As far as the production process is concerned, an externally-financed firm's shareholders may favour a level of investment which is greater than the level which would be favoured if the firm were internally financed firm. As for investment in the capital market, there may be externally-financed firms which purchase securities and internally-financed firms which do not.

APPENDIX A: NOTATIONS

U_i = time-separable utility function of investor i, assumed to be increasing and concave in its arguments;

u_{is} = investor i's marginal utility of state contingent date 1 consumption;

u_{i0} = investor i's marginal utility of date 0 consumption;

β_i = discount factor of investor i for date 1 consumption;

π_s = probability of occurrence of state s;

c_0^i = date 0 consumption of investor i;

$\bar{c}_0^i$ = endowment of date 0 consumption claims of investor i;

$c_1^i(s)$ = consumption of investor i at date 1 if state s occurs;

$x_i(s)$ = number of equity claims held by investor i at date 0, each of which pays 1$ at date 1 if state s occurs;

$\bar{x}_{ij}$ = fractional endowment of firm j's shares held by investor i;

$m_i(s)$ = number of municipal bond claims held by investor i at date 0, each of which pays 1$ at date 1 if state s occurs;

$\bar{m}_i(s)$ = endowment of bond claims for state s held by investor i;

v_j = market value of firm j at date 0, ex-dividend if the firm internally finances production, or after new shares have been issued to finance production if the firm is externally financed;

$p_e(s)$ = date 0 price of an equity claim to 1$ in state s at date 1;

$p_b(s)$ = price at date 0 of a 1$ municipal bond claim in state s at date 1;

$p_e^i(s)$ = investor i's marginal valuation of a one-unit equity claim in state s;

$p_b^i(s)$ = investor i's marginal valuation of a one-unit debt claim in state s;

$\bar{q}_j$ = internal funds held at date 0 by a firm j, which internally finances its production;

q_j = firm j's chosen input level at date 0;

α = fraction of the input cost ($0<\alpha<1$) assumed to be immediately deductible from corporate income at date 0;

$f_j(q_j;s)$ = output of firm j at date 1 if state s occurs, where $f_j(.;s)$ is increasing and concave in q_j;

t_c = corporate tax rate on income;

t^i_{0d} = shareholder i's tax rate at date 0;

t^i_{1d} = shareholder i's tax rate at date 1;

t_b = tax rate on bonds; and

δ_j = 1 if firm j pays a dividend at date 0, before investment decisions are made,
= 0 if firm j does not pay a date 0 dividend.

APPENDIX B: TAX CREDITS ON DIVIDENDS

Dividends - *i.e.*, the after-tax profit of the firm - are an income for shareholders, both individuals and corporates, and taxes must be paid on them. The Italian Tax Code provides that shareholders determine their amount of taxation on the dividend plus tax credits to completely avoid double taxation. Note that tax credits are exactly equal to the amount of taxation paid by the firm and that individual shareholders' tax rate varies as a function of their total income whereas corporates' tax rate is t_c. If the shareholder's tax rate is less than the rate of the firm, he has a tax rebate from the State whereas if his tax rate is higher he must pay the State the difference between taxation and tax credits. When a corporate receives a dividend the tax credit is exactly equal to the amount of taxation paid on the dividend, that is, there is neither a debt nor a rebate from the State.

If d is the dividend paid to a shareholder, t_c is the tax rate of the firm and t_d is the shareholder's tax rate, the amount of tax credits is equal to $\frac{t_c}{1-t_c}$ of the dividend, that is $d\frac{t_c}{1-t_c}$, the dividend plus tax credits is $d\left(1 + \frac{t_c}{1-t_c}\right)$, the correct amount of taxation is $d\frac{1}{1-t_c}t_d$, and the debt/credit to the State is $d\frac{1}{1-t_c}t_d - d\frac{t_c}{1-t_c} = \frac{d}{1-t_d}(t_d - t_c)$.

If t_d is greater than t_c the amount is positive (*i.e.*, the shareholder must pay it to the State) , if t_d is less than t_c the amount is negative (*i.e.*, he has a tax rebate from the State).

REFERENCES

BHATTACHARYA S (1979) Imperfect Information, Dividend Policy, and "The Bird in the Hand" Fallacy. Bell Journal of Economics: 259-270

BRENNAN M (1970) Taxes, Market Valuation and Corporate Financial Policy. National Tax Journal: 417-427

FARRAR D, SELWYN L (1967) Taxes, Corporate Financial Policy and Return to Investors. National Tax Journal: 444-454

HAKANSSON N (1982) To Pay or Not To Pay Dividends. Journal of Finance: 415-428

MASULIS RW, TRUEMAN B (1988) Corporate Investment and Dividend Decisions under Differential Personal Taxation. Journal of Financial and Quantitative Analysis: 369-385

MILLER M, MODIGLIANI F (1961) Dividend Policy, Growth and the Valuation of Shares. Journal of Business: 411-433

MILLER M, ROCK K (1985) Dividend Policy Under Asymmetric Information. Journal of Finance: 1031-1051

MILLER M, SCHOLES M (1978) Dividend and Taxes. Journal of Financial Economics: 333-364

ROSS SA (1977) The Determination of Financial Structure: The Incentive-Signalling Approach. Bell Journal of Economics: 23-40

ROZEFF M (1982) Growth, Beta and Agency Costs as Determinants of Dividend Payout Ratios. Journal of Financial Research: 249-259

A Decision Support System for the Evaluation of Bond Options in Imperfects Markets

Benoît Daenen[1] & Bertrand Mareschal[2]
(1)Banque Degroof Luxembourg S.A. & Solvay Business School (ULB-Belgium)
(2) Solvay Business School (ULB-Belgium)

Since the end of the Bretton Woods agreement in 1971 the volatility of interest rates has sharply increased. Moreover, the competition between banks has significantly reduced the net margin account. These cumulated effects have among others induced the emergence of major financial innovations. One of them is the option on bonds.

The option on a bond - is a financial contract that gives the buyer the right but not the obligation to buy (sell) a bond at a specified price (striking price) and at or until a definite date (maturity). Those options have taken a significant market share of the over-the-counter market in the last years even in Belgium. In this context, it is important for financial investors to be able to evaluate properly the theoretical value of bond options.

There are many models that give a solution to the bond option valuation problem. One of the differences between those models is the time required to describe the equilibrium i.e. the continuous time versus the discrete time. Very few papers deal with the problem of option valuation in imperfect markets and we mention Gilster & Lee (1984), Figlewski (1989) and Merton (1990). These authors arrive to the conclusion that using continuous time to describe equilibrium implies infinite transaction costs as far as the arbitrage free portfolio has to be rebalanced continuously. One solution to tackle this problem is to consider the equilibrium in discrete time. In that environment the arbitrage free portfolio is rebalanced at discrete points in time at which transaction costs can be calculated.

We propose to deal with the Ho & Lee (1986) model corrected for the occurence of negative interest rates by Ritchken & Beonawan (1990). This model defines the term structure as the state variable in contrast with the Cox-Ingersoll & Ross (1985) model that relies on the instantaneous interest rate as the state variable. We will take into account endogeneously the transaction costs we are faced up with when running the arbitrage free portfolio. In order to describe the equilibrium we will rely on the technique proposed by Boyle & Vorst (1990). They propose to calculate the arbitrage free portfolio that takes into account the transaction costs starting from the maturity and going backward along the lattice defined by the path followed by the term structure until the evaluation date. No transaction costs will be considered neither at the maturity nor at the beginning of the option. They will not take into account the bid and ask spread on the risk free rate.

This paper focuses on the problem of implementing a bond option valuation decision support system on a microcomputer that is entirely interactive, user-friendly and menu driven with permanent help facilities. It includes two main parts. First we derive the model of bond option valuation in imperfect market. Secondly we estimate the sensibility of the premium of the options against the main variables i.e. term structure and transaction costs providing an idea of the bid & ask spread and thirdly we describe the program and its utilities. Finally we conclude.

1 The Model

To describe the Boyle & Vorst (1990) model applied to the case of bond options, we suggest the following notations:

- P(t, i, T) the price of the bond P at time t for the state i of the nature and maturity T. This bond might be assimilated as a zero-coupon bond. Moreover we suppose that P(T, i, T)=1,
- B(t, i, T) the price of the bond B at time t for the state i of the nature and maturity T. That bond offers n coupons c_j with j = 1, ..., n. Suppose that the bond B is equivalent to a bond portfolio P(t, i, j) with j= 1, ..., n, we will then obtain:

$$B(t,i,T)=\sum_{j=1}^{n} c_j P(t,i,j)+B(T,i,T)P(t,i,T)$$

The path followed by the bond P(t, i, T) is consistent with the Ho & Lee (1986) model and for a two period case the bond P(t, i, T) follows the lattice:

$$\begin{array}{ccc} P(0,0,T) & P(1,1,T-1) & P(2,2,T-2) \\ & P(1,0,T-1) & P(2,1,T-2) \\ & & P(2,0,T-2) \end{array}$$

This process has to respect the principle of absence of risk free arbitrage AR and the hypothesis of independence of the path followed in the lattice - markov process. Suppose the perturbation functions are those of Ho & Lee (1986) i.e.: 1) h(T) the perturbation function in the upper case - increase of the bond price - and h*(T) in the lower case and 2) δ a constant. From the absence of risk free arbitrage Ho & Lee (1986) get the following equilibrium condition:

$$\frac{1-h^*(T)}{h(T)-h^*(T)}=p(t,i,T) \quad \forall t,i,T$$

(1)

with p(t,i,T) a constant noted p. With the independence of the path followed condition, they get the following relationship between h(T) and h*(T):

$$h^*(T)=\delta^T h(T)$$

(2)

Ho & Lee (1986) show that P(t,i,T) takes for $\forall t,i,T$ the value:

$$P(t,i,T)=\frac{P0,0,T+t)}{P(0,0,t)}*\left[\frac{h(T+t-1)h(T+t-2)\ldots h(T)}{h(t-1)h(t-2)\ldots h(1)}\delta^{T(t-i)}\right]$$

(3)

In order to get notations comparable with those employed by Cox, Ross & Rubinstein (1979) to describe the binomial model of stock options, we define u as the multiplicative factor in the upper case - increase of the price of P - and d the multiplicative factor for the lower case. We obtain:

$$\begin{cases}\dfrac{P(t,i,T-1)}{P(t-1,i-1,T)}=u\\ \dfrac{P(t,i-1,T-1)}{P(t-1,i-1,T)}=d\end{cases}$$

and R = (1 + r) with r the risk free rate over one period obtained by $P(t,i,1)^{-1}-1$.

Ho & Lee (1986) show that to avoid risk free arbitrage opportunities the following relation must hold at any time t in the lattice and for any state i of the nature:

$$\frac{R-d}{u-d}\equiv \text{constant}=p$$

As proved by Cox, Ross & Rubinstein (1979), p is equivalent to a binomial probability and implied by the model. In a risk neutral p is equal to ½.

Suppose we focus on the example of a bond which has the following characteristics: the coupon is 9 percent per year with a nominal value of 100 percent and maturity of ten years. The coupon is paid annually. Suppose p= 0.5 and d = 0.9998. Over two periods, with a discretisation step of one month we get the following lattice:

- For the bond P over two periods:

$P(0,0,2)=0.9875$	$P(1,1,1)=0.9938$	$P(2,2,0)=1$
	$P(1,0,1)=0.9936$	$P(2,1,0)=1$
		$P(2,0,0)=1$

- For the bond B over 120 periods:

$B(0,0,120)=100.53$	$B(1,1,119)=102.01$	$B(2,2,118)=103.48$
	$B(1,0,119)=100.33$	$B(2,1,118)=101.80$
		$B(2,0,118)=100.15$

It is then possible to evaluate any contingent claim against that lattice such as bond options.

In order to present the model of bond option valuation in imperfect markets, we will proceed with the two successive steps: 1) a description of the model in absence of transaction costs with the procedure suggested by Ho & Lee (1986) and 2) introduction of the transaction in the hedging portfolio following a procedure suggested by Boyle & Vorst (1990).

1.1. Absence of transaction costs

Suppose that there exists a portfolio that consists of *delta*, noted $\Delta(t, i)$, bonds $B(t, i, T)$ and an investment in a risk free portfolio which value is $E(t, i)$. If it is possible to adjust the proportion $\Delta(t, i)$ and the value $E(t, i)$ such that at any time t+1 and for any state i of the nature that portfolio has the same payoffs as the option, noted $C(t, i, \tau)$ for a call, then to avoid risk free arbitrage that portfolio must have at any time t, and in particular at time t=0, the same value as the option.

Suppose that we are looking for the evaluation of a call, C(t, i, τ). It follows the binomial lattice:

$$\begin{array}{ll} C(0,0,1) & C(1,1,0) \\ & C(1,0,0) \end{array}$$

The hedging portfolio must copy the payoffs of the option and be such that the proportion invested in the bond B(t, i, T) and the value invested in the risk free portfolio follows the binomial lattice:

$$\begin{array}{ll} (\Delta(0,0), E(0,0)) & (\Delta(1,1), E(1,1)) \\ & (\Delta(1,0), E(1,0)) \end{array}$$

At the maturity of the option we get the equations:

$$\begin{cases} \Delta(1,1)B(1,1,T-1)+E(1,1)=C(1,1,0)+Ac(1) \\ \Delta(1,0)B(1,0,T-1)+E(1,0)=C(1,0,0)+Ac(1) \end{cases} \tag{1}$$

with Ac(1) the accrued interest of the bond B at time $t=1$. In absence of risk free arbitrage opportunities, that portfolio will have a value at time t=0 equal to:

$$\Delta(0,0)B(0,0,T)+E(0,0)=C(0,0,1)$$

with,

$$\begin{cases} \Delta(0,0)=\dfrac{C(1,1,0)-C(1,0,0)}{B(0,0,T)(u-d)} \\ E(0,0)=\dfrac{uC(1,0,0)-dC(1,1,0)}{R(u-d)}+\dfrac{Ac(1)}{R} \end{cases}$$

the solutions of the system (1).

In the multiperiod case, the procedure is identical since we consider the final value of the option, time t=T, and go back to time t=0 by a backward technique identical for the one period case.

Consider the example of a call at a strike price of 100 for a six months period. The underlying asset is the bond for which the path followed across the lattice has been described above. The hedging or replicating portfolio for any time t and state i of the nature is given by the table 1.

t = 0	t = 1	t = 2	t = 3	t = 4	t = 51	t = 6
(0.46; -46.05)	(0.64; -64.67)	(0.83; -84.28)	(0.96; -98.86)	(0.09; -101.9)	(1; -103.88)	C(6, 6, 0)
	(0.29; -29.08)	(0.47; -47.45)	(0.71; -72.72)	(0.96; -99.49)	(1; -103.85)	C(6, 5, 0)
		(0.11; -11.74)	(0.23; -23.89)	(0.47; -48.62)	(0.95; -98.93)	C(6, 4, 0)
			(0, 0)	(0, 0)	(0, 0)	C(6, 3, 0)
				(0, 0)	(0, 0)	C(6, 2, 0)
					(0, 0)	C(6, 1, 0)
						C(6, 0, 0)

Table 1: replicating portfolio without transaction costs

The value of the replicating portfolio at time t=0 is:

$$0.4652*100.5339 - 46.0526 = 0.7205$$

We get for the call:

$$\begin{array}{cccc} C(0,0,6)=0.7205 & C(1,1,5)=1.1150 & \cdots & C(6,6,0)=4.9478 \\ & C(1,0,5)=0.3350 & \cdots & C(6,5,0)=3.2398 \\ & & \ddots & \vdots \\ & & & C(6,0,0)=0 \end{array}$$

The put case is managed equivalently to the appropriate boundary conditions. We now consider the case of bond option valuation with proportional transaction costs.

1.2. Presence of transaction costs

We suggest to modify the system (1) in order to explicitly take into account a market imperfection i.e. the presence of transaction costs. The transaction costs are proportional to the amount treated and apply exclusively to risky bonds. There are no transaction costs neither at the initiation nor at the end of the contract in contrast with the Merton (1990) model. This latter proposes to take explicitly account of those transaction costs but Merton builds up his model for a two periods case only. So Boyle & Vorst (1990) propose to simplify the model but extend it to a multiperiod case - more than two period. We will analyse 1) the case of the long call and the short put position and 2) the short call and long put position. The first point deals with options with a positive *delta*, noted $\Delta \geq 0$ and the second with negative *delta*, noted $\Delta \leq 0$.

1.2.1 $\Delta \geq 0$

Take the case of a long call position, noted C(t, i, τ) and to simplify suppose that τ = 2. The preliminary version of the model implemented in absence of transaction costs implies that for τ = 1, we have to adjust the proportion invested in the risky asset B(1, i, T-1) such that the proportion Δ(0,0) takes the value Δ(1, 1) in the upper case and Δ(1, 0) in the lower case. This modification of the proportion in the risky bond must be executed taking explicitly into account the transaction costs due, with k the transaction costs by unity of value treated. We get from (1) the following system of equations:

$$\begin{cases} \Delta(0,0)\,uB(0,0,T)+E(0,0)R=\Delta(1,1)\,uB(0,0,T)+E(1,1)+k\left|\Delta(0,0)-\Delta(1,1)\right|\left(uB(0,0,T)-Ac(1)\right) \\ \Delta(0,0)\,dB(0,0,T)+E(0,0)R=\Delta(1,0)\,dB(0,0,T)+E(1,0)+k\left|\Delta(0,0)-\Delta(1,0)\right|\left(dB(0,0,T)-Ac(1)\right) \end{cases} \quad (2)$$

Those equations explain that the portfolio must generate the necessary amount to endogeneously cover the transaction costs. Those are to be covered under any circumstances justifying the absolute value on Δ(0, 0) and Δ(1, i). We must mention that in practice the transaction costs are due on the price net of accrued interest, noted Ac(t). This particularity of the bond market modifies significantly the Boyle & Vorst (1990) model.

The resolution of the system of equation (2) for Δ(0, 0) et E(0, 0) is not straightforward. Indeed, the system is non linear because of these absolute values. We also suggest to take into account the theorem[1] 1 of Boyle & Vorst (1990). It shows that the system allows for a single and unique solution for $\Delta(0, 0)$ et $E(0, 0)$ <u>if and only if</u>:

$$\Delta(1,0) \leq \Delta(0,0) \leq \Delta(1,1)$$

The system (2) becomes:

$$\begin{cases} \Delta(0,0)uB(0,0,T)+E(0,0)R=\Delta(1,1)uB(0,0,T)+E(1,1)+k\big(\Delta(1,1)-\Delta(0,0)\big)\big(uB(0,0,T)-Ac(1)\big) \\ \Delta(0,0)dB(0,0,T)+E(0,0)R=\Delta(1,0)dB(0,0,T)+E(1,0)+k\big(\Delta(0,0)-\Delta(1,0)\big)\big(dB(0,0,T)-Ac(1)\big) \end{cases} \quad (3)$$

We then obtain for $\Delta(0,0)$ and $E(0,0)$ the following solutions with $\overline{u}=u(1+k)$ et $\overline{d}=d(1-k)$:

$$\Delta(0,0)=\frac{C(1,1,0)-C(1,0,0)+k\big[B(0,0,T)\big(\Delta(1,1)u+\Delta(1,0)d\big)-Ac(1)\big(\Delta(1,1)-\Delta(1,0)\big)\big]}{B(0,0,T)(\overline{u}-\overline{d})-2kAc(1)}$$

and,

$$E(0,0)=\frac{C(1,0,0)(\overline{u}B(0,0,T)-kAc(1))-C(1,1,0)(\overline{d}B(0,0,T)-kAc(1))}{R\big[B(0,0,T)(\overline{u}-\overline{d})-2kAc(1)\big]}$$
$$+\frac{k\big[\Delta(1,0)\big(\overline{u}B(0,0,T)-kAc(1)\big)\big(Ac(1)-dB(0,0,T)\big)+\Delta(1,1)\big(\overline{d}B(0,0,T)-kAc(1)\big)\big(Ac(1)-\overline{u}B(0,0,T)\big)\big]}{R\big[B(0,0,T)(\overline{u}-\overline{d})-2kAc(1)\big]}$$

Someone may want to change in the equilibrium condition of Cox, Ross et Rubinstein (1979) u by $\overline{u}$ and d by $\overline{d}$. But, as shown in Boyle & Vorst (1990) this modification of the equilibrium condition is not realistic since under those circumstances a systematic bias exists. Indeed, if we consider the upper case, C(1, 1, 1), to the fair value of the option $\Delta(1,1)uB(0,0,T)+E(1,1)$, is substituted the value $\Delta(1,1)\overline{u}B(0,0,T)+E(1,1)$ from the new equilibrium condition which is different from the fair value if $k \neq 0$.

1.2.2. $\Delta \leq 0$

The condition that allows the existence and unicity of the solution (2) for the unknowns $\Delta(0, 0)$ and $E(0, 0)$ is slightly different in the case $\Delta \leq 0$. The theorem 4 of Boyle & Vorst

---

1 Theorem 1 in Boyle & Vorst (1990)

(1990) proves that there exists a unique solution <u>if and only if</u> both following conditions are encountered:

$$\begin{cases} u(1-k) \geq R(1+k) \\ d(1+k) \leq R(1-k) \end{cases}$$

Relying on that theorem and with $\bar{u} = u(1-k)$ et $\bar{d} = d(1+k)$ we get for $\Delta(0, 0)$ and $E(0, 0)$ the solutions:

$$\Delta(0,0) = \frac{C(1,1,0) - C(1,0,0) - k\left[B(0,0,T)\left(\Delta(1,1)u + \Delta(1,0)d\right) - Ac(1)\left(\Delta(1,1) - \Delta(1,0)\right)\right]}{B(0,0,T)(\bar{u} - \bar{d}) + 2kAc(1)}$$

(4)

and,

$$E(0,0) = \frac{C(1,0,0)\left(\bar{u}B(0,0,T) + kAc(1)\right) - C(1,1,0)\left(\bar{d}B(0,0,T) - kAc(1)\right)}{B(0,0,T)(\bar{u} - \bar{d}) + 2kAc(1)} - \frac{k\left[\Delta(1,0)\left(\bar{u}B(0,0,T) - kAc(1)\right)\left(Ac(1) - dB(0,0,T)\right) + \Delta(1,1)\left(\bar{d}B(0,0,T) - kAc(1)\right)\left(Ac(1) - uB(0,0,T)\right)\right]}{B(0,0,T)(\bar{u} - \bar{d}) + 2kAc(1)}$$

(5)

We are now going to illustrate this model and provide calculation of bond options in presence of transaction costs. We suggest transaction costs of 5 basis points i.e. 0.05%[2].

Consider successively the case of the long call C(0, 0, 6) and the short put P(0, 0, 6) and secondly the short call and long put position. Remind that the option has a maturity date of 6 months and a striking price of 100 - the bond is identically defined for the valuation of bond options in absence of transaction costs. The table 2 gives the price, the delta[3] and the gamma[4].

---

2 That proportion of transaction costs corresponds to the mean bid and ask spread on the Belgian State Bonds or OLO.

3 It defines the sensibility of the price of the option to a marginal increase of the bond price.

4 It defines the sensibility of the delta of the option to a marginal increase of the bond price.

Option	Price	Delta	Gamma
Long C(0, 0, 6)	0.7814	0.4729	0.1976
C(0, 0, 6)[5]	0.7205	0.4652	0.2098
Short C(0, 0, 6)	-0.6822	-0.4667	-0.2210
Long P(0, 0, 6)	0.8237	-0.4747	0.1972
P(0, 0, 6)[6]	0.7697	-0.4742	0.2092
Short P(0, 0, 6)	-0.7310	0.4728	-0.2205

Table 2: Bond option valuation in presence of transaction costs

We will go into details about the case of the long call position. The portfolio that replicates the payoffs of the option is obtained by the composition of a portfolio invested in a long position of $\Delta(t, i)$ units in the underlying bond of coupon 9 and nominal value 100 and a short position in a risk free asset for a value of $E(t, i)$. That portfolio for which values will be given by the solutions of the equations (4) et (5), follows the binomial lattice described at table 3:

t = 0	t = 1	t = 2	t = 3	t = 4	t = 5	t = 6
(0.47; -46.79)	(0.64; -64.37)	(0.82; -83.17)	(0.96; -98.49)	(0.99, -102.2)	(1.00, -103.8)	C(6, 6, 0)
	(0.31; -30.79)	0.48; -48.30)	(0.70; -71.93)	(0..95, -98.2)	(1.00, -103.7)	C(6, 5, 0)
		(0.14; -13.68)	(0.26; -26.23)	(0.49; -50.26)	(0.93, -96.18)	C(6, 4, 0)
			(0.00; 0.00)	(0.00; 0.00)	(0.00; 0.00)	C(6, 3, 0)
				(0.00; 0.00)	(0.00; 0.00)	C(6, 2, 0)
					(0.00; 0.00)	C(6, 1, 0)
						C(6, 0, 0)

Table 3: replicating portfolio of a long call position with transaction costs.

[5] No transaction costs
[6] No transaction costs

The value of the replicating portfolio at time t equal to 0 is:

$$0.47*100.53-46.7$$

We are now going to estimate the sensibility of the price of the option - or premium to different explanatory variables.

2. Sensitivity Analysis

This section deals with the sensitivity of the premium of the option to variations of the main explanatory variables. The first explanatory variable - the term structure - can be estimated by different models. We will suggest the following models: McCulloch (1971), Vasicek & Fong (1982) and Cox-Ingersoll & Ross (1985). The second set of explanatory variables is the transaction costs level and main variables such as the maturity and the position of the striking price *vis-à-vis* the bond price. We will analyse these two explonatory variables.

2.1. Term structure estimation's method

If we consider the example described above and try to evaluate the bond with the different models we get for the long term bond the prices at time t equal to 30/10/1987:

- McCulloch (1971): 96.20
- Vasicek & Fong (1982): 102.19
- Cox-Ingersoll & Ross (1985): 100.53

We observe that the differences are large and will imply significant variation in bond option prices. In order to explain those differences, we must mention that at that time such a maturity did not exist. That would suggest that the approximations proposed by McCulloch (1971) and Vasicek & Fong (1982) are not reliable since the conditions to apply the theorem that allows the approximations of a continuous function by a suite of polynoms (Theorem of Weierstrass) are no more valid.

The graphics 1 for short term maturities and 2 for long term maturities illustrate the shape of the term structure estimated by the model of McCulloch (1971), Vasicek & Fong (1982) and Cox-Ingersoll & Ross (1985) for Belgium October 30th, 1991. This latter provides sufficiently stable shape across the maturities in comparison to the previous two models. We then retain the model of Cox-Ingersoll & Ross (1985) in order to manage the other premium sensibilities.

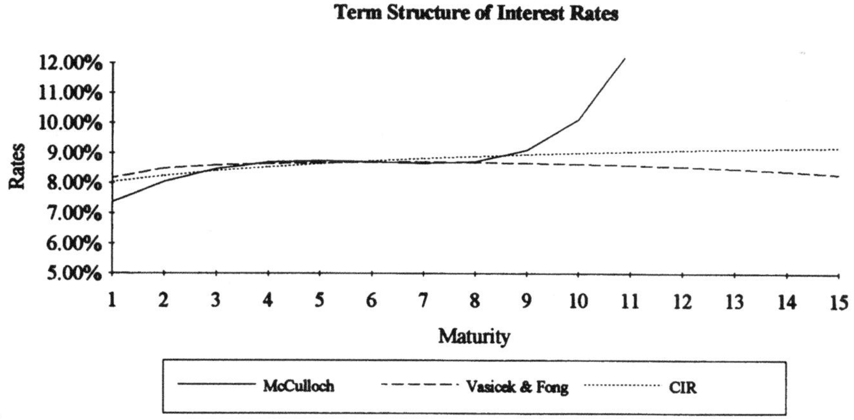

Graphic 1: comparison of techniques to estimate the term structure of interest rates 30/10/87- short term view

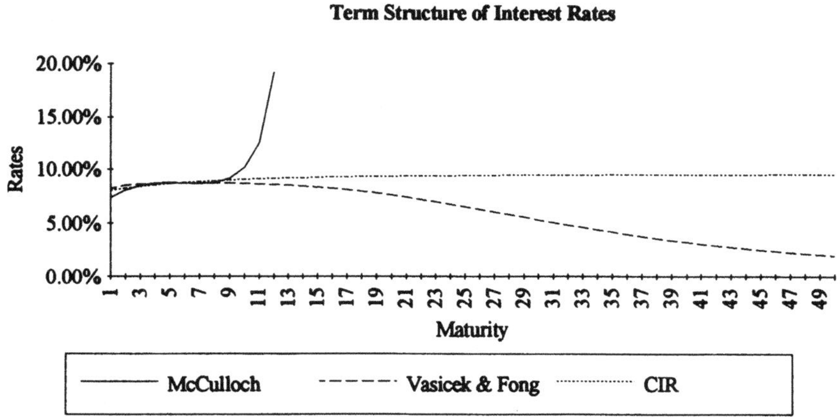

Graphic 2: comparison of techniques to estimate the term structure of interest rates 30/10/87 - long term view

2.2. Transaction costs and main variables

We are going to estimate the sensibility of the premium of the option to transaction costs as far as the maturity, the position of the striking price *vis-à-vis* the bond price and the slope of the term structure is concerned. We will consider the following characteristics:

- The term structure is estimated by the Cox-Ingersoll & Ross model (1985) with the estimates of end October 87 and October 91 for respectively the ascending and descending term structure. These are obtained by the procedure described by Brown & Dybvig (1986). For the flat term structure we will consider a rate of 8.5%.

- The bond on which the option will rely is the same as in section 1: 9 percent per year, 100 as nominal and a ten years maturity. The options considered will be defined for different maturities and striking prices. The maturity values enclose 6 months to 5 years and the striking price is either at-the-money or out-of-the-money and in-the-money by 2 units of value. For example with the flat term structure we will carry 103.28 as at-the-money striking price, 101.28 and 105.28 for the two other striking prices.
- The transaction costs are of 5 basis points.

All the results are presented in table 4.

We observe that the bid and ask spread, defined as the difference between the ask price less the bid price is an increasing function of the maturity of the option. A maximum of 0.7217 (in-the-money and descending term structure) to a minimum of 0.0443 (out-of-the-money and descending term structure) has been detected. For short term maturity, the spread of the at-the-money option is the highest except for the out-of-the-money call spread (descending term structure) and the in-the-money put spread (descending term structure). The explanation is to be found in the gamma of the at-the-money option which presents the highest value.

	Call spread					
In-the-money	6M	1Y	2Y	3Y	4Y	5Y
Ascending	0.0752	0.1864	0.3028	0.3831	0.4397	0.4842
Flat	0.081	0.1888	0.3203	0.4152	0.4748	0.5031
Descending	0.0701	0.1841	0.3479	0.4941	0.6184	0.7217
At-the-money						
Ascending	0.0875	0.1456	0.2107	0.2517	0.2754	0.286
Flat	0.1284	0.1684	0.2574	0.3185	0.3478	0.3473
Descending	0.098	0.1749	0.2951	0.4002	0.473	0.6394
Out-of-the-money						
Ascending	0.0528	0.0975	0.1472	0.1774	0.1907	0.1908
Flat	0.1284	0.1684	0.2574	0.3185	0.3478	0.3473
Descending	0.0591	0.1288	0.2257	0.3025	0.3567	0.3851

			Put spread			
Out-of-the-money						
Ascending	0.0512	0.1072	0.1895	0.256	0.3068	0.3313
Flat	0.0591	0.1075	0.1793	0.2367	0.2876	0.3255
Descending	0.0443	0.0776	0.1224	0.1491	0.1624	0.1614
At-the-money						
Ascending	0.0857	0.1483	0.2576	0.3607	0.4523	0.5189
Flat	0.0933	0.1489	0.237	0.3177	0.3947	0.4629
Descending	0.0895	0.1319	0.192	0.2335	0.2614	0.2741
In-the-money						
Ascending	0.0638	0.1478	0.2873	0.4235	0.5476	0.6477
Flat	0.0639	0.1513	0.2776	0.3945	0.5094	0.6219
Descending	0.068	0.1493	0.245	0.3144	0.3673	0.4051

Table 4: Bond option spread analysis

Graphics that present the evolution of the spread can be found in the appendix.

3. The Program

The following section describes the decision support system for the valuation of bond options in imperfect markets. It is written in Turbo Pascal under MS-Dos. This program provides us with the valuation of bond options and options on bond futures. It also identifies the expected value of the term structure and computes the control parameters that allow the construction of the hedging portfolio. It finally gives equilibrium prices for the bond and the future.

Utilities make possible the initialisation of the program by imposing a term structure to the system specified by the estimated parameters of the McCulloch (1971), Vasicek & Fong (1982) or Cox-Ingersoll & Ross (1985) models. For the monetary market for which spot rates exist the system allows the specification of rates for maturities of 1, 2, 3, 6 and 12 months. The term structure has to be defined by the mid rates in order to proceed to the valuation of bond option in imperfect markets.

Beside the parameters that characterise the term structure, the model allows the identification of those that synthesise the expected term structure. This implies that a procedure has been implemented that provides endogeneously the estimation of the optimal parameters π et δ for the model of Ho & Lee (1986) but also the possibility to implement exogeneously these parameters. In the case where the choice relies only on the volatility parameter, the system imposes the implicit probability π to be equal to 1/2. In that case we have to establish the correspondence between the volatility of the short term rate and the δ parameter of the Ho & Lee (1986) model. We obtain:

$$\delta = e^{-\left(\frac{\sigma / N_p^2}{\sqrt{0.25 \bullet N_p}}\right)}$$

where,

- σ is the volatility of the short term rate r
- Np is the number of periods between two years (i.e. if the period between two dates in the lattice is the month then Np will be equal to 12).

The endogenous research is executed using the downhill simplex method of Nelder & Mead (in Press, W.H. et al 1989) because of its tractability and convergence properties despite the speed that would suggest an other algorithm. The program also allows us to take into account proportional transaction costs that will be managed with the model described in section 1 and entered into the program in percent. Moreover all the results can be saved on ASCII files and initial settings such as term structure estimated parameters can be either exported or imported from ASCII files.

The user-friendliness of the program is enhanced by the availability of a context sensitive on-line help facility and the use of straightforward menus to access the different modules.

The diagram 1 presents a global insight into the program of bond option valuation in imperfect markets, detailing the main modules.

The main menu contains four modules: 1. Evaluations' programs, 2. Update of the current term structure, 3. Load an existing configuration and 4. the Control of the procedure.

The first module calculates the expected term structure and proceeds to the valuation of bond, future and options on bond and future with the term structure and deformation parameters available. This is the main module as far as valuation is concerned. We will describe it in more details.

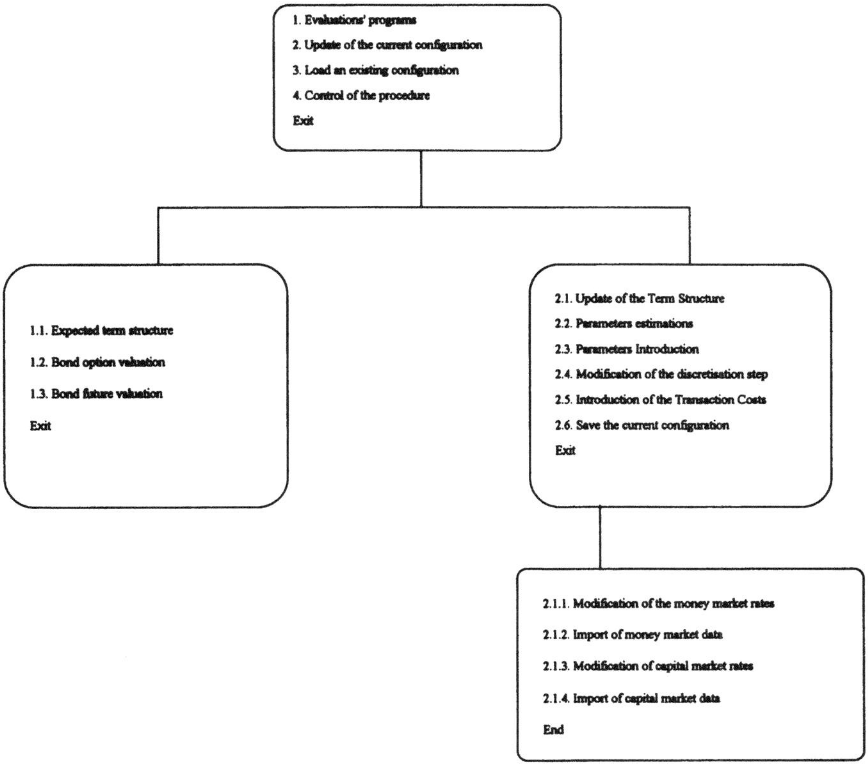

Diagram 1: Modules description

The expected term structure module calculates the average of expected term structures at discrete points in the future. The range of those points is limited to 12 months and the expected term structure accessible by pressing arrow keys. The bond option valuation module contains two main parts: the first part is dedicated to the input of the bond characteristics i.e. the final payoff, the coupon, first coupon date and the maturity date. The time spread between coupon dates is 12 periods, the period Δt is defined as one month. Then the decision support system provides the option screen. This final screen allows the option characteristics to be loaded and by pressing on the F10 key calculates the option price, its delta and gamma. The same sequence is to be found in the future and future option module.

The second main module entitled "Update of the current term structure", gives the opportunity to update the parameters that resume the evolution of the term structure. Selecting this module we get six choices: 2.1. Update of the term structure, 2.2. Parameters estimation, 2.3. Parameters introduction, 2.4. Modification of the discretisation step, 2.5. Introduction of transaction costs and 2.6. Save the current configuration.

The Update of the term structure allows the input of the rates of the monetary market either manually or by loading an ASCII file. It also allows the input of the current term structure expressed by the parameters of McCulloch (1971) or Vasicek & Fong (1982) or Cox-Ingersoll & Ross (1985) model. To be more specific for this latter model, the parameters are those estimated by the Brown & Dybvig (1986) method.

The other screens are designed to configure the lattice i.e. the evaluation of the Ho & Lee (1986) parameters π et Δ or their introduction exogeneously, the modification of the path of discretisation, the introduction of proportional transaction costs and finally the opportunity to save the configuration.

4. Conclusion

This paper describes a decision support system that evaluates bond and future bond options in imperfect markets. We rely on a discrete time model that allows us to take into account proportional transaction costs. We have developed the formula for the call and for the put and applied those.

We have estimated the sensibilities of the bond option price to different explanatory variables and identified the importance of an appropriate term structure estimation. We confirm the superiority of the Cox-Ingersoll & Ross (1986) method of estimation. We have empirically observed that the transaction costs increase with the maturity of the option, are influenced by the slope of the term structure and the relative position of the price in comparison with the exercise price. We have estimated the bid and ask spread at 0.0443 to 0.7217 for 5 basis points of spread in the underlying asset i.e. the bond. This level confirms the Figlewski (1989) empirical finding that the bid and ask spread in option does not cover the transaction costs accrued when running the hedge.

We have described the decision support system that generates the option prices and calculates the delta and gamma. Those control parameters take into account the transaction costs and allow to establish the coverage position in imperfect makets.

References

Boyle & Vorst (1990), " Option Replication in Discrete Time with Transaction Costs", AFFI proceedings, July 1991

Brown & Dybvig (1986), "The Empirical Investigation of the Cox-Ingersoll & Ross Theory of the Term Structure of Interest Rates", *Journal of Finance*, july

Cox-Ingersoll & Ross (1985), "A Theory of Term Structure of Interest Rates", *Econometrica*, mars, n°2

Cox, Ross & Rubinstein (1979), "Option Pricing: a simplified approach", *Journal of Financial Economics*, vol.7, pp. 229-263

Figlewski (1989), "Options Arbitrage in Imperfect Markets", Journal of Finance, vol.44, pp. 1289-1311,

Gilster & Lee (1984), "The Effect of Transaction Costs and Different Borrowing and Lending Rates on the Option Pricing Model: a Note", Journal of Finance, vol 43, pp. 1215-1221,

Ho & Lee (1986), " Term Structure Movements and Pricing Interest Rate Contingent Claims", *Journal of Finance*, vol.41, pp. 1011-1029

McCulloch, J. (1971)," Measuring the Term Structure of Interest Rates", *Journal of Business*, January,

Merton (1990), "Continuous Time Finance", Basil Blackwell Ltd., Oxford, (see Chapter 14, Section 14.2),

Press W.H., Vetterling B.P., Tenkolsky S.A. & W.T. Vetterling (1989), "Numerical Recipes in Pascal", *Cambridge University Press*

Ritchken & Beonawan (1990), " On Arbitrage-free Pricing of Interest Rate Contingent Claims", *Journal of Finance*, vol.45, pp. 259-264

Vasicek, O. & G. Fong (1982)," Term Structure Modeling Using Exponential Splines", *Journal of Finance*, vol 37,

Pure Capital Rationing Problems: How to Bury Them and Why

Maria Elena De Giuli Umberto Magnani *

(University of Pavia, Italy)

Abstract

A usual version of *pure capital rationing problems* with *consistent optima* is recalled in Sec. 1. Sec. 2 criticizes some known results and clarifies the assumptions hidden there; their proofs are made quicker in Sec. 4. By means of a very general theorem of the alternative for linear systems (see Sec. 7), three theorems in Sec. 3 put forward necessary and sufficient conditions for the existence of consistent optima, according to the various assumptions on the discounting factors. Sec. 5 points out that such an optimum leads to a vicious circle in fixing the budgets and looks like a machine which doubles their financial value. Sec. 6 shows that these worrying results come from an improper fitting of a well-known application of linear programming in activity analysis. These conclusions claim for *non-pure* capital rationing problems, *i.e.* with borrowing and lending opportunities.

KEYWORDS: projects selection, capital rationing, linear programming, theorems of the alternative.

1 Introduction

Following [9], [11] and [12], a *problem* $\mathcal{P}$ of *pure capital rationing* (C.R. in the following) may be sketched as follows.

- Take a row vector $v \in R^m$ of discounting factors v_i, with

$$1 > v_1 > v_2 > \ldots > v_m > 0, \tag{1}$$

and a real matrix $A = [a_{ij}]$ of order (m, n); its j-th column A^j shows the net cash flows of a safe project $\mathrm{A}^{(j)}$; according to their signs (> 0 or < 0), they are to be cashed or paid at the times $1, 2, \ldots, m$.

- Take a column vector $b \in R^m$ defining the *budgets* b_i; b_i measures the additional internal funds coming in or out of the management of the n projects at time i.

*Research projects *Cariplo* and *Murst*.

- Define the column vector $u \in R^n$ whose entries are all ones (prime denotes transposition) $u = [1, 1, \ldots, 1]'$ and the column vector $x = [x_1, x_2, \ldots, x_n]'$, whose entry x_j defines the *activation level* of $A^{(j)}$. Any non-integer x_j may be viewed as the measure of our share in the full activation of the j-th project.

- Denote with $[0]$ the zero vector of suitable order and solve the L.P. (linear programming) problem $\mathcal{P}$:

$$\mathcal{P}: \quad \begin{cases} \operatorname*{Max}_x vAx \\ Ax + b \geqq [0] \\ [0] \leqq x \leqq u. \end{cases}$$

Its financial meaning is well-known: the search of an optimum vector x^*, *i.e.* of a *project mix* leading to the maximum net present value of the n projects. Alternatively, the budget constraint may involve, instead of A, a matrix defining the gross capital outlays required by the various projects, as in [13], [14] and [15], but we prefer, following [9], [11] and [12], to drop this variant.

Before going on, we must note that a bit of confusion is present in the literature, as for what regards the assumptions on the discount factors, on the cash flows of the projects and on the budgets. Our relation (1) assumes that the interest rates embedded in v are all positive and finite, but some Authors do not explicitly rule out the case $v = [0]$, especially when the simple assumption $v_i \geq 0, \forall i$, is made, or when the case $v > [0]$ is taken as a special one (see [9], property 6). Moreover, the assumption that each project starts with a cash outflow is sometimes implicitly made and is hidden (as in [9]); the same happens for the assumption $b_i \geq 0, \forall i$ (as in [12]). In order to avoid any misunderstanding, we will always specify the further assumptions to be made on A, b and v, if any.

2 Some Known Results

The dual $\mathcal{P}'$ of problem $\mathcal{P}$ is

$$\mathcal{P}': \quad \begin{cases} \operatorname*{Min}_{y,w} \{yb + wu\} \\ -yA + w \geqq vA \\ y \geqq [0], w \geqq [0]. \end{cases}$$

The entries of y^* in an optimum $[y^*; w^*]$ for $\mathcal{P}'$ should measure how much the capital which flows into and comes out of the projects through the budgets is useful and scarce for $\mathcal{P}$, *i.e.* in the maximization of the net present value of the projects. This has led to the notion of *consistent optimum*: when problem $\mathcal{P}$ is solvable, an optimum x^* is called consistent if, among the optima $[y^*; w^*]$ for $\mathcal{P}'$, a vector y^* exists such that

$$y^* = v. \tag{2}$$

This notion was put forward by [2] and has raised much interest. Some rather recent results are contained in the following Theorems 1 (see [9]) and 2 (see [11], [12]).

Theorem 1 . *If x^* is a consistent optimum for $\mathcal{P}$, then the following properties hold:*

$$x_j^* = 0 \Rightarrow vA^j \le 0; \quad 0 < x_j^* < 1 \Rightarrow vA^j = 0; \quad x_j^* = 1 \Rightarrow vA^j \ge 0;$$

$$y^*Ax^* = \tfrac{1}{2}w^*u = -y^*b; \tag{3}$$

$$y^*Ax^* \neq 0 \Rightarrow b \text{ has mixed sign entries}; \tag{4}$$

$$v > [0] \Rightarrow Ax^* + b = [0].$$

Theorem 2 . *If problem $\mathcal{P}$ admits a consistent optimum x^*, then:*

$$vAx^* \le 0, \tag{5}$$

$$y^* = [0]. \tag{6}$$

Remark 1 . Some remarks on Th. 1 are needed. No assumption is explicitly made on v, but $v \geqq [0]$ seems assumed. Moreover, the assumption

$$a_{1j} < 0, \forall j \in \{1, 2, \dots, n\} \tag{7}$$

is only hidden (see end-note 4 of [9], p. 59), but it is quite essential for implication (4), otherwise (4) is false, as the following counter-example shows:

$$A = \begin{bmatrix} 2 & -1 \\ -3 & 4 \end{bmatrix}, \quad b = \begin{bmatrix} -1 \\ -1 \end{bmatrix}, \quad v = [.8 \quad .5],$$

$$x^* = [1 \quad 1]', \quad y^* = [.8 \quad .5], \quad w^* = [.2 \quad 2.4].$$

Finally, Th. 6 below simplifies the original proof of Th. 1, without assuming (7).

Remark 2 . Th. 2 claims to show that, thanks to (6), properties (3) and (4) of Th. 1 are simply meaningless. In order to refuse this claim, we may get a case where (5) and (6) do not hold by taking

$$A = \begin{bmatrix} -2 & -3 \\ 5 & 8 \end{bmatrix}, \quad b = \begin{bmatrix} 5 \\ -13 \end{bmatrix}, \quad v = [.8 \quad .6],$$

and checking that the vectors

$$x^* = [1 \quad 1]', \quad y^* = [.8 \quad .6], \quad w^* = [2.8 \quad 4.8]$$

define optima for $\mathcal{P}$ and $\mathcal{P}'$. x^* and $[y^*; w^*]$ are feasible and lead the objective function to the value 3.8 in both problems; moreover, x^* is consistent, as $y^* = v$, and yet neither (5) nor (6) holds. A similar counter-example put forward in [1] does not fit, as it proves (6) false, but its optimum is not consistent.

All becomes clear if we note that nothing is said in [12] on the signs of b, but the assumption $b_i \ge 0, \forall i$, is needed to show that $x = [0]$ is a feasible vector in $\mathcal{P}$ (see [12], p. 257). If one realizes this, then (5) trivially follows from (3) of Th. 1. Moreover, relation (6) is obtained by means of the well-known L.P. *basis theorem*, but without checking whether, when b changes, the optimal basis looses neither its feasibility nor its consistency.

3 Some Existence Theorems

Curiously enough, nobody has already tried, as far as we are aware, to get necessary and sufficient conditions on the data A, b and v for the existence of consistent optima. This is just the content of Theorems 3 to 5 below.

Theorem 3 . *Define*

$$\tilde{b} = \left[\tilde{b}_1, \tilde{b}_2, ..., \tilde{b}_m\right]', \text{ with } \tilde{b}_i = b_1 + b_2 + ... + b_i, \tag{8}$$

$$\tilde{A} = [\tilde{a}_{ij}], \text{ with } \tilde{a}_{ij} = a_{1j} + a_{2j} + \ldots + a_{ij}, \tag{9}$$

and use the notation $\geq [0]$ *for semi-positive vectors. Then Problem* $\mathcal{P}$ *admits consistent optima which satisfy* (1)*:*

$$1 > v_1 > v_2 > \ldots > v_m > 0, \tag{10}$$

iffi *the system*

$$\begin{cases} Ax + b = [0] \\ [0] \leqq x \leqq u \end{cases} \tag{11}$$

admits some solution x*, but no solution* q *exists for the system*

$$\begin{cases} \tilde{A}q + \tilde{b} \geq [0] \\ [0] \leqq q \leqq u. \end{cases} \tag{12}$$

Proof . Each consistent optimum satisfies (2), hence $y^* = v$ is a positive vector. Thanks to the L.P. *complementarity theorem*, this allows to get

$$Ax^* + b = [0]. \tag{13}$$

Multiplying both sides of (13) by v gives

$$vAx^* = -vb. \tag{14}$$

Moreover, if x^* solves $\mathcal{P}$ and $[y^*; w^*] = [v; w^*]$ solves $\mathcal{P}'$, then the L.P. *optimality theorem* gives $vAx^* = vb + w^*u$, and also, thanks to (14),

$$w^*u = -2vb. \tag{15}$$

Define the column vector $e \in R^m$ and the matrix $Z = [z_{ij}]$ of order (m, m) as follows:

$$e = [1,\ 0,\ 0, \ldots,\ 0]', \quad Z = [z_{ij}], \text{ with } z_{ij} = \begin{cases} 1, & \text{if } i = j \\ -1, & \text{if } i = j+1 \\ 0, & \text{otherwise,} \end{cases}$$

just in order to write (10) as

$$vZ > [0], \quad ve < 1. \tag{16}$$

Being $y^* = v > [0]$, $w_j^* \geq 2vA^j, \forall j$, comes from the constraints system of $\mathcal{P}'$. Thus we may identify all the vectors $[x^*; y^*; w^*] = [x^*; v; w^*]$ defining a consistent optimum in the sense (2) as follows: $x = x^*$ solves system (11) and $[v; w^*]$ solves the following one:

$$\begin{cases} w^* \geqq 2vA \\ w^*u + 2vb = 0 \\ ve < 1 \\ w^* \geqq [0], \quad vZ > [0]. \end{cases} \tag{17}$$

By means of a general *alternative theorem* for linear systems (see Sec. 7) we realize that (17) is solvable in $[v; w^*]$ if and only if no vector $[q; s]$ exists which solves the system

$$\begin{cases} Aq + b = Zs \\ [0] \leqq q \leqq u \\ s \geq [0], \end{cases} \tag{18}$$

which may be translated into system (12) by computing the inverse Z^{-1} of Z as

$$Z^{-1} = [\eta_{ij}], \text{ with } \eta_{ij} = \begin{cases} 1, & \text{if } i \geq j \\ 0, & \text{if } i < j. \end{cases}$$

□

Theorem 4 . *Problem $\mathcal{P}$ admits consistent optima satisfying the property*

$$v_1 > v_2 > \ldots > v_m > 0$$

iffi *$\mathcal{P}$ admits consistent optima which satisfy* (10).

Proof . The proof fully runs as in Th. 3, simply the second inequality in (16) is absent; hence, to unify proofs, substitute e with $[0]$. □

Theorem 5 . *Problem $\mathcal{P}$ admits consistent optima satisfying the property $v > [0]$* iffi *system* (11) *admits a solution x, but no solution q exists for the system*

$$\begin{cases} Aq + b \geq [0] \\ [0] \leqq q \leqq u. \end{cases} \tag{19}$$

Proof . The proof fully runs as in Th. 3; to unify proofs, substitute e with $[0]$ and Z with the identity matrix I. □

Remark 3 . The financial meaning of the solvability of system (11) is evident: if we are seeking for a consistent optimum, then the budgets must exactly balance, at each time, the cash requirements generated by some project mix. Note that in Th. 3 vector (8) defines all the sums of the first i budgets, for i running from 1 to m, while the $(i; j)$-entry of matrix (9) is simply the sum of the first i cash flows of project $A^{(j)}$. On this ground, the non-solvability of system (12) in Th. 3 and Th. 4 means that no project mix q exists which leads to net cumulated cash balances which are all non-negative, but positive for some time. The non-solvability of system (19) in Th. 5 says the same things with regard to simple (not cumulated) net cash balances.

4 Some Old and New Properties

Theorems 1 to 5 and Remarks 1 to 3 suggest to dig more on consistent optima. The following Th. 6 just tries to do this.

Theorem 6 . *Let v verify the property $v > [0]$ and x^* be a consistent optimum for problem $\mathcal{P}$. Then the financial value vb of all the budgets is non-positive and verifies the relations:*

$$vb = -vAx^* = -\tfrac{1}{2}w^*u = -\tfrac{1}{2}w^*x^* \leq 0 \quad (< 0 \text{ if } vA^j > 0 \text{ for some } j), \tag{20}$$

$$Ax^* + b = [0], \tag{21}$$

and the following implications hold:

$$\begin{cases} x_j^* = 0 \Rightarrow vA^j \leq 0;\ 0 < x_j^* < 1 \Rightarrow vA^j = 0;\ x_j^* = 1 \Rightarrow vA^j \geq 0; \\ vA^j < 0 \Rightarrow x_j^* = 0;\ vA^j > 0 \Rightarrow x_j^* = 1. \end{cases} \tag{22}$$

Proof . Th. 6 is quite similar to Th. 1 but it does not require assumption (7) on the negativeness of the first cash flow of each project, since it does not claim to get property (4). Its proof, which is much quicker than the one of Th. 1, is almost trivial. We may get (21) and the first two equalities in (20) just in the same way we already got relations (13) to (15) in the proof of Th. 3. The last equality in (20) follows from the L.P. *complementarity theorem* applied to the constraint $x_j \leq 1, \forall j$, in problem $\mathcal{P}$, while the weak inequality in (20) directly follows from the signs of u and w^*.

The consistency of x^* and the L.P. theorem quoted above give

$$x^* \geqq [0], \quad w^* - 2vA \geqq [0], \quad (w^* - 2vA)x^* = 0, \tag{23}$$

$$w^* \geqq [0], \quad u - x^* \geqq [0], \quad w^*(u - x^*) = 0, \tag{24}$$

hence from (23):

$$w_j^* \geq 2vA^j,\ \forall j, \tag{25}$$

$$x_j^* > 0 \Rightarrow w_j^* = 2vA^j, \tag{26}$$

and from (24):

$$w_j^* \geq 0,\ \forall j, \tag{27}$$

$$x_j^* < 1 \Rightarrow w_j^* = 0. \tag{28}$$

When $x_j^* = 0$, (25) and (28) give $vA^j \leq 0$. When $0 < x_j^* < 1$, the vanishing of vA^j follows from (26) and (28). When $x_j^* = 1$, (26) and (27) ensure the non-negativeness of the present value of $A^{(j)}$. The first three implications in (22) are therefore proven, while the last two ones may be quickly deduced from them. If some profitable (*i.e.* with positive present value) project exists, then, thanks to (22), some project will be fully activated, while the other ones, if any, will be not activated or will enter into vAx^* with a vanishing weight. This leads to a positive value for vAx^*: $vAx^* = \sum_j^+(vA^j) > 0$, $\sum_j^+$ being the sum that covers only the profitable projects. As (20) gives $vb = -vAx^*$, the strong inequality in (20) follows. □

Remark 4 . Th. 6 shows that, if $v > [0]$, the non-positiveness of the net present value vb of the budgets is a necessary condition for the existence of a consistent optimum for $\mathcal{P}$. Being $v > [0]$, it is now clear that no optimum of this kind can exist if b is semi-positive, as in this case $q = [0]$ solves (12) and (19). Remark 2 shows an example with $vb < 0$, but it is quite easy to set up a problem $\mathcal{P}$ which admits consistent optima with $vb = 0$: simply choose a matrix A without profitable projects, then compute

$$b = -Ax^*, \quad x_j^* \begin{cases} = 0, & \text{if } vA^j < 0 \\ \in [0;1] & \text{and arbitrary, if } vA^j = 0. \end{cases}$$

Note that x^* and $[y^*; w^*] = [v; [0]\,]$ are feasible in $\mathcal{P}$ and $\mathcal{P}'$; moreover, they fulfill all the complementarity relations. Hence they define a pair of optima for those problems and x^* is consistent. Being $vAx^* = 0$, $vb = 0$ follows from (20). A forthcoming paper [7] deals with some computational features of problem $\mathcal{P}$.

5 How to Bury Pure C.R. Problems and Why

The most relevant consequence of Th. 6 is that, when a pure C.R. problem $\mathcal{P}$ admits a consistent optimum, then this problem works just as a *machine to double the value of the money* it involves. Indeed, a positive [negative] entry in the budget b_i planned for time i by the *problem solver* (who solves $\mathcal{P}$), is a negative [positive] cash flow for the *cash manager* (who provides that budget). Obviously, since the latter provides the former with all the budgets, he will also withdraw the optimal value vAx^*. Therefore, if the whole financial value vb of the budgets is negative, then the cash manager gets a first gain vb before the problem is solved and a second one, for the same amount, after its solution: thus a C.R. problem of this kind deserves some suspicion, as it seems to work as a trick to exactly double the wealth it moves.

Relation (21) shows a necessary condition that vector b must fulfill for the existence of a consistent optimum. This means that the cash manager must know in advance all the right cash balances required by such an optimum, *i.e.* must exactly guess b before defining $\mathcal{P}$. But $\mathcal{P}$ cannot be solved before it is fully formulated, hence before b is fixed: here is another serious criticism to pure C.R. problems. A way-out from this trap may be to treat the budgets as decision variables, not as data. This approach leads to the maximization of the gain $(vAx - vb)$ in the net present value, under the usual constraints of $\mathcal{P}$. In this case, thanks to (21) and (22), $\mathcal{P}$ and $\mathcal{P}'$ (which becomes trivial) are easily solved:

$$x_j^* \begin{cases} = 0, & \text{if } vA^j < 0, \\ \in [0;1], & \text{if } vA^j = 0, \\ = 1, & \text{if } vA^j > 0, \end{cases} \quad b^* = -Ax^*, \quad y^* = v, \quad w_j^* = \text{Max}\,\{2vA^j; 0\}\,, \forall j,$$

x^* is consistent and the optimal value for both problems equates $\sum_j^+(2vA^j)$.

6 Conclusions

Summing up: on one side, as soon as we require that v must measure how much cash funds are useful and scarce, pure C.R. problems with no consistent optima are to be refused; on the other side, consistent optima may well exist (A and b may pass the test of Theorems 3 to 5), but the results of Sec. 5 show that they seem a trick to double the value of the cash funds and lead to a *vicious circle* in the choice of the budgets vector. On this ground, the best thing we can do is perhaps to keep us off any pure C.R. problem.

The main troubles to which pure C.R. problems lead come from a hidden basic mistake. These problems recall a well-known application of L.P. to *linear production models* (*e.g.*, see [5], [8]), which may be summarized as follows. n *activities* with *constant returns to scale* may be activated at the levels measured by a non-negative vector x. Let c be the row vector of the net direct *profits* c_j coming from those activities, each activated at unit intensities. Moreover, a non-negative column vector r shows the fixed availability of the m *resources*, whose consume is measured by Ax, A being a matrix of order (m, n). Then the search of the best program x leads to the problem

$$\begin{cases} \max\limits_{x} cx \\ Ax \leqq r \\ x \geqq [0]\,. \end{cases} \tag{29}$$

Note that here the resources lead to no new cost, as they are assumed already available from past decisions; moreover, they cannot be used otherwise. If alternative uses are allowed, first the objective function in problem (29) should be reformulated as $\{cx + d(r - Ax)\}$, d being the vector of the profits coming from alternative uses; then some additional constraints, if any, should be added.

Obviously, any resource whose availability turns out to be redundant for what is needed by an optimum x^* must have a zero *shadow value* (this recalls the *free commodities rule*), as shown by the corresponding entry in the vector y^* which solves the dual problem

$$\begin{cases} \min\limits_{y} yr \\ yA \geqq c \\ y \geqq [0]\,. \end{cases}$$

Also in pure C.R. problems, constant returns to scale apply, but a point deserves attention: budgets cannot be treated in the same way the resources are handled in problem (29), as they measure the internal capital flowing into and out of the management of the projects. In other words, money is a resource which is expensive [worth] when it is paid [cashed] and is one of the most movable ones. Hence a C.R. problem *must* host the opportunity to move money by means of borrowing and lending external projects: this is an old story. Using some ideas already employed for the optimal management of one project (see [3], [4]), paper [6] tries to widen many well-known proposals for *non-pure* C.R. problems.

7 Appendix

Here is how to get (18) of our Th. 3. Th. 3 in [10] states that the system

$$\begin{cases} \sum_{j=1}^{q} A_{1j}x^j = b^1 \\ \sum_{j=1}^{q} A_{2j}x^j \leqq b^2 \\ \sum_{j=1}^{q} A_{3j}x^j < b^3 \\ \sum_{j=1}^{q} A_{ij}x^j \leq b^i,\ i \in \{4,\dots,p\} \\ x^1 \text{ arbitrary},\ x^2 \geqq [0]\,,\ x^3 > [0]\,,\ x^j \geq [0]\,,\ j \in \{4,\dots,q\} \end{cases} \tag{30}$$

admits a solution $x = [x^1; x^2; \dots; x^q]'$ *iff* the system

$$\begin{cases} \sum_{i=1}^{p} y^i A_{i1} = [0] \\ \sum_{i=1}^{p} y^i A_{ij} \geqq [0]\,,\ j \in \{2,\dots,q\} \\ \sum_{i=1}^{p} y^i b^i \leqq 0, \\ y^1 \text{ arbitrary},\ y^i \geqq [0]\,,\ i \in \{2,\dots,p\} \end{cases} \tag{31}$$

admits no solution $y = [y^1; y^2; \dots; y^p]$ which verifies at least one of the following properties:

$$\begin{cases} \sum_{i=1}^{p} y^i b^i < 0, \\ y^3 \geq [0]\,, \\ y^i > [0] \text{ for some } i \in \{4,\dots,p\}\,, \\ \sum_{i=1}^{p} y^i A_{i3} \geq [0]\,, \\ \sum_{i=1}^{p} y^i A_{ij} > [0] \text{ for some } j \in \{4,\dots,q\}\,. \end{cases}$$

Choose the elements in system (30), all of suitable order, as follows:

$p = q = 4$, $x^1 = v'$, $x^2 = (w^*)'$, $A_{11} = 2b'$, $A_{12} = u'$, $A_{21} = 2A'$, $A_{22} = -I$ (the identity matrix of order n), $A_{31} = [-Z; e]'$, all other A_{ij} zero and all A_{4j} with one row, $b^1 = 0$, $b^2 = [0] \in R^n$, $b^3 = [\,[0]\,; 1]' \in R^{m+1}$, $b^4 = t > 0$ and arbitrary.

Then treat the alternative system (31) as follows: write y^3 as $[h; \beta]$ (with $h \in R^m$, $\beta \in R$) and note that the signs of y^3, y^4 and t imply $\beta = y^4 = 0$. If $y^1 < 0$, then $y^1 u' - y^2$ cannot be non-negative, hence system (31) is unsolvable. The same happens if $y^1 = 0$, as in this case $y^2 = [0]$ but no $h \geq [0]$ can solve $hZ' = [0]$, being Z non-singular. Finally, if $y^1 > 0$, define $q = (1/y^1)(y^2)'$ and $s = (y^1/2)h'$ to get system (18).

References

[1] Baum S., *Observations on "Discount Rates in Linear Programming Formulations of the Capital Budgeting Problem"*, The Engineering Economist, *30* (1985), n. 3, 292-293.

[2] Baumol W.J., Quandt R.E., *Investment and Discount Rates Under Capital Rationing - A Programming Approach,* The Economic Journal, *75* (1965), n. 298, 317-329.

[3] Carezzano E., De Giuli M.E., Magnani U., *C'era una volta il tasso interno: uso e misuso di leggi finanziarie interne* (L.F.I.) *nella valutazione e scelta di progetti alternativi* (V.E.S.P.A.), Fasc. Dip.to Ricerche Aziendali, Sez. Matem. Gen. ed Appl., Univ. Pavia, n. 28, a.a. 1991-92.

[4] Carezzano E., De Giuli M.E., Magnani U., *Project Analysis Using a Linear Approach* (P.A.U.L.A.), 1993 (forthcoming).

[5] Charnes A., Cooper W.W., Miller M.H., *Applications of Linear Programming to Financial Budgeting and the Costing of Funds,* Journal of Business, *32* (Jan. 1959), 20-46.

[6] De Giuli M.E., Magnani U., *More Scope for Capital Rationing and Valuation,* Atti XVI Convegno AMASES, Treviso, 10-13.9.1992, 263-276.

[7] De Giuli M.E., Magnani U., *Consistent Optima in Pure Capital Rationing Problems,* 1993 (forthcoming).

[8] Dorfman R., Samuelson P.A., Solow R.M., Linear Programming and Economic Analysis, McGraw-Hill, 1958.

[9] Freeland J.R., Rosenblatt M.J., *An Analysis of Linear Programming Formulations for the Capital Rationing Problem,* The Engineering Economist, *24* (1978), n. 1, 49-61.

[10] Giorgi G., *Un approccio unificante ai teoremi dell'alternativa per sistemi lineari,* Atti X Convegno AMASES, Siena, 8-10.9.1986, 103-136.

[11] Hayes J.W., *Discount Rates in Linear Programming Formulations of the Capital Budgeting Problem,* The Engineering Economist, *29* (1984), n. 2, 113-126.

[12] Hayes J.W., *Dual Variables in Pure Capital Rationing Linear Programming Formulations,* The Engineering Economist, *34* (1989), n. 3, 255-260.

[13] Kornbluth J., Salkin G., The Management of Corporate Financial Assets: Application of Mathematical Programming Models, Academic Press, 1987.

[14] Salkin G., Kornbluth J., Linear Programming in Financial Planning, Haymarket Publ. Ltd., London, 1973.

[15] Weingartner H.M., Mathematical Programming and the Analysis of Capital Budgeting Problems, Prentice-Hall, 1963.

APV Sensitivity with Respect to Interest Rates Fluctuations

Maria Luisa Gota
Istituto di Matematica Finanziaria
dell'Università di Torino
Facoltà di Economia e Commercio
Piazza Arbarello, 8—I-10122 Torino (Italy)

1 Introduction

The aim of this paper is to provide some simple relations in order to evaluate how much the yield is influenced by a change in the internal rate of return in a contract of division into instalments. These relations can be used to get some hedging results (see, i.e., Platt (1986)). I consider three parameters useful to describe the yield of the investment:

- Total amount of interests;
- Net Present Value;
- Adjusted Present Value.

The choice of one of these measures of the operation income depends on the knowledge of the financial context in which one acts. For example, to use the total amount of interests implies that only equity capital is employed and that the opportunity cost is zero or that a pure accounting viewpoint is adopted, while with the use of the NPV a positive opportunity cost is involved. The APV is the most detailed model among the ones introduced; it is suitable when loan capital is partially employed and the opportunity cost is positive. Later on I will point out the effects of a contractual rate fluctuation, assuming, where it makes sense, that changes in the contractual rate are caused by changes in cost rates. This cause-effect relation is absolutely realistic being the actor I am considering a financial mediator. Finally I will develop a sensitivity analysis for period results on the basis of the APV decomposition presented in Peccati (1987). The results of this paper are currently used *a priori* for simulation purposes by a leading Italian financial Company.

2 Sensitivity of the total amount of interests

Consider a cash-flow through n periods (months) ruled by the parameters defined below. My purpose is to give an approximation of the *sensitivity* of the total sum of interests, meaning by sensitivity the ratio K of the variation of interests to the spread of the contractual rate. Let S denote the amount to be returned through n periods, R_s the s-th instalment, $\phi(t_s, 0)$, $s = 1, ..., n$ the internal financial law holding the operation. If $\delta(t)$ indicates the force of interest at t, then:

$$\phi(t_s, 0) = \exp\left(-\int_0^{t_s} \delta(u)\mathrm{d}u\right)$$

Let M be the total interests amount:

$$M = \sum_{s=1}^{n} I_s = -S + \sum_{s=1}^{n} R_s$$

I assume that $R_s = R_1\rho_s$, where $\rho_2, ..., \rho_n$ are fixed and $\rho_1 = 1$.
The main issue is to study what it happens if a parallel change in the contractual rate affects the force of interest soon after the beginning time, say at 0^+, in the shape of a shift k, $k \in \mathbf{R}$, so that the new force of interest results $\delta^*(t) = \delta(t) + k$. As a consequence the amounts R_s are modified and the new ones are:

$$R_s^* = R_1^*\rho_s$$

with R_1^* such that:

$$S = R_1^* \sum_s \rho_s\phi^*(t_s, 0)$$

and:

$$\phi^*(t_s, 0) = \exp\left(-\int_0^{t_s} \delta^*(u)\mathrm{d}u\right) =$$

$$= \phi(t_s, 0)e^{-kt_s}$$

Obviously also M changes, becoming:

$$M^* = -S + R_1^* \sum_s \rho_s$$

Now the purpose is to find a relation providing an approximation for the spread between M^* and M, say ΔM. It's easy to prove that it results:

$$\Delta M = Dk\sum_s R_s + \mathrm{o}(k)$$

and, for small enough k:

$$\Delta M \approx Dk \sum_s R_s$$

where D denotes the duration of the cash-flow with $\{\phi(t_s, 0)\}$, $s = 1, ..., n$ as a discount rule.
It follows for the sensitivity K:

$$K = DR_1 \sum_s \rho_s + \frac{\mathrm{o}(k)}{k}$$

Remark. A test of the goodness of the last approximations can be provided by a simple numerical example, assuming constant instalments and:

$$\phi(t_s, 0) = (1 + x)^{-t_s}$$

In this particular case, I make a small change in the model supposing the shift affects the interest rate x instead of the force of interest; this choice is quite natural when the financial law is so simple. The relations found above become:

$$K = nR\,\frac{D}{1+x} + \frac{\mathrm{o}(\Delta x)}{\Delta x}$$

and:

$$\Delta M = nR\,\frac{D}{1+x}\,\Delta x + \mathrm{o}(\Delta x)$$

Let the financed amount be $S = 1,000,000$, the term $n = 36$ months and the contractual monthly rate $x = 1\%$. The monthly instalment results:

$$R = 33,214.31$$

Now let the contractual rate x change by $\Delta x = 0.1\%$. The exact variation of M is:

$$\Delta M = 20,738$$

while the approximated value is:

$$\Delta M \approx 20,633$$

3 Sensitivity of the Net Present Value

In this section my attention is focused on the NPV as an index of the investment income when the employed capital costs according with the discount law:

$$\psi(t_s, 0) = \exp\left(-\int_0^{t_s} \gamma(u)\mathrm{d}u\right)$$

Let G denote the NPV and H its sensitivity under rate fluctuations (sensitivity has an analogous meaning as above). Then:

$$G = -S + \sum_s R_s \psi(t_s, 0)$$

If at 0^+ the contractual force of interest $\delta(t)$ is affected by a shift k, G is modified and becomes $G^* = G + \Delta G$. So it's easy to obtain for H and ΔG:

$$H = D(G+S) + \frac{\mathrm{o}(k)}{k}$$

$$\Delta G = D(G+S)k + \mathrm{o}(k)$$

where D, as usual, denotes the duration.

Remark. Under the same simplified hypotheses as the ones made in the preceeding remark I get:

$$H = (G+S)\,\frac{D}{1+x} + \frac{\mathrm{o}(\Delta x)}{\Delta x}$$

$$\Delta G = (G+S)\,\frac{D}{1+x}\,\Delta x + \mathrm{o}(\Delta x)$$

The numerical example introduced before offers a test driver for both last formulas, providing for the exact and the approximated variation respectively:

$$\Delta G = 17,956.997$$

$$\Delta G \approx 17,866.232$$

4 Consequences of cost rate fluctuations

In this section an improvement over the former model is introduced: cost rate variation is considered as a cause for contractual rate variation. Let us suppose that at 0^+ the force of interest $\gamma(t)$ is affected by a shift h. We can assume that there is some functional dependence of k on h. Because of this connection expressed by means of the function f: $k = f(h)$, also $\delta(t)$ changes according with $k = f(h)$. It follows that the NPV, $G(h,k) = G(h, f(h))$, is modified. Let ΔG be the variation of G; one gets for the sensitivity H' and ΔG respectively:

$$H' = (G+S)\left[Df'(0) - D_\gamma\right] + \frac{o(h)}{h}$$

$$\Delta G = (G+S)\left[Df'(0) - D_\gamma\right] h + o(h)$$

where D_γ denotes the duration under $\{\psi(t_s, 0)\}$. From the preceeding equations a suggestion for checking H' can be drawn. That is to manage f so that:

$$Df'(0) - D_\gamma \approx 0$$

Again I recall the numerical example of section 1 in order to test the new relation and practise the suggested hedging method.

Remark. Under the usual simplified hypotheses (x is the contractual rate, i the cost rate, $\Delta x = f(\Delta i)$) the last relations are:

$$H' = (G+S)\left[\frac{D}{1+x} f'(0) - \frac{D_i}{1+i}\right] + \frac{o(\Delta i)}{\Delta i}$$

$$\Delta G = (G+S)\left[\frac{D}{1+x} f'(0) - \frac{D_i}{1+i}\right] \Delta i + o(\Delta i)$$

indicating by D_i the duration with $\psi(t_s, 0) = (1+i)^{-t_s}$ as a discount factor. It can be useful to look into the structure of:

$$(G+S)\left[\frac{D}{1+x} f'(0) - \frac{D_i}{1+i}\right]$$

In standard conditions ($x > i$) the following result can be easily proved:

Proposition 1 *If f is differentiable at 0 then an hedged NPV implies $f'(0) > 1$ as a necessary condition.*

This proposition is a trivial consequence of the well known result:

Proposition 2 *The duration D decreases if the discount rate x increases.*

This proposition can also be proved in the following way.

Proof. Using the derivative of D with respect to x, it's immediate to obtain the following condition. If it holds, then the thesis is verified.

$$\sum_s t_s^2 (1+x)^{-t_s} R_s \sum_s (1+x)^{-t_s} R_s - \left[\sum_s t_s (1+x)^{-t_s} R_s\right]^2 > 0$$

Now I consider the random variable **X** assuming the values t_s, $s = 1, ..., n$, with probability:

$$p(t_s) = (1+x)^{-t_s} \frac{R_s}{\sum_s (1+x)^{-t_s} R_s}$$

The relation found above is the same of the following:

$$E(\mathbf{X}^2) - [E(\mathbf{X})]^2 > 0$$

which is obviously true. •

From a practical viewpoint Proposition 1 signals that a successful hedging policy requires that the rate x rises more than the rate i.

Coming back to the numerical example, assume: $i = 0.006$, $\Delta i = 0.001$ and $f(\Delta i) = 2\Delta i$. Then the exact amount for ΔG is:

$$\Delta G = 17,932.27$$

while the approximated one is:

$$\Delta G \approx 17,979$$

5 APV and interest rates fluctuations

In this section I bring a further issue into action, that is the resort to debt capital. So the investment:

$$\{-S, R_1, ..., R_n\}$$

is supported by the following financing:

$$\{Q, -P_1, ..., -P_n\}$$

Also for the financing the ratio of P_s $(s = 1, ..., n)$ to P_1, say π_s, doesn't change though the cost of Q does. Let the debt capital cost according with the force of interest $\theta(t)$. As above $\delta(t)$ and $\gamma(t)$ denote respectively the contractual rate and the opportunity cost. Let the discount factor related to $\theta(t)$ be:

$$\chi(t_s, 0) = \exp\left(-\int_0^{t_s} \theta(u)du\right)$$

so that:

$$Q = \sum_{s=1}^{n} P_s \chi(t_s, 0)$$

The (Generalized) APV, say A, turns to be:

$$A = -S + Q + \sum_{s=1}^{n} (R_s - P_s)\psi(t_s, 0)$$

The question is to understand what consequences can be produced on the APV by shifts of γ, θ, δ, assuming that the shift of δ, k, is a function of both the others, respectively h, m: $k = F(h, m)$. As above I suppose that the change in the force of interest works at 0^+. If ΔA denotes the variation of A, it's almost immediate to obtain:

$$\Delta A = \mathbf{R}[\psi]\left[D\Delta F(0,0) - D_\gamma h\right] +$$
$$\mathbf{P}[\psi]\left[DF_\gamma h - DFm\right] + \mathrm{o}\left(\sqrt{\Delta h^2 + \Delta m^2}\right)$$

with:

$$\mathbf{R}[\psi] = \sum_s R_s \psi(t_s, 0)$$
$$\mathbf{P}[\psi] = \sum_s P_s \psi(t_s, 0)$$
$$\Delta F(0,0) = F_h'(0,0)\Delta h + F_m'(0,0)\Delta m$$

DF and DF_γ respectively the duration of the financing under $\{\chi(t_s, 0)\}$ and under $\{\psi(t_s, 0)\}$.

Remark. Again I assume simplified hypotheses and let j be the internal rate of return of the financing operation. ΔA reduces to:

$$\Delta A = \mathbf{R}[\psi]\left[\frac{D\Delta F(0,0)}{1+x} - \frac{D_i \Delta i}{1+i}\right] +$$
$$\mathbf{P}[\psi]\left[\frac{DF_i \Delta i}{1+i} - \frac{DF\Delta j}{1+j}\right] + \mathrm{o}\left(\sqrt{\Delta i^2 + \Delta j^2}\right)$$

with:

$$\psi(t_s, 0) = (1+i)^{-t_s}$$

DF and DF_i respectively the duration of the financing under j and under i. It is interesting to remark that in the last formulas there is a partial set off between different addenda.

6 Period results sensitivity analysis

Sometimes it can be useful to know how the profitability forms through the duration of the financial operation and how the profitability related to the s-th period depends on rates fluctuations.

In developing a period results sensitivity analysis I follow the APV decomposition worked out by Peccati (1987).

I assume self-financing, compound interest law and constant contractual rate and opportunity cost.

Supposing that a shift affects the contractual rate, the opportunity cost being unchanged, an interesting result appears:

$$\Delta G_s \approx \frac{w_{s-1}}{(1+i)^s}\left[(D_0 - D_{s-1})\frac{x-i}{1+x} + 1\right]\Delta x$$

where:

G_s is the share of NPV formed through the $s-$th period;

w_{s-1} is the outstanding at the time $s-1$;

D_0, D_{s-1} are the *durations* computed at 0 and at $s-1$ respectively;

x, i are the contractual rate and the opportunity cost;

Δx is the shift of the contractual rate.

The previous relation shows the possibility that an increase in the contractual rate causes a drop in G_s. For an investment with $x > i$ this situation is particularly realistic if the financial barycentre, in terms of *duration*, is low.

REFERENCES

L. PECCATI (1987): 'DCF e risultati di periodo', *Atti dell'XI Convegno A-MASES*, Aosta.

R.B. PLATT (1986): *Controlling Interest Rate Risk*, John Wiley & Sons, New York.

A Note on the Existence of Equilibrium Price Measures

Marco Li Calzi

Istituto di Matematica "E. Levi"
Università di Parma
43100 Parma, Italy

Introduction

A series of key results in the modern theory of prices in financial markets links the existence of an equilibrium price measure with the absence of arbitrage opportunities. In discrete-time models, this link is particularly sharp: an equilibrium price measure exists if and only if there are no arbitrage opportunities.

As it often happens, the available proofs of this result use different techniques to establish the necessity and the sufficiency part. More precisely, necessity is shown by a simple argument of elementary linear algebra while sufficiency requires the usage of the separating hyperplane theorem. The purpose of this short note is to provide an alternative route to the proof of sufficiency which is based on the mixture space theorem by Herstein and Milnor (1953). The interest of this approach, which is perhaps simpler than the existing ones, is twofold: first, it emphasizes the order-preserving properties of the price functional and thus leads to a more natural interpretation of the construction used; second, it points out that results and theorems from decision theory can be usefully applied to asset pricing models. See also Chateauneuf et alii (1992).

1. The mixture space theorem

We recall the mixture space theorem proved by Herstein and Milnor in 1953. Let I be the unit interval in $\mathbf{R}$ and I^0 be the interior of I. A set X is said to be a mixture set if for any $x, y \in X$ and any $\alpha \in I$ there exists another element in X, denoted

$\alpha x + (1 - \alpha)y$, such that

$$1x + (1-1)y = x$$
$$\alpha x + (1-\alpha)y = (1-\alpha)y + \alpha x$$
$$\beta[\alpha x + (1-\alpha)y] + (1-\beta)y = (\alpha\beta)x + (1-\alpha\beta)y$$

for all $x, y \in X$ and all $\alpha, \beta \in I$. Interpreting the expressions above as multiplication by scalars and vector addition, it is easily seen that a convex set in a real vector space is a mixture space.

Given a binary relation $\succ$ on X, we consider the following axioms:

A1. Preference relation $\succ$ is a preference relation, i.e. $\succ$ is asymmetric and negatively transitive;

A2. Independence $x \succ y$ implies $\alpha x + (1-\alpha)z \succ \alpha y + (1-\alpha)z$ for all $z \in X$ and all $\alpha \in I^0$;

A3. Continuity $x \succ y \succ z$ implies that there exist $\alpha, \beta \in I^0$ such that $\alpha x + (1-\alpha)z \succ y \succ \beta x + (1-\beta)z$.

The mixture space theorem states that these three axioms hold if and only if there exists a linear order-preserving function F on X.

Theorem 1 (Mixture space theorem) *Let X be a mixture space and $\succ$ a binary relation on X. Then A1–A3 hold if and only if there exists a function $F : X \to \mathbf{R}$ such that*

1. *$x \succ y$ if and only if $F(x) > F(y)$, and*
2. *$F[\alpha x + (1-\alpha)y] = \alpha F(x) + (1-\alpha)F(y)$.*

Moreover, F is unique up to an increasing affine transformation.

We note two points. First, the statement of the theorem given here is slightly different from the original but can be shown to be equivalent (see Fishburn 1970). Second, and much more important for our purposes, a careful reading of Herstein and Milnor's proof shows that the unit interval I in the definition of a mixture space can be replaced by any connected superset of I in $\mathbf{R}$ without affecting the result. In the following, in fact, we replace I with $\mathbf{R}$ itself.

2. A discrete one-period model

We begin with the description of a standard one-period model for prices in a financial market. Notation and presentation are borrowed from Dothan (1990) to which we refer for more extensive discussions.

There is a finite time interval $[0,T]$, with initial date 0 and terminal date T. Uncertainty is represented by a finite state space Ω with K elements $\omega_1,\ldots,\omega_K$ each of which occurs with probability $P(\omega_k) > 0$, for $k = 1,\ldots,K$. There is only one perishable consumption good, which is also used as the *numéraire* for the economy.

There is a finite number N of securities, which are all endogenous and infinitely divisible. Trading in securities takes place only at time 0; short sales are permitted and there are no taxes or trading costs. Each security yields only a final payout at time T, which is contingent on the prevailing state. Formally, for $n = 1,\ldots,N$, security n is a random variable d_n on Ω. More generally, securities can be combined in a portfolio θ by following the trading strategy which buys at time 0 and holds until time T θ_i units of security i, for $i = 1,\ldots,N$. When necessary, we denote by v^k, $k = 1,\ldots,K$, the portfolio which realizes a state contingent claim paying one if state ω_k occurs and zero otherwise.

Given current prices $p_1,\ldots,p_N$ for securities $1,\ldots,N$, the price of portfolio θ is $p(\theta) = \sum_{n=1}^N \theta_n p_n$ and its payout at time T is the random variable $d(\theta) = \sum_{n=1}^N \theta_n d_n$. It is convenient to think of $d(\theta)$ as a K-dimensional column vector where the k-component $d(\theta)(\omega_k)$ is the payout of portfolio θ in state k. Also, note that the prices of the N securities determine the price of any possible portfolio θ: we say that they form a price system p for the market.

There is a finite set I of traders, who are all price takers. For each trader i, the following holds: 1) he knows the set Ω of possible states at time 0 and the prevailing state $\omega \in \Omega$ at time T; 2) he receives an endowment $e^i(0)$ of the consumption good at time 0 and another endowment $e^i(T,\omega)$ at time T contingent on the prevailing state ω; 3) he consumes a certain amount $c^i(0)$ at time 0 and a random amount $c^i(T)$ at time T which depends on his uncertain terminal endowment and the payouts of securities in his possession; 4) he has a complete preference ordering on the consumption process $c^i = \{c^i(0), c^i(T)\}$ which is continuous, increasing and convex.

Given a price system p, each trader i faces a budget set given by all the consumption processes that he can attain by acquiring at time 0 and holding until time T a portfolio θ^i. The market is said to be in equilibrium at time 0 if there are a price system p and trading strategies θ^i for each trader $i = 1,\ldots,I$ such that θ^i optimizes i's preferences over his feasible consumption processess and the market clears, i.e. $\sum_{i=1}^I \theta_n^i = 0$, for all $n = 1,\ldots,N$. The price system of a market in equilibrium is called an equilibrium price system.

An arbitrage opportunity is a trading strategy θ that gives a trader with zero endowment a nonnegative and nonzero consumption process. This can happen in two cases. Either the initial value of the portfolio θ implemented by the trading strategy is $p(\theta) \leq 0$ and the terminal payout $d(\theta) \geq 0$ for all $\omega \in \Omega$ with the strict inequality holding for at least one ω; or its initial value is (strictly) negative and the terminal payout is not negative for all $\omega \in \Omega$. As it is easy to show, arbitrage trading strategies do not exist in equilibrium. See for instance Dothan (1990), thm. 1.6, p. 18.

3. One-period equilibrium price measures

Assume that one of the securities in the market is a zero-coupon bond with positive initial price and a positive final payout which does not depend on the prevailing state. If the bond is security 1, then, $p_1 > 0$ and $d_1(\omega) = d_1$ for all $\omega \in \Omega$. We interpret the quantity $r = (d_1/p_1) - 1$ as the rate of interest on the bond.

Denote by q a K-dimensional vector and associate its k-th component q_k with state $\omega_k \in \Omega$. Given a price system p for a financial market, we say that q is an equilibrium price measure for p if

$$d(\theta)' q = (1 + r)\, p(\theta) \tag{1}$$

for any portfolio θ and $q_k > 0$ for all $k = 1, \ldots, K$. By linearity of $d(\theta)$ and $p(\theta)$ in the weights θ_n, it is apparent that this is equivalent to requiring that (1) holds only for the K contingent claims. Moreover, when θ is the portfolio composed only of one unit of security 1 (the bond), (1) simplifies to

$$\sum_{k=1}^{K} q_k = 1.$$

Together with the positivity of q, this shows that q is a probability measure on the state space Ω.

The justification of the name equilibrium price measure rests on two observations. First, it is possible to show that an equilibrium price measure q exists if and only if the price system p is an equilibrium price system for some population of traders with continuous, increasing, and convex preferences. See Dothan (1990), cor. 2.1, p. 27. Second, q is a price measure because the initial cost of any attainable consumption process is given by its expected value relative to any equilibrium price measure discounted at the bond rate of interest r. See Dothan (1990), thm. 2.3, p. 30. In particular, if we denote by E_q the expected value taken with respect to q, this implies that $p(\theta) = \mathrm{E}_q[d(\theta)]/(1 + r)$.

Note that in the definition q is not requested to be unique; in fact, it is easily shown that this is the case if and only if the market is complete, i.e. there is a contingent claim for each state. See Dothan (1990), thm. 2.2, p. 28. If we join the N vectors d_n representing each security $n = 1, \ldots, N$ into the $K \times N$-dimensional matrix

$$D = \begin{bmatrix} d_1(\omega_1) & \cdots & d_N(\omega_1) \\ \cdots & \cdots & \cdots \\ d_1(\omega_K) & \cdots & d_N(\omega_K) \end{bmatrix} \tag{2}$$

where each row represents a state and each column represents a security, an equivalent condition for completeness is that the rank of D is K.

We now move to the announced proof of the sufficiency part of the following theorem. See Dothan (1990), thm. 2.1, p. 24.

Theorem 2 *An equilibrium price measure q for a price system p exists if and only if there are no arbitrage opportunities.*

The proof proceeds in three steps. First, we observe that if there are no arbitrage opportunities, then all trading strategies yielding the same payout in every state must have the same initial price. Formally, if θ^1 and θ^2 are two portfolios such that $d(\theta^1)(\omega) = d(\theta^2)(\omega)$ for all $\omega \in \Omega$, then $p(\theta^1) = p(\theta^2)$. Therefore, in the absence of arbitrage opportunities, there is a one-to-one correspondence between attainable terminal payout profiles and initial price.

Second, we note that the set of all attainable portfolios is a linear subspace and hence a mixture space where I has been replaced by $\mathbf{R}$.

The third crucial observation is that, given a price system, we can define a binary relation on the set of attainable terminal payout profiles by letting $d(\theta^1) \succ d(\theta^2)$ if and only if $p(\theta^1) > p(\theta^2)$. In the absence of arbitrage opportunities, this relation is well-defined. Moreover, the binary relation $\succ$ thus defined satisfies axioms A1–A3. Therefore, by the mixture space theorem, there exists a linear order-preserving functional F on the set of attainable payout profiles, which is unique up to an increasing affine transformation.

Now, suppose for the moment that the market is complete so that there exist state contingent claims $v^1, \ldots, v^K$ for each state. By a standard induction argument, the functional F can be written as

$$F[d(\theta)] = \sum_{k=1}^{K} d(\omega_k) f_k \tag{3}$$

where $f_k = F(v^k)$ for $k = 1, \ldots, K$. Since F is unique only up to an increasing affine transformation, we have two degrees of freedom in the choice of the weights $f_1, \ldots, f_K$ which can be used to normalize them so that $\sum_k f_k = 1$ and $F[cd(\theta)] = cF[d(\theta)]$, for any $c \in \mathbf{R}$. The normalized weights $f_1, \ldots, f_K$ thus obtained determine the (unique) equilibrium price measure for the complete market.

If the market is not complete, we can add $K - \text{rank}(D)$ arbitrary column vectors to the matrix D in (2) to increase its rank to K. Each of these column vectors represents a fictitious security which is necessary to span an additional coordinate in the $\mathbf{R}^K$ vector space. Then, repeating the construction above, we obtain again an equilibrium price measure. Note that, although the price measure obtained is unique, there exist infinite possible ways to complete the market by choosing fictitious securities and therefore an incomplete market has infinite different equilibrium price measures. This is hardly surprising, given the already quoted result that an equilibrium price measure is unique if and only if the market is complete.

4. Discussion

A natural modification of the proof given above works also in the case of a discrete multiperiod model with a finite number of trading dates. See Garlappi (1992). The multiperiod model is broken into several one-period models and an equilibrium price measure is derived for each of them. The multiperiod equilibrium price measure is then defined as the product of the one-period measures, which are thus interpreted as the conditionals of the multiperiod measure.

For infinite state spaces, instead, the extension requires some additional assumptions. To see why, let us go back to (3) and to our usage of the mixture space theorem. As it is well-known, the mixture space theorem is usually applied to establish some version of the expected utility theorem. In (3), it is d and f that respectively play the roles usually associated with probability and utility. The trick in the proof is to use these traditional elements in a nontraditional way. For instance, the "probability" distribution d can take negative values and may not sum to 1, while the "utility" function f is interpreted (after a normalization) as a price measure. See Castagnoli (1990) and Castagnoli and Li Calzi (1993) for more about an alternative interpretation of the expected utility model where the utility function is read a probability distribution.

To make possible the normalization that transforms the "utility" function f into a price measure, the function f must be bounded. Since this is not guaranteed when the state space is infinite, the extension of our construction requires additional assumptions analogous to the sufficient conditions for the boundedness of the utility function in the expected utility representation. See Fishburn (1982).

Extending the approach, finally, one might consider what might be obtained when trying to apply decision theories different from expected utility to asset pricing models. For a significant step in this direction, see Chateauneuf et alii (1992).

References

[1] E. Castagnoli (1990), "Qualche riflessione sull'utilità attesa," *Ratio Mathematica* **1**, 51–59.

[2] E. Castagnoli and M. Li Calzi (1993), "Expected utility without utility," presented at the Colloquium on Decision Making towards the XXI Century, June 2–5, Madrid, Spain.

[3] A. Chateauneuf, R. Kast and A. Lapied (1992), "Choquet pricing for financial markets with frictions," presented at the XII Meeting of the EURO Working Group on Financial Modelling, November 26–28, Turku, Finland.

[4] M.U. Dothan (1990), *Prices in financial markets*, Oxford University Press.

[5] P.C. Fishburn (1970), *Utility theory for decision making*, Wiley.

[6] P.C. Fishburn (1982), *The foundations of expected utility*, Reidel.

[7] L. Garlappi (1992), *Misure di prezzo di equilibrio nei mercati finanziari*, B.A. thesis, Università "L. Bocconi", Milano.

[8] I.N. Herstein and J. Milnor (1953), "An axiomatic approach to measurable utility," *Econometrica* **21**, 291–297.

Bond Pricing through Bargaining

Elisa Luciano
Istituto di Matematica e Statistica
dell'Università di Lecce
Facoltà di Economia e Commercio
Via Dalmazio Birago 64 73100 Lecce (Italy)

The purpose of this paper is that of studying an highly simplified thin market, where price and quantity are set by bargaining. First we do not explicitly model the bargaining process (axiomatic approach), then we do (strategic one). The traded amount is the same in both cases, since we demonstrate that it depends on Pareto efficiency, not on trade rules. Price on the contrary varies according not only to the approach, but also on the agents' utility function. In the strategic context it depends also on the last mover's advantage.

1 Introduction

The evaluation of financial assets in thin markets acquires a central importance in explaining the behavior of prices and quantities in less developed financial markets, such as most Italian ones. Financial analysts in fact would not hesitate in defining several of our markets as thin, a thin market being defined as one

- with a small number of agents,
- where small demand-supply changes may be connected with significant price effects.[1]

Due to the nature of thin markets – in the above sense – bargaining theory seems to be a truly appropriate instrument for studying their asset pricing.

Even tough we are stimulated by the Italian examples, we do not attempt – for the time being – at focusing on one of them.

The purpose of the paper, on the contrary, is that of using bargaining theory in order to study the equilibrium price and trade volume in symmetric-information financial markets with few buyers and few sellers. They act on their own account, with no intermediaries, and put forward limit orders only.[2]

[1]We do not study thin markets in the sense of markets with a low frequency of transactions.

[2]However, it can be shown that in the presence of limit orders only – as supposed below – and an intermediary, all others equal, price indeterminacy arises, which justifies the present study.

For the sake of simplicity we treat the case of only one bidder and one seller, who trade in a single risky asset. We analyze the case of institutional investors, who maximize the value of their final wealth over a finite horizon.

We adopt two bargaining models, Nash's axiomatic one (Nash, 1950) and Rubinstein's one (Rubinstein, 1982). Both of them are seen as a benchmark, due to their widespread use in the literature and to the fact that they may be self-enforcing (Osborne and Rubinstein, 1990, chapter 4). As a consequence, Rubinstein's approach appears less arbitrary than other models of bargaining. In addition, it is chosen for future developments, since the conditions under which it supports a competitive analysis are quite well known (Osborne and Rubinstein, 1990).

The application of these games however is not straightforward, since not only we have both endogenous prices and quantities, while the standard games are for a normalized quantity, but also we have additional constraints on the choice variables, which call for a detailed study of the set of possible agreements. As a result, the study of our model departs from the standard bargaining situation.

The structure of the paper is as follows. The first part of the paper (sec. 2) uses a cooperative approach, Nash's axiomatic one. Within this framework, subsection 2.1 sets up the model, while subsection 2.2 demonstrates the dependence of the traded amount (price times quantity) on the Pareto-efficiency of the solution; subsection 2.3 characterizes the equilibrium, while 2.4 points out solution properties for the decreasing marginal utility of money case. The second part of the paper (sec. 3) uses a non-cooperative, strategic approach. Within this, subsection 3.1 sets up the model and studies Nash equilibria. Subsection 3.2 studies the subgame perfect equilibria with a finite number of possible offers and counterproposals. Subsection 3.3 investigates the same equilibria when, after any rejection, another offer is allowed. Subsection 3.4 considers the constant marginal utility of money or linear-utility function subcase. Section 4 summarizes and concludes.

2 Nash's axiomatic approach

2.1 Model set-up

The set-up of our model in this case is the following: the market is characterized by the presence of a bidder (a) and a seller (b), who trade at time 0 in a single asset – a bond – against cash. The agents a and b have constant marginal utility of money and are interested only in the value at time n of their portfolio.

Their initial endowments of cash are respectively α and β, both positive. Before any trade is carried out, only the seller owns the bond, in quantity $q > 0$. Short-selling is ruled out.

The bond has an initial price – before any trade occurs – normalized to one. We denote with Φ the (positive) final value of the bond.

Cash at time 0 is invested in the financial market at the conditions represented by a compound factor from 0 to n denoted with ϕ.

Whenever cash and the bond produce cash-flows, they are supposed to be invested again up to the final horizon, which is common to both agents. The factors Φ, ϕ then already inorporate the use of cash-flows on the way. In addition, the factor ϕ

is supposed to depend on the cash amount which is applied to. This dependence is meant to represent the different financial opportunities open to agents with different wealth[3] – due to the presence both of minimal order sizes, and of information and transaction costs. As a consequence, the function ϕ – which is positive whenever its argument is – is supposed to be strictly increasing .

In order to complete the set-up of the model, define also A, the expenditure by a, and ψ, the bond-price determined by bargaining.

As a consequence of the previous assumptions – if we assume that there is no private information[4] – the set of possible agreements between the players a and b is described by the couples of final values

$$(\alpha - A)\phi(\alpha - A) + A\Phi/\psi,$$
$$(\beta + A)\phi(\beta + A) + (q - A/\psi)\Phi\ '$$

provided that

- there is any net gain from trading for at least one of the two players, *i.e.*

$$(\alpha - A)\phi(\alpha - A) + A\Phi/\psi \geq \alpha\phi(\alpha),$$

$$(\beta + A)\phi(\beta + A) + (q - A/\psi)\Phi \geq \beta\phi(\beta) + q\Phi, \tag{1}$$

  with at least one of the two inequalities strict.

- the expenditure for a is non-negative and not greater than his wealth:

$$0 \leq A \leq \alpha.$$

- the bond is not short-saled:

$$A/\psi \leq q.$$

Since in correspondence to the agreement

$$(\alpha - A)\phi(\alpha - A) + A\Phi/\psi = \alpha\phi(\alpha),$$

$$(\beta + A)\phi(\beta + A) + (q - A/\psi)\Phi = \beta\phi(\beta) + q\Phi,$$

the two bargainers are indifferent with respect to trade, that outcome is described as the disagreement event.

If we choose now among the class of linear utility functions the identity[5], the set of all of the utility pairs which can be the outcome of bargaining is:

[3]The use of two different compound functions for the two agents wouldprovide minor changes in the model in the equilibrium. The particular case of compound factors constant with respect to the cash amount – which generates trade iff the factors of the two agents differ – is sketched in Appendix 1.

[4]This rules out the possibility of studying markets with a low frequency of transactions.

[5]This choice is not restrictive, since – as stated below – the first Nash's axiom assumes independence of the equilibrium with respect to preference representations.

$$
\begin{aligned}
S \stackrel{d}{=} \{(s_a, s_b) \in R^2 :\\
(s_a, s_b) = ((\alpha - A)\phi(\alpha - A) + A\Phi/\psi, (\beta + A)\phi(\beta + A) + (q - A/\psi)\Phi),\\
(\alpha - A)\phi(\alpha - A) + A\Phi/\psi \geq \alpha\phi(\alpha),\\
(\beta + A)\phi(\beta + A) + (q - A/\psi)\Phi \geq \beta\phi(\beta) + q\Phi,\\
0 \leq A \leq \alpha, A/\psi \leq q\},
\end{aligned} \tag{2}
$$

At least one of the two inequalities in (1) and (2) must be strict. We are interested first of all in the axiomatic Nash's bargaining outcome of this model.

In order for the Nash solution to be well defined, we must have a couple of agreements (s_a, s_b) which are strictly preferred to the disagreement event. The two conditions which must be satisfied at the same time for this are:

$$
\begin{aligned}
(\alpha - A)\phi(\alpha - A) + A\Phi/\psi > \alpha\phi(\alpha),\\
(\beta + A)\phi(\beta + A) + (q - A/\psi)\Phi > \beta\phi(\beta) + q\Phi.
\end{aligned} \tag{3}
$$

Define the difference in the investment from cash – respectively after and before trade – for the seller, p, and for the buyer, $-P$:

$$
\begin{aligned}
p \stackrel{d}{=} (\beta + A)\phi(\beta + A) - \beta\phi(\beta),\\
P \stackrel{d}{=} (A - \alpha)\phi(\alpha - A) + \alpha\phi(\alpha),
\end{aligned}
$$

and note that $p \geq 0, P \geq 0$, with the inequality strict for $A > 0$. We will regard both of this differences as functions of the traded amount, $p = p(A), P = P(A)$, even when we drop their functional dependence in the formulas. With these definitions the first inequality in (3) above is satisfied by $A > 0$ iff

$$
A\Phi/\psi > P,
$$

while the second holds with $A > 0$ iff

$$
A\Phi/\psi < p.
$$

Obviously, these inequalities mean that the final bond value must be greater than the final cash loss for the buyer, while it must be smaller than the cash gain for the seller. Define now, for $\phi' \neq 0$,

$$
\mathcal{G}(x) \stackrel{d}{=} x\phi''(x)/\phi'(x)
$$

Appendix 2 proofs that the following condition is sufficient [6].

[6] An alternative set of hypotheses is (4) and $q \geq \alpha\phi(\alpha)/\Phi$. If we do not assume (5) in fact, the constraint $A/\psi \leq q$, which can be read as a constraint on ψ – $\psi \geq A/q$ – is binding whenever $A > 0$ and $\Phi/p < 1/q$ (When $\Phi/p \geq 1/q$ it coincides or it is implied by $\psi \geq A\Phi/p$, while for $A = 0$ it is irrelevant). When the constraint is binding for the set of admissible values of ψ to be non-empty we need

$$
1/q \leq \Phi/P
$$

i.e.

$$
q \geq \frac{P}{\Phi}.
$$

Since under (4) the rhs of this inequality is increasing in A, a sufficient condition for it to hold for every A is that $q \geq \alpha\phi(\alpha)/\Phi$. We do not discuss the set of hypotheses (4) and $q \geq \alpha\phi(\alpha)/\Phi$ in the paper.

for the existence of an agreement not worse than the disagreement one for every $A > 0$:

$$\mathcal{G}(x) < -2 \tag{4}$$

both at $x = \alpha - A$ and at $x = \beta + A$.

$$\mathcal{G}(x) \stackrel{d}{=} x\phi''(x)/\phi'(x)$$

The same Appendix proofs also that the no short-sale constraint is satisfied if

$$q \geq \frac{(\alpha+\beta)\phi(\alpha+\beta) - \beta\phi(\beta)}{\Phi}\,. \tag{5}$$

This condition can be re-written as

$$q\Phi \geq p(\alpha)$$

which means that the final value of the bond endowment is not smaller than the maximum cash gain for the seller.

Theorem 2.1.1 *Under the hypotheses (4) and (5),*

- *for each* $0 < A \leq \alpha$ *the set of admissible values for* ψ *has a non-empty interior*
- *the requirement in (1) above, with at least one inequality strict, is satisfied*
- *the no-short sales constraint is redundant.*

As a consequence, the set S described by (2) can be re-written as

$$\mathbf{S} = \{(\mathbf{s}_a, \mathbf{s}_b) \in R^2 :$$

$$(\mathbf{s}_a, \mathbf{s}_b) = ((\alpha - A)\phi(\alpha - A) + A\Phi/\psi, (\beta + A)\phi(\beta + A) + (q - A/\psi)\Phi)\,,$$

$$\frac{A\Phi}{p} \leq \psi \leq \frac{A\Phi}{P}$$

$$(\text{if } A \neq 0), 0 \leq A \leq \alpha\}. \tag{6}$$

2.2 Pareto efficiency

The agreement reached by the two parties is as usual assumed to be Pareto-efficient, *i.e.* to lie on the contract curve. When $A \neq 0$, the latter is characterized by the equation

$$\frac{\frac{\partial \mathbf{s}_a}{\partial A}}{\frac{\partial \mathbf{s}_a}{\partial \psi}} = \frac{\frac{\partial \mathbf{s}_b}{\partial A}}{\frac{\partial \mathbf{s}_b}{\partial \psi}}\,,$$

which in turn can be rewritten as

$$(A^* - \alpha)\phi'(\alpha - A^*) + (\beta + A^*)\phi'(\beta + A^*) - \phi(\alpha - A^*) + \phi(\beta + A^*) = 0. \tag{7}$$

The Pareto-efficiency of the solution [7] then determines the value of the traded amount (price times quantity). Since, as we will demonstrate, (7) holds for investors with non-linear utility functions too, the specific bargaining rules – in our terminology, the axiomatic or the strategic approach, with finite or infinite offers – are responsibile only for the price level. When no solution exists for (7), there is no trade, while the existence of one or more solutions opens the way to price-bargaining.

First of all, we note that α cannot solve (7), since ϕ strictly increasing implies that its lhs be positive:

$$(\beta + A)\phi'(\beta + A) + \phi(\beta + A) - \phi(0) > 0.$$

We are then left with the cases of no solution – which implies no trade – and of solutions smaller than α. Having defined

$$M \stackrel{d}{=} \max_{A,\psi}(\mathbf{s}_a + \mathbf{s}_b)$$

subject to

$$0 < A < \alpha,$$

in the sequel we distinguish the two cases by saying respectively that $A^* = 0$ and $A^* = \arg M < \alpha$.

In fact, the following property holds:

Theorem 2.2.1 *if $A^* = \arg M$, then (7) holds.*

In turn, this property can be demonstrated by performing the following steps:

- compute $\mathbf{s}_a$ in $\arg M$ and isolate ψ:

$$\psi = \frac{\Phi \arg M}{\mathbf{s}_a - (\alpha - \arg M)\phi(\alpha - \arg M)},$$

- substitute ψ into $\mathbf{s}_b$, so as to obtain the following equality, which holds along the contract curve:

$$\mathbf{s}_a + \mathbf{s}_b = (\alpha - \arg M)\phi(\alpha - \arg M) + (\beta + \arg M)\phi(\beta + \arg M) + q\Phi.$$

[7] Note that the contract curve is well-defined, if we assume that the sum of the elasticities of substitutions between A and ψ for the two agents is positive. In fact, with linear utility functions, the indifference curves of both agents have the slope of the same sign. This slope is

$$\frac{\psi}{A}\,[-1 + \psi(x\phi(x) + \phi'(x))/\Phi]$$

with $x = \alpha - A$ for a and $x = \beta + A$ for b. Substituting the condition (7) into this expression and recalling that both A and ψ are positive, the statement on the slopes follows. Given that, the locus of the tangency points defines the Pareto-optimal trades iff the elasticities of substitution have the same sign or – having different signs – the positive one prevails in the sum. The two cases in fact represent indifference curves in the Edgeworth box with opposite concavity and indifference curves with the same concavity, which – when tangent – do not stand in the direction of increase of the other agent's utility.

- Finally, substitute this expression for the sum of the payoffs into M:

$$M = q\Phi + \max_A ((\alpha - A)\phi(\alpha - A) + (\beta + A)\phi(\beta + A)). \tag{8}$$

By so doing it is evident that the first necessary condition for M is (7) above.

Two comments are immediate on the effects of Pareto optimality, represented by (7):

- the value A^* depends on both the seller's and the buyer's wealth – as well as on the investment conditions other than the bond ones – and it is independent of the bond profitability (Φ);
- When trade exists ($A^* > 0$), a wealth effect applies, since A^* can be proved to be decreasing in β and increasing in α. This effect is then positive for the buyer and negative for the seller, producing an increase in trade when either the buyer's wealth increases or the seller's one decreases. [8]

2.3 Equilibria

Having outlined the consequences of Pareto-efficiency, we define the set of agreements:

$$\begin{gathered} \mathbf{S}' \stackrel{d}{=} \{(\mathbf{s}_a, \mathbf{s}_b) \in R^2 : \\ (\mathbf{s}_a; \mathbf{s}_b) = [(\alpha - A)\phi(\alpha - A) + A\Phi/\psi, (\beta + A)\phi(\beta + A) + (q - A/\psi)\Phi], \\ \mathbf{s}_a + \mathbf{s}_b \leq M, \\ \alpha\phi(\alpha) \leq \mathbf{s}_a \leq \mathbf{s}'_a, \beta\phi(\beta) + q\Phi \leq \mathbf{s}_b \leq \mathbf{s}'_b\}, \end{gathered} \tag{9}$$

The upper bounds $\mathbf{s}'_a$ and $\mathbf{s}'_b$ are determined in Appendix 3 (to be obtained from the author upon request). The set $\mathbf{S}'$ is compact, convex and connected.

We define also its Pareto frontier, represented in the figure below:

$$\mathcal{F}(\mathbf{S}') \stackrel{d}{=} \{(\mathbf{s}_a, \mathbf{s}_b) \in \mathbf{S}' : \mathbf{s}_a + \mathbf{s}_b = M\}.$$

Appendix 3 demonstrates the following property:

Theorem 2.3.1 *Along the Pareto frontier $F(\mathbf{S}')$ the constraints on the payoffs become:*

$$\alpha\phi(\alpha) \leq \mathbf{s}_a \leq M - q\Phi - \beta\phi(\beta),$$

$$\beta\phi(\beta) + q\Phi \leq \mathbf{s}_b \leq M - \alpha\phi(\alpha).$$

[8] The results follow simply from the implicit function theorem applied to (7):

$$\frac{\partial A^*}{\partial \beta} = - \frac{\phi'(A^* + \beta)[2 + \mathcal{G}(A^* + \beta)]}{\phi'(\alpha - A^*)[2 + \mathcal{G}(\alpha - A^*)] + \phi'(A^* + \beta)[2 + \mathcal{G}(A^* + \beta)]},$$

$$\frac{\partial A^*}{\partial \alpha} = \frac{\phi'(\alpha - A^*)[2 + \mathcal{G}(\alpha - A^*)]}{\phi'(\alpha - A^*)[2 + \mathcal{G}(\alpha - A^*)] + \phi'(A^* + \beta)[2 + \mathcal{G}(A^* + \beta)]}.$$

The theorem is applicable because we assumed ϕ stricly increasing and (4), which excludes also $\phi'(x) = 0$ at $x = \alpha - A, \beta + A$. In turn, (4) implies that both the numerator and the denominator of the second derivative above be negative. Also, it implies that the first derivative is negative.

To the bargaining problem defined on the set $\mathbf{S}'$ we can apply Nash's theorem (Nash, 1950):

Theorem 2.3.1 (Nash) *There is a unique bargaining solution satisfying the axioms of*

- *invariance to equivalent utility representation,*
- *symmetry of utility pairs,*
- *independence of irrelevant alternatives,*
- *Pareto efficiency.*

In our case the solution in Nash's theorem is given by:

$$\arg \max_{(\mathbf{s}_a,\mathbf{s}_b)\in\mathbf{S}'} (\mathbf{s}_a - \alpha\phi(\alpha))\,(\mathbf{s}_b - \beta\phi(\beta) - q\Phi)\,.$$

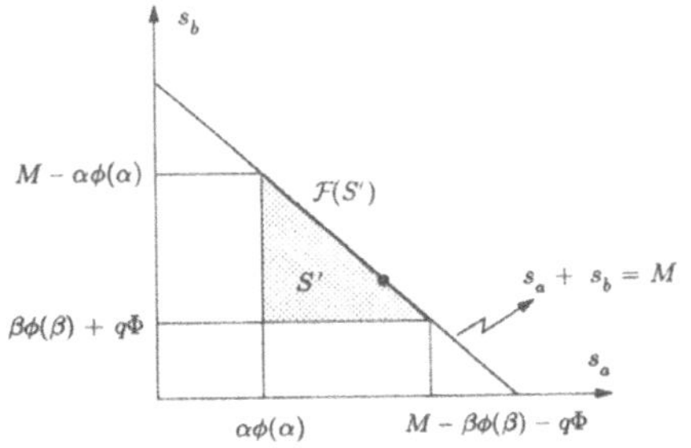

Figure #1

Due to the hypothesis of Pareto efficiency, the solution on $\mathbf{S}'$ is the same than on $\mathbf{S}$. In any case in fact the solution is on the Pareto frontier of $\mathbf{S}'$, $\mathcal{F}(\mathbf{S}')$.

Due to the Pareto assumption, the maximization process leads to $A^* = \arg M$ when (7) has solutions, to $A^* = 0$ otherwise.

As concerns the optimal price, which is worth considering only when $A^* > 0$, it must be

$$\arg\max_{\psi} ((\alpha - A^*)\phi(\alpha - A^*) + A^*\Phi/\psi - \alpha\phi(\alpha)) \times \qquad (10)$$
$$\times\, ((\beta + A^*)\phi(\beta + A^*) - A^*\Phi/\psi - \beta\phi(\beta))\,,$$

subject to:

$$\frac{A\Phi}{p(A)} \leq \psi \leq \frac{A\Phi}{P(A)}\,. \qquad (11)$$

The function to be maximized in (10) can be written as

$$-pP + A\Phi(p+P)/\psi - A^2\Phi^2/\psi^2.$$

It is increasing (decreasing) w.r.t. ψ if

$$\psi < (>) A\Phi/(p+P).$$

The first part of the constraint (11) together with the fact that P is positive ($A > 0$), implies that the optimal value of ψ is

$$\psi^* = 2A\Phi/(p+P), \tag{12}$$

which lies strictly between the constraint boundaries.

We have then proved the following theorem:

Theorem 2.3.1 *The Nash solution for the traded amount is* $A^* = \arg M$, *when (7) holds, and* $A^* = 0$ *otherwise. In the first case the optimal price is given by (12).*

Several comments can be made about the price which characterizes this solution, or, equivalently, positive trade.

- First of all, ψ^* is chosen so as to give the following payoffs:

$$\mathbf{s}_a = \alpha\phi(\alpha) + (p - P)/2,$$

$$\mathbf{s}_b = \beta\phi(\beta) + q\Phi + (p - P)/2.$$

  Both players then receive the same payoff increase with respect to their no-trade final wealth.

- Secondly, the payoffs to the two players are equal, whenever

$$\alpha\phi(\alpha) = \beta\phi(\beta) + q\Phi,$$

  and $(\mathbf{s}_a, \mathbf{s}_b)$ belongs to $\mathbf{S}'$ iff $(\mathbf{s}_b, \mathbf{s}_a)$does. In this peculiar case, represented in figure 2, the symmetry axiom implies the symmetry of the Nash's solution, which means the equality of the equilibrium payoffs [9].

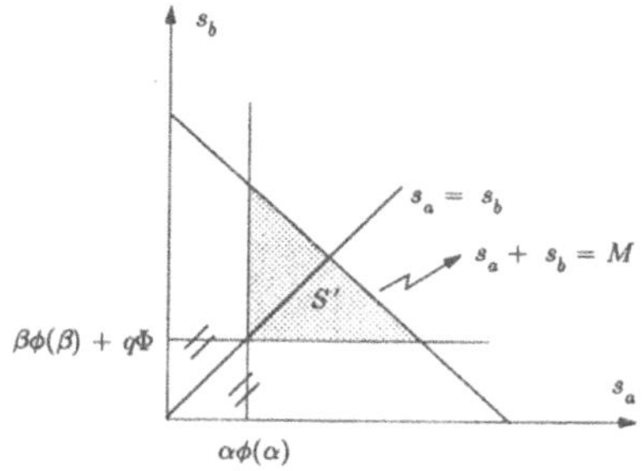

Figure #2

[9] Please note that we have payoff equality, not symmetry of the solutions $\arg M$ and ψ^*. In the latter case in fact we should have $\arg M = A^* = \alpha/2$ and $\psi^* = A\Phi(P+p)/(2pP)$.

- the optimal price is strictly increasing (linearly) with the bond's profitability (Φ).
- the price changes due to changes in the traded amount or in the agent's wealth do not have a constant or *a priori* known sign, since

$$\frac{\partial \psi^*}{\partial A} = 2\Phi \frac{-A\{(\beta + A)\phi'(\beta + A) + (\alpha - A)\phi'(\alpha - A)\} + \beta\Delta\phi(b) + \alpha\Delta\phi(a)}{(p(A) + P(A))^2}$$

where

$$\Delta\phi(b) \stackrel{d}{=} \phi(\beta + A) - \phi(\beta)$$
$$\Delta\phi(a) \stackrel{d}{=} \phi(\alpha) - \phi(\alpha - A)$$

In particular, an increase in the traded amount can be the result of both price and quantity increases as well as of a price increase accompanied by a quantity decrease (or viceversa). As a consequence, the phenomenon of small demand-supply changes connected with significant price-effects – mentioned in the introduction – is allowed for.

2.4 Decreasing marginal utility of money

Assume now that – all other things equal – our agents' utilities are not linear any more. On the contrary, suppose that they are continuous, strictly increasing and concave. Since in our context this simply produces a distortion in the monetary outcomes, we do not expect the model to be very sensitive to this new assumption, except that as a consequence of the differences in the two agents' utilities.

As a matter of fact, the problem is non-degenerate if conditions (3) are satisfied. The sufficient conditions for them to hold are (4) and (5), the same as above. As above, we suppose that (4) above hold for every A, so that ϕ is twice differentiable. The set which now plays the rôle of $\mathbf{S}'$ above is:

$$\begin{aligned} \overline{\Sigma} \stackrel{d}{=} \{(\sigma'_a, \sigma'_b) \in R^2 : \\ (\sigma'_a, \sigma'_b) = [u_a(\mathbf{s}_a), u_b(\mathbf{s}_b)], \qquad & \mathbf{s}_a + \mathbf{s}_b \le M, \\ u_a[\alpha\phi(\alpha)] \le \sigma'_a \le \overline{\sigma}'_a, \quad & u_b[\beta\phi(\beta) + q\Phi] \le \sigma'_b \le \overline{\sigma}'_b\}. \end{aligned} \tag{13}$$

where M is defined as above, and the upper and lower bounds on utilities are a consequence of those on the payoffs together with the monotonicity of the utility functions. In particular, if $\mathbf{s}_a + \mathbf{s}_b = M$, the upper constraints become – for the same reasons than in the linear case –

$$\overline{\sigma}'_a = u_a[M - \beta\phi(\beta) - q\Phi],$$

$$\overline{\sigma}'_b = u_b[M - \alpha\phi(\alpha)].$$

We then note that – due to the strict monotonicity of the utility functions – the constraint

$$\mathbf{s}_a + \mathbf{s}_b \le M$$

can be re-written as

$$u_a^{-1}(\sigma_a') + u_b^{-1}(\sigma_b') \leq M$$

where u_i^{-1} $(i = a, b)$ is the inverse of the function u_i. At least when the conditions for applying twice the implicit function theorem to the constraint $u_a^{-1}(\sigma_a')+u_b^{-1}(\sigma_b') = M$ apply, concavity of the utility functions is sufficient for the set $\overline{\Sigma}$ to be compact and convex. By applying the aforementioned theorem with concave utility functions in fact the constraint $\mathbf{s}_a + \mathbf{s}_b \leq M$ can be shown to produce a concave Pareto frontier – $\mathcal{F}(\overline{\Sigma})$ – for the set $\overline{\Sigma}$, as represented in the following picture.

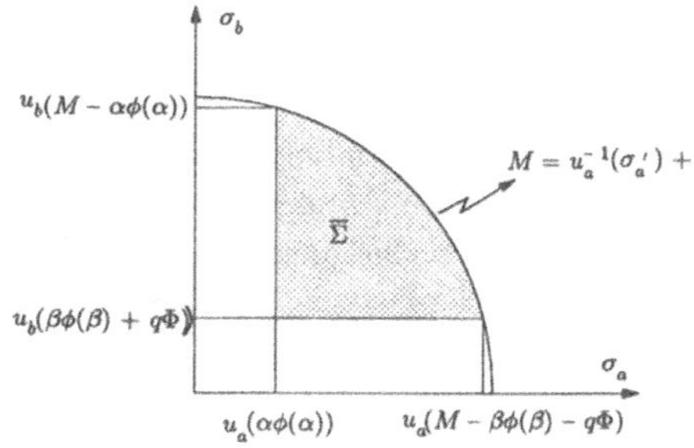

Figure #3

Due to the properties of the set $\overline{\Sigma}$ Nash's theorem again applies.

Since the solution lies on the Pareto frontier of $\overline{\Sigma}$, A is bounded to be 0 or $\arg M$, as determined by (7). In the second case we can write the Nash solution for the equilibrium price as

$$\arg\max_{\psi} \left[u_a(\mathbf{s}_a) - u_a(\alpha\phi(\alpha))\right] \left[u_b(\mathbf{s}_b) - u_b(\beta\phi(\beta) + q\Phi)\right], \tag{14}$$

with the payoffs computed in A^* and in the optimal value of ψ, ψ^*. The maximum is subject to

$$A^*\Phi/p(A^*) \leq \psi \leq A^*\Phi/P(A^*).$$

As a consequence, the same remarks than in the linear interior case apply to the equilibrium trade.

As for ψ^*, in the internal case with differentiable utility functions the necessary condition for (14) – discussed in Appendix 4 – reduces to:

$$\frac{u_a'(\mathbf{s}_a)}{u_a(\mathbf{s}_a) - u_a(\alpha\phi(\alpha))} = \frac{u_b'(\mathbf{s}_b)}{u_b(\mathbf{s}_b) - u_b(\beta\phi(\beta) + q\Phi)} \tag{15}$$

with $\mathbf{s}_a$ and $\mathbf{s}_b$ computed in $A^* = \arg M$ and in the optimal value of ψ, ψ^*.

In the internal case then – since the strict concavity of the utility functions guarantees that the sufficient conditions for the maximum with respect to ψ are satisfied – the Nash solution of our problem has the following property, which is proved in Appendix 4:

Theorem 2.4.1 *If the agents'utility functions are C^2 on an open set containing ψ^* and $A^* = \arg M$, then the equilibrium value of ψ is strictly increasing (strictly decreasing) with respect to $A^* > 0$ if it is smaller (greater) than $\Phi/[\phi(\alpha - A^*) + (\alpha - A^*)\phi'(\alpha - A^*)]$.*

However, in this case, since we do not have an explicit solution for ψ^*, we cannot give conditions on the price increase $(\psi^* - 1)$ for the model to be consistent.

3 The strategic approach

3.1 The model

In the strategic approach we take as set of possible agreements **S** defined in section 2.1. However, we suppose that agents are interested not only in the result of the bargaining procedure, but also in the epoch at which the agreement – or the final decision not to trade – is reached. This assumption is justified by the standard hypothesis of opportunity cost in financial markets. To do this, we need to explicitly model the negotiation process.

We imagine that at each time of a discrete sequence $t = 0, 1, \ldots,$ either the buyer or the seller tenders an amount A and a price ψ. The counterpart may accept or reject the offer. In the first case the game ends up. In the second the players wait up to the next time of the sequence, when the one who was formerly the proponent accepts or refuses the tender of the other, who moves first. The time sequence denoted with t can be either finite ($t \leq T$) or infinite. In the first case the solution of the bargaining process can be determined by backward induction; under the assumptions specified below in this section, the backward-induction solution can be proved to have the property that it converges – for divergent T – to the solution of the infinite-bargaining game (Binmore 1987). Please note that we allow for possibly infinite proposals within the finite agents' horizon for a main reason, discussed at lenght by Osborne and Rubinstein (1990):"the significant difference in the two models is not in the realism of the horizon they posit, but in the strategic reasoning of the two players", since"the model with a finite horizon fits a situation in which the players perceive that, after any rejection of an offer, there is room for a counterproposal...the model with a finite horizon fits a situation in which the final stage of the game is perceived clearly by the players, who fully take it into account when formulating their strategies.". Even in a finite context the possibility of counterproposals may be crucial for some agents, so that the infinite model makes sense even without making the usual reference to the infinite horizon as a proxy for a very long, finite one. [10]

In the sequel we analyze first the finite-horizon case and then the infinite one.

As stated before, we then assume that each player is interested not only in his payoff from the couple $(\mathbf{s}_a, \mathbf{s}_b)$ in **S**, but also in the epoch t at which this agreement is reached. The standard time-preference hypothesis applies.

[10]Note also that in the model below the discrete index takes integer values: however, we could easily make it run over an infinite sequence converging to a finite epoch.

On the triplets $(\mathbf{s}_a, \mathbf{s}_b, t)$ we assume that the two players have a complete, transitive and reflexive preference ordering, $\succeq_i$, $i = a, b$, satisfying the assumptions of [6]:

- 1) disagreement is the worst outcome,
- 2) M is desirable,
- 3) time is valuable,
- 4) preferences are continuous,
- 5) preferences are stationary.

We will eventually introduce also the hypothesis of

- 6) loss to delay increasing with the payoff.

The third and sixth hypotheses depend on our assumption that $(\mathbf{s}_a, \mathbf{s}_b)$ are final payoffs. If there is a delay in agreement, the agents lose opportunities for investing their rewards. Whenever assumption 6 holds, opportunity costs are increasing, as standard in a financial context. Assumptions 1 to 5 imply that each player's preferences are represented - for every $\delta_i \in (0, 1)$ - by a function

$$\delta_i^t u_i(\mathbf{s}_i) \quad i = a, b. \tag{16}$$

Both u_i must be continuous and strictly increasing (Fishburn and Rubinstein, 1982).

Under the hypotheses 1 to 5 we can define – both for the finite and the infinite horizon model – two standard types of equilibrium:

- the Nash equilibrium,
- the subgame perfect equilibrium, which is a Nash equilibrium both for the entire game and for each subgame.

Since we are still working with Nash equilibria, the Pareto efficiency of the solution implies $A = A^*$, as defined in section 2.1. Either trade is not carried out, or it is characterized by the amount $\arg M$.

As concerns the Nash equilibria, we do not end up with a unique solution for our bargaining procedure, be it finite or not. On the contrary, it can be shown, even without assumption 6, that each agreement $(\mathbf{s}_a, \mathbf{s}_b)$ belonging to the Pareto frontier of $\mathbf{S}$ – defined as $\mathcal{F}(\mathbf{S}')$ in section 2.1 – is a Nash equilibrium both for the finite and the infinite horizon game [11]. As a consequence of this infinity of equilibria, price is undetermined.

As concerns subgame perfect equilibria, we must truly distinguish the finite and the infinite horizon games.

---

[11] As in Osborne and Rubinstein (1990, p.42): suppose that the buyer a always proposes $(s_a, s_b$ and accepts an offer from b iff its own payoff in it is not less than s_a. Suppose analogously that the seller b always proposes (s_a, s_b) and accepts a buyer's offer iff its own payoff in it is not less than s_b. The equilibrium is then reached at time 0, when the first mover proposes (s_a, s_b) , and the other player accepts. This equilibrium is Nash, because – under the assumption 1 above and given the first move – it is the best result that the second player can attain.

3.2 Finite offers

In the finite horizon case, the equilibrium is studied through backward induction, as in Rubinstein (1982).

If period T is reached and it is a's turn to make the offer, he chooses

$$\max_{A,\psi} u_a(\mathbf{s}_a),$$

where the maximum is subject to the constraints in (6) and to $\mathbf{s}_a + \mathbf{s}_b = M$. When trade is positive, ψ – the corresponding price – is chosen so as to maximize a's utility. The problem above transforms into:

$$\max_{\psi} u_a(\mathbf{s}_a),$$

with $A = \arg M$ and under the constraint (11). This maximum is reached by minimizing the payoff to b, since the utility function is assumed to be increasing. In turn, the payoff to b is minimized by choosing $\psi^* = A\Phi/p$.

As a consequence, a offers to b his indifference-payoff $q\Phi + \beta\phi(\beta)$, and gets $M - q\Phi - \beta\phi(\beta)$, which, if the set $\mathbf{S}$ has a non-empty interior, is greater than $\alpha\phi(\alpha)$.

In period $T - 1$, when it is b's turn to make an offer, he proposes to a the minimum acceptance cash-flow. Since at T a gets $M - q\Phi - \beta\phi(\beta)$, b's proposal at $T - 1$ is $\mathbf{m}_a$ defined by:

$$u_a(\mathbf{m}_a) = \delta_a u_a[M - q\Phi - \beta\phi(\beta)],$$

or, due to the properties of u_a,

$$\mathbf{m}_a = u_a^{-1}\left\{\delta_a u_a[M - q\Phi - \beta\phi(\beta)]\right\}.$$

Obviously, this proposal is valid if it generates values of A and ψ such that the corresponding cash-flow for b, $\mathbf{m}_b$, makes him at least indifferent between getting it at $T - 1$ or getting $q\Phi + \beta\phi(\beta)$ at T. This fact – evident in Rubinstein's model – in our context can be proved as follows. Agent b is not only indifferent, but he gains from waiting his turn: in fact, he gets

$$u_b(M - \mathbf{m}_a).$$

Since $\mathbf{m}_a$ permits a to reach a utility level which is only a fraction $0 < \delta_a < 1$ of his former utility, $u_a[M - q\Phi - \beta\phi(\beta)]$, then

$$\mathbf{m}_a < M - q\Phi - \beta\phi(\beta).$$

It follows that

$$\Phi + \beta\phi(\beta) < M - \mathbf{m}_a,$$

and, since u_b is increasing and $0 < \delta_b < 1$:

$$delta_b u_b(q\Phi + \beta\phi(\beta)) < u_b(M - \mathbf{m}_a),$$

which means that the value at $T - 1$ of the "satisfaction" of b at T is smaller than the one at $T - 1$.

At $T-1$ then the seller, who is the first mover, gains with respect to T – in present value terms – while the buyer is indifferent.

At time $T-2$ a offers to b

$$\mathbf{m}_b = u_b^{-1}\left(\delta_b u_b(M - \mathbf{s}_a)\right),$$

so that b is indifferent between getting this payoff at $T-2$ or stopping the bargain at $T-1$. At the same time, a obtains

$$u_a(M - \mathbf{m}_b).$$

With a reasoning analogous to that reported for period $T-1$, it can be shown that

$$\delta_a u_a(\mathbf{m}_a) < u_a(M - \mathbf{m}_b).$$

There is then a net gain for the buyer a – also in present value terms – in passing from $T-1$ to $T-2$, when he is the first-mover. The seller b on the contrary is indifferent between stopping the bargain at $T-1$ or going to $T-2$.

Organizing the results in a table, we get:

TABLE 1

time	T	$T-1$	$T-2$
first mover	a	b	a
utility of a	$u_a[M - q\Phi - \beta\phi(\beta)]$	$u_a(\mathbf{m}_a)$	$u_a(M - \mathbf{m}_b)$
utility of b	$u_b[q\Phi + \beta\phi(\beta)]$	$u_b(M - \mathbf{m}_a)$	$u_b(\mathbf{m}_b)$

By continuing in our reasoning, and then going onwards instead of backwards, it can be shown that at each time t there is at least one player which loses from going on in the bargaining procedure, while the other is indifferent. Based on the first assumption of section 2.1. the equilibrium of the game exists and is the first offer ($t = 0$).

In this equilibrium, the optimal price value depends on the agents'utilities and on the number of moves which the agents can exploit. In particular, if T is even, so that at $t = 0$ it is a's turn to move first, he is advantaged with respect to the case in which T is odd. In the latter b makes the first and final offer. The equilibrium then reflects the last-mover advantage structure of the game, as in Rubinstein (1982). As in that case, however, this is not proper to the bargaining structure, but only to some of its features. The equilibrium in fact could be changed simply by assuming that b moves first at the last bargaining stage, T. Alternatively, a symmetric solution can be searched for – as in the axiomatic approach – reducing the length of time between two successive offers or making the choice of the first mover random (with probability 1/2 for each) at each stage of the game (Osborne and Rubinstein, 1990, sections 3.10.3 and 4.4.).

3.3 Infinite offers

In the infinite horizon market, the assumptions 1 to 6 above are sufficient for the following result of [8] to hold:

Theorem 3.3.1 (Rubinstein) *Every bargaining game of alternating offers in which the players' preferences satisfy assumptions 1 to 6 has a unique subgame perfect equilibrium, in which player a (b) always proposes the agreement* $(\mathbf{s}_a^*, \mathbf{s}_b^*)((\mathbf{v}_a^*, \mathbf{v}_b^*))$ *in the previous lemma whenever it is her turn to make an offer, and accepts an offer* $(\mathbf{v}_a, \mathbf{v}_b)((\mathbf{s}_a, \mathbf{s}_b))$ *of b (a) iff* $\mathbf{v}_a \geq \mathbf{v}_a^*((\mathbf{s}_b \geq \mathbf{s}_b^*))$. *Player a proposes* $(\mathbf{s}_a^*, \mathbf{s}_b^*)$ *in the first period, and b immediately accepts.*

We now specify the marginal utility of money of the agents – analogously to what we did in section 2 above – in order to

- give an example of convergence of the finite-horizon equilibrium to the infinite-horizon one, and to
- appreciate the consequences of the propositions just stated in selecting from an infinite number of Nash's equilibria a single subgame perfect one.

3.4 Linear utility functions

We suppose from now on that the buyer and the seller in our bargaining procedure have linear utility functions within each period. The functions in (16) become:

$$U_i(T-t) \stackrel{d}{=} \delta_i^t \mathbf{s}_i.$$

As usual $A^* = 0$ or $A^* = \arg M$. In the latter case, as concerns the perfect equilibrium with a finite number of offers, the solution proposed in section 3.2 above transforms into:

TABLE 2

time	1st mover	utility of a	utility of b
T	a	$U_a(T)$	$U_b(T)$
$T-1$	b	$U_a(T-1)$	$U_b(T-1)$
$T-2$	a	$U_a(T-2)$	$U_b(T-2)$
...	...	...	...
$T-2n^*$	a	$U_a(T-2n)$	$U_b(T-2n)$
$T-(2n+1)^{**}$	b	$U_a[T-(2n+1)]$	$U_b[T-(2n+1)]$

* $(1 \leq n \leq T/2)$, ** $(0 \leq n \leq (T-1)/2)$

where:

$$\begin{aligned}
&U_a(T) = M - q\Phi - \beta\phi(\beta)\\
&U_b(T) = q\Phi + \beta\phi(\beta)\\
&U_a(T-1) = \delta_a(M - \beta\phi(\beta) - q\Phi)\\
&U_b(T-1) = M - \delta_a(M - \beta\phi(\beta) - q\Phi)\\
&U_a(T-2) = M - \delta_b[M - \delta_a(M - \phi(\beta) - q\Phi)]\\
&U_b(T-2) = \delta_b[M - \delta_a(M - \beta\phi(\beta) - q\Phi)]\\
&U_a(T-2n) = M(1-\delta_b)\textstyle\sum_0^{n-1}\delta_a^j\delta_b^j + \delta_a^n\delta_b^n(M - q\Phi - \beta\phi(\beta))\\
&U_b(T-2n) = M - M(1-\delta_b)\textstyle\sum_0^{n-1}\delta_a^j\delta_b^j - \delta_a^n\delta_b^n(M - q\Phi - \beta\phi(\beta))\\
&U_a[T-(2n+1)] = M - M(1-\delta_a)\textstyle\sum_0^{n}\delta_a^j\delta_b^j - \delta_a^{n+1}\delta_b^n(q\Phi + \beta\phi(\beta))\\
&U_b[T-(2n+1)] = M(1-\delta_a)\textstyle\sum_0^{n}\delta_a^j\delta_b^j + \delta_a^{n+1}\delta_b^n(q\Phi + \beta\phi(\beta))
\end{aligned}$$

This equilibrium can be interpreted exactly as the one in section 3.2 above. As a consequence, the strategic approach under linear utility has no effect neither on the equilibrium trade nor on the epoch at which trade takes place. Price on the contrary will be chosen so as to make the payoff correspond to those in table 2. All others equal, it will then be different from that in section 3.2, which guarantees the payoffs in table 1.

As concerns the infinite-offers game, since in this case the theorem in section 3.3 above applies, we know that – for $A^* = \arg M$ – there exists a unique perfect equilibrium for our bargaining procedure, which is reached at time 0. Considering the form of the utility function, at time 0 a proposes

$$\mathbf{v}_a^* = \delta_a \mathbf{s}_a^*, \tag{17}$$

$$\mathbf{s}_b^* = \delta_b \mathbf{v}_b^*, \tag{18}$$

and b immediately accepts.

Rubinstein's results however can be enriched, since not only we can solve for $\mathbf{s}_a^*, \mathbf{s}_b^*, \mathbf{v}_a^*, \mathbf{v}_b^*$, but also for the equilibrium values of ψ.

As regards the former problem, since we know that we are in a Nash's equilibrium, so that

$$\mathbf{v}_a^* + \mathbf{v}_b^* = \mathbf{s}_a^* + \mathbf{s}_b^* = M, \tag{19}$$

we can use the conditions (17),(18),(19) in order to solve for $\mathbf{s}_a^*, \mathbf{s}_b^*, \mathbf{v}_a^*, \mathbf{v}_b^*$:

$$\begin{aligned} \mathbf{s}_a^* &= M\,\frac{1-\delta_b}{1-\delta_a\delta_b}\,, \\ \mathbf{s}_b^* &= M\,\frac{\delta_b(1-\delta_a)}{1-\delta_a\delta_b}\,, \\ \mathbf{v}_a^* &= M\,\frac{\delta_a(1-\delta_b)}{1-\delta_a\delta_b}\,, \\ \mathbf{v}_b^* &= M\,\frac{1-\delta_a}{1-\delta_a\delta_b}\,. \end{aligned} \tag{20}$$

The reader can easily appreciate the fact that this values are the limits of the perfect equilibrium ones under finite offers, when we can work back an infinite number of periods. To be precise, we have:

$$\begin{aligned} \mathbf{s}_a^* &= \lim_{n\to+\infty} U_a(T-2n) \\ \mathbf{s}_b^* &= \lim_{n\to+\infty} U_b(T-2n) \\ \mathbf{v}_a^* &= \lim_{n\to+\infty} U_a(T-2n-1) \\ \mathbf{v}_b^* &= \lim_{n\to+\infty} U_b(T-2n-1) \end{aligned}$$

They still reflect a's advantage, which disappears under the hypothesis suggested in section 3.2 above.

As concerns the equilibrium value of ψ, ψ^*, it equates $\mathbf{s}_a$ to $\mathbf{s}_a^*$ and $\mathbf{s}_b$ to $\mathbf{s}_b^*$:

$$\psi^* = \frac{A\Phi}{\mathbf{s}_b^* + (A+\beta)\phi(A+\beta) + q\Phi}$$

or, equivalently:

$$\psi^* = \frac{A\Phi}{\mathbf{s}_a^* - (\alpha - A)\phi(\alpha - A)}$$

When $A^* = \arg M$, since

$$\mathbf{s}_a = M - (\beta + A)\phi(\beta + A) + A\Phi/\psi - q\Phi,$$

and (20) holds, ψ^* can be rewritten as:

$$\psi^* = \frac{A^*\Phi(1 - \delta_a\delta_b)}{(1 - \delta_b)[(\beta + A^*)\phi(\beta + A^*) + q\Phi] - \delta_b(1 - \delta_a)(\alpha - A^*)\phi(\alpha - A^*)} . \tag{21}$$

We have then proved the following theorem:

Theorem 3.4.1 *The subgame perfect equilibrium value for the traded amount is $A^* = \arg M$, when (7) holds, and $A^* = 0$ otherwise. In the first case the bond price is given by (21).*

Two remarks can be done on the expression of ψ^*.

- This price depends on trade, on the value of δ compatible with a linear representation of the utility function, and on the wealth of both agents, as well as on the returns of both bonds and cash.
- Since

$$\frac{\partial \psi^*}{\partial A} = \Phi \frac{\mathbf{s}_b^* + q\Phi + \phi(A + \beta)\beta - A(\beta + A)\phi'(\beta + A)}{(\mathbf{s}_b^* + q\Phi + \phi(A + \beta)(A + \beta))^2} = \tag{22}$$

$$= \Phi \frac{\mathbf{s}_a^* - \alpha\phi(\alpha - A) + A(\alpha - A)\phi'(\alpha - A)}{(\mathbf{s}_a^* - \phi(\alpha - A)(\alpha - A))^2} \tag{23}$$

- the optimal price is increasing with respect to A if the returns on non-bond wealth satisfy one of the following inequalities:

$$\phi(A + \beta)\beta - A(\beta + A)\phi'(\beta + A) > -\mathbf{s}_b^* - q\Phi$$

$$\phi(\alpha - A)\alpha + A(\alpha - A)\phi'(\alpha - A) < \mathbf{s}_a^*$$

As in section 2.3, (21, 22 23) entail that small demand-supply changes may be accompanied by discrete price variations.

4 Summary and conclusions

We have studied bond equilibrium prices and traded quantities in a thin market with limit orders and bargaining.

Our results are the following.

Both in an axiomatic and in a strategic context, the traded amount (price times quantity) is determined by the hypothesis of Pareto efficiency of the outcome. Its properties have been studied in section 2.2.

As concerns the price at which trade takes place – when it indeed does – we have distinguished axiomatic Nash bargaining solutions from strategic Nash and subgame perfect equilibria. In the strategic context, in addition, we have characterized both the case in which a finite number of proposals is allowed – so that agents take into account this fact while bargaining – and the case in which after any proposal there is room for a counteroffer.

In the axiomatic context, price is implicitly determined by the Nash's solution necessary conditions. Under linear utility, in particular, it can be found explicitly. Its properties have been explored in section 2.

In the strategic bargaining game it is well known that

- every agreement – in our case every price which produces for at least one player a payoff preferred to the no-trade one – is a Nash's equilibrium, reached with the first offer.

- among Nash's equilibria, both under finite and infinite bargaining a unique subgame perfect equilibrium exists, reached with the first offer.

In our model this equilibrium is characterized by the bond price.

Under finite bargaining, price reflects the last mover's advantage: since we assume that the seller offers at the final stage, the equilibrium price is in his favour.

Under infinite bargaining, the seller maintains a price-determined advantage, the last mover's one of the finite offer case. In the linear-utility case, in particular, we are able to determine explicitly the equilibrium price, as in the axiomatic linear case.

Two comments are in order, as concerns respectively the level and the variability of equilibrium prices, when trade is positive.

As regards the first point, the absolute price level depends on the particular structure of the payoffs and on some bargaining rules. We have indicated which assumptions make the result asymmetric and which would not.

As regards the second problem, when the equilibrium price is explicitly characterized, its non-linearity in traded amounts and quantities is evident: this justifies the existence of significant price shocks with small demand changes, which is proper of thin markets. By comparing the results with those in Appendix 1, where different hypotheses on the agents' portfolio choices are introduced, the reader can appreciate the fact that these conclusions are robust with respect to the portfolio assumptions.

Finally, we remind that in a bargaining game in which a single player makes all the offers he reduces his counterpart to the indifference payoff. As opposite to Jang (1986), the model with limit orders and an intermediary then produces no spread for the latter, who does not make offers. By exploiting this case however we readily proved that price indeterminacy arises. Our bargaining model then is robust also to the presence of an intermediary – acting as a broker – since bargaining between buyers and sellers can be interpreted as the response to the blind, unconclusive placement of limit orders with the broker.

References

[1] Binmore, K.G. (1987), Perfect Equilibria in Bargaining Models, in Binmore and Dasgupta (1987), pp. 77-105.

[2] ——, and P. Dasgupta (1987), *The Economics of Bargaining*, Oxford, Blackwell.

[3] Fishburn, P.C., and A. Rubinstein (1982), Time Preference, *International Economic Review* 23, pp. 677-694.

[4] Hasung Jang (1986), Efficient Security Trading with a Specialist: an Application of Non-Cooperative Bargaining Theory, *Working Paper*, The Wharton School.

[5] Nash, J.F. (1950), The Bargaining Problem, *Econometrica* 18, pp.152-162.

[6] Osborne, M.J.,and A. Rubinstein (1990), *Bargaining and Markets*, New York, Academic Press.

[7] Rasmusen, E. (1989), *Games and Information*, Oxford, Blackwell.

[8] Rubinstein, A. (1982), Perfect Equilibrium in a Bargaining Model, *Econometrica* 50, pp. 97-109.

Appendix 1

Increasing returns to scale in the use of money – introduced in the text with the monotonic function ϕ – are meant to represent either decreasing transaction costs – information costs included – or alternative real investments, as opposite to purely financial ones. Another case in which trade occurs between two agents as those in the text is that in which the portfolio choice of the two agents is different. This hypothesis, which is well suited to the model with different utility functions, transforms the buyer's and seller's payoffs respectively into:

$$(\alpha - A)\mu + A\Phi/\psi,$$

$$(\beta + A)\nu + (q - A/\psi)\Phi,$$

with μ and ν two positive constants.

Under these portfolio choices, the constraint on ψ – stemming form the existence only of agreements not worse than the disagreement event – becomes:

$$\Phi/\nu \leq \psi \leq \Phi/\mu,$$

and is non-empty iff $\nu \geq \mu$, it i.e. iff the return on cash due to the portfolio choices of the seller is not smaller than that of the buyer.

Trade however occurs iff the previous inequality is strict. When $\mu = \nu$ in fact the constraint on ψ leads to $\psi = \Phi/\mu = \Phi/\nu$, and the payoffs for a and b reduce – for whatever A – to the disagreement (initial) ones.

In addition, when trade occurs, it takes its maximum value, α: the buyer transforms the whole of his wealth into bonds. When $\nu > \mu$ in fact

$$M = q\Phi + \alpha\mu + \beta\nu + \max_A A(\nu - \mu),$$

so that $\arg M = \alpha$.

As concerns the equilibrium price, ψ^*, we distinguish the following cases:

- in Nash's bargaining solution, which exists unique under the hypotheses of Nash's theorem, we have

  $$\psi^* = \arg\max[u_a(\alpha\Phi/\psi) - u_a(\alpha\mu)]\{u_b[(\beta + A)\nu + (q - \alpha/\psi)\Phi - u_b(\beta\nu + q\Phi)\}.$$

  If the utility functions are linear, in particular, we get:

  $$\psi^* = 2\Phi/(\mu + \nu).$$

- in the dynamic game Nash's equilibria, every price can obtain, since all of the agreements are possible.

- in the finite-horizon dynamic-game unique perfect equilibrium a's last mover advantage leads to:

  $$\psi^* = \Phi/\nu,$$

  which implies the following payoffs for a and b respectively:

  $$\alpha\nu = M - \beta\nu - q\Phi,$$

  $$\beta\nu - q\Phi.$$

- in the infinite-horizon dynamic game a unique perfect equilibrium exists, because of Rubinstein's theorem. That equilibrium is characterized by the following payoffs:

  $$\alpha\Phi/\psi^* = M\,\frac{1 - \delta_b}{1 - \delta_a\delta_b},$$

  $$(\beta + \alpha)\nu + (q - \alpha/\psi^*)\Phi = M\,\frac{\delta_b(1 - \delta_a)}{1 - \delta_a\delta_b}.$$

Exploiting the fact that

$$M = q\Phi + (\alpha+\beta)\nu,$$

from the first payoff we obtain

$$\psi^* = \frac{\alpha\Phi(1-\delta_a\delta_b)}{[q\Phi + (\alpha+\beta)\nu](1-\delta_b)} \cdot$$

The same result can be obtained using the second payoff.

Appendix 2

A sufficient condition for the existence of an agreement not worse than the disagreement outcome is that there exists an amount A such that $P \leq p$. The transaction corresponding to turning the whole wealth of the first player into bonds ($A = \alpha$) satisfies this inequality strictly[12]. This means that there is at least a transaction strictly preferred by both players to doing nothing.

In addition, since the lhs and the rhs of the above inequality are strictly increasing in $0 < A \leq \alpha, 0 \leq A \leq \alpha$ respectively, while the inequality is satisfied as an equality if $A = 0$ and in the strict sense if $A = \alpha$, a sufficient condition for it to hold in a strict sense for every $0 < A \leq \alpha$ is that its lhs be strictly convex and its rhs be strictly concave, as – with continuous ϕ – in the following picture.

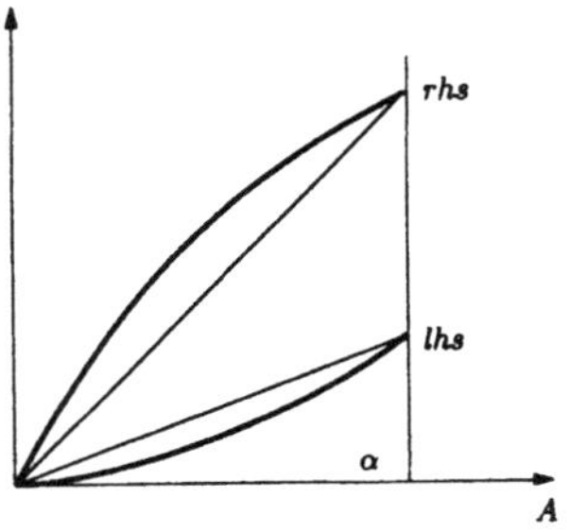

Figure #4

If ϕ is twice differentiable, the aforementioned concavity conditions are satisfied for $\phi' \neq 0$ if, having defined

$$\mathcal{G}(x) \stackrel{d}{=} x\phi''(x)/\phi'(x),$$

we have $\mathcal{G}(x) < -2$ both at $x = \alpha - A$ and at $x = \beta + A$ for every $A \in (0, \alpha)$.

When $\phi' = 0$, a sufficient condition for strict convexity of the lhs and strict concavity of the rhs is that $\phi''(x) < 0$ for the same x as above.

[12]Since α and β are both positive and ϕ is strictly increasing $0 < \alpha[\phi(\beta+\alpha) - \phi(\alpha)]$ and $-\beta[\phi(\beta+\alpha) - \phi(\beta)] < 0$. As a consequence $\alpha[\phi(\beta+\alpha) - \phi(\alpha)] > -\beta[\phi(\beta+\alpha) - \phi(\beta)]$ or $\alpha(\phi(\alpha) < (\beta+\alpha)\phi(\beta+\alpha) - \beta\phi(\beta)$ which demonstrates the statement in the text.

In both cases for ϕ', the sufficient conditions above – which are assumed to hold throughout the paper when the case of positive trade is investigated – imply ϕ concave at $\alpha - A, \beta + A$ for $0 < A < \alpha$.

In addition, we have the constraint

$$A/\psi \leq q,$$

which coincides with the lower constraint previously discussed when $A = 0$. When $A > 0$, it is not binding whenever

$$q \geq \frac{p}{\Phi}.$$

Since the rhs of this inequality is strictly increasing and strictly concave in A, due to the hypothesis on G, a sufficient condition for the no short-sale constraint to be respected for every A is that

$$q \geq \frac{(\alpha+\beta)\phi(\alpha+\beta) - \beta\phi(\beta)}{\Phi},$$

as illustrated in the following picture:

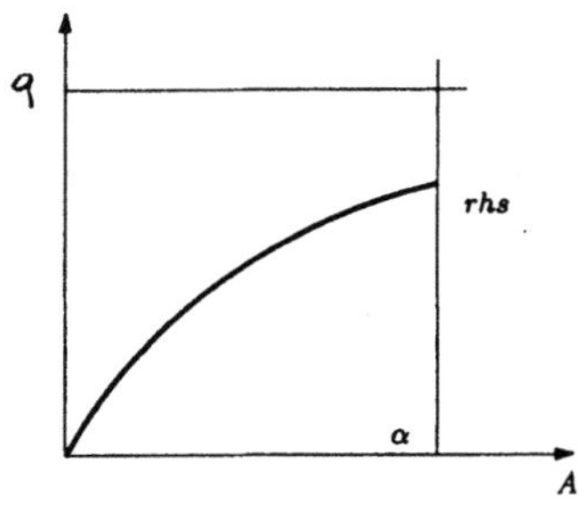

Figure #5

Appendix 4

When the value of A on the Pareto frontier is positive (so that the problem of determining a price makes sense) and the utility functions are at least once differentiable the first-order necessary condition for an internal solution to the optimization problem (14) is:

$$\frac{u_a'(\mathbf{s}_a)}{u_a(\mathbf{s}_a) - u_a(\alpha\phi(\alpha))} \frac{\partial \mathbf{s}_a}{\partial \psi} = -\frac{u_b'(\mathbf{s}_b)}{u_b(\mathbf{s}_b) - u_b(\beta\phi(\beta) + q\Phi)} \frac{\partial \mathbf{s}_a}{\partial \psi},$$

with the payoffs computed in $A = \arg M$ and in the optimal price, $\psi = \psi^*$.

This can be simplified to:

$$\frac{u'_a(\mathbf{s}_a)}{u_a(\mathbf{s}_a)-u_a(\alpha\phi(\alpha))}=\frac{u'_b(\mathbf{s}_b)}{u_b(\mathbf{s}_b)-u_b(\beta\phi(\beta)+q\Phi)}\,. \tag{24}$$

with the same caveats as above on the payoffs.

From this condition the following theorem can be proved:

Theorem 2.2.1. *If the utility functions of the two agents are C^2 on an open set containing ψ^* and A^*, then the equilibrium value of ψ is strictly increasing (strictly decreasing) with respect to $A^* > 0$ if it is smaller (greater) than $\Phi/[\phi(\alpha-A^*)+(\alpha-A^*)\phi'(\alpha-A^*)]$.*

Proof – When $A^* > 0$, define as $f(\psi, A)$ the difference between the two members of (17), and denote with U_a and U_b the following quantities:

$$U_a \stackrel{d}{=} u_a(\mathbf{s}_a)-u_a(\alpha\phi(\alpha)),$$

$$U_b \stackrel{d}{=} u_b(\mathbf{s}_b)-u_b(\beta\phi(\beta)+q\Phi).$$

In a neighbourhood of the equilibrium values we have:

$$\partial f(\psi,A)/\partial\psi =$$

$$-\frac{A\Phi}{\psi^2}\left\{\frac{1}{U_a}\left[u''_a(\mathbf{s}_a)-\frac{u'^2(\mathbf{s}_a)}{U_a}\right]+\frac{1}{U_b}\left[u''_b(\mathbf{s}_b)-\frac{u'^2(\mathbf{s}_b)}{U_b}\right]\right\},$$

$$\partial f(\psi,A)/\partial A =$$

$$\frac{\partial\mathbf{s}_a/\partial A}{U_a}\left[u''_a(\mathbf{s}_a)-\frac{u'^2(\mathbf{s}_a)}{U_a}\right]-\frac{\partial\mathbf{s}_b/\partial A}{U_b}\left[u''_b(\mathbf{s}_b)-\frac{u'^2(\mathbf{s}_b)}{U_b}\right].$$

Since from the necessary condition for M

$$\frac{\partial\mathbf{s}_a}{\partial A}=\frac{-\partial\mathbf{s}_b}{\partial A}=-\phi(x)-x\phi'(x)+\Phi/\psi,$$

where $x = A+\beta$ or $x=\alpha-A$, $\partial f(\psi,A)/\partial A$ can be rewritten as:

$$[-\phi(x)-x\phi'(x)+\Phi/\psi]\left\{\frac{1}{U_a}\left[u''_a(\mathbf{s}_a)-\frac{u'^2(\mathbf{s}_a)}{U_a}\right]+\frac{1}{U_b}\left[u''_b(\mathbf{s}_b)-\frac{u'^2(\mathbf{s}_b)}{U_b}\right]\right\}.$$

As a consequence, since under the above assumptions the implicit function theorem applies,

$$\frac{\partial\psi}{\partial A}=\frac{\psi}{A}\,[1-\psi(\phi(x)+x\phi'(x))/\Phi],$$

and the sign of this derivative depends on the quantity in square brackets.

Choosing $x=\alpha-A$ we then have $\partial\psi/\partial A>0$ iff

$$\psi < \Phi/[\phi(\alpha-A)+(\alpha-A)\phi'(\alpha-A)].$$

This completes the proof.□

RISK MEASUREMENT AND SIZE EFFECT ON THE DUTCH STOCK MARKET

A. Corhay

University of Liège (Belgium) and University of Limburg (The Netherlands)

and

A. Tourani Rad

University of Limburg (The Netherlands)

Abstract

In this paper it is shown that there is an intervalling effect in the beta coefficients of the Dutch firms. The sign of the intervalling effect coefficient is generally negative, implying that most betas measured on short differencing intervals underestimate their asymptotic values. This further points out a significant relationship between the intervalling effect and the firm size.

1 Introduction

A considerable body of research in finance has been concerned for some years with the existence of market anomalies in security markets. The anomalous empirical regularities can be classified into cross-sectional empirical regularities or seasonal regularities. The anomalous cross-sectional regularities, or anomalies related to some firm or market attributes, are systematic and persistent deviations from the equity pricing models such as the Capital Asset Pricing Model (CAPM). An example of cross-sectional empirical regularity is the Size Effect (Banz, 1981) according to which firms with a relatively lower market value of equity seem to achieve returns above those warranted by the CAPM. The existence of such market anomaly can also be interpreted as a misspecification of the CAPM. That means there may exist a risk factor in addition to systematic risk which is relevant in the pricing of securities, or at least a factor influencing the pricing. As to the seasonal empirical regularities which can be considered as violations of the efficient market hypothesis, the most common ones are: the January Effect (Rozeff and Kinney, 1976 and Gultekin and Gultekin, 1983), that is average monthly returns are larger in January relatively to the rest of the year, the Weekend or Monday Effect (French, 1980, Gibbons and Hess, 1981 and Lakonishok and Levi, 1982), that is, average return on Monday is significantly less than the average return over the other days of the week, and the Turn-of-month (Ariel, 1987 and Lakonishok and Smidt, 1988), that is, returns at the turn of the month are significantly higher than those of the rest of the year.

Both types of anomalies have been observed in many security markets. Despite efforts and time devoted to their study, they remain a puzzle insofar as suggested explanations are not unanimous and do not explain, at least not completely, their existence.

We are concerned in this paper with the first type of anomalies, more specifically with the size effect and its relationship with the bias in the measurement of the systematic risk due to the choice of the length of the differencing interval used to calculated the returns. The latter, which is commonly called the intervalling effect, can be due to nonsynchronous trading or, more generally, to delays in the price adjustment which can be caused by the microstructure of the market and the reaction of investors to the arrival of news. The first models dealing with this intervalling effect bias in beta were presented by Scholes and Williams (1977) and Dimson (1979). Both imputed the intervalling effect bias in beta to infrequent trading. Their models consist in regressing observed returns against synchronous or lagged market returns in order to avoid the problem of serial correlation, and then in aggregating the slope coefficients obtained to calculate a beta estimate. Cohen, Hawawini, Maier, Schwartz and Whitcomb, henceforth CHMSW, (1980), developed a more general model for correcting the empirical estimates of beta for the intervalling effect due to any type of delays in the price adjustment. According to their theory the expected magnitude of the price adjustment delays is related to the thinness of the securities: thinner securities have greater adjustment delays than frequently and highly traded securities. They also demonstrated that thin securities have a downward bias in their betas for short differencing intervals, while relatively frequently traded securities have an upward bias.

As the market value of a firm is generally used as a proxy variable for the thinness of a security, the relationship between intervalling effect bias in beta and thinness would suggest that the intervalling effect could explain the size or small firm effect. Roll (1981) argued that trading infrequency, which induces some autocorrelation in the market indexes, seems to be a powerful cause of bias in the systematic risk estimation and could explain the small firm effect. And, according to CHMSW, the adjustment for the intervalling effect bias should be more important for small firms than for large firms.

The rest of the paper is organised as follows. Section 2 presents the data and section 3 discusses CHMSW procedure to obtain an asymptotic beta. Section 4 deals with the relationship between systematic risk for different interval length and the size effect. Section 5 concludes and presents a brief summary.

2 Data

Our sample consists of 50 Dutch firms. The daily closing prices for a period starting 28/10/87 and ending 1/3/92 are used to calculate the returns. Returns for any interval length are calculated as the difference between the natural logarithm of two closing prices, $R_t=\ln(P_t+D_t)-\ln(P_{t-1})$, where D_t denotes the dividend. The CBS general index, the most appropriate index available in the Netherlands, is used as a proxy of the market index. It is a weighted average of a number of sector indices and is adjusted for dividends. As for the market value of the firms, it is that of 31 December 1990. This date which is the midpoint of our sample period was chosen such that the market value of the outstanding shares are close to their actual average over this period.

3 Measurement of Systematic Risk

We assume that the security returns are generated by the Market Model of Sharpe (1963),

$$R_{it} = \alpha_i + \beta_i R_{mt} + \varepsilon_{it} \qquad t=1,\ldots,T \tag{1}$$

where β_i, the security beta, measures the change in R_{it} as a result of a change in the market index return R_{mt}, α_i measures the change in R_{it} that is independent of a change in R_{mt}, and ε_{it} is the random error term. According to this model, β_i should not depend on the length of the differencing interval used to calculate the returns. However, empirical studies showed that there is an impact of the length of the differencing interval used to measure the returns on the estimated betas. Examples can be found in, among others, Berglund, Liljeblom, and Löflund (1989) for Finland, Corhay (1992) for Belgium and Corhay and Tourani Rad (1992) for the Netherlands.

CHMSW (1983) presented two procedures for correcting the empirical estimates of beta for the intervalling effect. Their first procedure consists in estimating an asymptotic beta by increasing the length of the differencing interval, and the second one consists in adjusting the beta estimates by cross-sectional differences in the intervalling effect. A proxy variable for the security thinness, for example, the market value of the outstanding shares, is used to determine the cross-sectional differences. These procedures were tested by CHMSW (1983), by Fung, Schwartz and Whitcomb (1985) and by Corhay (1988) on samples of 50 American, 52 French and 250 Belgian securities respectively. The results of these three studies support CHMSW's theory while another study of McInish and Wood (1986), using intermediate results of CHMSW, does not.

We calculate the asymptotic betas for the firms in our sample. But, since the size of the sample cannot be increased without bounds and β_i is not necessarily stationary across time, we follow Cohen et al. (1983) second procedure to obtain asymptotic betas. This requires two steps. First the security beta coefficients are estimated using equation (1) for a finite set of lengths of the differencing interval. These betas are then used in a second pass regression to calculate estimates of the security asymptotic beta, as well as a measures of the intervalling effect:

$$\hat{\beta}_{iL} = \hat{\beta}_i + \hat{\gamma}_i \; f^{-n}(L) + \upsilon_{iL} \qquad (2)$$

where $\hat{\beta}_i$ is the estimator of the asymptotic beta coefficient, $\hat{\gamma}_i$ is a measure of the intervalling effect on the beta of security i, L is the length of the differencing interval and υ_{iL} is the error term, υ_{iL}~N[0,1]. As CHMSW noted, functional forms which converge to an asymptote, the value of the asymptotic beta, and for which the difference between the dependent variable and the asymptote decreases with L, could be used in (2). Any decreasing function of L satisfies these requirements. Furthermore, in order to use only linear regressions, they suggested to use powers of the inverse functions of L, the value of the power being determined experimentally. In their study on the U.S. data, CHMSW simply used the inverse of the length of the differencing interval L^{-n}, while Fung, Schwartz and Whitcomb (1985) found the function $\ln(1+L^{-n})$ fitted the French data best. We tested various decreasing functions of L for the Dutch market, that is, L^{-n}, $\ln(1+L^{-n})$ and $\exp(-L^{-n})$, and it appeared that the function $L^{-.8}$ fits the data best. Estimated asymptotic betas and intervalling effect coefficients for the 50 firms are reported in table 1. It can be noticed that the sign of the intervalling effect coefficient is generally negative, which means that observed betas for small differencing intervals underestimate their asymptotic values. The firms with large market values, which tend to be thicker than our index have, however, a positive intervalling effect coefficient, which is consistent with CHMSW theoretical model and the empirical findings on US and other equity markets.

Table 1 : Asymptotic betas and intervalling effect coefficients

Firm	Asymptotic betas $\hat{\beta}_i$	Intervalling effect $\hat{\gamma}_i$
1	0.7121	-0.3670
2	1.0049	0.1759
3	1.0817	0.1389
4	1.1813	0.0889
5	1.1237	0.3357
6	1.4197	0.3160
7	1.6381	1.3379
8	0.8863	0.5365
9	0.8760	0.2779
10	0.7143	0.6711
11	1.1283	1.2061
12	1.5015	0.4008
13	0.5145	0.0130
14	1.0768	0.3512
15	0.9126	0.6458
16	0.9696	0.6218
17	1.4115	0.0469
18	0.6914	0.6377
19	1.1160	0.2392
20	1.4600	-0.0740
21	1.8489	-1.0329
22	1.3647	-0.8314
23	0.8519	-0.3312
24	0.7855	-0.4859
25	0.5591	-0.4627
26	0.9622	-0.3694
27	0.6532	-0.1695
28	0.7461	0.0560
29	0.6124	0.4050
30	0.8716	-0.6373
31	0.4923	-0.4256
32	1.4627	-0.2008
33	0.1973	-0.0934
34	-0.0028	0.0643
35	1.0222	-0.6976
36	1.2831	-0.9004
37	0.2522	-0.1586
38	1.1573	-1.3009
39	0.9903	-0.5024
40	-0.1573	0.2977
41	0.9822	-0.3778
42	0.9581	-0.2889
43	0.5885	-0.6407
44	1.0633	-0.3641
45	1.1456	0.2051
46	0.7790	-0.6130
47	1.3546	-0.8301
48	1.1801	-0.2316
49	1.6952	-1.1926
50	0.6226	-0.1684
Mean	0.9548	-0.3915

4 Intervalling Effect and Firm Size Effect

In this section we investigate the relationship between the intervalling effect and the size effect. The model we used was proposed by CHMSW (1983). According to them the adjustment for the intervalling effect should be more important for small firms than for large firms. This means that for small differencing intervals, estimated betas should be related to the size of the firms, and when the differencing interval is lengthened, they should become independent of the size of the firm. Their test consists in a cross-sectional regression with the natural logarithm of the market value (LMV) of the firms as independent variable and the betas $\hat{\beta}_{iL}$, measured on a differencing interval of length L, or the asymptotic beta estimate $\hat{\beta}_i$ as dependent variables (ψ). That is:

$$\psi = \psi_0 + \psi_1 \, \text{LMV} \tag{3}$$

Results of this model for betas calculated using intervals of 1 to 5, 10, 15, 20 days and for the asymptotic one are reported in table 2. These results are taken from Corhay and Tourani Rad (1993) who have thoroughfully examined the relationship between the two effects. The slope coefficients (ψ_1) are all positive and statistically significant. The R^2 of the regressions are also quite high. This indicates clearly that betas are related to the market value of the firms. The examination of the behaviour of the slope coefficient with regards to the length of the interval is interesting. One should expect that if the firm size effect is explained by the intervalling effect, the slope coefficient should decrease and become insignificant for long intervals. This pattern can be observed in the results, the value of the coefficient decreases when the differencing interval is lengthened, and is the lowest when the asymptotic beta estimate is the dependent variable. All coefficients are, however, statistically significant, which means that after being adjusted for the intervalling effect bias, betas are still related to the market value. The adjustment for the intervalling effect bias in the Dutch firm betas only decreases the magnitude of the size effect.

Table 2: Intervalling Effect and Firm Size *

$$\psi = \psi_0 + \psi_1 \text{ LMV}$$

ψ	ψ_0	ψ_1	R^2
$\hat{\beta}_{i1}$	-1.6400	.1997	.6345
$\hat{\beta}_{i2}$	-1.4099	.1820	.5977
$\hat{\beta}_{i3}$	-1.3139	.1744	.5806
$\hat{\beta}_{i4}$	-1.1933	.1662	.5563
$\hat{\beta}_{i5}$	-1.1184	.1611	.5427
$\hat{\beta}_{i10}$	-1.0749	.1650	.4751
$\hat{\beta}_{i15}$	-0.8699	.1554	.3798
$\hat{\beta}_{i20}$	-0.7525	.1515	.3184
Asymptotic Beta ($\hat{\beta}_i$)	-0.8099	.1506	.3738

* All coefficients are significant at the one percent level.

5 Conclusions

The objective of this paper was to investigate the relationship between size effect and the bias in the measurement of the systematic risk on the Dutch stock market. We found first that there is an intervalling effect in the beta coefficients. The sign of the intervalling effect coefficient is generally negative, implying that betas measured on short differencing intervals underestimate their asymptotic values. We also found a significant relationship between the intervalling effect and the size of the firms. Our results further show that the magnitude of this relationship is reduced when the interval length is increased, but remains statistically significant which means that adjusting for the intervalling effect only decreases the importance of the size effect.

6 References

Ariel R.A. (1987) A Monthly Effect in Stock Returns. *Journal of Financial Economics* 17, 161-174.

Banz R.W.(1981) The Relationship between Return and Market Value of Common Stocks*Journal of Financial Economics* 9, 3-18.

Berglund T., Liljeblom, E., Löflund A. (1989) Estimating Betas Using Daily Data for a Small Stock Market. *Journal of Banking and Finance* 13, 41-64.

Cohen K.J., Hawawini G.A., Maier S.F., Schwartz R.A., Whitcomb D.K. (1980) 'Implications of Microstructure Theory for Empirical research on stock Price Behavior. *Journal of Finance* 35, 249-257.

Cohen K.J., Hawawini G.A., Maier S.F., Schwartz R.A., Whitcomb D.K. (1983) Estimating and Adjusting for the Intervalling Effect Bias in Beta. *Management Science* 29, 135-148.

Cohen K.J., Hawawini G.A., Maier S.F., Schwartz R.A., Whitcomb D.K. (1983) Friction in the Trading Process and the Estimation of Systematic Risk'. *Journal of Financial Economics* 12, 263-278.

Corhay A. (1988) The Adjustment for the Intervalling Effect Bias in Beta: A Broader and Multiperiod Test. Working paper 88-26, European Institute for Advanced Studies in Management, Brussels.

Corhay A. (1992) The Intervalling Effect Bias in Beta: a Note. *Journal of Banking and Finance* 16, 61-73.

Corhay, A., Tourani Rad A. (1992) Beta Estimate of Dutch Firms: Alternate Methods. *Vereniging van Beleggings Analisten Journaal* 4, 1992, 2-6.

Corhay, A., Tourani Rad A. (1993) Return Interval, Firm Size and Systematic Risk on the Dutch Stock Market. Forthcoming in *Review of Financial Economics.*

Dimson, E. (1979) Risk Measurement when Shares are Subject to Infrequent Trading. *Journal of Financial Economics* 7, 197-226.

French K. (1980) Stock Returns and the Weekend Effect. *Journal of Financial Economics* 8, 55-69.

Fung W.K.H., Schwartz R.A., Whitcomb D.K. (1985) Adjusting for the Intervalling Effect Bias in Beta: A test Using Paris Bourse Data. *Journal of Banking and Finance,* 9, 443-460.

Gibbons, N.R., Hess P. (1981) Day of the Week Effects and Asset Returns. *Journal of Business* 54, 579-596.

Gultekin, M.N., Gultekin N.B. (1983) Stock Market Seasonalities: International Evidence. *Journal of Financial Economics* 12, 469-485.

Lakonishok J., Levi M. (1982) Weekend Effects on Stock Returns: A Note. *Journal of Finance 37*, 883-889.

Lakonishok J., Smidt, J. (1988) Are Seasonal Anomalies Real? A Ninety-Year Perspective. *Review of Financial Studies* 1, 403-425.

McInish T.H., Wood, R.A. (1986) 'Adjusting for Beta Bias: An Assessment of Alternate Techniques: A Note. *The Journal of Finance*, 41, 277-286.

Roll R. (1981) A Possible Explanation of the Small Firm Effect. *Journal of Finance* 36, 879-888.

Rozeff M.S. Kinney WR. (1976), 'Capital Market Seasonality: the Case of Stock Returns. *Journal of Financial Economics* 3, 379-402.

Scholes M., Williams J. (1977) Estimating Betas from Nonsynchronous Data. *Journal of Financial Economics* 5, 309-327.

CONDITIONAL RISK AND PREDICTABILITY OF FINNISH STOCK RETURNS

Markku MALKAMÄKI*
Bank of Finland, P.O. Box 160, 00101 Helsinki, FINLAND

ABSTRACT

This paper studies the driving forces of predictable variation in Finnish stock returns. The dynamics of Ferson and Harvey's (1991) methodology are extended and applied within the Sharpe–Lintner CAPM. We find that market risk is conditionally priced in the Finnish stock market. Most of the predictable variation of stock returns is attributed to the time-varying risk premium, which supports the hypothesis of rational behavior by Finnish investors in setting stock prices. However, the conditional residual term accounted for a larger part of the predictable variation of the stock returns than is found in the US market.

* I am grateful to Ray Ball, Tom Berglund, Pierre Hillion, S.P. Kothari, Juha Tarkka, Jouko Vilmunen, Matti Virén and two anonymous references for helpful comments. This research has benefited from workshops at the Bank of Finland, the 12th Meeting of the Euro Working Group on Financial Modelling, the Finnish Economic Association and the University of Vaasa. Financial support provided by Suomen Arvopaperimarkkinoiden Edistämissäätiö is gratefully acknowledged. A previous version of this paper appeared in Bank of Finland Discussion Papers.

1 INTRODUCTION

The predictability of stock returns has been documented in several recent studies. Keim and Stambaugh (1986) reported this phenomenom first for US returns, and they were followed by Campbell (1987), Fama and French (1988), Poterba and Summers (1988) and others. Virtanen and Yli-Olli (1987) were the first to find return predictability in the Finnish stock market. Similar results were reported later, eg in Knif and Högholm (1991) and Malkamäki (1993a). There are two major explanations for this predictability. Either the market is inefficient or the required rate of return is changing over time. Both explanations have been supported by empirical evidence. If the asset pricing models provide a reasonable description of the expected returns of assets, then the predictable variation in the expected returns should be driven by variation in (1) risk exposures, ie the betas, (2) the price of beta, ie the risk premiums, and/or (3) the riskless rate of return.

Ferson and Harvey (FH) (1991) specify a list of risk factors similar to Chen, Ross and Roll (1986). However, FH focus on predictable variation in expected asset returns in order to analyse the relative importance of the above explanations (1) and (2) for predictability of US monthly portfolio returns. FH suggest that if the rational expectations hypothesis is true, then the expected returns implied by an asset pricing model should mimick the expected returns generated by the type of regression analysis that they employ in the study. If this holds, the predictable variation in the model's returns is driven by predictable variation in the betas, the price of betas or a combination of the two, ie if the predictable variation in the model's expected returns closely matches the predictable variation from the regression analysis in forecasting stock returns, then the rational expectations view is supported.

FH (1991) found that most of the predictability (some 81 %) is driven by changes in the expected betas and expected price of betas. They called what is left over "the part due to market inefficiency". This part was generally small (some 10 %). They also found that the primary source of predictability was the time variation in the expected risk premiums – not the betas. Interestingly, the market risk was only weakly priced on average, yet it was extremely important in accounting for variation in the predicted returns in the US stock portfolios.

Recent conditional tests of the Sharpe—Lintner CAPM with Finnish data suggest that market risk is rewarded in the Finnish stock market if the betas are allowed to vary through time according to a mean-reverting AR1 process (see Berglund and Knif (1992) and Malkamäki (1993b) and (1993c)). This provides motivation to replicate the study of FH (1991) to find out to what extent the Kalman filtered, conditional firm-specific betas and conditional market risk premium are able to explain the return predictability in the Finnish stock Market.

This paper aims to extend FH (1991) in four ways. Firstly, we replicate the FH (1991) study with greater dynamics in the parameter estimation for the CAPM, as the betas are allowed to vary through time according to a mean-reverting AR1 process. Secondly, we employ firm-specific betas and thus, in this sense, allow far more idiosyncratic variation in the betas. Thirdly, empirical analysis on the source of the predictable variation in the expected returns is carried out for a thin security market, ie the Finnish stock market. Moreover, the data employed here include the highly volatile years around the 1987 stock market crisis. Finally, we use stock returns in excess of the short-term money market rate used for the first time in Malkamäki (1993a) in analysing the predictability of Finnish returns.

This paper finds that most of the predictable variation is due to the time-varying risk parameters of the CAPM. Actually, almost none of the predictability was attributed to the betas. However, the conditional residual term mimics fairly well the predictable variation, suggesting that the inefficiency factor in the sense of FH (1991) is considerably larger for the Finnish stock market than for the US market. Our findings concerning the risk premium are very similar to those of FH, ie that the risk premium is conditionally time varying and that the conditional risk premium is the primarly source of predictability. Expectation concerning changes in the future order stock for Finnish industry and unexpected changes in inflation are found to capture the variation in the risk premium; and the unexpected changes in inflation, in combination with an instrument for the lagged influence of Finnish, German, Swedish, UK and US stock market returns on the Finnish market, are found to predict firm-specific excess returns fairly well.

The remainder of the paper is organized as follows. Section two discusses the methodologies employed. Section three describes the stock market data and conditioning variables. Empirical results are presented in the next section, and section five concludes with the key findings of the paper.

2 METHODOLOGIES

2.1 Conditional Market Risk

Sharpe-Lintner version of the CAPM states that expected returns on an asset are linearly related to the systematic risk, which is measured by the asset's beta. Actually, the CAPM is not testable, as stated in Roll (1977), because the true market portfolio is not observable. Therefore, the CAPM, as applied in empirical work, is just a statement about the mean-variance efficiency of a given market portfolio. Thus, in our empirical analysis, we test whether the observed stock market portfolio is mean-variance efficient. The test is then a joint test of whether the given market portfolio is mean-variance efficient and whether the market is information efficient.

Unfortunately, the true beta coefficient, β_i, implied by the CAPM cannot be observed. It is usually estimated, under the assumption of constant market risk, by computing iteratively an OLS regression over Sharpe's well-known time series (TSR) market model. However, we relax the assumtion of constant market risk and estimate the market model (2) by applying the dynamic Kalman filter estimation procedure, which accounts for time variation in the betas. The market model is now rewritten in state space form as

$$r_{it} = X_t' \theta_t + \varepsilon_t, \tag{1}$$

where $X_t' = [1, r_{mt}]$

$\theta_t' = [\alpha_{it}, \beta_{it}]$

ε_t = a random error with variance v_t.

The parameter vector θ_t is assumed to vary according to the stationary first order autoregressive (AR1) model

$$\theta_t - \bar{\theta} = F(\theta_{t-1} - \bar{\theta}) + u_t, \tag{2}$$

where $\bar{\theta}$ = mean vector of the parameters

F = weights for the AR1 and mean parameters

u_t = random error with covariance matrix M_t.

The state space representation of the market model is now

$$r_{it} = \begin{bmatrix} X'_t & X'_t \end{bmatrix} \begin{bmatrix} \bar{\theta}_t \\ \theta_t - \bar{\theta}_t \end{bmatrix} + \varepsilon_t . \tag{3}$$
$$= B'_t \gamma_t + \varepsilon_t$$

and the parameter vector

$$\gamma_t = \begin{bmatrix} \bar{\theta}_t \\ \theta_t - \bar{\theta}_t \end{bmatrix} = \begin{bmatrix} I & 0 \\ 0 & F \end{bmatrix} \begin{bmatrix} \bar{\theta}_{t-1} \\ \theta_{t-1} - \bar{\theta}_{t-1} \end{bmatrix} + \begin{bmatrix} 0 \\ u_t \end{bmatrix} \tag{4}$$
$$= A\gamma_{t-1} + e_t,$$

where F = diag $[\omega_1, \omega_2]$

$\bar{\theta}_1$ = $\bar{\theta}_{t-1}$ for all t

e_t = random error with covariance matrix N_t.

The random errors ε_t and e_t are independent of each other. The corresponding variance v_t and covariance matrix N_t are estimated. The maximum likelyhood (ML) method is employed to estimate minimum mean square values for γ_{t-1} and its covariance matrix Σ_{t-1}. The estimates for the Σ_t and γ_t, given r_{it} and X_t, are updated at each time t by means of the Kalman filter updating equations (see eg Harvey (1989) or Malkamäki (1993b)).

The Kalman filter technique used here is actually a three-step procedure.[1] First, a maximum likelihood solution for the parameter vector is found by means of the above forward recursive Kalman equations, which use past and current information. Next, the information from the whole sample period is used to find another set of ML estimators by applying the backward recursions of the Kalman smoother. As a final step, the AR(1) model is employed to estimate the forecasted beta series.

The forecasted betas are used later in Fama and MacBeth (1973) type cross-sectional (CSR) analyses of the price of risk and in conditional tests of predictability. In the first phase, the following second-pass CSR is estimated for each month:

$$r_{it} = \lambda_{0t} + \lambda_{1t}\hat{\beta}_{it-1} + e_{it}, \tag{5}$$

where r_{it} = expected excess return implied by the CAPM on asset i for period t

λ_{0t} = intercept term (= 0 according to the CAPM)

λ_{1t} = risk premium at time t

$\hat{\beta}_{it-1}$ = beta coefficient estimated for the previous period

e_{it} = random error term.

The final Fama–MacBeth estimates for the intercept and risk premium are the sample means from the time series of these coefficients. In the univariate test of the CAPM, the estimates for the intercept and average risk premium are the sample means from the time series of these coefficients. The computation of the standard errors is based on the assumption that the time series of cross-sectional estimates are independent and distributed identically with the means of the final estimates. However, we know that the independence assumption is not strictly satisfied due to the use of estimated betas instead of true betas as the explanatory variable. An errors-in-variables (EIV) problem is introduced in the second-pass regression, since the betas are subject to measurement error (for a review of

[1] For details on the maximization algorithms, see Goodrich (1989).

EIV problems, see eg Shanken (1992) and for thin markets, Malkamäki (1993b)). The EIV problem is reduced at least to some extent in the case of the mean-reverting AR1 model, since forecasted betas are used as the independent variable in the second-pass regressions. This procedure reduces the EIV problem assuming that the changing residual variance of the market model is dependent on the time variation of beta.[2]

2.2 Predictable Variation of Stock Returns

The monthly risk premiums from the CSR are regressed on the instrumental variables in order to see whether the variation in premiums can be explained by the instruments. If the risk premiums are constant over time, then the regression of these coefficients on the information variables should not be significant. The model for the conditional risk premium is

$$\lambda_{1t} = \delta_0 + \delta_1 Z_{1,t-1} + \delta_2 Z_{2,t-1} + \delta_3 Z_{3,t-1} + \varepsilon_{jt}, \tag{6}$$

where λ_1 represents the estimated risk premium associated with the market risk and Z_{t-1} represents an instrumental variable with a lag structure (not necessarily t−1).

The CSR provides the following decomposition of the driving forces of predictable variation in stock returns:

$$r_{it} = \{\beta_{i,t-1}\lambda_{1t}\} + \{\lambda_{0t} + \varepsilon_{it}\}.^{3} \tag{7}$$

---

[2] The critisism regarding the standard deviations of the univariate tests could be avoided at least to some extent by eg computing just one regression over pooled return and beta series, as in Malkamäki (1993b) or using a weighted least squares approach, as eg in Berglund and Knif (1992). Since our primary interest is in the source of predictability, we proceed to test it.

[3] The conditional variance decomposition is:
$Var\{r_{it}|Z\} = Var\{\beta_{i,t-1}\lambda_{1t}|Z\} + Var\{\lambda_{0t} + \varepsilon_{it}|Z\} + Cov\{(\beta_{i,t-1}\lambda_{1t}, \lambda_{0t} + \varepsilon_{it})|Z\}.$

The first term is related to the cross-sectional structure and price of the conditional market risk. The second term $(\lambda_{0t} + \varepsilon_{it})$ is not related to systematic risk and should be unpredictable, assuming that the CAPM is the correct model and the pricing of stocks is rational in the sense of Ferson and Harvey (1991).[4]

Two variance ratios can be formed. The first one (VR1) is the ratio of the variance of the model's conditionally predicted returns to the variance of expected returns from a linear regression on the set of instruments (Z). That is

$$VR1 = \frac{Var[E(\beta_{i,t-1}\lambda_{1t}|Z)]}{Var[E(r_{it}|Z)]}, \tag{8}$$

where the expected values are obtained by regressing on the information variables. The second variance ratio (VR2) is the ratio of the variance of the conditional part of a return that is not explained by the model to the variance of the conditionally expected return. Thus

$$VR2 = \frac{Var[E(r_{it} - \beta_{i,t-1}\lambda_{1t}|Z)]}{Var[E(r_{it}|Z)]}. \tag{9}$$

If most of the predictable variation in returns is due to the changing structure of the risk parameters, then VR1 should be close to one and VR2 close to zero.

A further decomposition of variance ratios reveals whether time-varying expected risk premium or time-varying risk sensitivities drive the predictable variation in stock returns. The variance is decomposed as:

$$\begin{aligned} Var[E(\lambda\beta)|Z] = [E(\beta)]^2 Var[E(\lambda|Z)] + [E(\lambda)]^2 Var[E(\beta|Z)] \\ + \text{interaction term}, \end{aligned} \tag{10}$$

where $E(\lambda)$ and $E(\beta)$ are the unconditional means of estimated parameters and $E[\lambda|Z)$ and $E(\beta|Z)$ are linear projections on the λ and β on the instruments. The interaction term arise because of covariance between the time-varying risk premium and betas.

[4] Ferson and Harvey provides a discussion of cases where predictability may enter via the λ_{0t} term also.

3 THE DATA

This study uses end-of-month stock returns in excess of the short-term interest rate on all 25 restricted[5] ordinary stocks listed on the Helsinki Stock Exchange (HSE) throughout the period 1972–1989 (see Table 1). Returns are measured as logarithmic changes in the indices. The HSE market index, which is used here, is value weighted (see Berglund–Wahlroos–Grandell (1983)). In the index, prices are corrected for cash dividends, splits,

Table 1. **Stocks included in the analysis: all restricted ordinary shares listed throughout the period 1972–1989**

Stock	Designation
Bank of Åland Ltd K	AB
Effoa-Finland Steamsip Co Ltd K	EFFO
Enso-Gutzeit Ltd A	ENSOA
Fiskars Corporation	FISKK
Huhtamäki Corporation K	HUHTK
Instrumentarium Corporation	INSTA
Kemi Corporation	KEMI
Kesko Corporation	KESK
KANSALLIS-OSAKE-PANKKI	KOP
Kymmene Corporation	KYMI
Lassila & Tikanoja Ltd	LASS
Lohja Corporation A	LOHJA
Nokia Corporation	NOKIK
Otava Publishing Company Ltd	OTAVK
Partek Corporation	PART
Rauma-Repola Corporation	RAUM
Finnish Sugar Co Ltd I	SOKEI
Stockman A	STOCA
Suomen Trikoo Corp. A	TRIK
Union Bank of Finland Ltd A	SYPA
Tamfelt Group K	TAMF
Tampella Ltd	TAMP
Talous-Osakekauppa Co	TAOK
Wärtsilä Co I	WARTI
United Paper Mills Ltd K	YHTYK

[5] Only domestic investors are allowed to buy restricted stocks. An observation at an end-of-month day when there was no transaction in a stock is the last bid price for that day.

stock dividends and new issues. The correction is based on the principle that all income from a stock is reinvested in that stock with no transaction cost. No portfolios are formed for the analysis, as is usually done in US studies. This is because of the extremely limited number of actively traded stocks. The excess returns are computed by using the one-month return entailed in the three-month Eurorate on the Finnish markka. This interest rate series is introduced in Malkamäki (1993b). The whole period is used to estimate the betas. Predictability analyses are carried out on data beginning with 1977.

Table 2. **Summary statistics for the excess returns (per cent per month) for 1972:2—1989:12 (215 observations)**

Asset	Mean	St.dev.	Skewness	Kurtosis
	Excess Returns			
AB	0.746	10.683	1.332	16.702
EFFO	0.423	8.204	0.348	1.448
ENSOA	-0.234	7.922	0.645	3.114
FISKK	1.292	7.252	0.296	1.959
HUHTK	0.782	6.610	1.056	2.655
INSTA	1.156	7.118	0.607	3.206
KEMI	-0.360	10.646	-0.694	4.457
KESK	0.658	5.147	1.060	2.481
KOP	0.104	6.644	0.751	4.821
KYMI	-0.002	6.410	0.597	1.908
LASS	1.298	9.240	1.336	7.143
LOHJA	0.930	7.333	0.141	0.295
NOKIK	-0.009	6.910	0.159	0.684
OTAVK	1.234	9.496	1.773	10.212
PART	0.522	6.594	0.242	0.555
RAUM	0.034	6.741	1.042	2.112
SOKEI	0.694	8.094	0.762	2.001
STOCA	0.895	6.645	0.521	2.684
SYPA	0.433	6.083	1.230	4.425
TAMF	0.717	9.835	-0.486	6.468
TAMP	0.051	7.788	1.276	5.215
TAOK	1.866	9.520	-0.031	1.863
TRIK	0.136	11.697	0.255	6.330
WARTI	0.613	7.480	0.764	1.155
YHTYK	0.707	7.459	0.380	0.934
VWI[a]	0.254	4.230	0.265	0.976

[a] The stock market index return.

Summary statistics for monthly excess returns for 25 firms and for the HSE market index are shown in Table 2. The statistics indicate that the return distributions are somewhat skewed to the right and leptokurtic, as is usual (see eg Taylor (1986)).

We use three information variables, which are usually called instruments in the literature. These variables are assumed to describe the information that investors use to set prices in the stock market (see Table 3). The instruments are FSM, an instrument for the influence of lagged excess returns on the stock markets in Finland, Germany, Sweden, the United Kingdom and the United States, UNEXINF, change in unexpected inflation, and BARIP, expected change in order stock for Finnish industry.[6] FSM is based on Malkamäki (1993a). He applied Johansen's (1988) multidimensional vector autoregressive (VAR) technique, which accounts also for the multivariate cointegration of stock market indices in the above countries and found that the Finnish stock market is clearly Granger caused by these countries' market returns with Germany having the strongest foreign impact. FSM is the fit of the VAR model for the Finnish stock market. The second instrument, UNEXINF, is the difference between actual and forecasted inflation. The forecast is obtained from an ARIMA (1,0,1)(0,0,2) model for percentage changes in the seasonally unadjusted consumer price index.[7] The third instrument, BARIP, is an estimate of the aggregated future cash-flow expectations of firms. BARIP is the percentage change

Table 3. **Instrumental variables**

Instrument	Definition
FSM	An instrument for influence of lagged stock market returns in Finland, Germany, Sweden, UK and US.
UNEXINF	Change in unexpected inflation.
BARIP	Expected change in future order stock for Finnish industry.

[6] We also tried most of the instruments that are commonly employed in US studies (see also next paragraph). However, these variables did not show any forecasting power for excess stock returns or risk premium.

[7] The model is stable according to the F-test at the 5 % level of significance.

in negative answers regarding expected change in order stock for Finnish industry in the quarterly questionaire of the Confederation of the Finnish Industries. The monthly series is interpolated from the quarterly series.

Summary satistics for the instruments are given in Table 4. Only FSM is somewhat skewed and leptokurtic. The lower part of the table shows that cross-correlation of the insrumental variables is not a matter of concern. However, one should keep in mind that all the instruments are generated variables. Pagan (1984) discusses econometric issues concerning generated variables and shows that their use may lead to biased estimates in OLS regressions. On the other hand, the market-based instrumental variables most commonly used in US studies were tested here as conditioning instruments before turning to the generated variables, but no significant relations were found. The variables studied include change in the difference between long- and short-term interest rates, change in the difference between medium and short-term interest rates, nominal and real three month Euromarket returns for the Finnish markka, a bond return index, nominal inflation and real per capita growth of personal consumption (seasonally adjusted). From preliminary analysis of the above instruments, we concluded that the information that is relevant to Finnish investors in setting stock prices differs from that which is relevant in the US market.

Table 4. **Summary statistics for the instrumental variables, 1972:2–1989:12**

Instrument	Mean	Std. dev.	Skew.	Ex. Kurt.
FSM	−.032	.021	−.834	3.396
UNEXINF	.005	.006	.069	−.227
BARIP	−4.300	10.230	−.348	−.043

Correlation matrix

Instrument	FSM	UNEXINF	BARIP
FSM	1.000		
UNEXINF	.176	1.000	
BARIP	−.085	−.044	1.000

4 EMPIRICAL RESULTS

4.1 Unconditional vs Conditional Price of Risk

Cross-sectional regressions of the excess returns on the conditional betas are performed for each month. The model estimated is that of equation (5). The slope coefficient for the betas is the monthly risk premium. The results from these regressions are reported in Table 5. The upper part of the table gives the results from the unconditional analysis of the price of beta risk. These results are taken from Malkamäki (1993c). The table shows that the unconditional price of risk is not significant for the period 1977:2–1989:12, and furthermore, the sign of the coefficient is negative. The t-ratios reported in parenthesis are calculated as in Fama–MacBeth (1973). The hypothesis tested, as in numerous other studies, is that the mean premium equals zero. However, as stated in FH (1991), a premium may be the most significant premium even if it has zero mean. This is possible if the premium is changing through time or there is a sudden structural change in the return-generating process for a particular period, as reported in Booth et al. (1991) or there are several structural changes, as found in Malkamäki (1993b). In such a case, our tests of the significance of average risk premium would be weak.

We test the conditional pricing of market risk by regressing the ex post risk premiums from the monthly cross-sectional regressions on the instrumental variables in order to detect the predictable variation in the premium. If the conditional ex post risk premium is constant, the regression should not detect a significant relation. The outcome of this test is given in the lower part of Table 5. We see that some of the observed variability of the ex post risk premium can be explained by the instruments. The coefficient of determination, 8.7 %, is reasonable in light of the results of FH. Note also that the period studied here includes two extraordinary periods for the Finnish economy, which are found to have a dominating role in unconditional tests of the CAPM. These are the period of three devaluations, 1977:4–1978:2, and the year 1989, when the drastic slowdown of the Finnish economy started. Malkamäki (1993b and 1993c) shows that these periods have a strong impact on the risk-return relationship under the assumption of constant risk premium. The above analysis shows that the conditioning instruments are able to predict the behavior of the ex post premium also for these extraordinary periods.

Table 5. **Unconditional and conditional price of market risk 1977:2—1989:12 (155 observations)**

Unconditional model

λ_0	λ_1	R^2
0.011	−0.003	6.3
(1.85)	(−0.40)	

The model estimated is: $r_{it} = \lambda_{0t} + \lambda_{1t}\hat{\beta}_{it-1} + e_{it}$, where $\hat{\beta}_{it-1}$ is actually a beta forecasted for the period t based on the mean-reverting AR1 model: $\beta_t = \omega\beta_{t-1} + (1-\omega)\beta$.

Conditional model[a]

δ_0	δ_1	δ_2	δ_3	R^2	DW
0.051	0.161	−2.559	0.005	8.7	2.16
(1.28)	(0.78)	(−2.08)	(3.26)		

The model estimated is: $\lambda_{it} = \delta_0 + \delta_1 FSM(t) + \delta_2 UNEXINF(t-3) + \delta_3 BARIP(t-4) + u_t$. BARIP was second-order differenced in the regression (see text).

[a] Heteroscedasticity-consistent t-values in parenthesis, White (1980).

UNEXINF and BARIP turned out to have the greatest effect on the risk premium, BARIP having the strongest influence according to the t-statistics. BARIP had significant t-values and coefficients of same size but opposite sign at lags 4 and 5. It was, therefore, differenced a second time in order to increase the power of the regression analysis. It follows from the second-order differencing that the positive regression coefficient implies a decrease in the expected ex post risk premium as the percentage of negative answers regarding the future order stock for Finnish industry increases, which seems reasonable enough. The negative coefficient of the unexpected inflation at lag 3 implies that an unanticipated increase in inflation reduces the expected ex post premium associated with stock investments. This supports the view that unexpected inflation is bad news for Finnish stock investors. A lag structure of this size between economic variables and stock price reactions is also found in Virtanen and Yli-Olli (1987). A possible explanation for this is that macro-information is usually available with a lag of several months.

4.2 Decomposing the Predictable Variation

The cross-sectional regression provides a decomposition of the predictable variation in stock returns. The first term is related to the cross-sectional structure of risk. The second term is a residual that should be unpredictable (see equation (7)). The estimated λ's and β's are assumed to be unbiased estimates of the "true" parameter values. Therefore, we construct artificial data which satisfy the hypothesis that the model captures the predictable variation of the returns when conditioning on the instruments (Z) (see also FH (1991)). We compute mean-centred residuals mcu_{it} by subtracting the mean of $\lambda_{ot} + \varepsilon_{it}$ from $\lambda_{ot} + \varepsilon_{it}$ ($\lambda_{ot} + \varepsilon_{it} = r_{it} - \lambda_{1t}\beta_{i,t-1}$) and form the pseudo-returns (r_i) as the sum $mcu_{it} + \lambda_{1t}\beta_{i,t-1}$. Two variance ratios can be formed based on the above components. The first one, VR1, is the ratio of the variance of the model's predicted returns $E(\lambda\beta|Z)$ to the variance of expected (pseudo) returns (see equation (8)). The expected values are obtained from a linear regression on the instruments. The second variance ratio, VR2, is the ratio of the variance of the expected part of a return that is not explained by the model, ie the mean-centred residual, to the variance of the expected return (see equation (9)). This ratio is compared to VR1. If the first variance ratio is close to unity, then most of the predictable variation in returns is due to the changing structure of risk.

Ferson and Harvey (1991) found that some 81 % of the predictability in US returns was driven by changes in the expected betas and expected price of betas. Table 6 gives the corresponding analysis with Finnish stock data. The variance ratio VR1 has, in all cases except three, a bigger value than VR2, which indicates that the predictability of Finnish returns is driven mainly by the component that is related to the cross-sectional structure of risk and the cross-section of expected returns. We characterize this part of predictability as rational. The irrational source of predictability is driven by the variance of the expected error term in equation (9). This component, VR2, clearly has a smaller mean than VR1. We do not have a specific test for the significance of the variance ratios. However, the irrational component of the predictability seems to be bigger in Finland than in the US.

Table 6. **Decomposition of predictable variation of stock-specific returns, 1977:6–1989:12 (151 observations)**

Stock	VR1	VR2
AB	1.056	0.768
EFFO	1.342	0.438
ENSOA	1.361	0.475
FISKK	1.752	1.704
HUHTK	0.900	0.776
INSTA	4.434	3.384
KEMI	1.349	0.898
KESK	4.115	2.835
KOP	1.680	1.424
KYMI	1.307	0.553
LASS	1.077	1.392
LOHJA	2.652	0.512
NOKIK	1.301	0.428
OTAVK	0.913	1.270
PART	3.118	2.045
RAUM	6.884	2.960
SOKEI	1.314	0.859
STOCA	1.190	0.440
SYPA	2.399	1.346
TAMF	1.371	0.129
TAMP	1.110	0.908
TAOK	1.438	1.253
TRIK	1.406	1.449
WARTI	2.666	0.608
YHTYK	3.996	1.704
Mean	2.085	1.222

$$VR1 = \frac{Var[E(\lambda\beta|Z)]}{Var[E(r|Z)]}$$

$$VR2 = \frac{Var[E(r-\lambda\beta|Z)]}{Var[E(r|Z)]} = \frac{Var[E(mcu|Z)]}{Var[E(r|Z)]}$$

The variance ratios are often greater than one, which indicates that the covariance of the numerators in the variance ratios is negative. It should be noted that the conditioned return in the denominator is the firm-specific pseudo-return instead of the portfolio return used in Ferson and Harvey. This implies that we also condition an aggregate variable, ie the risk premium, in addition to the firm-specific betas in the numerator, whereas only the firm-specific returns are conditioned in the denominator. It is not surprising, given this background, that the conditional variance of the denominator is often smaller than that of the numerator.

A closer look at the conditioning regressions reveals that BARIP is the major source of negative covariation. This is illustrated clearly by the t-values for BARIP on pseudo-returns (Appendix 1A) and mean-centred residuals (Appendix 1B), given that BARIP was the most significant forecasting instrument for the ex post risk premium. Appendix 1A shows that ENSOA, LOHJA, NOKIK, TAMF and WARTI are the only stocks whose returns BARIP is able to predict significantly. None of these firms has significant t-value on BARIP in Appendix 1B, and all of these firms have reasonable VR2 values in Table 6. This evidence suggests that the high VR2 values are due to the data construction method, where the negative covariance between the $\lambda\beta$s and mcus is introduced via the estimated λ term if returns on a stock are not predicted by BARIP.

All in all, the large variance ratios seem to be related to small sample problems, which at times introduce extra variability, via the λ term, to the artificial data used in the numerator of the variance ratios. However, the extra variance is approximately the same in both of the numerators and hence does not alter the relative order of size between the two.

Appendix 1A also shows further that the coefficients of determination for regressions of the pseudoreturns are reasonable enough. The interpretation of FSM is quite straightforward. It is the most significant predictor of firm-specific returns, having a significant t-value (at the 5 % level) in 14 regressions. Unexpected inflation turned up with a significant t-value in 11 regressions out of 25.

4.3 Risk Premium vs Risk Sensitivity

The numerator of the first variance ratio, VR1, can be decomposed further to determine whether the time-varying expected risk premium or risk sensitivities are driving the predictable variation in the excess stock returns. In the third variance ratio, VR3, the variance of the conditional risk premium is multiplied by the square of the unconditional mean of the betas (see equation (10)). The interaction terms arise because of covariance between the time-varying risk premium and the betas. $E(\lambda)$ and $E(\beta)$ are the unconditional means – which are assumed to be constants. The constancy assumption is accurate at least with respect to the betas, according to Malkamäki (1993b), who found that the betas of the stocks analysed here follow a stationary AR1 process.

Table 7 shows us that some 61 % of the rational part of predictability is due to the predictable variation of the risk premium. No predictable variation is attributed to the conditional betas, according to VR4 in the table. This supports the findings of FH. They also pointed out that the variance of expected risk premium is on the order of the variance of expected stock returns, and the betas are on the order of 1.0. Furthermore, Malkamäki (1993b) found that the mean-reverting AR1 betas employed here are in most cases constant. Thus, it is not surprising that the predictable variation of Finnish stock returns is attributed to the time-varying risk premium.

Table 7. **Decomposition of predictable variation between betas and the price of the betas, 1977:6–1989:12 (151 observations)**

Stock	**VR3**	**VR4**	**Interaction effects**
AB	61.092	0.0000	38.908
EFFO	61.104	0.0000	38.896
ENSOA	61.350	0.0000	38.650
FISKK	61.252	0.0000	38.748
HUHTK	60.561	0.0000	39.439
INSTA	61.121	0.0000	38.879
KEMI	59.516	0.0000	40.484
KESK	61.664	0.0000	38.336
KOP	61.103	0.0000	38.897
KYMI	60.598	0.0000	39.402
LASS	59.436	0.0000	40.564
LOHJA	61.056	0.0000	38.944
NOKIK	61.417	0.0000	38.583
OTAVK	59.072	0.0002	40.928
PART	61.084	0.0000	38.916
RAUM	61.312	0.0000	38.688
SOKEI	61.438	0.0000	38.562
STOCA	61.135	0.0000	38.865
SYPA	60.683	0.0000	39.317
TAMF	58.387	0.0000	41.613
TAMP	60.863	0.0000	39.137
TAOK	61.139	0.0000	38.861
TRIK	64.004	0.0004	35.996
WARTI	61.094	0.0000	38.906
YHTYK	61.022	0.0000	38.978
Mean	60.900	0.000	39.100

$$VR3 = \frac{[E(\beta)]^2 Var[E(\lambda | Z)]}{Var[E(\lambda\beta | Z)]} x 100$$

$$VR4 = \frac{[E(\lambda)]^2 Var[E(\beta | Z)]}{Var[E(\lambda\beta | Z)]} x 100$$

5 CONCLUSIONS

This paper studies the driving forces of predictable variation in Finnish stock returns. We apply a modified version of the research design of Ferson and Harvey (1991) in order to divide the driving forces of predictabity into rational and irrational parts. However, the analysis is conducted within the Sharpe—Lintner CAPM instead of using the multifactor approach of FH. The rational expectations view is supported in the analysis if the predictable variation of excess stock returns is driven by predictable variation in the betas, the price of the betas or a combination of the two. We allow for greater dynamics in the beta estimation than FH, since the betas are allowed to vary over time according to a mean-reverting AR1 process. We also use firm-specific returns instead of portfolio returns as in FH.

We find that market risk is conditionally priced on the thin Finnish stock market. Finnish investors were found to use change in unexpected inflation, expected change in future order stock for Finnish industry and an instrument for the influence of lagged excess returns on stock markets in Finland, Germany, Sweden, the United Kingdom and the United States, in setting prices in the stock market. The interest-based variables that have been found to be relevant information to US investors did not succeed as conditioning variables in this analysis. Most of the predictable variation in the stock returns is attributed to the time-varying risk premium, which supports the rational behavior of Finnish investors in setting the prices in the market. However, the conditional residual term accounted for a greater part of the predictable variation of the stock returns than that which was found by Ferson and Harvey. The bigger "irrational" part of predictability may be partly due to the data employed, as we used firm-specific returns instead of portfolio returns. Another reason could be that the CAPM is not an adequate model. A conditional multifactor replication of this study could provide further information concerning the pricing of Finnish stocks.

REFERENCES

Berglund, T. and Knif, J. (1992) Time Varying Risk and CAPM Tests on Data from a Small Stock Market. Swedish School of Economics and Business Administration, Helsinki and Vaasa. Working paper.

Berglund, T., Wahlroos, B. and Grandel, L. (1983) The KOP and the UNITAS Indexes for the Helsinki Stock Exchange in the Light of a New Value Weighted Index. Swedish School of Economics and Business Administration. Working Paper.

Booth, G.G., Hatem, J., Virtanen, I. and Yli-Olli, P. (1992) Stochastic Modelling of Security Returns: Evidence from the Helsinki Stock Exchange. Fothcoming in the European Journal of Operational Research.

Campbell, J.Y. (1987) Stock Returns and the Term Structure, Journal of Financial Economics 18, 373–399.

Chen, N.-F., Roll, R. and Ross, S.A. (1986) Economic Forces and the Stock Market, Journal of Business 59:3, 383–403.

Fama, E.F. and French, K.R. (1988) Dividend Yields and Expected Stock Returns, Journal of Financial Economics 22, 3–25.

Fama, E.F. and MacBeth, J.D. (1973) Risk, Return, and Equilibrium: Empirical Tests, Journal of Political Economy 81:May, 607–636.

Ferson, W, and Harvey, C. (1991) The Variation of Economic Risk Premiums, Journal of Political Economy 99:2, 385–415.

Goodrich, R.L. (1989) Applied Statistical Forecasting. Belmont, MA, USA, Business Forecast Systems, Inc.

Harvey, A.C. (1989) Forecasting, Structural Time Series Models and the Kalman Filter, Cambridge University Press.

Harvey, C. (1989) Time-Varying Conditional Covariances in Tests of Asset Pricing Models, Journal of Financial Economics 24, 289–317.

Johansen, S. (1988) Statistical Analysis of Cointegration Vectors, Journal of Economic Dynamics and Control 12, 231–254.

Keim, D.B. and Stambaugh, R.F. (1986) Predicting Returns in the Stock and Bond Markets, Journal of Financial Economics 17, 357–390.

Knif, J. (1989) Parameter Variability in the Single Factor Market Model, An Empirical Comparison of Tests and Estimation Procedures Using Data from the Helsinki Stock Exchange, Commentationes Scientiarum Socialium 40, Societas Scientatiatrum Fennica.

Knif, J. and Högholm, K. (1991) Forecasting Stock Returns for Different Time Aggregation Levels. Swedish School of Economics and Business Administration, Helsinki, 46, 125–150.

Lintner, J. (1965) The Valuation of Risk Assets and the Selection of Risky Investments in Stock Portfolios and Capital Budgets, Review of Economics and Statistics 47:1, 347–400.

Malkamäki, M. (1993a) Cointegration and Causality of Stock Markets in Two Small Open Economies and Their Major Trading Partners. Manuscript. Bank of Finland.

Malkamäki, M. (1993b) In the Defence of the CAPM: Evidence Using Time Varying Betas on a Thin Stock Market. Manuscript. Bank of Finland.

Malkamäki, M. (1993c) The Superiority of Time-Varying Betas in the Finnish Stock Market, Journal of Multinational Financial Management, Forthcoming.

Pagan, A. (1984) Econometric Issues in the Analysis of Regressions with Generated Regressors, International Economic Review 25:1, 221–247.

Poterba, J.M. and Summers, L.H. (1988) Mean Reversion in Stock Prices: Evidence and Implications, Journal of Financial Economics 22, 27–59.

Shanken, J. (1992) On the Estimation of Beta-Pricing Models, Review of Financial Studies 5:1, 1–33.

Sharpe, W.F. (1964) Capital Asset Prices. A Theory of Market Equilibrium under Condition of Risk, Journal of Finance. 19:3, 425–442.

Taylor, S. (1986) Modelling Financial Time Series. John Wiley.

Virtanen, I. and Yli-Olli, P. (1987) Forecasting Stock Market Prices in a Thin Security Market, Omega 15:2, 145–155.

White, K.J. (1980) A Heteroscedasticity-Consistent Covariance Matrix Estimator and Direct Test of Heteroscedasticity, Econometrica, 817–838.

Appendix 1A

Pseudo-returns (r_{it}) conditioned on the instruments* 1977:2—1989:12 (155 observations)

r_{it}	Constant	FSM(t)	UNEXINF(t−3)	BARIP(t−4)	R^2	DW
AB	0.030	0.789	−1.328	0.001	3.3	2.47
	(1.79)	(1.96)	(−0.93)	(0.76)		
EFFO	0.028	0.675	−1.631	0.002	5.1	1.71
	(1.97)	(2.00)	(−1.36)	(1.59)		
ENSOA	0.028	0.751	−1.072	0.003	8.0	1.96
	(2.20)	(2.51)	(−1.01)	(2.44)		
FISKK	0.026	0.672	−1.274	0.000	4.1	1.92
	(2.11)	(2.26)	(−1.21)	(0.01)		
HUHTK	0.022	0.581	−0.858	0.001	3.7	1.76
	(1.90)	(2.12)	(−0.88)	(0.78)		
INSTA	0.010	0.399	0.325	0.001	2.4	2.15
	(0.90)	(1.48)	(0.34)	(1.09)		
KEMI	0.010	−0.151	−3.391	0.001	3.3	2.19
	(0.55)	(−0.34)	(−2.16)	(0.34)		
KESK	0.013	0.286	−1.089	0.000	2.8	1.47
	(1.59)	(1.44)	(−1.54)	(0.13)		
KOP	0.032	0.614	−3.014	−0.000	10.8	2.42
	(3.18)	(2.54)	(−3.51)	(−0.26)		
KYMI	0.032	0.652	−2.663	0.002	11.2	1.75
	(3.25)	(2.77)	(−3.18)	(1.47)		
LASS	0.021	0.276	−2.812	−0.001	3.6	1.97
	(1.37)	(0.75)	(−2.16)	(−0.61)		
LOHJA	0.020	0.384	−2.019	0.003	7.2	2.19
	(1.77)	(1.42)	(−2.10)	(2.38)		
NOKIK	0.036	0.773	−2.634	0.002	11.1	1.88
	(3.11)	(2.85)	(−2.73)	(2.02)		
OTAVK	0.022	0.282	−2.958	−0.001	5.0	2.31
	(1.60)	(0.87)	(−2.57)	(−0.71)		
PART	0.026	0.579	−1.864	0.000	6.2	2.05
	(2.51)	(2.36)	(−2.14)	(0.40)		
RAUM	0.004	−0.028	−1.225	0.001	2.3	1.99
	(0.33)	(−0.11)	(−1.37)	(1.27)		
SOKEI	0.034	0.868	−1.531	0.002	6.5	1.86
	(2.55)	(2.77)	(−1.38)	(1.08)		
STOCA	0.029	0.531	−2.828	0.002	9.2	1.89
	(2.70)	(2.08)	(−3.11)	(1.38)		
SYPA	0.027	0.596	−1.990	0.001	8.7	1.90
	(2.97)	(2.76)	(−2.60)	(0.85)		
TAMF	0.022	0.457	−1.523	0.004	6.5	1.81
	(1.69)	(1.49)	(−1.39)	(2.54)		
TAMP	0.039	0.894	−2.395	0.001	8.4	1.85
	(3.07)	(3.00)	(−2.26)	(0.49)		
TAOK	0.017	0.461	−0.533	0.001	1.1	2.20
	(1.03)	(1.21)	(−0.39)	(0.30)		
TRIK	0.036	1.046	−0.868	0.000	2.9	2.38
	(1.69)	(2.05)	(−0.48)	(0.08)		
WARTI	0.016	0.373	−1.072	0.003	4.4	1.99
	(1.27)	(1.28)	(−1.04)	(2.09)		
YHTYK	0.021	0.484	−1.533	0.002	4.1	2.06
	(1.76)	(1.69)	(−1.51)	(1.24)		

* The model estimated: $r_{it} = \gamma_0 + \gamma_1 FSM(t) + \gamma_2 UNEXINF(t\text{-}3) + \gamma_3 BARIP(t\text{-}4) + e_{it}$

Appendix 1B

**Mean-centred residuals (mcu_{it}) conditioned on the instruments*
1977:2–1989:12 (155 observations)**

(mcu_{it})	Constant	FSM(t)	UNEXINF(t–3)	BARIP(t–4)	R^2	DW
AB	0.017	0.612	0.536	–0.002	1.7	2.43
	(0.82)	(1.24)	(0.30)	(–0.93)		
EFFO	0.012	0.468	0.583	–0.002	1.4	2.02
	(0.66)	(1.06)	(0.37)	(–0.84)		
ENSOA	0.010	0.515	1.427	–0.001	2.4	2.28
	(0.60)	(1.33)	(1.04)	(–0.78)		
FISKK	0.012	0.486	0.701	–0.004	4.4	1.94
	(0.78)	(1.30)	(0.53)	(–2.16)		
HUHTK	0.013	0.470	0.417	–0.001	2.2	1.78
	(0.98)	(1.49)	(0.37)	(–0.92)		
INSTA	–0.005	0.195	2.489	–0.003	4.2	2.12
	(–0.34)	(0.53)	(1.89)	(–1.60)		
KEMI	–0.007	–0.368	–1.055	–0.004	2.6	2.08
	(–0.33)	(–0.78)	(–0.63)	(–1.66)		
KESK	0.002	0.139	0.626	–0.003	3.6	1.92
	(0.13)	(0.48)	(0.60)	(–2.22)		
KOP	0.013	0.362	–0.350	–0.005	6.9	2.25
	(0.86)	(0.98)	(–0.27)	(–3.13)		
KYMI	0.015	0.430	–0.325	–0.003	3.1	1.98
	(1.04)	(1.23)	(–0.26)	(–1.76)		
LASS	0.008	0.102	–1.016	–0.004	3.3	2.09
	(0.43)	(0.23)	(–0.63)	(–2.11)		
LOHJA	–0.001	0.103	0.957	–0.003	2.0	2.34
	(–0.07)	(0.27)	(0.71)	(–1.56)		
NOKIK	0.017	0.522	0.030	–0.002	2.8	2.18
	(1.05)	(1.40)	(0.02)	(–1.47)		
OTAVK	0.009	0.104	–1.234	–0.004	4.0	2.21
	(0.54)	(0.25)	(–0.85)	(–2.29)		
PART	0.007	0.322	0.843	–0.005	6.0	2.12
	(0.44)	(0.91)	(0.67)	(–2.85)		
RAUM	–0.014	–0.270	1.233	–0.003	3.7	1.91
	(–0.99)	(–0.79)	(1.02)	(–2.04)		
SOKEI	0.017	0.649	0.772	–0.003	3.3	1.96
	(0.99)	(1.57)	(0.53)	(–1.47)		
STOCA	0.014	0.327	–0.660	–0.002	2.2	1.95
	(0.89)	(0.91)	(–0.52)	(–1.48)		
SYPA	0.009	0.356	0.524	–0.004	4.6	2.05
	(0.61)	(1.02)	(0.42)	(–2.43)		
TAMF	0.004	0.218	0.731	–0.001	0.6	2.31
	(0.23)	(0.60)	(0.57)	(–0.47)		
TAMP	0.021	0.643	–0.157	–0.004	4.9	2.28
	(1.33)	(1.69)	(–0.12)	(–2.14)		
TAOK	0.008	0.351	0.649	–0.002	0.9	2.27
	(0.41)	(0.74)	(0.39)	(–0.78)		
TRIK	0.014	0.670	1.630	–0.004	3.8	2.28
	(0.62)	(1.27)	(0.87)	(–1.84)		
WARTI	–0.002	0.137	1.422	–0.002	1.6	2.08
	(–0.13)	(0.35)	(1.03)	(–1.06)		
YHTYK	0.001	0.217	1.339	–0.004	3.6	2.10
	(0.05)	(0.55)	(0.95)	(–2.07)		

* The model estimated: $(mcu_{it}) = \gamma_o + \gamma_1 FSM(t) + \gamma_2 UNEXINF(t\text{-}3) + \gamma_3 BARIP(t\text{-}4) + e_{it}$

Linear Models for Portfolio Selection and their Application to the Milano Stock Market

M.G. Speranza
Dept. of Quantitative Methods
University of Brescia
Corso Mameli, 27, I-25122 Brescia

In this paper we recall a linear model presented in Speranza (1992) in which the risk is measured by means of a linear combination of the semi-absolute deviations and which has been shown, for a suitable choice of the coefficients, to be equivalent to and more efficient than the model introduced in Konno and Yamazaki (1991). In order to give some insight on the model, the analytic solution of some particular case is derived. A weighted version of the model is also reviewed which gives rise to different models for different choices of the weights. Different linear unweighted and weighted models and Markowitz's model are compared on two different sets of data of 117 stocks of the Milano Stock Market. Global information on the obtained portfolios are reported, together with more detailed information, for a high value of the required rate of return, which show similarities and dissimilarities of the portfolios. The ex-post analysis shows the weighted models in general perform better, especially on the short horizon. In particular, one of the weighted models guarantees a rate of return always higher than the required one.

1. Introduction

The portfolio selection problem consists in deciding, given a set of investment alternatives, the percentage of money to be invested in each of the alternatives so that a good return rate is guaranteed at a low level of risk. Although the problem has a number of applications, the most classical and celebrated model, Markowitz's model, has not been applied as much as one would expect. This may be due to several reasons and probably to a combination of these reasons. We do not intend to enter here the discussion and refer to Konno and Yamazaki (1991) for a review of the difficulties which may be encountered in the application of Markowitz's model. However, given the practical relevance of the problem and the difficulties in the application of Markowitz's model, it remains of relevant interest the investigation of models for the individual portfolio selection problem.

In the direction of simplifying Markowitz's model, some attempts have been made to linearize the quadratic objective function (see, in particular, Sharpe, 1967, Sharpe, 1971 and Stone, 1973). More recently, Konno and Yamazaki (1991) proposed a model which has directly a linear programming form, where a L_1 (absolute deviation) instead of a L_2 (variance) risk function is adopted. In case the rates of return of the securities have a multivariate normal distribution, the model has been shown to be equivalent to Markowitz's model. In Speranza (1992) a more general model has been introduced in which the risk is measured by a linear combination of the semi-absolute deviations of the portfolio rate of return. A suitable selection of the coefficients of the linear combination gives rise to a model equivalent to the one of Konno and Yamazaki which halves its number of constraints. The computational results showed that it halves the computational time as well. A weighted version of the model based on the linear combination of the semi-absolute deviations is also introduced in Speranza (1992) which aims at maintaining the simplicity of the unweighted one, achieving at the same time a higher flexibility in the definition of the investor's preferences and the interpretation of the historical data upon which the model is based.

In this paper we review the models introduced in Speranza (1992). In order to give some insight on the basic unweighted model, the analytic solution of some particular case is derived. Moreover, computational results made on a set of 117 stocks taken from the Milano Stock Market are reported for a required rate of return of 2.2% per month. The ex-post analysis shows that in general the weighted models perform better than the unweighted one and than Markowitz's model, especially on the short horizon. In particular, one the weighted models always guarantees a rate of return higher than the required one.

The paper is organized as follows. In Section 2 we recall the unweighted model presented in Speranza (1992) and in Section 3 the analytic solution of some particular case is derived. The weighted model is introduced in Section 4 and the computational results obtained on the Milano Stock Market are discussed in Section 5.

2. The Semi Absolute Deviation Model

In this Section we recall the model which has been proposed by Speranza (1992).

A capital C has to be invested in a set J of securities in such a way that an expected rate of return ρ is guaranteed and that the portfolio risk is minimized. We assume, as in Konno and Yamazaki (1991), that the expected rate of return r_j of security $j \in J$ can be approximated by the average derived from a set of data $\{r_{jt} | t = 1, \ldots, T\}$, where r_{jt} is the rate of return observed (or predicted) at time t for security j, that is

$$r_j = \frac{\sum_{t=1}^{T} r_{jt}}{T}.$$

An upper bound u_j can be introduced on the investment in security j.

We will assume, without loss of generality, that the capital C is normalized to 1. The decision variables x_j represent the percentage of capital to be invested in security j. We denote by $R(x)$ the rate of return of the portfolio determined by variables x and by $\mu(x) = \sum_j r_j x_j$ its mean value.

The model presented in Speranza (1992) differs from other portfolio selection models on the risk function. The risk $N(x)$ associated to a portfolio given by the variables x is defined as a linear combination of the semi absolute deviations of the portfolio rate of return from the mean value, that is

$$N(x) = E\{-\alpha \min(0, R(x) - \mu(x)) + \beta \max(0, R(x) - \mu(x))\}. \tag{1}$$

We briefly recall the interpretation of this risk function in terms of investor's utility and refer to Markowitz (1987) and Elton and Gruber (1987) for a general introduction to utility analysis. The risk function $N(x)$ represents the investors for whom the utility of the portfolio determined by the variables x with mean return rate $\mu(x)$ is measured by the function

$$U(x) = \gamma R(x) + \alpha \min(0, R(x) - \mu(x)) - \beta \max(0, R(x) - \mu(x)).$$

The investor, who aims at maximizing his/her expected utility, chooses among the alternative portfolios the one which maximizes the mean value of $U(x)$. As a function of $R(x)$, $U(x)$ is a piecewise linear function. The quantities $\gamma + \alpha$ and $\gamma - \beta$ are the derivatives of the utility function below and above $\mu(x)$, respectively. In other words, the investor who uses this model has a constant utility for a unit deviation from the mean portfolio rate of return, different for the case in which the deviation is below and above the mean. In order to have a non-decreasing $U(x)$ it must be $\gamma + \alpha \geq 0$ and $\gamma - \beta \geq 0$. The utility function is concave, representing a risk averse investor, if $\gamma - \beta < \gamma + \alpha$, that is if $\alpha + \beta > 0$. A risk seeking and a risk neutral investor are represented by the cases $\alpha + \beta < 0$ and $\alpha + \beta = 0$, respectively.

We will refer to the above model as the Model(α, β). The model presented in Konno and Yamazaki (1991) (KY model) is a particular case, obtained with $\alpha = \beta = 1$. In Speranza (1992) it has been shown that, if $\alpha + \beta > 0$, then Model(α, β) always generates the same portfolio. On the contrary, if $\alpha + \beta < 0$, finding the portfolio which, for a given rate of return, minimizes the linear combination of the semi absolute deviations is equivalent to finding a portfolio which maximizes the mean absolute deviation. Observe that, in this case, the associated utility function is convex representing, as already mentioned, a risk seeking investor. Taking into account Theorem 3.1 in Konno and Yamazaki (1991), it follows that, if $\alpha + \beta > 0$ and the rates of return have a multivariate normal distribution, Model(α, β) is equivalent to Markowitz's model.

A suitable selection of the parameters α and β, namely

$$\alpha = 1 \qquad \beta = 0,$$

allows the formulation of a model equivalent to the KY model and to Markowitz's model, in case the normality assumption is satisfied. The model can be formulated as follows and will be referred to as the Absolute Deviations (AD) model

$$\min \frac{-\sum_{t=1}^{T}(\min(0, \sum_{j\in J}(r_{jt} - r_j)x_j))}{T}$$

$$\sum_{j\in J} r_j x_j \geq \rho$$

$$\sum_{j\in J} x_j = 1$$

$$0 \leq x_j \leq u_j \qquad j \in J.$$

The AD model takes the following linear form

$$\min \frac{\sum_{t=1}^{T} y_t}{T}$$

$$y_t + \sum_{j \in J} (r_{jt} - r_j) x_j \geq 0 \qquad t = 1, \ldots, T$$

$$\sum_{j \in J} r_j x_j \geq \rho$$

$$\sum_{j \in J} x_j = 1$$

$$0 \leq x_j \leq u_j \qquad j \in J$$

$$y_t \geq 0 \qquad t = 1, \ldots, T.$$

Observe that the AD model has $T + |J|$ variables and $T + 2$ constraints, while the KY model has $T + |J|$ variables and $2T + 2$ constraints and is therefore simpler and more efficient. Computational results showed that the computational time required by the AD model halves the time required by the KY model. Obviously, the portfolios obtained for the same value of ρ are identical.

3. The analytic solution of some particular cases

In order to give some insight on the AD model, in this Section we derive the analytic solution of some particular cases.

Let us first consider the case of two securities whose interest rates have opposite behaviour. This corresponds, in the Markowitz's modelization, to the case of a perfect negative correlation coefficient between the two securities, $\rho = -1$. More formally, let us suppose $r_{2t} - r_2 = -k(r_{1t} - r_1)$, $\forall t$. In this case the solution of the model can be analytically derived. Let us suppose u_1 and u_2 are upper unbounded. If not so, the results can be immediately generalized. Let us first consider the case $r_1 \neq r_2$ and suppose, with no loss of generality, that $r_1 > r_2$.

Proposition 1: If $n = 2$, $r_1 > r_2$ and $r_{2t} - r_2 = -k(r_{1t} - r_1)$, with $k \geq 0$, $\forall t$, then the optimal solution of the K-Y model is

a) if $\rho \leq \frac{kr_1+r_2}{k+1}$

$$x_1^* = \frac{k}{k+1} \quad \textit{and} \quad x_2^* = \frac{1}{k+1}$$

b) if $\frac{kr_1+r_2}{k+1} < \rho \leq r_1$

$$x_1^* = \frac{\rho - r_2}{r_1 - r_2} \quad \textit{and} \quad x_2^* = \frac{r_1 - \rho}{r_1 - r_2}$$

c) if $\rho > r_1$

no feasible solution.

Proof: Let us denote $a_t = r_{1t} - r_1$, $\forall t$. The AD model can be written as

$$\min - \sum_t \min(0, (k+1)a_t x_1 - k a_t)$$

$$x_1 \geq \frac{\rho - r_2}{r_1 - r_2}.$$

Then, observe that, for any given t, the function $y_t = -\min(0, (k+1)a_t x_1 - k a_t)$ is piecewise linear, with an unconstrained minimum in $k/(k+1)$, where $y_t = 0$. Moreover, observe that the feasible value of x_1 closest to $x_1^m = k/(k+1)$ minimizes y_t, for any t, and thus minimizes the whole objective function.

Let $b_0 = \frac{\rho - r_2}{r_1 - r_2}$ denote the minimum feasible value of x_1. Cases a, b and c correspond to the cases in which $b_0 \leq x_1^m$, $x_1^m < b_0 \leq 1$ and $b_0 > 1$, respectively. □

It can be interesting to note that in case a the portfolio is risk free. Observe that, as it is obviously expected, if the required rate of return is not too high, that is $\rho \leq \frac{r_1 + r_2}{2}$, and if the two securities have exactly opposite behaviour, that is $k = 1$, the optimal solution is to split the capital equally between security 1 and 2, that is $x_1^* = x_2^* = 1/2$. Let us now consider the case in which $r_1 = r_2$.

Proposition 2: If $n = 2$, $r_1 = r_2 = r$ and $r_{2t} - r = -k(r_{1t} - r)$, with $k \geq 0$, $\forall t$, then the optimal solution of the K-Y model is

a) if $\rho \leq r$

$$x_1^* = \frac{k}{k+1} \quad \textit{and} \quad x_2^* = \frac{1}{k+1}$$

b) if $\rho > r$

no feasible solution.

Proof: The proof follows immediately from the observation of the problem

$$\min - \sum_t \min(0, (k+1)a_t x_1 - k a_t)$$

$$r \geq \rho.$$

□

Unfortunately, in the more general case in which $r_{2t} - r_2 = -k_t(r_{1t} - r_1)$, with $k_t \geq 0$, it is not possible to find a simple analytic form for the solution of the model. In this case the objective function is

$$- \sum_t \min(0, (k_t+1)a_t x_1 - k_t a_t)$$

and each function $y_t = -\min(0, (k+1)a_t x_1 - k a_t)$ has a minimum unconstrained value of x_1 in $k_t/(k_t+1)$, which depends upon t.

Let us now consider the case in which the two securities have a similar behaviour. Formally, let us suppose $r_{2t} - r_2 = k_t(r_{1t} - r_1)$, with $k_t \geq 0$, $\forall t$. The case of perfect positive correlation coefficient between the two securities, $\rho = +1$, is obtained when $k_t = k$, $\forall t$. The analytic solution of the AD model can be obtained for the case $k_t \leq 1$, $\forall t$, and the case $k_t \geq 1$, $\forall t$. When $k_t = k$, $\forall t$, the former situation corresponds to the case of perfect positive correlation in which the least risky security has the lowest expected return rate, while the latter situation to the case in which the least risky security has the highest return rate.

Proposition 3: Let $n = 2$, $r_1 \geq r_2$ and $r_{2t} - r_2 = k_t(r_{1t} - r_1)$, with $0 \leq k_t \leq 1$, $\forall t$. Then, if $r_1 > r_2$, the optimal solution of the AD model is

a1) if $\rho \leq r_2$

$$x_1^* = 0 \qquad \textit{and} \qquad x_2^* = 1$$

b1) if $r_2 < \rho \leq r_1$

$$x_1^* = \frac{\rho - r_2}{r_1 - r_2} \qquad \textit{and} \qquad x_2^* = \frac{r_1 - \rho}{r_1 - r_2}$$

c1) if $\rho > r_1$

no feasible solution.

If $r_1 = r_2 = r$, the optimal solution is

a2) if $\rho \leq r$

$$x_1^* = 0 \qquad \textit{and} \qquad x_2^* = 1$$

b2) if $\rho > r$

no feasible solution.

Proof: The AD model can be written as

$$\min - \sum_t \min(0, (1 - k_t)a_t x_1 + k_t a_t)$$

$$x_1 \geq \frac{\rho - r_2}{r_1 - r_2}.$$

The function $y_t = -\min(0, (1 - k_t)a_t x_1 + k_t a_t)$ either is constantly 0 or has an unconstrained minimum in $x_1 = 0$. It follows that the whole objective function is always increasing and thus the analytic solution follows immediately. Cases $a1$, $b1$ and $c1$ correspond to the cases $b_0 = \frac{\rho - r_2}{r_1 - r_2} \leq 0$, $0 < b_0 \leq 1$ and $b_0 > 1$, respectively. □

Proposition 4: If $n = 2$, $r_1 \geq r_2$ and $r_{2t} - r_2 = k_t(r_{1t} - r_1)$, with $k_t \geq 1$, $\forall t$, then the optimal solution of the AD model is

a) if $\rho \leq r_1$

$$x_1^* = 1 \qquad \textit{and} \qquad x_2^* = 0$$

b) if $\rho > r_1$

no feasible solution.

Proof: In this case the function $y_t = -\min(0, (1-k_t)a_t x_1 + k_t a_t)$ either is constantly 0 or is decreasing. It follows that the whole objective function is always decreasing. □

The result of Proposition 4 is obvious observing that the case in which $k_t \geq 1$, $\forall t$, corresponds to the situation in which security 1 has always higher expected rate of return, as it has been assumed $r_1 \geq r_2$, and lower risk than security 2.

4. Models with Weighted Risk Functions

In this Section we briefly recall a model presented in Speranza (1992) which aims at maintaining the characteristic of simplicity of the AD model, but also at giving a more flexible interpretation of the historical data.

The data r_{jt} at time t can be seen as a scenario to which a certain measure of risk w_t^1 can be attributed and which, with a certain degree of belief w_t^2, will happen in the near future. On the basis of this simple interpretation of the data, a new risk function $N'(x)$ can be defined as

$$N'(x) = -\alpha \sum_{t:g(t)\leq 0} w_t^1 g(t) + \beta \sum_{t:g(t)\geq 0} w_t^1 g(t),$$

where it has been defined

$$g(t) = \sum_{j\in J}(r_{jt} - r_j^w)x_j.$$

The constant factor $1/\sum_t w_t^1$ has been disregarded, as it does not influence the identification of the points of the efficient frontier. The quantity r_j^w is an estimation of the rate of return of security j in the next period and is defined as

$$r_j^w = \frac{\sum_t w_t^2 r_{jt}}{\sum_t w_t^2}. \tag{2}$$

The function $N'(x)$ can be seen as a weighted discretized version of (1). In the case $w_t^1 = w_t^2 = w_t$, $\forall t$, it has been shown that any selection of the parameters α and β, with $\alpha + \beta > 0$, generates the same portfolio, in general different from the portfolio generated by the AD model. This equivalence result does not hold if the two types of weights do not coincide.

Like for the Model(α, β), a suitable selection of the parameters limits at a minimum the number of constraints of the resulting linear programming model. Selecting $\alpha = 1$ and $\beta = 0$, the model, referred to as model W0 in the following, turns out to be a weighted version of the AD model and can be formulated as

$$\min \sum_{t=1}^{T} w_t y_t$$

$$y_t + \sum_{j\in J}(r_{jt} - r_j^w)x_j \geq 0 \qquad t = 1, \ldots, T$$

$$\sum_{j\in J} r_j^w x_j \geq \rho$$

	α	β	w_t^1	w_t^2
AD	1	0	1	1
W0	1	0	δ^t	δ^t
W1	1	0	δ^t	1
W2	1	1	δ^t	1
W3	1	0	1	δ^t

Table I: The characteristics of the linear models

$$\sum_{j \in J} x_j = 1$$

$$0 \leq x_j \leq u_j \qquad j \in J$$

$$y_t \geq 0 \qquad t = 1, \ldots, T,$$

where, according to (2), it is

$$r_j = \frac{\sum_t w_t r_{jt}}{\sum_t w_t}.$$

The weight w_t may be chosen, for example, to be a smoothing coefficient $w_t = \delta^t$, with $0 < \delta < 1$. This corresponds to assuming that more recent scenarios will happen with higher probability in the near future.

If the weights w_t^1 and w_t^2 are different for some t, different portfolios are obtained for different values of α and β. Setting $w_t^2 = 1$, $\forall t$, corresponds to calculating the mean rate of each security by attributing the same degree of belief to all the historical data under consideration. Setting $w_t^1 = \delta^t$, $\forall t$, corresponds to considering the more recent deviations of the portfolio rate of return from the mean more risky than the less recent ones. For this choice of the weights and for $\alpha = 1$ and $\beta = 0$, the model represents an investor who prefers portfolios which recently did not generate rates of return below the mean. For $\alpha = 1$ and $\beta = 1$, the model represents an investor who prefers portfolios which recently did not deviate from the mean value at all. For this investor recent stability is a more important value than for the previous one, for whom of high value is a recent history of increasing portfolio rates of return.

5. Computational results

We have compared the models discussed in this paper on a set of data taken from the Milano Stock Market. A set of 117 stocks has been considered, which represent about the 35% of the complete set of stocks. This was the largest set available with data covering a large period. In particular, the data cover the time period going from January 1986 to June 1991 and have been divided in two sets, D1 and D2, relative to the periods 86-89 and 87-90, respectively. The month has been taken as time unit. The models whose characteristics are summarized in Table I and Markowitz's model have been compared.

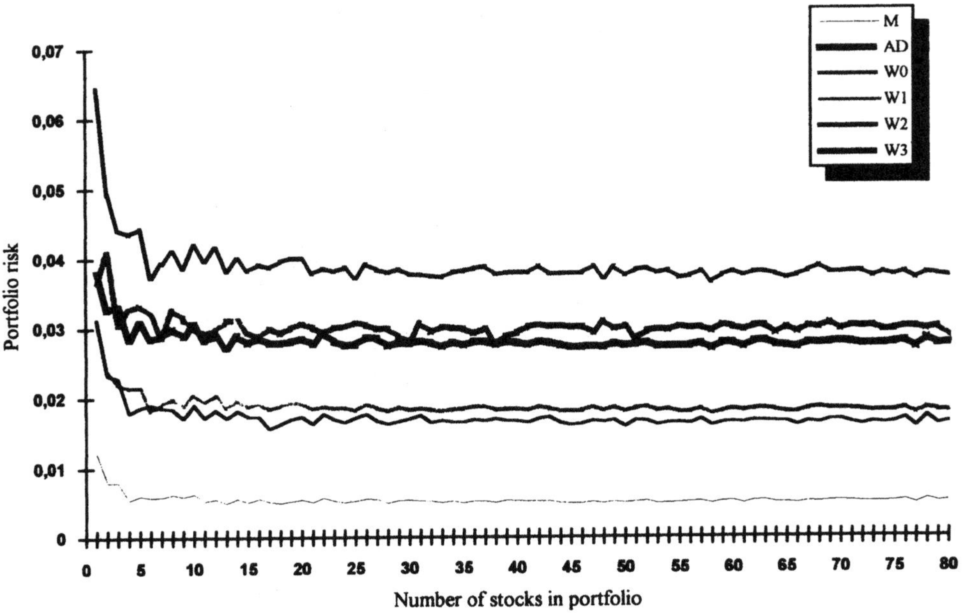

Figure 1: The diversification effect

Before discussing the portfolios generated by the models, we show the effect of diversification in the different models. In Figure 1 the value of risk is shown for different numbers of stocks. Each value of the risk is obtained by taking the mean over 10 random samples of a set of stocks of given size. The results show that the effect of diversification is similar in all the models. The risk decreases with the number of stocks in the portfolio and becomes almost constant above 15.

The efficient frontier has been obtained for each of the above models, discretizing the expected rate of return between 1.0% and 2.2% per month. In order to test the sensitivity of the weighted models to the value of the smoothing coefficient, we tested different values of δ. Markowitz's model has been solved by means of a compiled version of the routine reported in Bookstaber (1985). All the linear models have been solved using the linear programming routine of the SAS package on a personal computer. In all cases the computational time has been below one minute per point of the efficient frontiers. However, the W0 model requires about twice the time required by the other linear models. This is due to the fact that the number of constraints is twice the number of the other models.

We report here the results obtained for $\rho = 2.2\%$ per month on the two sets of data D1 and D2 with values of the smoothing coefficient $\delta = .9$ and $\delta = .95$. In Tables II and III some global characteristics of the portfolios obtained on D1 and D2, respectively, are shown. The rankings of the stocks in the different portfolios are shown in Tables IV and V, again for the two sets of data D1 and D2, respectively. The results suggest that Markowitz's model and the AD model generate similar portfolios, confirming the results obtained by Konno and Yamazaki. However, differences exist which in some case are quite relevant. Given the equivalence of the models under the normality assumption on the rates of return, the differences can be regarded as a

			$\delta = .9$				$\delta = .95$			
	M	AD	W0	W1	W2	W3	W0	W1	W2	W3
Number of stocks	12	10	13	10	15	9	12	11	15	11
Stock with max share (%)	18.7	23.8	16.4	41.7	19.1	23.7	16.3	17.8	26.2	24.3
Stock with min share (%)	0.1	2.1	2.1	1.3	0.5	1.1	0.3	0.2	0.6	0.4
Share of the first 3 stocks (%)	49.5	52.5	40.8	69.4	44.2	60.2	46.3	48.2	52.7	61.4
Stocks with share $\leq 3\%$	3	1	1	2	2	1	3	2	6	3

Table II: Portfolios obtained with $\rho = 2.2\%$ per month on D1

			$\delta = .9$				$\delta = .95$			
	M	AD	W0	W1	W2	W3	W0	W1	W2	W3
Number of stocks	4	5	5	5	4	5	6	8	5	7
Stock with max share (%)	55.7	73.3	53.1	58.8	46.1	66.0	45.3	51.4	35.3	54.6
Stock with min share (%)	11.6	1.2	2.4	2.0	2.1	5.2	0.1	0.01	2.0	1.6
Share of the first 3 stocks (%)	88.4	95.2	93.4	95.8	98.0	87.5	80.0	87.7	88.2	82.7
Stocks with share $\leq 3\%$	0	1	1	2	1	0	1	3	1	2

Table III: Portfolios obtained with $\rho = 2.2\%$ per month on D2

			$\delta = .9$				$\delta = .95$			
	M	AD	W0	W1	W2	W3	W0	W1	W2	W3
Aedes	12	6	7	4	14	7	10		11	7
Alcatel	4	4	6	2	6	5	1	4	4	5
Auschem					10				9	
BAV			2	3	11		9			
BNA	1	1	4	7	5	1	4	3	7	1
Espresso	7	9	13	6	2	2	7	7	2	2
Eridania								11		
Euromobil.									8	
Fiscam H.	5	5	1		1		3	9	1	8
Fiscam H. n.c.			11							
Fochi			9	10	8		5	5		
Gim	11									
Italcable				5						
Jolly H.	6	10			15	8	11		10	6
Magona	10	8						10	12	10
Mediobanca									13	
Mi. Ass. n.c.			8	8	12					
Pierrel					9					
Pierrel n.c.			10							
Rejna	9	7				4				4
Schiappar.	3	3	3		4	3	2	2	3	3
Serfi	8				7	9			6	11
Sip n.c.			5				12		15	
Sirti					3				14	
Sme				9						
Sopaf			12		13		6	8	5	
Unicem							8	6		
Zucchi	2	2		1		6		1		9

Table IV: Rankings for $\rho = 2.2\%$ per month on D1

			$\delta = .9$				$\delta = .95$			
	M	AD	W0	W1	W2	W3	W0	W1	W2	W3
Alcatel										7
BNA	4	3								4
Banco Lar.				5	3		6	4	5	5
Dalmine			5	3			3			
Eridania										6
Espresso	3	2							2	
FMC			3			4	4	6		
Fochi	2	4	1	1	1	1	1	1	3	1
Fondiaria			2	4			2	5		
Italcable								7		
Italgas						5		8		
Sasib Priv.			4			2	5			
Serfi		5			2	3				2
Standa				2				2	4	
Zucchi	1	1			4			3	1	3

Table V: Rankings for $\rho = 2.2\%$ per month on D2

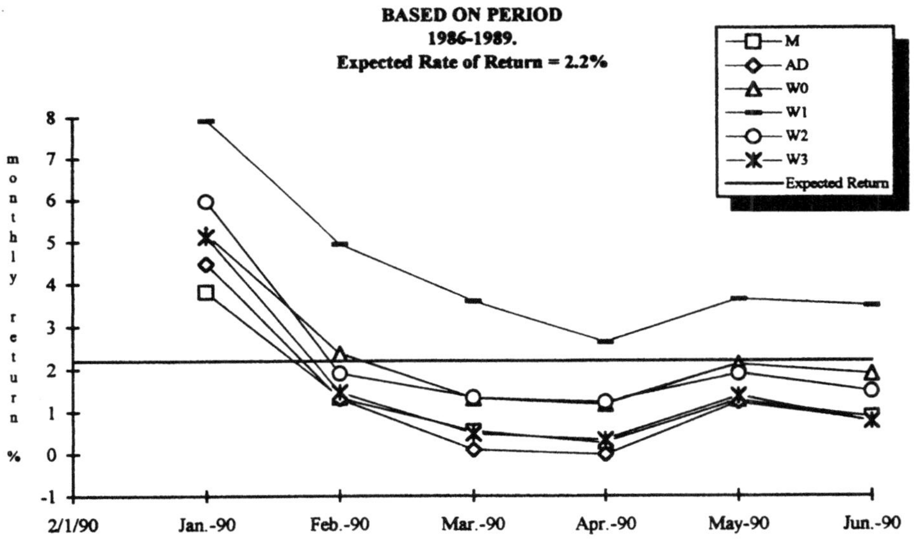

Figure 2: Ex-post analysis for $\rho = 2.2\%$ per month and $\delta = .9$ on D1

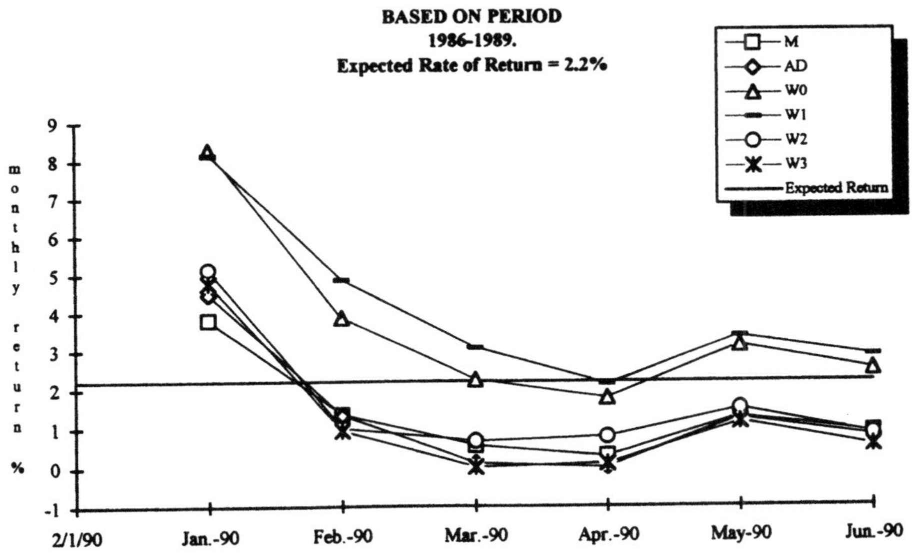

Figure 3: Ex-post analysis for $\rho = 2.2\%$ per month and $\delta = .95$ on D1

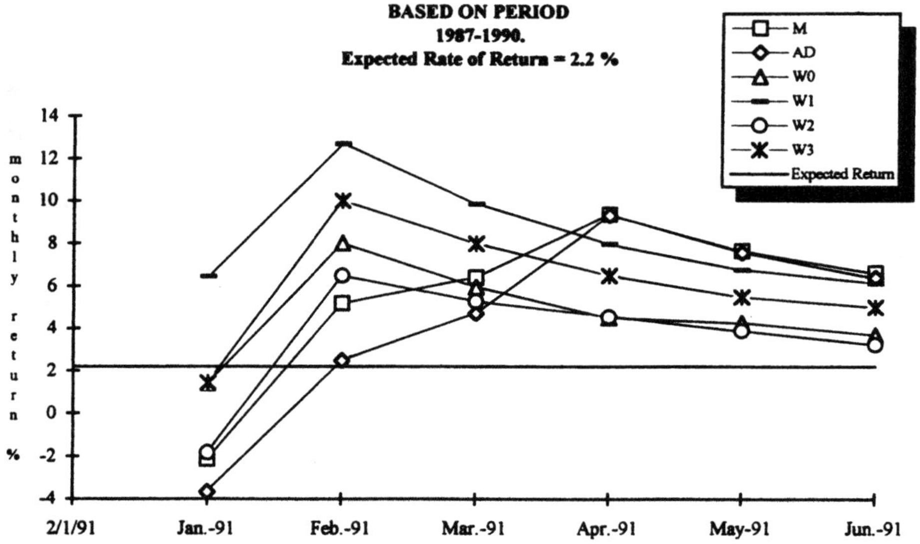

Figure 4: Ex-post analysis for $\rho = 2.2\%$ per month and $\delta = .9$ on D2

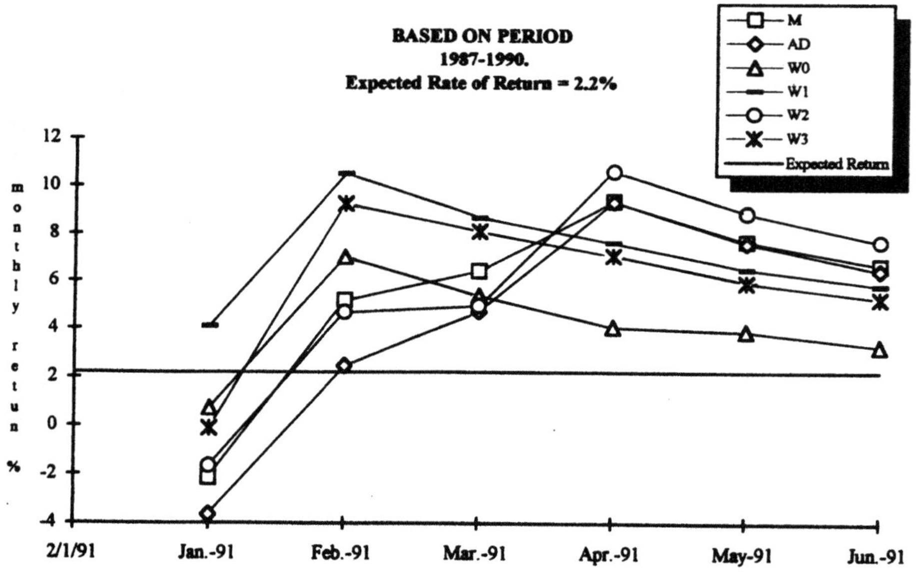

Figure 5: Ex-post analysis for $\rho = 2.2\%$ per month and $\delta = .95$ on D2

violation of the normality assumption.

The weighted models in general produce portfolios quite different from those generated by Markowitz's and the AD models and different from each other. Moreover, the structure of the portfolios generated by the weighted models seems to be quite sensitive to the value of the smoothing coefficient, as it could be expected.

In order to evaluate the performance of the models, an ex-post analysis has been performed. The results are shown in Figures 2 and 3 for the set of data D1 and in Figures 4 and 5 for the set of data D2. In both cases and for both values of the smoothing coefficient, the weighted models show a better performance, especially on the short horizon. In particular, model W1 always guarantees a return rate higher than the required one.

References

Bookstaber, R. (1985), *The Complete Investment Book*, Scott, Foresman and Company, Glenview, Illinois.

Elton, E.J. and Gruber, M.J. (1987) *Modern Portfolio Theory and Investment Analysis*, John Wiley and Sons, New York.

Konno, H. and Yamazaki, H. (1991), Mean Absolute Deviation Portfolio Optimization Model and Its Applications to Tokyo Stock Market, *Management Science* 37, 519-531.

Markowitz, H. (1959), *Portfolio Selection: Efficient Diversification of Investments*, John Wiley and Sons, New York.

Markowitz, H. (1987), *Mean-Variance Analysis in Portfolio Choice and Capital Markets*, Basil Blackwell, Oxford.

Sharpe, W.F. (1967), A Linear Programming Algorithm for Mutual Fund Portfolio Selection, *Management Sci.* 13, 499–510.

Sharpe, W.F. (1971), A Linear Programming Approximation for the General Portfolio Analysis Problem, *Journal of Financial and Quantitative Analysis*, December 1971, 1263-1275.

Speranza, M.G. (1992), Linear Programming Models for Portfolio Optimization, to appear in *Finance.*

Stone, B.K. (1973), A Linear Programming Formulation of the General Portfolio Selection Problem, *Journal of Financial and Quantitative Analysis*, September 1973, 621–636.

WHEN TO USE CURRENCY SWAPS
Determining the expected profit and variance

Robert C. Coppes / University of Groningen

ABSTRACT

In this paper, different uses of currency swaps will be discussed. One of the uses relates to possible cost reduction or yield enhancement, which may be realized when swapping to a lower interest currency. But in such a case it is uncertain whether a profit will actually be realized, as this depends on the exchange rate development. Therefore, it is more interesting to have some information about the variance of the expected profit. In this paper a method is presented to determine both the expected profit and its variance. Examples are given for specific currency swaps, involving the US dollar, the Swiss franc and the main EMS-currencies.

1. Introduction.

In 1980 the swap market was virtually non-existent. Ten years later, the market has expanded to about 2900 billion USD (measured by notional amount) and is expanding even further. Some 80% of this amount consists of interest rate swaps. The rest are currency swaps (see figure 1). Swaps are contractual agreements between two parties to exchange cash flows at specified future dates and can be used for treasury management purposes.

Figure 1. The interest rate and currency swap market.

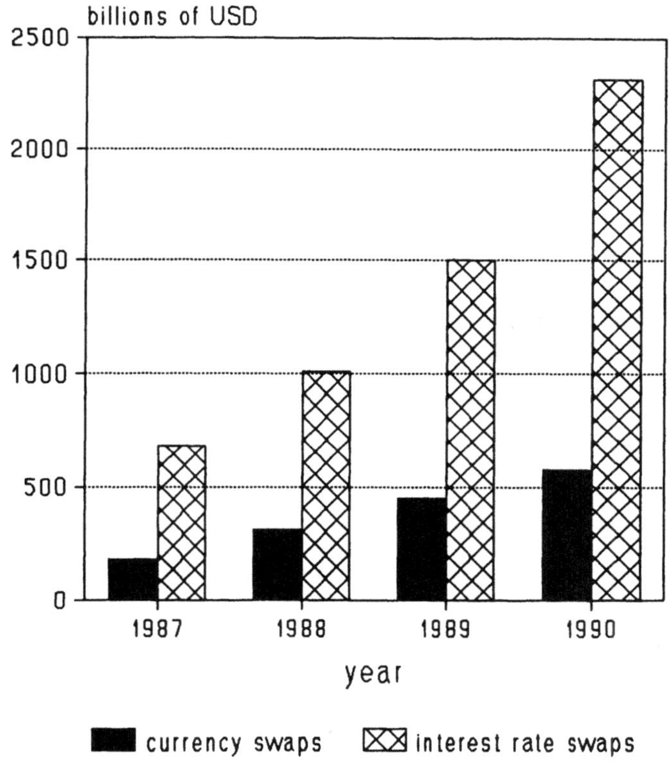

The two cash flows in currency swaps are denominated in different currencies and are based on the prevailing interest rates in the two countries. Although they only determine 20% of the swap market, currency swaps play a significant role in integrating the world's capital markets. Their significance is that they can be used to skip easily from one currency into another. This makes it possible to overcome some of the barriers to international capital movements.

Before using currency swaps for treasury management purposes, it is necessary to have some understanding of the possible development of their values. This is especially true when swap contracts are concluded, in the expectation of obtaining a cost reduction or yield enhancement. This may, for instance, be realized when swapping to a lower interest currency. But an adverse development of the exchange rate may turn an expected profit into a loss. Therefore it is of interest to the financial manager to have more information about the variability of the expected profit.

In this paper a method is presented to determine not only the contract value but also its variance. First, the different purposes for which currency swaps can be used are distinguished in section 2. Then, in section 3 and 4, the expected profit and its variance are shown to depend on the expected currency development. When the International Fisher Effect[1] is valid, the expected profit will be zero. Managers may, however, have a different view of the exchange rate development. An example could be a random walk process without drift. Also a mean reverting process is introduced for the movement of the exchange rates within the European Monetary System. The variance of the possible profit from currency swaps is determined by simulations (section 5). Conclusions will follow in section 6.

2. Uses of currency swaps.

In the literature on swaps many reasons are mentioned for the use of

---

[1] In this theory it is stated that the change in currency value is equal to the relative difference in interest rates between the two countries.

currency swaps[2]. After close examination these can be reduced to three main items: (a) managing interest and exchange rate exposure, (b) diversification of investment or funding, (c) cost saving or yield enhancement.

a. Managing interest and exchange rate exposure.

The domestic currency value of assets, liabilities, income and debt service costs depend to some extent on the volatility of interest and exchange rates. Like other derivatives, currency swaps can be helpful to manage the exposure to interest and exchange rate changes.

They can be seen as being composed of a series of currency forward contracts. But regular forward contracts cannot be arranged for periods of more than a few years. Swaps, however, can be used to eliminate longer term currency exposure. For instance, one can engage into a five year currency swap, neutralizing during this period an existing foreign currency cash flow and creating a domestic currency cash flow.

Currency swaps can also be used to manage interest exposure. Swapping from foreign to domestic currency will eliminate the exposure to the foreign interest rate, creating a new exposure to the domestic interest rate.

b. Diversification of investment or funding.

Currency swaps can be used to change the specifications of any existing investment or funding. A specification that can be changed is the currency in which the investment or funding is denoted. The investment basis of a US Treasury Bond can be changed from US Dollars (USD) into Swiss Francs (CHF), when it is combined with a USD-CHF swap. An other specification that changes is the cash flow. When the swap is agreed, a Swiss Franc interest will be received instead of a US Dollar interest.

Changing the specifications can be desirable from a diversification point of view. Moreover, swaps may reduce the transaction costs of diversification. An interest paying asset, like the US Treasury Bond above, does not have to be liquidated before investing in an other interest paying asset. With a USD-CHF swap the US

---

[2] See for instance Hargreaves (1991), Das (1989), Smith et al. (1986)

Treasury Bond can artificially be changed into a Swiss Treasury Bond. The same reasoning can be followed for changing of funding.

c. Real cost saving or yield enhancement.

Cost reduction by using currency swaps can either be real or expected. It is real when it can be achieved free of risk, through financial arbitrage or arbitrage of capital market imperfections[3]. The importance of financial arbitrage for the explanation of the continuing growth of the swap market has been questioned by - Smith, Smithson and Wakeman (1988), Das (1989) and Wall (1989). In efficient markets the process of arbitrage should lead to the elimination of the arbitrage opportunity.

As opposed to the financial arbitrage, arbitrage of market imperfections does not necessarily lead to the elimination of the arbitrage opportunity. These capital market imperfections relate to dissimilarities in taxation and regulation between countries for the same kind of financial instrument. This causes arbitrage opportunities, which will only disappear when the underlying dissimilarities in taxes and regulations have disappeared[4].

Cost reduction or yield enhancement can also be expected. This is the case when the anticipation of cost reduction or yield enhancement is based on the forecasts of financial managers concerning the future interest rates and exchange rates. In contrast to situations where arbitrage is involved, the expected cost reduction is not certain. It will depend on whether or not the manager's forecast was right.

An example of expected cost reduction is when a financial manager perceives an acceptable balance between a low foreign interest rate and a moderate appreciation of the foreign currency. The manager can either pick up a foreign currency funding directly by issuing foreign currency debt, or indirectly by

---

[3] In the case of interest rate swaps it is suggested that real cost reduction can be achieved through arbitrage of the quality spread differential. See Loeys (1985), Bicksler and Chen (1986), Whittacker (1977) and Chen and Millon (1989). However, cost reduction can only be achieved at the expence of higher risk. Therefore it is no arbitrage in the strict sense. See Wall and Pringle (1989).

[4] See Das, p.92-93.

swapping from domestic debt to the desired foreign currency debt. A real cost reduction will be realized only if the foreign currency appreciation proved to be moderate. This will be shown in more detail in the following section.

3. The expected profit of currency swaps.

From the example in the last section it has become clear that the profit of the swap is not certain. It will depend on the actual development of the exchange rate, which in the following analysis is considered to be a stochastic variable.

Assume a fixed (domestic) to fixed (foreign) currency swap with an initial exchange of principal amounts. The possible profit (or loss) from the swap is determined by the differences in the contractual payments and receipts at the respective payment dates. In order to arrive at one value for the profit or loss, the respective differences have to be discounted. The value of the cash flow in domestic currency, discounted to the first day, is:

$$-P + \sum_{T-t=1}^{n} i_D \, P \, z_D(t,T) + P \, z_D(t,n) \tag{1}$$

in which:

P	= principal amount in domestic currency
i_D	= fixed domestic interest
$z_D(t,T)$	= the value at the current time t of one unit of domestic currency received at payment date T
n	= the expiry date of the currency swap

The foreign currency cash flow has to be evaluated from the domestic point of view. Therefore, all foreign currency amounts have to be translated against the exchange rates of the respective payment dates. The resulting amounts are then discounted with the domestic zero-coupon discount rate. The initial receipt of the principal amount in foreign currency (P/SER) is also exchanged back into domestic currency at the current exchange rate S_t. The resulting value is:

$$\frac{P}{SER} S_t - \sum_{T-t=1}^{n} i_F \frac{P}{SER} S_T z_D(t,T) - \frac{P}{SER} S_n z_D(t,n) \tag{2}$$

in which:

P/SER = principal amount in foreign currency calculated with the contractual swap exchange rate (SER)

i_F = fixed foreign interest

S_T = exchange rate prevailing at payment date T using direct quotation (domestic currency value of one unit of foreign currency)

The profitability (π) of the currency swap as percentage of the notional amount is equal to[5]:

$$\pi = \frac{S_t - SER}{SER} + z_D(t,n) \frac{SER - S_n}{SER} + \sum_{T-t=1}^{n} z_D(t,T) \left(i_D - i_F \frac{S_T}{SER}\right) \tag{3}$$

The first part of the equation refers to the initial exchange of the principal amount at the beginning of the contract. A swap party can make an initial profit when it can sell the initially received (foreign currency) principle to a third party at a higher rate than the swap exchange rate. In a perfect market the swap exchange rate and the third party quote will of course be the same. In reality slight differences might occur and could lead to a small profit. If no higher third party quote can be found, the first part of the equation will be negative. It might be better to do the swap without the initial exchange of principal.

The second part of the equation refers to the exchange back again of the principal amount at the end of the contract period. The firm has a disadvantage when S_n is higher than the initial swap exchange rate. It has to return a high value (foreign currency) principal and it receives a comparably lower value (domestic currency) principal.

The third part of the equation refers to the difference in interest payments

---

[5] For a swap in the other direction (a foreign to domestic currency swap) the same equation holds, but with opposite signs.

and receipts. It depends on the respective exchange rates at any of the payment dates, whether this cash flow will be positive or negative.

It is clear from the equation that all factors are known at time 0, except for the stochastic variable: the future exchange rate[6]. When the future exchange rates are expected to be in line with the International Fisher Effect, the expected swap value will be zero for all swaps: the interest (dis)advantage will be completely compensated by the exchange rate development. The expected value of the swap will deviate from zero when a manager has a different view of the exchange rate development.

This, for instance, is the case when the exchange rate movements are expected to be approximated by a random walk without drift[7]. When this is assumed, the change in currency value can be described as follows:

$$dS = \sigma S dz \tag{4}$$

in which σ refers to the standard deviation of the exchange rate and dz to a Wiener process, $\epsilon \sqrt{dt}$. (ϵ is a random sample from a standardized normal distribution and dt is a small interval of time)

This model applies to currencies that float freely, like the US Dollar. However, there are currencies that exhibit a managed float, like the European currencies participating in the European Monetary System (EMS). For these currencies a mean reverting process would be more appropriate[8]:

$$dS = \kappa(\theta - S)dt + \sigma S dz \tag{5}$$

In which $\kappa(\theta - S)$ is the drift back to the mean θ at any point in time, and κ the speed at which this happens.

---

6 The zero-coupon discount rates can be derived from the actual yield curve.

7 Several studies indicate that this may be the case. For instance Giddy and Dufy (1975), Cornell and Dietrich (1978), Meese and Rogoff (1983), Longworth (1981), Chiang (1986).

8 See for a discussion on mean reversion Cox et al. (1985) and Courtadon (1982).

It should be noted that equation 4 is a special case of equation 5, namely where there is no mean reversion and thus $\kappa=0$. The expected future exchange rates at payment dates, given the present spot rate, can be calculated. In appendix A it is shown to be equal to:

$$E(S_T|S_t) = S_t\, e^{-\kappa(T-t)} + \theta(1-e^{-\kappa(T-t)}) \tag{6}$$

In case of a mean reversion process the expected future exchange rate will eventually be equal to the presupposed mean. The higher κ, the sooner the mean θ will be reached. If there is no mean reversion process, the expected future spot rate at any time is equal to the present spot rate.

When the expected future exchange rates are known, it is easy to calculate the expected profit of a swap: simply substitute equation 6 in equation 3. However, for the financial manager it is more interesting to have information about the uncertainty of realizing the expected profit (the variance).

4. The variance of the expected profit.

The eventual realized profitability of a certain swap can only be determined after the last swap payment has been made. It depends on the realized exchange rates at all payment dates, which may deviate from the expected exchange rate. Consequently the realized profitability may also deviate from the expected profit. The variance of the profit depends on the variances of the exchange rates at the respective payment dates.

These variances can be calculated for every expected spot rate in the future. This is shown in appendix B[9]. But it is insufficient for the calculation of the variance of the profit. The different exchange rate variances cannot just simply

---

[9] See also Cox et al. (1985).

be added because there is a correlation between the spot rates of each future payment date. For the calculation of the exact variance of the profit the correlation coefficients should be known. Fortunately, simulation techniques make a direct determination of the variance possible.

The exchange rate movement can be simulated by sampling repeatedly from a standardized normal distribution and calculating subsequent changes with equation 5. The computer simulates as many exchange rate developments as desired; in this paper 5000. The generated exchange rates at payment dates can be substituted in equation 3 to calculate a possible profit or loss. From the simulated profit and loss positions the variance can be determined.

5. Simulation study

Simulations can be performed for any desired currency swap. In this paper the results for specific 5-year currency swaps are shown. These concern fixed to fixed EMS-USD, EMS-CHF and EMS-EMS currency swaps[10]. In the simulated currency swaps, the domestic interest was supposed to be 8,5%, which is about the actual average in France, Germany and the Netherlands. This percentage was also used to discount the simulated differences in payments and receipts at the respective payment dates. The foreign interest was fixed at 6.5% and was increased in each next simulation by 0.5% to 9.5%. Each simulation consisted of 5000 iterations.

Before the simulation could be started some assumptions had to be made. These were the following:

- For intra EMS exchange rates, κ was estimated to be about 0.6. With this reversion factor, the exchange rates have a 95% chance to

---

[10] USD refers to the US Dollar, CHF to the Swiss Franc and EMS to the European currencies participating in the European Monetary System, having a maximum deviation from the European Currency Unit of 2.25%.

remain within their preset EMS-boundaries[11]. κ is fixed at 0 for the other exchange rates, to simulate a free float.

- A perfect currency market was assumed. Consequently there is no difference between the swap exchange rate (SER) and the spot rate at time 0. Therefore the initial exchange of the principal does not lead to an initial profit as described in section 3.
- For the calculation of the exchange rate movements average standard deviations (σ) were used for the European currencies versus the USD (10.8%), the CHF (4.6%) and each other (1.5%)[12].

Given the interest difference between the currencies, the combination of the expected profitability and variance of a swap was derived from the simulation. The output of the intra-EMS swap is shown in table 1 and for the other swaps in appendix C. For all the currency swaps the expected profit is the same because with a random walk the expected exchange rate is assumed to be constant. But the uncertainty concerning the expected profit is not the same for the three swaps. It is highest for the EMS-USD swaps: the standard deviation is about 17.5%. The standard deviation for the EMS-CHF swap is a moderate 8% and for the intra EMS swap it is only about 1%.

The financial manager has to evaluate the combination of expected profit and variance when a swap is considered for reasons of cost reduction or yield enhancement. For example in the case of an interest differential of 1.5% (8.5% domestic to 7% foreign currency swap) the expected profit over a 5 year period is 5.91%. But the spread around this expectation can be very low as for the intra-EMS swap (see figure 2) or quite considerable as for the EMS-USD swap (see appendix D).

---

11 $\kappa = 0.6$ applies to simulations where dt = one week

12 These were calculated from daily exchange rate changes during 1988-1991. Information from Datastream.

Table 1. Simulation results for the EMS-EMS currency swap.

foreign interest	expected profit % of principal	standard deviation	probability of profit
6.5 %	7.88 %	1.08 %	100.0 %
7.0 %	5.91 %	1.08 %	100.0 %
7.5 %	3.94 %	1.09 %	99.9 %
8.0 %	1.97 %	1.10 %	96.1 %
8.5 %	- 0.0 %	1.11 %	49.6 %
9.0 %	- 1.97 %	1.13 %	3.8 %
9.5 %	- 3.94 %	1.13 %	0.5 %

In the case of an intra EMS swap it seems there is an outstanding opportunity for cost reduction or yield enhancement when the interest differential exceeds 0.5%. Two remarks need to be made. The first is that the expected profit is based on the mean reversion process explained before. It may turn into a loss when the central banks of the relevant countries suddenly decide to adjust the central exchange rates (the mean). The second remark is that the interest differentials between the mentioned EMS countries tend to be small. Therefore, not even with intra-EMS swaps is an almost risk-free cost reduction within easy reach.

Figure 2.

Intra EMS currency swap from 8.5% to 7%: a probability diagram
expected profit is 5.91%, the standard deviation is 1.08%

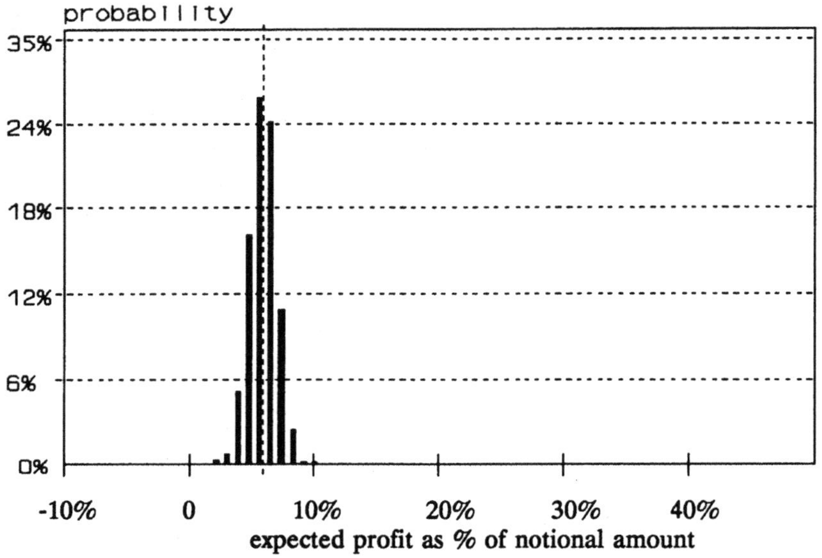

6. Conclusion.

From the discussion above it is clear that swaps are certainly profitable in three situations. The first situation is when a financial manager considers it sensible to hedge a pre-existing open position. In that case the obtainable profit relates to a lower volatility of the value of assets, liabilities, income or debt service costs. The second situation is when a financial manager considers it sensible to diversify investment or funding. The obtainable profit then relates to a more optimal investment or liability position. The third situation is when arbitrage opportunities exist.

Profitability is not equally evident when a swap is based on the (subjective) expectations of the financial manager concerning the future exchange rate development. Of course, the expected profit can easily be calculated, but it will always be uncertain whether the profit can be realized. It is, therefore, more interesting for the manager to have some information about the variance.

In this paper a method has been presented to calculate the expected value and variability of currency swaps. It has been concluded that both depend heavily on the expected development of the exchange rate, for which a random walk process is assumed. When the International Fisher Effect is expected to hold, the drift of the process will be equal to the difference in interest rates. Consequently, there will be no expected cost reduction or yield enhancement possibilities. But when no drift is assumed, the expected profit will deviate from zero.

The variance depends on the variance of the underlying currency and whether or not the currency floats freely. Simulations were performed to determine the variance for specific currency swaps. This can be done for all possible currency swaps. With the derived information the manager can decide whether the expected profit is acceptable, given the spread of the possible outcomes.

APPENDIX A

Calculation of the expected future spot exchange rate.

Given the present spot exchange rate, let the expected spot exchange rate at time T be:

$$E(S_T|S_{t_0}) = \bar{S} \qquad \text{A.1}$$

Given

$$dS = \kappa(\theta - S)dt + \sigma\, S\, dz \qquad \text{A.2}$$

then

$$d\bar{S}/dt = \kappa(\theta - \bar{S}) \qquad \text{A.3}$$

If κ and $\kappa\theta$ are continuous in the time interval $(t_0 - T)$, then the general solution for the expected future spot rate is:

$$\bar{S} = S_{t_0}\, e^{-A(T)} + e^{-A(T)} \int_{t_0}^{T} \kappa\theta e^{A(t)} dt \qquad \text{A.4}$$

$$\text{where} \quad A(T) = \int_{t_0}^{T} \kappa\, dt = \kappa(T - t_0)$$

Thus the expected future spot exchange rate is:

$$\bar{S} = S_t\, e^{-\kappa(T-t_0)} + e^{-\kappa(T-t_0)} \left[\theta e^{\kappa(T-t_0)} - \theta\right]$$

$$= S_{t_0} e^{-\kappa(T-t_0)} + \theta(1 - e^{-\kappa(T-t_0)}) \qquad \text{A.5}$$

APPENDIX B

Calculation of the expected variance of the future spot ex-change rate.

Given the present spot exchange rate, let the expected value of the squared exchange rate at time T be:

$$E(S_T^2 | S_{t_0}) = \overline{S^2} \qquad \text{B.1}$$

Then the variance of the future spot exchange rate is:

$$Var\ (S_T | S_0) = \overline{s^2} - (\bar{S})^2 \qquad \text{B.2}$$

From Ito's Lemma it is known that

$$d\ S^2 = 2\kappa\theta S dt + (\sigma^2 - 2\kappa) S^2 dt + 2\sigma S^2 dz \qquad \text{B.3}$$

then

$$d\ \overline{S^2}/dt = 2\kappa\theta S + (\sigma^2 - 2\kappa) S^2 \qquad \text{B.4}$$

If $2\kappa\theta$ and $(\sigma^2 - 2\kappa)$ are continuous in the time interval $(t_0 - T)$ then the general solution for the expected value of the squared future spot rate is:

$$\overline{S^2} = S_{t_0}^{\ 2}\, e^{-A(T)} + e^{-A(T)} \int_{t_0}^{T} 2\kappa\theta S_t e^{A(t)} dt \qquad \text{B.5}$$

where

$$A(T) = \int_{t_0}^{T}(2\kappa-\sigma^2)dt = (2\kappa-\sigma^2)(T-t_0)$$

Thus:

$$\overline{S^2} = S_{t_0}^{\,2}\, e^{(\sigma^2-2\kappa)(T-t_0)} + 2\kappa\theta e^{(\sigma^2-2\kappa)(T-t_0)} \int_{t_0}^{T} e^{(2\kappa-\sigma^2)(t-t_0)} S_t \, dt \qquad \text{B.6}$$

By using the formula for the expected future exchange rate (equation A.5), the following solution to the integral in equation B.6 appeares:

$$\int_{t_0}^{T} e^{(2\kappa-\sigma^2)(t-t_0)} S_t \, dt =$$

$$\int_{t_0}^{T} S_0 e^{(\kappa-\sigma^2)(t-t_0)} dt + \int_{t_0}^{T} \theta e^{(2\kappa-\sigma^2)(t-t_0)} dt - \int_{t_0}^{T} \theta e^{(\kappa-\sigma^2)(t-t_0)} dt =$$

$$\frac{S_0}{\kappa-\sigma^2}\left[e^{(\kappa-\sigma^2)(T-t_0)} - 1\right] + \frac{\theta}{2\kappa-\sigma^2}\left[e^{(2\kappa-\sigma^2)(T-t_0)} - 1\right] - \frac{\theta}{\kappa-\sigma^2}\left[e^{(\kappa-\sigma^2)(T-t_0)} - 1\right]$$

B.7

Combining equations B.7 and B.6 with B.2 and A.5 gives the expression for the variance of the future spot exchange rate:

$$Var(S_T|S_{t_0}) = S_{t_0}^{\,2}\, e^{(\sigma^2-2\kappa)(T-t_0)} + \frac{2\kappa\theta(S_{t_0}-\theta)}{\kappa-\sigma^2}\left[e^{-\kappa(T-t_0)} - e^{(\sigma^2-2\kappa)(T-t_0)}\right] +$$

$$\frac{2\kappa\theta^2}{2\kappa-\sigma^2}\left[1 - e^{(\sigma^2-2\kappa)(T-t_0)}\right] - \left[S_{t_0} e^{-\kappa(T-t_0)} + \theta(1 - e^{-\kappa(T-t_0)})\right]^2 \qquad \text{B.8}$$

APPENDIX C

Simulation results for the EMS-CHF currency swap.

foreign interest	expected profit % of principal	standard deviation	probability of profit
6.5 %	7.88 %	7.6 %	84.7 %
7.0 %	5.91 %	7.7 %	77.9 %
7.5 %	3.94 %	7.7 %	69.7 %
8.0 %	1.97 %	7.8 %	60.1 %
8.5 %	- 0.0 %	7.8 %	50.0 %
9.0 %	- 1.97 %	7.9 %	39.9 %
9.5 %	- 3.94 %	7.9 %	30.82 %

Simulation results for the EMS-USD currency swap.

foreign interest	expected profit % of principal	standard deviation	probability of profit
6.5 %	7.88 %	17.2 %	67.4 %
7.0 %	5.91 %	17.3 %	63.4 %
7.5 %	3.94 %	17.4 %	58.9 %
8.0 %	1.97 %	17.5 %	54.4 %
8.5 %	- 0.0 %	17.6 %	50.0 %
9.0 %	- 1.97 %	17.7 %	45.6 %
9.5 %	- 3.94 %	17.8 %	40.9 %

APPENDIX D

8.5% EMS to 7% CHF currency swap: a probability diagram.
Expected profit is 5.91%, the standard deviation is 7.7%.

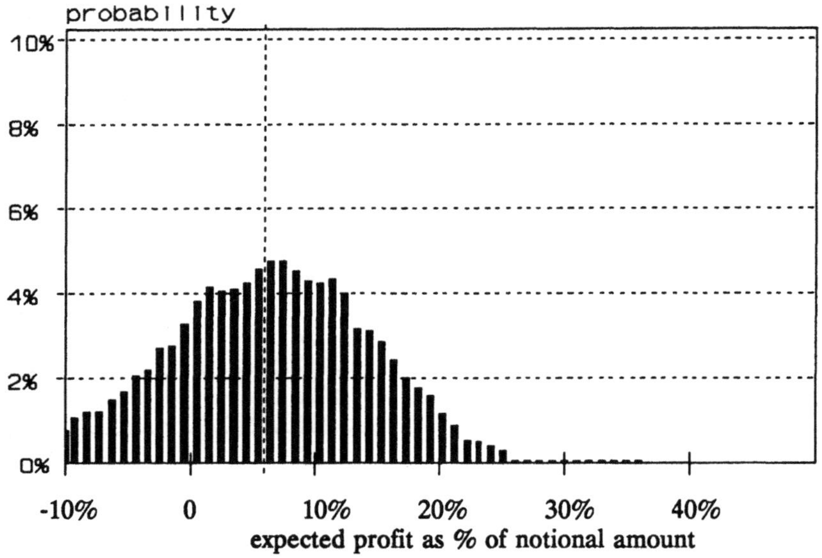

8.5% EMS to 7% USD currency swap: a probability diagram.
Expected profit is 5.91%, the standard deviation is 17.3%.

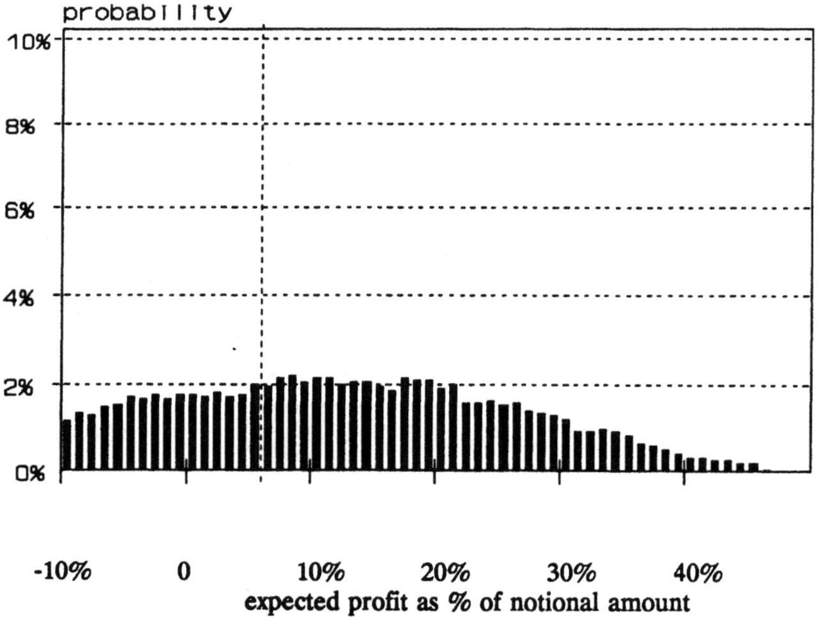

REFERENCES

Bicksler, J. and A.H. Chen, "An Economic Analysis of Interest Rate Swaps", Journal of Finance, Vol XLI, No.3, July 1986, p.645-655.

Chen, A.H. and M.H. Millon, "The Secondary Market and Dynamic Swap Management", in: Khoury, S.J. and A. Gosh (eds), "Recent Developments in International Banking and Finance", Probus Publishing Co. Chicago, Illinois, 1989, p. 131-148.

Chiang, T.C., "Empirical Analysis on the Predictors of Future Spot Rates", in: The Journal of Financial Research, Vol.IX, no.2, summer 1986, pp.153-162.

Cornell, W.B. and J.K. Dietrich, "The Efficiency of the Foreign Exchange Market under Floating Exchange Rates", in: Review of Economics and Statistics, February 1978, pp. 111-120.

Courtadon, G.,"The Pricing of Options on Default-Free Bonds", Journal of Financial and Quantitative Analysis, Vol.XVII, No.1, March 1982, p.75-100

Cox, J.C., Ingersoll, J.E. and S.A. Ross, "A Theory of the Term Structure of Interest Rates", Econometrica, Vol.53, No.2, March 1985, p. 385-405.

Das, S., "Swap Finance", 1989, p. 84-106 and p. 540-553.

Giddy, I.H. and G.Dufey, "The Random Behaviour of Flexible Exchange Rates", in: Journal of International Business Studies, no. 6, spring 1975, pp.1-32.

Hargreaves, D.K., "Swaps: versatility at controlled risk", World Financial Markets, Morgan Guaranty Trust Company of New York, New York, 1991, issue 2, p. 1-28.

Loeys, J.G., "Interest Rate Swaps: A New Tool For Managing Risk", in Federal Reserve Bank of Philidelphia Business Review, May/June 1985, pp 17-25.

Longworth, D., "Testing the Efficiency of the Canadian - U.S.Exchange Market Under the Assumption of No Risk Premium", in: Journal of Finance, March 1981, pp.43-49.

Meese, R.A. and K.Rogoff, "Empirical Exchange Rate Models of the Seventies: Do They Fit Out of Sample?", in: Journal of International Economics, no.14, February 1983, pp. 3-24.

Smith C.W., C.W. Smithson and L.M. Wakeman, "The Evolving Market for Swaps", Midland Corporate Finance Journal, Vol.3, No.4, winter 1986, p.20-32.

Smith C.W., C.W. Smithson and L.M. Wakeman, "The market for Interest Rate Swaps", Financial Management 17, no.4, winter 1988, p. 34-44.

Wall, L.D. and J.J. Pringle, "Alternative Explanations of Interest Rate Swaps: A Theoretical and Emperical Analysis", Financial Management, summer 1989, p. 59-69.

Whittacker, J.G., "Interest Rate Swaps: Risk and Regulation", in: Federal Reserve Bank of Kansas City Economic Review, March 1987, pp 3-13.

CURRENCY FORECASTING: AN INVESTIGATION INTO PROBABILITY JUDGEMENT ACCURACY

Mary E Wilkie
Department of Psychology, Glasgow Caledonian University

Andrew C Pollock
Department of Mathematics, Glasgow Caledonian University

1 Introduction

Judgemental forecasting techniques are extensively used in business and industry (eg. Dalrymple, 1987; Klein and Linneman, 1984). Currency forecasting is no exception. Professionals in the currency market often rely on judgement alone or, at the very least, incorporate some sort of subjective procedure into their forecasts. Despite this, however, academic research has tended to focus on the behaviour of statistical models and has neglected what appears to be the most important aspect of real-world forecasting: human judgement.

The present study focuses on judgement involved in the initial stage of currency forecasting - extrapolation from past and present data. Time series extrapolation has been given considerable attention in psychology and decision science literature and much of this research has shown human judgement to be surprisingly good (cf. Goodwin and Wright, in press); but this work has tended to examine the performance of student subjects rather than that of individuals with professional knowledge of the series in question. Since experts' different, and often more complex, cognitive strategies do not always lead to better decisions (Ayton, 1992), it is difficult to draw conclusions from the existing time series studies. However, specific cognitive strategies can be identified by using a probabilistic approach to examine performance (cf. Yates, 1982). Such an approach allows accuracy to be decomposed into various unique aspects of performance. The present study moves away from the traditional concern about sophisticated statistical models and uses a probabilistic approach to explore three important judgemental issues. These issues are:

i) Do professional currency forecasters make more or less accurate predictions than individuals with relevant analytical ability but no knowledge of currency series?

ii) Do professional forecasters make more or less accurate predictions than a simple *random walk* forecaster?

iii) Does aggregating forecasts (which is typically done in real-world practice) improve accuracy?

2 Method

Subjects: Forty subjects took part in the study. Twenty of the subjects were currency professionals employed by academic and financial institutions in several European countries. The other twenty were mathematicians with no experience of financial markets.

Task: Thirty four actual currency series (containing 60 monthly data points) were presented graphically to the subjects. Each series consisted of the end-of-month cross exchange rate between two countries and was expressed as the first country's currency per unit of the second. However, the subjects were given no information concerning the particular cross rates used or the time period under consideration. The subjects were required to study each series and make directional forecasts for month 61, 63 and 66. They were also required to indicate how certain they were about each prediction by providing a probability between 0.5 and 1.

The reasons behind asking for directional predictions and not providing subjects with contextual information need, perhaps, to be explained.

Directional forecasts were requested, rather than value forecasts, due to the requirement of a probability with each prediction. Probability assessment is much more difficult for value forecasts since the subjects must undertake either direct fractile assessment (Lichtenstein, Fischhoff and Philips, 1982), or assess confidence intervals (Lawrence and Makridakis, 1989) or define parameters for a subjective probability distribution (Pollock and Wilkie, 1991). It was considered that increased difficulty of this kind would give unfair advantage to the mathematicians.

The only way that time series extrapolative judgement can be specifically examined is by controlling contextual information. As pointed out by O'Connor and Lawrence (1989), if information is not controlled very little can be said about the possible causes of either good or bad judgement: it is impossible to determine whether poor judgement (for instance) is the result of salient non-time series information (Tversky and Kahneman, 1973) or factors relating to the series.

After the subjects' task was carried out a *composite forecaster* was obtained for each group (professionals and mathematicians) by aggregating the results for all the subjects within that group. For a particular subject and series, the probability assigned was compared to the forecast direction. These probabilities were transformed to give the probability of a rise in the exchange rate. For a given series, these values were obtained for all 20 individuals in each group. If the mean probability was .5 or above, the composite forecaster was defined to give a directional forecast of a rise with the assigned probability equal to the mean probability. If the mean probability was below .5, the composite forecaster was defined to give a directional forecast of a fall with the assigned probability equal to unity less the mean probability. These values for the composite forecasters were obtained for each series to form a complete set of probability forecasts.

Several probability performance measures were then computed for each subject.

Two measures of overall accuracy were calculated: the *proportion correct* (c) and the *mean probability score* (MPS). The proportion correct is simply the number of times the subject makes the correct response divided by the total number of responses. The MPS, which is associated with Brier (1950), is defined as:

$$MPS = \sum_{i=1}^{n} (r_i - c_i)^2 / N \qquad (1)$$

where r_i is the probability response for forecast i, c_i takes the value of unity for a correct forecast of i and zero for an incorrect forecast of i and N denotes the total number of forecasts.

The MPS can be decomposed into various components.

One decomposition approach, set out by Murphy (1973) points to the contribution of *calibration* and *resolution*. In this approach, *calibration* or *reliability* refers to the closeness of an individuals assigned probabilities to actual occurrences. This measure is obtained by grouping the assigned probabilities into categories. This component, which has a positive effect on the MPS, is zero for a perfectly calibrated individual. *Resolution* or *discrimination*, which is distinct from calibration, refers to the ability of the individual to group events into categories. The higher the value of this component the better as it has a negative effect on the MPS. Poor resolution is indicated by a value close to zero.

One of the main limitations of Murphy's approach, however, arises from the choice of the grouping of the assigned probabilities which is invariably necessary with this technique. This issue is discussed by Pollock and Wilkie (1992).

The difference between the calibration and the resolution measures provides a useful measure of what Yates (1982) describes as a *skill index* (SI). This is not influenced by the grouping of values. SI can alternatively be defined as the difference between the MPS and the variance of the proportion correct V(c) [note:V(c)=c(1-c)]. That is:

$$SI = MPS - V(c) \tag{2}$$

The skill index of zero reflects no skill. The higher the negative value (in absolute terms) of this statistic the better. The measure, however, can give positive values, which reflects a skill factor below that of a *random walk* forecaster (ie. who assigns probabilities of .5 with an arbitrary direction).

An alternative decomposition is provided by the covariance approach of Yates (1982). Equation (3) sets out a simplified form of this approach. That is:

$$MPS = V(c)(1-SL)^2 + SC + B^2 \tag{3}$$

with

$$B = (r - c)$$
$$SC = \{(N_1V(r_1) + N_0V(r_0)\} / (N_1+N_0)$$
$$SL = r_1 - r_0$$

where r, r_1 and r_0 are the average probability judgements for all, correct and incorrect forecasts respectively, $V(r_1)$ and $V(r_0)$ measures the variation around r_1 and r_0 respectively and N_1 and N_0 are the number of occasions the correct and incorrect judgement is made respectively.

The *bias* (B) component, which is closely related to calibration, is a term that measures the degree of under/overconfidence. B is positive in cases of overconfidence and negative in cases of underconfidence. It is zero for perfect confidence.

The *scatter* component (SC) is also closely related to calibration and arises from forecast errors that are independent of rises and falls in the series. This can occur when the forecaster's interpretation of similar situations results in differing forecasts as can be the case where he or she relies on inefficient heuristics (rules of thumb) that are not closely related to the behaviour of the series. It is measured by a statistic based on the composite variation around the mean when predictions are correct and incorrect. A value of zero is best on this measure.

The *slope* component (SL) is an alternative measure of resolution which uses the difference between the mean number of correct predictions and the mean number of incorrect predictions. This measure is not affected by the grouping of probabilities so it is more suitable to use in comparisons between individuals. A value of zero on this measure indicates no resolution. The larger the value the better the performance.

Once the MPS and its components were obtained for the professional forecasters and mathematicians, the distribution for each group was compared by computing a number of statistics. Comparisons were made between the groups and with the random walk forecaster.

To examine the distribution for each group the mean and standard deviation were computed. Further, the test suggested by Lilliefors was applied to examine whether the distributions were normal. This test is is a modification of the Kolmogorov goodness of fit test which can be applied when the population mean and variance are unknown. This test involves the comparison of the normalised relative cumulative distribution of the data with the cumulative distribution of the standard normal. The hypothesis is rejected if a Lilliefors statistic value, in absolute terms, is critical. Critical values for this test are given in Lilliefors (1967).

To compare the distribution of the two groups (professional forecasters and mathematicians) the Student t test was used to examine the difference between means .

3 Results

An examination of the distribution of the accuracy measures for the two groups (professional forecasters and mathematicians) and a comparison between the two sets of results using the Student t (difference between means) test are set out in Table 1. The table also includes the results for the composite (Com.) forecasters and random walk (RW) forecaster. These results, in general, show that the professional forecasters did not perform better than the mathematicians, although they performed better than the random walk forecaster. Aggregating the individual results to obtain a composite forecaster for both groups resulted in some slight improvement in overall accuracy. This resulted from an improvement in the components relating to calibration at the expense of components relating to resolution. The results did, however, show considerable variation between the individuals, especially the professional forecasters. This is consistent with the findings of the review of survey data undertaken by Takagi (1991). He illustrated that exchange rate expectations of market participants tend to be heterogeneous. The results for the overall accuracy measures and components are outlined below.

Overall Accuracy

Proportion Correct (c): Table 1 shows that the professional forecasters did not perform better on this measure than the mathematicians on any of the three horizons. The two sample t test, however, illustrates that there was no significant differences between the groups' means (Lilliefors test [Norm.] supported the hypothesis that the distributions were approximately normal). The results also illustrate that the professional forecasters improved on the random walk forecaster on all three horizons. This was significant for the 3 and 6 month horizons. One sample t tests for the null hypothesis of a mean of .5 against an alternative greater than .5 showed significance at the 1% level on the three month horizon (t=5.75) and at the 5% level on the six month horizon (t=1.83). The composite forecasts improved on the individual forecasts, in general, for the respective groups for all horizons except in the case of the professionals for the six month horizon.

Table 1

Summary Statistics, Professional Forecasters and Mathematicians.

Measure	Professionals				Mathematicians				RW	t-Two
	Mean	SD	Norm.	Com.	Mean	SD	Norm.	Com.	For.	Sample
One Month Horizon										
c	.507	.077	.161	.529	.507	.068	.175	.529	.500	0.00
MPS	.274	.033	.166	.257	.288	.026	.098	.266	.250	-1.50
B	.122	.110	.138	.067	.149	.091	.133	.087	.000	0.87
r	.629	.076	.161	.596	.657	.071	.253**	.616	.500	-1.20
SC	.008	.005	.121	.003	.010	.005	.160	.004	.000	-1.47
SL	.008	.026	.170	-.001	-.007	.026	.153	-.012	.000	1.79
SI	.029	.034	.168	.008	.043	.025	.118	.017	.000	-1.42
Three Month Horizon										
c	.581	.063	.165	.676	.596	.070	.143	.676	.500	-0.68
MPS	.246	.024	.166	.230	.241	.019	.098	.227	.250	0.66
B	.033	.082	.101	-.100	.021	.088	.149	-.103	.000	0.43
r	.614	.071	.241**	.576	.617	.049	.212*	.573	.500	-0.16
SC	.006	.004	.099	.002	.007	.003	.160	.003	.000	-0.67
SL	.017	.031	.157	.002	.022	.025	.195*	.012	.000	-0.58
SI	.007	.020	.142	.012	.005	.015	.110	.011	.000	0.33
Six Month Horizon										
c	.537	.090	.116	.529	.568	.072	.152	.647	.500	-1.89
MPS	.261	.030	.134	.239	.249	.024	.192*	.234	.250	1.20
B	.087	.105	.130	.040	.022	.085	.134	-.094	.000	2.14*
r	.624	.069	.104	.569	.590	.042	.148	.553	.500	1.89
SC	.009	.007	.151	.002	.008	.004	.196*	.001	.000	1.57
SL	.014	.032	.127	.027	.015	.032	.139	.010	.000	-0.14
SI	.019	.032	.149	-.010	.008	.022	.145	.006	.000	1.26

Significant values are denoted for a two tailed test-
*denotes significance at 5%; **denotes significance at 1%.

Mean Probability Score (MPS): The results show that the mean of the individual values for the professional forecasters on this measure was only better than the mathematicians for the one month horizon with worse values for the three and six month horizons. The two sample t test, however, illustrates that there was no significant difference between the groups' mean MPS values on any of the horizons (Lilliefors test supported the hypothesis that the distributions were approximately normal for five out of the six cases). The professionals had mean MPS values worse than the random walk forecaster for the one and six month horizons. Furthermore, a one sample t tests for the null hypothesis of a mean of .25 against an alternative less than .25 was non-significant for the professionals on the three month horizon. These results show that the professionals did not clearly perform better than the random walk forecaster on this measure. The composite forecasts, however, improved clearly on the group means for all horizons for both groups.

Accuracy Components

Under/overconfidence or bias (B): Table 1 illustrates that both groups showed overconfidence in their forecasts over all horizons. The professional forecasters were slightly less overconfident on the one month horizon than the mathematicians but slightly more overconfident for the other horizons. This overconfidence reflected average probability response rates in excess of the average proportion correct. It is interesting to note that the mean response rate (r) for the professionals was similar across all horizons while that of the mathematicians declined as the length of the forecast horizon increased. This appears to be due to a fundamental difference in the way the two groups approached the forecasting task. The mathematicians appeared to take the view that the longer the horizon the more difficult the task and gave probabilities accordingly. The professionals, however, may have taken the view that currency movements in shorter horizons are more subject to noise than in longer horizons such that an offsetting effect occurred. The difference between the two groups as regards overconfidence tended to reflect the different approaches used as well as the proportion correct. The random walk forecaster, of course, had no bias. The composite forecasters over all horizons were clearly less overconfident (and even underconfident in several cases) than the individuals as a whole for their respective groups.

Scatter (SC) or unexplained variation: The results show that this was relatively low as the response rates tended to be generally in the lower half of the .5 to 1 range. The random walk forecaster, of course, had no scatter. The Composite forecaster in both cases, over all horizons, had clearly lower values for scatter than the mean for the individuals.

Resolution or slope (SL): The results illustrate that the professional forecasters over all horizons and the mathematicians over the three and six month horizons showed only a slight positive slope indicating poor resolution. The mathematicians showed a slight negative slope for the one month horizon which implied that lower responses, in general, were given for situations when the correct forecast was made than when the incorrect forecast was made. The two sample t test illustrates, however, that there did not appear to be any difference between the means for each group (Lilliefors test results supported the null hypothesis of normality for five out of the six series). The random walk forecaster, of course, had no resolution. The poor resolution exhibited by both groups did not appear to be improved by aggregating the individual results. The composite forecaster except in the case of the professionals for the six month horizon had lower slope values than the individuals.

Skill index (SI): This component should have a negative value for individuals who perform better than the random walk forecaster, the lower the better. The results, however, show that both groups over all horizons had positive mean group values. In addition, there did not appear to be a clear difference between the two groups on the basis of a two sample t test. The random walk forecaster, of course, had a value of zero for this measure. The composite forecasters improved on the individual means but was only negative in one case. Aggregating the results, again, did not clearly appear to improve this measure .

4 Conclusion

The results illustrated that professional currency forecasters failed to perform better than mathematicians; and although the professionals generally performed better than the random walk forecaster in terms of the proportion correct, this was clearly not the case on the MPS measure. Aggregating individual forecasts to give composite forecasts slightly improved overall accuracy and factors related to calibration, but had a detrimental effect on resolution. Resolution, which is the most difficult aspect of forecasting to improve was only made worse by aggregating individual forecasts. This suggests that composite forecasts, as published in commercial sources such as *The Currency Forecasters' Digest,* are of limited use if resolution is the main consideration.

The major finding of the study was that currency professionals were no better at making directional forecasts of currencies than mathematicians. Although no contextual information was made available to the subjects in the experiment, it would not have been unreasonable to expect the professionals to be more able to capture and extrapolate accurately the underlying structure of the series. Furthermore, even if contextual information was available to the subjects, some professionals may have thought that the most desirable option was to make forecasts purely on the basis of the series. Chartists take this view, believing that past and present prices contain all the relevant information necessary to predict future movements. Since all of the professionals who took part in the study had some knowledge of classical chartist techniques, the results may have serious implications for the use of such techniques in practice.

There were, however, differences in the way the respective groups approached the task. In particular, the professional forecasters tended to give similar response probabilities over all horizons while the mathematicians reduced their probabilities as the forecast horizon lengthened. As previously indicated, this led to greater overconfidence on the part of the professionals on the three and six month horizons.

In practical currency forecasting situations, the problem of overconfidence or positive bias can lead to calibration weaknesses. It is, however, a relatively easy problem to correct. With appropriate feedback forecasters would be expected to lower their mean response rates to reduce overconfidence even where their proportion correct stayed the same. Furthermore, attempts can be made to identify biases that might lead to overconfidence and efforts can be made to reduce their impact.

Wilkie, Tuohy and Pollock (1993) have, in fact, discussed how several types of bias might affect judgemental currency forecasting. One such bias is the *illusory correlation* (Chapman and Chapman, 1969). This refers to the human tendency to see relationships or associations in data which are not statistically present, but which are expected to take place on the basis of prior beliefs. This particular bias could easily cause chartists to go for a 'random walk'. In the context of the present study, another important bias is *anchoring and adjustment* (Tversky and Kahneman, 1974), which refers to the tendency to make insufficient adjustments away from a given initial value. In currency forecasting situations, experts often make predictions by starting at an initial value which is then adjusted as the assessment proceeds. Psychological literature suggests that such adjustments are typically too conservative, and that the increments by which extrapolation is made depend crucially on the relative magnitude of the initial value (*the anchor*). These and several other biases can easily lead to overconfidence in currency forecasting.

The subjects' poor resolution and its effect on overall accuracy was an additional finding to emerge from the present investigation. Perhaps, in retrospect, it is not too surprising to find that both groups were poorly resolved. Perfect resolution is only possible if the judge fundamentally 'knows' what will or will not happen: something rather unlikely with volatile currency series.

However, given that poor resolution appears to have had such an impact on overall accuracy its rectification warrants close attention. This opinion is shared by Yates (1982, 1990) who stresses that good resolution provides a more solid foundation for accurate judgement than does good calibration, but as Yates points out, too many previous studies have ignored resolution completely; and even when it is included in analyses its implications tend to be overlooked. However, there exists evidence that resolution can be improved.

Sharp, Cutler and Penrod (1988) have demonstrated, for example, that training can substantially improve resolution skills. Their subjects were given feedback in terms of probability concerning the appropriateness of their judgements. This experiment involved students and general knowledge questions; but there is no reason why similar training sessions could not be carried out in real-world forecasting situations to improve judgemental accuracy. In the context of currency forecasting, individuals are not required to assign probabilities to their forecasts. Assigning appropriate probabilities is a skill that requires training and practice; but, as pointed out by Wilkie, Tuohy and Pollock (1993), the valuable feedback it provides is likely to improve forecasting performance enormously. This was certainly the case with weather forecasters who, incidentally, did not perform particularly well until probabilistic forecasting became a requirement of the job.

The present investigation could be extended in a number of ways. For instance, probabilistic forecasts from statistical models could be provided for subjects along with the graphical information. Pollock and Wilkie (1992) found that autoregressive and time series regression models showed higher probabilistic accuracy than professionals. Using such models to provide the initial input would allow the integration of statistical forecasting models with judgemental forecasting. Forecasting procedures that use both human judgement and statistical models are, of course, commonly used in practice, but not in an integrated probabilistic framework.

It must be said in conclusion that while this study has confined itself to time series extrapolations using currency data, the methodology can easily be applied to practical forecasting situations in a full information context. The procedure can examine a forecaster's accuracy for a given cross exchange rate over a number of non-overlapping forecast horizons. This aspect of the methodology is perhaps as important to currency forecasting as the results obtained. Professionals can use it to examine their own judgement.

References

Ayton P. (1992). On the Competence and Incompetence of Experts. In Wright G. and Bolger F. eds., Expertise and Decision Support. Plenem Press, New York.

Brier G.W. (1950). Verification of Forecasts Expressed in Terms of Probability. Monthly Weather Review, **78**:1-3.

Chapman L.J. and Chapman J.P. (1969). Illusory Correlation as an Obstacle to the Use of Valid Psychodiagnostic Signs. Journal of Abnormal Psychology, **74**:271-280.

The Currency Forecasters' Digest (monthly periodical). Tech A. (publisher), White Plains, New York.

Dalrymple D.J. (1987). Sales Forecasting Practices. International Journal of Forecasting, **3**:379-391.

Goodwin, P. and Wright G. (in press). Improving Judgemental Time Series Forecasting: A Review of the Guidance Provided by Research, International Journal of Forecasting.

Klein H.E. and Linneman R.E. (1974). Environmental Assessment: An International Study of Corporate Practice. Journal of Business Strategy, **5**:66-84.

Lawrence M.J. and Makridakis S. (1989). Factors Affecting Judgemental Forecasts and Confidence Intervals. Organisational Behavior and Human Decision Processes, **43**:172-187.

Lichtenstein S., Fischhoff B. and Phillips L.D. (1982). Calibration of Probabilities: The State of the Art to 1980. In Kahneman D., Slovic P. and Tversky A . (ed). Judgment Under Uncertainty: Heuristics and Biases. Cambridge University, London.

Lilliefors H.W. (1967). On the Kolmogorov-Smirnov Test for Normality with Mean and Variance Unknown. Journal of the American Statistical Association, **62**:399-402.

Murphy A.H. (1973). A New Vector Partition of the Probability Score. Journal of Applied Meteorology, **12**:595-600.

O'Connor M. and Lawrence M. (1989). An Examination of the Accuracy of Judgemental Confidence Intervals in Time series Forecasting. Journal of Forecasting, **8**:141-155.

Pollock A.C. and Wilkie M.E. (1991). Briefing - Forex Forecasting, Euromoney, June, 123-124.

Pollock A.C. and Wilkie M.E. (1992). Currency Forecasting: Human Judgement or Models? VBA-Journaal, September, 21-29 .

Sharp G.L., Cutler B.L. and Penrod S.D. (1988). Performance Feedback Improves the Resolution of Confidence Judgments. Organisational Behaviour and Human Decision Processes, **42**:271-283.

Takagi S. (1991). Exchange Rate Expectations. IMF Staff Papers, **38**:156-183.

Tversky A. and Kahneman D. (1973). Availability: A Heuristic for Judging Frequency and Probability. Cognitive Psychology, **5**:207-232.

Tversky, A. and Kahneman D. (1974). Judgement under uncertainty: Heuristics and biases. Science, **185**:1124-1135.

Wilkie M.E., Tuohy A. and Pollock A.C. (1993). Examining Heuristics and Biases in Judgemental Currency Forecasting. VBA-Journaal, June, 12-17.

Yates J.F. (1982). External Correspondence: Decompositions of the Mean Probability Score. Organisational Behavior and Human Performance, **30**:132-156.

Yates J.F. (1990) Judgement and Decision Making. Prentice Hall, New Jersey.

GPSR Compliance

The European Union's (EU) General Product Safety Regulation (GPSR) is a set of rules that requires consumer products to be safe and our obligations to ensure this.

If you have any concerns about our products, you can contact us on ProductSafety@springernature.com

In case Publisher is established outside the EU, the EU authorized representative is:

Springer Nature Customer Service Center GmbH
Europaplatz 3
69115 Heidelberg, Germany

Batch number: 10725973

Printed by Printforce, the Netherlands